THE CANADIAN DISTINCTIVENESS
INTO THE XXIST CENTURY

LA DISTINCTION CANADIENNE
AU TOURNANT DU XXIE SIÈCLE

A gift from the
Canadian Consulate
General Seattle

The International Canadian Studies Series
La Collection internationale d'études canadiennes

The *International Canadian Studies Series* offers a unique collection of high-quality works written primarily by non-Canadian academics. The Series includes conference proceedings, collections of scholarly essays, and various forms of reference works. The Series publishes works written in either English or French.

La *Collection internationale d'études canadiennes* présente des ouvrages de premier ordre, rédigés surtout par des universitaires non canadiens. Elle comprend des actes de colloque, des recueils d'articles et divers types d'ouvrages de référence. La collection publie en français et en anglais.

Editorial committee / Comité éditorial
Chad Gaffield
Guy Leclerc

ISSN 1489-713X

International Canadian Studies Series
Collection internationale d'études canadiennes

THE CANADIAN DISTINCTIVENESS
INTO THE XXIST CENTURY

LA DISTINCTION CANADIENNE
AU TOURNANT DU XXIE SIÈCLE

Edited by / Sous la direction de
Chad Gaffield
Karen L. Gould

UNIVERSITY OF OTTAWA PRESS
LES PRESSES DE L'UNIVERSITÉ D'OTTAWA

National Library of Canada Cataloguing in Publication

The Canadian distinctiveness into the XXIst century / edited by Chad Gaffield, Karen L. Gould = La distinction canadienne au tournant du XXIe siècle / dirigé par Chad Gaffield, Karen L. Gould.

(International Canadian studies series = Collection internationale d'études canadiennes, ISSN 1489-713X)
Text in English and French.
Proceedings of a conference held at University of Ottawa, 18-20 May 2000.
Includes bibliographical references.
ISBN 0-7766-3022-9 (bound).—ISBN 0-7766-0551-8 (pbk.)

1. Canada—Congresses. 2. Canada—Civilization—Congresses. 3. Canada—Forecasting—Congresses. 4. Canada—Civilization—Forecasting—Congresses. I. Gaffield, Chad, 1951– II. Gould, Karen, 1948– III. Title: La distinction canadienne au tournant du XXIe siècle. IV. Series: International Canadian studies series.

FC97.C273 2003   971.064'8   C2003-902378-8E
F1021.2.C375 2003

Catalogage avant publication de la Bibliothèque nationale du Canada

The Canadian distinctiveness into the XXIst century / edited by Chad Gaffield, Karen L. Gould = La distinction canadienne au tournant du XXIe siècle / dirigé par Chad Gaffield, Karen L. Gould.

(International Canadian studies series = Collection internationale d'études canadiennes, ISSN 1489-713X)
Texte en anglais et en français.
Comptes rendus d'une conférence présentée à l'Université d'Ottawa, 18-20 mai 2000.
Comprend des références bibliographiques.
ISBN 0-7766-3022-9 (relié).—ISBN 0-7766-0551-8 (br.)

1. Canada—Congrès. 2. Canada—Civilisation—Congrès. 3. Canada—Prévision—Congrès. 4. Canada—Civilisation—Prévision—Congrès. I. Gaffield, Chad, 1951– II. Gould, Karen, 1948– III. Titre: La distinction canadienne au tournant du XXIe siècle. IV. Collection: International Canadian studies series.

FC97.C273 2003   971.064'8   C2003-902378-8F
F1021.2.C375 2003

University of Ottawa Press gratefully acknowledges the support extended to its publishing programme by the Canada Council and the University of Ottawa.

We acknowledge the financial support of the Government of Canada through the Book Publishing Industry Development Program (BPIDP) for our publishing activities.

 UNIVERSITY OF OTTAWA
UNIVERSITÉ D'OTTAWA

© University of Ottawa Press, 2003
542 King Edward, Ottawa, Ont. Canada K1N 6N5
press@uotttawa.ca   http://www.uopress.uottawa.ca

First reprint 2003. Printed and bound in Canada

Contents
Table des matières

Préface

C et ouvrage est le résultat d'une collaboration importante entre l'Institut d'études canadiennes, de l'Université d'Ottawa et le Conseil international des études canadiennes (CIEC), un organisme qui représente vingt associations nationales et plurinationales d'études canadiennes de partout dans le monde. La conférence sur « La distinction canadienne au tournant du XXIe siècle », qui s'est tenue à l'Université d'Ottawa en mai 2000, a attiré des chercheurs canadiens et étrangers de marque qui représentaient toute une gamme de disciplines et d'approches différentes et contrastées du thème choisi. Les articles que vous trouverez réunis dans ce livre sont donc le résultat d'un dialogue particulier, et qui tombe tout à fait à point, sur ce qui a été et ce qui est sans doute appelé à demeurer spécifiquement canadien au Canada.

On a invité les auteurs qui ont collaboré à cet ouvrage à envisager tant le passé que l'avenir dans leurs discussions et analyses du caractère spécifique de la société, de la culture et de la politique canadiennes. En conséquence, les lecteurs constateront que les contextes où s'inscrit ce dialogue savant relèvent de l'histoire autant que des préoccupations de notre époque. En cette ère de mondialisation et d'élaboration d'une vision de plus en plus mondiale des problèmes internationaux, la question de la spécificité canadienne exige que l'on porte une attention renouvelée aux traits distincts et à des aspects particuliers de la vie canadienne qui continuent de définir le Canada comme un espace politique et culturel à nul autre pareil. Par ailleurs, notre thème se prête également à plusieurs analyses comparatives pénétrantes et particulièrement révélatrices du point de vue des canadianistes étrangers. Tant la conférence de mai 2000 que les textes réunis ici témoignent du vif intérêt qui anime les chercheurs canadiens et étrangers lorsqu'ils parlent du Canada et de la place toute particulière qu'il occupe en Amérique du Nord et dans le monde.

Karen L. Gould
présidente du CIEC, 1999-2001
Doyenne du McMicken College of Arts and Sciences
University of Cincinnati

Preface

This volume is the result of an important collaboration between the Institute of Canadian Studies at the University of Ottawa and the International Council for Canadian Studies, an organization that represents twenty national and multi-national associations of Canadian Studies around the world. Held at the University of Ottawa, the May 2000 conference on "The Canadian Distinctiveness into the XXIst Century" attracted the participation of leading Canadian and international scholars from a variety of disciplines whose approaches to the topic were wide-ranging. The essays assembled here are therefore the fruits of a particular and especially timely dialogue about what has been and is likely to remain uniquely Canadian in Canada.

Contributors to this volume have been asked to look backward as well as forward in their discussion and analysis of the distinctive character of Canadian society, culture, and politics. As a result, readers will find that the contexts for this scholarly dialogue are historical as well as contemporary. In an era of globalization and increasingly global perspectives on international issues, the subject of Canadian distinctiveness calls for renewed attentiveness to the distinguishing features and particular aspects of Canadian life that continue to define Canada as a unique political and cultural space. At the same time, our topic also lends itself to a number of comparative analyses that are insightful and particularly revealing for international Canadianists. Both the May 2000 conference and the volume of essays collected here mark the keen interest that Canadian and international scholars share in the subject of Canada and its special place in North America and in the world.

Karen L. Gould
President of the ICCS, 1999-2001
Dean of McMicken College of Arts and Sciences
University of Cincinnati

Remerciements

Plusieurs personnes et organismes ont encouragé les directeurs de ce livre. Celui-ci est le résultat d'une conférence internationale fructueuse qui a été organisée par le Conseil international des études canadiennes et l'Institut d'études canadiennes à l'Université d'Ottawa du 18 au 20 mai 2000. Le programme de la conférence est le fruit du travail d'un comité superbe composé de Caroline Andrew, Chad Gaffield, Karen Gould, Alain Guimont, David Staines et Jean-Pierre Wallot. La conférence a bénéficié de nombreuses subventions des organismes suivants : la division Éducation internationale et relations universitaires du ministère des Affaires étrangères et du Commerce international, la Direction de l'identité canadienne du ministère du Patrimoine canadien, ainsi que l'Université d'Ottawa.

Pendant tout le processus de publication, les directeurs ont reçu l'aide de Ivana Caccia, Houria Messadh, Louise Verner, Angela Mattiacci de l'Institut d'études canadiennes, et de Guy Leclair du Conseil international des études canadiennes.

Acknowledgements

The editors of this book have been supported and encouraged by many organizations and people. This book is the result of a successful international conference, organized by the International Council for Canadian Studies and the Institute of Canadian Studies at the University of Ottawa, that took place 18-20 May 2000. The conference program was the result of a splendid committee composed of Caroline Andrew, Chad Gaffield, Karen Gould, Alain Guimont, David Staines, and Jean-Pierre Wallot. The conference benefited from generous grants from the following organizations: the International Academic Relations Division of the Department of Foreign Affairs and International Trade, Canadian Identity Directorate of the Department of Canadian Heritage, and the University of Ottawa.

Throughout the publication process, the editors have received assistance from Ivana Caccia, Houria Messadh, Louise Verner, Angela Mattiacci at the Institute of Canadian Studies, and from Guy Leclair at the International Council for Canadian Studies.

Perspectives sur la distinction canadienne au tournant du XXIe siècle

Chad Gaffield

Quels sont les origines, le statut actuel et les perspectives de la distinction canadienne au tournant du vingt et unième siècle ? C'est cette question complexe qui a préoccupé les conférenciers de renommée internationale et les délégués de douzaines de pays réunis lors d'une conférence de trois jours du 18 au 20 mai 2000. Cet événement du millénaire fut organisé par le Conseil international des études canadiennes et l'Institut d'études canadiennes de l'Université d'Ottawa. La conférence « La distinction canadienne au tournant du XXIe siècle » a exploré les dynamiques clés du présent et du passé du Canada afin de fournir des perspectives pertinentes sur l'avenir de celui-ci. Le fruit de cette conférence fut une discussion intense toujours pénétrante et stimulante, tout en étant à la fois rassurante, dérangeante, encourageante, décourageante, visionnaire, pragmatique, optimiste et pessimiste.

Puis vint le 11 septembre 2001. Au moment où nous nous apprêtions à publier les actes de la conférence, la destruction des tours jumelles du World Trade Center à New York a remis en question la pertinence à long terme de ces textes. Si le monde était changé à tout jamais, comme on semblait le croire, ne devions-nous pas demander aux auteurs de réviser leurs perspectives ? Ou ferions-nous mieux de renoncer tout simplement à la publication des résultats de la conférence si ces analyses et ces idées n'étaient plus pertinentes dans un monde d'après le 11 septembre ?

Un an après la tragédie du 11 septembre, il est possible d'élaborer une perspective sur la signification de cette journée. Même s'il faudra plusieurs années avant de connaître son importance à long terme, de nombreux analystes croient en l'importance de situer tous les événements courants, qu'ils provoquent ou non des cataclysmes, dans un

Perspectives on the Canadian Distinctiveness into the XXIst Century

Chad Gaffield

W hat are the origins, current status, and prospects for the distinctiveness of Canada into the twenty-first century? This infinitely complex question was at the heart of a three-day conference that brought together internationally-acclaimed speakers and delegates from dozens of countries from May 18 to 20, 2000. Organized as a millennium event by the International Council for Canadian Studies and the Institute of Canadian Studies at the University of Ottawa, the conference, "The Canadian Distinctiveness into the XXIst Century," probed the key dynamics of Canada's past and present in order to provide timely perspectives on the future. The result was an intense and profound discussion that was consistently insightful and stimulating, as well as being, at various times, reassuring, disturbing, encouraging, discouraging, visionary, pragmatic, optimistic, and pessimistic.

And then came 11 September 2001. Just as we were ready to publish the revised conference papers, the destruction of the twin towers of the World Trade Center in New York City caused us to wonder about the continued relevance of these papers. If the world were really fundamentally changed as so often claimed, should we not ask all the authors to reconsider their perspectives? Or, perhaps, we should simply abandon the plan to publish the results of the conference if indeed the analyses and insights no longer had currency in the post–9/11 world.

One year after the 11 September tragedy, some perspective on the meaning of this day is possible, and although its long-term importance will not be known for many years, an increasing number of analysts are now insisting on the need to situate all current events, no matter how cataclysmic, within larger contexts across space and time. Moreover, these analysts are emphasizing that 11 September exposed

contexte plus large dans l'espace et le temps. De plus, ces analystes maintiennent que le 11 septembre a exposé l'importance de deux considérations, jusque-là ignorées, comme facteurs déterminants du vingt et unième siècle : l'état-nation et les valeurs culturelles. En effet, pour une grande partie du vingtième siècle, il semblait que la mondialisation remettait en question l'importance de l'état-nation et que l'urbanisation, les entreprises multinationales et d'autres formes de liens et d'organisations avaient tôt fait d'amoindrir la pertinence d'entités politiques comme le Canada. De même, la poussée de la mondialisation semblait relever de l'économie et de la technologie plutôt que de la culture. Les valeurs, les priorités et l'histoire étaient considérées, tout au plus, comme des épiphénomènes, voire comme étant détachées des phénomènes portant à conséquence.

Un an après le 11 septembre, toutefois, personne ne doute de la pertinence de l'état-nation ni de l'importance des valeurs culturelles. Il est également évident que nous n'aurions jamais dû douter de la pertinence à long terme des contributions exceptionnelles faites en mai 2000 pour mieux comprendre le Canada à l'aube d'une ère nouvelle. Ces analyses justes ont mis l'accent sur la culture et la nature du Canada comme juridiction politique au sein de laquelle un changement profond s'opère. L'importance des chapitres qui suivent s'est donc accrue au lieu de s'affaiblir avec le temps.

La première partie rapproche les idées innovatrices des trois conférenciers de marque, c'est-à-dire John Ralston Saul, Jocelyn Létourneau et Margaret Atwood. Chacun s'est attardé aux questions clés de la distinction canadienne dans une perspective historique et contemporaine. Ce sont leurs visions du Canada au début d'une ère nouvelle qui sont à la base des chapitres suivants où quatre thèmes majeurs sont abordés. Dans la deuxième partie intitulée « Individus, collectivités et État », Gilles Paquet et Susan D. Phillips présentent des analyses du développement historique du Canada afin d'aborder d'une nouvelle façon les questions de gouvernance et des relations entre l'État et la société civile au vingt et unième siècle. Denis Lacorne et Alan C. Cairns, pour leur part, donnent un contexte à la diversité de la société canadienne dans des perspectives comparatives, longitudinales et critiques. Dans la troisième partie, W. Michael Wilson, Monique Bégin et Maya Dutt examinent « Le caractère de la société canadienne » du point de vue des cultures d'affaires, des cultures sociales et politiques et de diverses cultures littéraires. Le lien entre ces cultures forme le thème de la quatrième partie, « Culture, identité et

the critical character of two considerations that previously had been increasingly dismissed as determining factors for the twenty-first century: the nation-state and cultural values. Indeed, for much of the later twentieth century, it had been argued that globalization was undermining the importance of the nation-state, and that with the rise of cities, multinational businesses, and other forms of connection and organization, the relevance of political entities such as Canada was declining rapidly. Similarly, the driving forces of this globalization were often said to be economic and technological rather than cultural. Questions of values, priorities, and, in fact, of history were often considered epiphenomenal at best and, perhaps, completely detached from those of real consequence.

One year after 9/11, however, no one is doubting that the nation-state is still relevant or that cultural values are fundamentally important. And it is clear that we should never have doubted for a minute the enduring relevance of the outstanding contributions made in May 2000 to understanding Canada at the dawn of a new era. These penetrating analyses emphasize both culture and the nature of Canada as a political jurisdiction within which complex change is now underway. The urgency of the following chapters has thus increased rather than diminished with the passage of time.

Part One brings together the innovative and profound insights of the conference's three keynote speakers, John Ralston Saul, Jocelyn Létourneau, and Margaret Atwood, each of whom focuses on central questions of Canadian distinctiveness from both historical and contemporary perspectives. Their visions of Canada on the eve of a new era provide the foundation for the following chapters that address four major themes. In the next section entitled, "Individuals, Collectivities, and the State," Gilles Paquet and Susan D. Phillips offer analyses of Canada's historical development in order to propose new ways of thinking about questions of governance and state–civil society relationships in the twenty-first century while Denis Lacorne and Alan C. Cairns contextualize Canadian society's diversity in comparative, longitudinal, and critical perspectives. In Part Three, W. Michael Wilson, Monique Bégin, and Maya Dutt examine "The Texture of Canadian Society" in terms of business cultures, social and political cultures, and diverse literary cultures. The connections between these cultures are the focus of the theme of Part Four, "Culture, Identity, and the Market" which is analyzed by C. Michael Hall in the context of tourism; by Shirley L. Thomson with reference to Canada's cultural

marché ». Ce thème est analysé par C. Michael Hall dans le contexte du tourisme, Shirley L. Thomson quant à la politique culturelle du Canada, Jean-Louis Roy dans le contexte des forces internationales et Maria Teresa Gutiérrez-Haces quant à la « diplomatie de citoyenneté ». La cinquième partie confronte directement le contexte international instable du Canada sous le thème « Le rôle du Canada sur la scène internationale au vingt et unième siècle ». Dans cette section, Donna Winslow étudie la sécurité mondiale dans la perspective de l'armée canadienne, tandis qu'Huguette Labelle examine les préoccupations quant à la qualité de vie de tous les peuples par rapport au rôle international qui reviendra au Canada. Dans les derniers chapitres, Terry Cook explore la signification des techniques de l'information et des communications en vue d'une voix canadienne distincte, alors que Jean Laponce et Lorna Irvine s'intéressent à l'avenir dans la perspective des tendances sociétaires, des métaphores et des cartes littéraires.

Pris dans leur ensemble, les chapitres de ce livre rejettent toute notion de fatalité relative au Canada, qu'elle soit historique ou future. Les analyses s'intéressent plutôt au fait que, quel que soit leur vécu, passé ou présent, qu'ils soient ou non victimes, les individus, les groupes et les collectivités sont en mesure de jouer un rôle significatif dans la construction de leur destinée et de celle du Canada. De plus, les auteurs mettent systématiquement l'accent sur l'importance de la culture, de la créativité, de l'imagination, de même que des forces du marché et des changements technologiques. Leurs interprétations s'éloignent du déterminisme, économique ou autre, pour rejoindre une interrogation plus complexe qui explore les liens et non-liens entre ce qui est dit et ce qui est fait, entre les idées et les comportements, entre la pensée et l'action, entre l'intellectuel et le matériel. Enfin, ces auteurs présument qu'il est nécessaire de se concentrer sur l'avenir à partir d'une perspective qui englobe le passé et le présent. Cette approche suppose non seulement la reconnaissance et l'analyse de la complexité de la réalité canadienne, mais aussi l'examen de l'ensemble des qualités en perpétuelle mutation qui ont défini le Canada à travers son histoire, mais qui ne sont pas nécessairement toutes appropriées à la vie au vingt et unième siècle.

En interrogeant la distinction canadienne, les auteurs identifient à maintes reprises les questions clés portant sur l'équilibre existant entre les diverses forces en rapport compétitif. Ils ont souvent recours aux termes « complexité », « contingence », « ambiguïté », « inclusion »,

policy; by Jean-Louis Roy in terms of international forces; and by Maria Teresa Gutiérrez-Haces with respect to "citizenship diplomacy." Part Five then directly confronts Canada's changing international context under the theme, "The Place of Canada in the World of the XXIst Century." In this section, Donna Winslow addresses the question of global security from the perspective of the Canadian military and Huguette Labelle explores concerns about the quality of life of all peoples in terms of Canada's expected international role. In the concluding chapters, Terry Cook probes the meaning of information technologies and communications for a distinct Canadian voice while Jean Laponce and Lorna Irvine peer into the future from the vantage points of current societal trends and literary metaphors and maps.

Taken together, the chapters of this book reject any notions of inevitability about Canada, either historically or for the future. Rather, the analyses focus on agency, on the idea that however much victimization has occurred and occurs now, individuals, groups, and collectivities can in fact play a meaningful role in determining their own destinies, and indeed, the destiny of Canada. Second, the authors consistently emphasize the importance of culture, of creativity, of imagination, as well as of market forces and technological change. Their interpretations back away from concepts of determinism, either economic or otherwise, to embrace a more complex interrogation in which they explore the connections and disconnections between what is said and what is done, between ideas and behaviour, between thought and action, between the intellectual and the material. Third, these authors assume that it is necessary to focus on the future from the perspective of the past and the present. This approach calls not only for recognition and analysis of the complexity of the Canadian reality, but also for examination of the changing constellation of qualities that have defined Canada historically, and that may or may not be appropriate as we move forward into the twenty-first century.

In addressing the question of Canadian distinctiveness, the authors repeatedly identify key questions of balance, of equilibrium, in the context of competing forces. They frequently use such words as "complexity", "contingency", "ambiguity", "inclusivity", "chaos", "coherence", "identities", "contradictions", and "continuities" – all of which have become familiar in international debate not only in the social sciences and humanities but across all disciplines.

« chaos », « cohérence », « identités », « contradictions » et « continuité ». Ces termes sont d'usage courant dans les débats internationaux non seulement en sciences sociales et humaines, mais dans toutes les disciplines.

C'est dans ce contexte que Jocelyn Létourneau fait référence à la complexité délicate des mobiles de l'artiste Alexander Calder. Même si celui-ci est né à la fin du dix-neuvième siècle, sa vie et ses intérêts s'appliquent bien à nos réflexions sur le vingt et unième siècle. De fait, c'est par sa formation en génie mécanique que Calder a fait le lien entre les arts et les sciences avant de devenir l'un des sculpteurs les plus innovateurs de son temps. Ses mobiles sont d'ailleurs le résultat de son intérêt pour les constructions qui se modifient gracieusement en réponse à des stimuli externes. Certains contesteront l'idée que l'œuvre d'un Américain puisse refléter de façon métaphorique la dynamique canadienne, tandis que d'autres verront que les caractéristiques des mobiles de Calder sont pertinentes à plusieurs aspects de la société canadienne contemporaine.

Que des exemples comme les mobiles d'Alexander Calder soient vus ou non comme des images utiles au moment où nous allons de l'avant dans le vingt et unième siècle, les discussions de la conférence accentuent le fait que des changements complexes ont fini par caractériser la réalité canadienne. Dans leur ensemble, les diverses présentations ont insisté sur l'espoir et la prudence qui doivent entourer ces changements. Avant tout, les conférenciers ont mis en évidence que le véritable défi n'est plus simplement de se connaître soi-même en tant que Canadien, mais plutôt de mettre en pratique cette connaissance de manière à créer une société meilleure et plus juste, et ce dans le contexte international en évolution où se situe « le monde d'après le 11 septembre ».

It is in this context that Jocelyn Létourneau refers to the delicate complexity of artist Alexander Calder's mobiles. Even though Calder was born at the end of the nineteenth century, his life and interests may serve us well in thinking about the twenty-first century. Indeed, before becoming one of the more innovative sculptors of his time, Calder was to bridge the arts and sciences through his education as a mechanical engineer. Similarly, his mobiles resulted from his interest in creating constructions that shift and change gracefully in response to new external pressures. The idea that the art of an American is able to capture metaphorically the Canadian dynamic will undoubtedly be contested by some while others will agree that the characteristics of Calder's mobiles do, indeed, seem relevant to many aspects of contemporary Canadian society.

Whether or not examples such as Calder's mobiles will be seen to be useful images as we move forward in the twenty-first century, the discussions at the conference emphasized that profound and complex changes have come to characterize the Canadian reality. Taken together, the various presentations emphasized that these changes called for both hope and caution. Above all, the speakers stressed that the challenge is no longer simply to know ourselves as Canadians, but rather to use this knowledge to create a healthier and more just society in a rapidly changing international context within which the 'changed world' after 9/11 must be situated.

LOCUS IN QUO

The Inclusive Shape of Complexity

John Ralston Saul

AT THIS TIME, ALL OF US – JUST ABOUT EVERYWHERE IN THE WORLD, especially in democracies or countries where the free market prevails – are victims of what could be called the Tristan and Isolde syndrome. What is the Tristan and Isolde syndrome? It is what has been taught in schools of economics for about 25 years. It says that if we all drink a magic potion – a love potion – we will suddenly lose our sense of responsibility as citizens, and it will be replaced by inevitable, passionate, romantic forces that will determine the direction of the world. This sense of responsibility will also be replaced by the dominance of what is called 'self-interest.' The French term is less descriptive: *amour propre*, or *intérêt personnel*. Prince Hassan has suggested *narcissisme économique*, which is an interesting translation.

This syndrome has lasted for a quarter century. But we have been seeing the beginning of a change of direction over the past two years or so. In various places around the globe, we sense that the magic potion has worn off a little bit. People no longer really believe in inevitable forces.

They are beginning to remember the fact that while self-interest is necessary, absolutely necessary, it is too mediocre a concept to guide a civilization. And embrace inevitable forces? That is far too romantic, too emotional an idea for citizens who, over the past 2,500 years, have become accustomed to feeling responsible for their actions and the directions of their society.

This does not mean that because we taught Tristan and Isolde in schools of economics for a quarter century, we are now going to lapse into the opposite – idiotic protectionism or whatever. It does not mean that the nation-state of the 19th century will return. Or that it must return. I hope that it will not. That kind of nation-state has already given us two world wars. This is not the time to revisit all of that again.

But it does mean that the great syndrome of inevitability will not appear either. And that we are looking for something between the two, a kind of reasonable globalization where citizens in nation-states will play a very important role. After all, you can't say in the same text, as many people do, "Thank God democracy won ten years ago, democracy won throughout the world," and then three sentences later, "how wonderful, the nation-state is dead." Because democracy was created and exists only within nation-states. Therefore, if nation-states are dead, democracy is dead, because we have not done what is necessary to transfer democracy to other regional or global levels.

So at this time, individuals and citizens just about everywhere in the West are looking for ways to become involved, or rather to become re-involved, in the debates on the major questions of the day – all kinds of major questions. The way we see ourselves as citizens, in whatever territory or country we may live, is therefore very important; the way we see ourselves within our civilization, the way we see other citizens in other civilizations. Carlos Fuentes said: [in translation] "Culture comes before the nation, and culture can organize itself in many ways." And you know that when Carlos Fuentes uses the word culture – rather in the same way as Robin Blaser of British Columbia when he said that "poetry comes first" – we are not talking about culture in the strict sense of the term, but culture in the sense of great concepts of civilization. This is what comes first in a nation. Not interests, but how citizens see themselves, that is, culture.

And I will add two things that must be repeated again and again in order to understand a country, countries, nations, peoples. First, as many other people have said, history is the past moving through the present into the future. It does not consist of three chapters or periods. It is a single event. Second, nations, countries, peoples do not really change that much over time. In our civilizations we have deep memories. And I use the word "memories" in its broadest sense – those memories that exist at many levels. Over time, those memories are lost and then, curiously, from out of nowhere, they are rediscovered, often 5, 50, 100, 200 years later. It is amazing how deep are the memories that exist in human cultures, memories which are often there, hidden, slumbering, asleep, but which will always resurface. The memories of civilizations are not wiped out. They will always appear in different or similar combinations, new or old interpretations, or a combination of both. It is interesting to note – the Ambassador of France is here, and I believe he will agree with me – that the peoples of Europe, we could say the states or nations of Europe, are in the process of rebuilding themselves, of finding themselves once again within a framework that they previously used in another way, more or less during the Middle Ages. And this is a compliment. They are rediscovering the continent, the continental concept as it existed before the advent of the nation-state in the 18th and 19th centuries. But they are rediscovering the Middle Ages, with the advantages and without the disadvantages of the late 19th century and the 20th century.

They are memories that are constantly acting within civilizations. In these memories, there are, however, key moments, events, crises that signal changes, that slightly alter the direction of various developments, that fix memories or certain interpretations of memories. I do not believe that there are that many "wild cards" in history. They turn up from time to time, but not as often as people say. Today, we talk as if, I don't know, e-mail is something that came at us out of nowhere and will change our history. In twenty years, we will surely laugh at this kind of small, amusing event, this small technology.

As for key events, aren't there two kinds – the worst and the best? Half a century ago, we murdered seven million Jews. That was a key moment in the history of the West. In our memory, it changed everything, but at the same time it is part of the catastrophic continuation of a certain part of our memory. There are also some extremely positive events. It is incredible that these two things can coexist. But experienced memory and real memory make up real experience.

I want to talk to you a little bit about some of these moments in Canada's past and also in the present and future. They are tools we have right now for discussion and for change.

Let me begin with the questions of murder or political death. Whenever I mention this subject, I'm amazed by the reaction. There is either an embarrassed silence, or a look of surprise, as if to say, 'why would you think that was important?', or 'what possible importance could that have?' or 'what's that got to do with the characteristics of a civilization?'

Confederation represents an artificial kick-off date, but let's use it. Since 1867 this country has killed in the course of internal political strife, in various ways, by hanging, battle, riots and so on, depending on how you do the numbers, approximately 85 people. With all due respect to other cultures, many of whom may be represented here today, this is an extremely unusual characteristic for a nation-state. At this moment, in New York, there's an enormous discussion going on about the fact that 3,000 American blacks were lynched, in the late 19th century and the 20th century. That's just one form of political murder for one group. There have also been various riots during which hundreds of blacks were killed. And, as I said, that is only one category of citizen. Think of the British in Ireland and the deaths over the last quarter century alone. The French in Corsica and in the Basque region. The Spanish and the Basques. And so on and so on and so on.

This country is constructed with all the elements which should have led to internal violence in the late 19th and 20th centuries – religions which oppose each other, racial, cultural groups which in other places opposed each other, enormous differences of richness and poverty. All of those things elsewhere led automatically to violence in the 19th century nation-state. Somehow, we avoided the worst of it in Canada. I don't think it's because we're more intelligent or nicer. I think it has to do with all sorts of circumstances which shape society and events – distance, the North, marginality, poverty. Of course, some choices have been made; there have been some clever moments. But you know, one shouldn't take credit for these things. And of course we must not forget all the catastrophic things that happened. I could spend the entire morning listing them. The stupid things. The scandalous things. The people whose lives we have ruined. In spite of this, the casualties have only crept up to about eighty-five, and we can name them all. It's an astonishing thing to say that in 133 years we can actually name everybody who has died as a result of civil strife.

My feeling is that if you want to understand a nation-state, you begin by asking: "How many of its own citizens has it killed?" Then you can move on to other matters – Were good paintings painted? Very good paintings? Is there wonderful architecture? In other words, you begin not with glory but with modesty. And modesty means believing that you don't have the right to kill your own citizens.

I believe very strongly that the key historic moment, when it was decided formally that we would go down this relatively non-violent road (because it was not automatic), came on the 27th of April 1849, two days after the elite of Canada burnt down our Parliament Buildings because they didn't want to lose power (I am grossly simplifying the way it's normally taught but I think it's an accurate interpretation.) They came out of their houses in Montreal, burnt down the Parliament Buildings, and then tried to stone the Governor General and assassinate the Prime Minister and Deputy Prime Minister. Just a minor event. We tend not to talk about it. Two days later, on the 27th, in the midst of ongoing civil disorder, the Cabinet met. This was at a time when, throughout Europe and the United States, there was enormous disorder in the streets, cavalry was charging down main avenues everywhere on a regular basis, opening fire to clear the streets. And they were not simply firing on working class citizens, they were firing on the middle class and the upper middle class and the minor aristocracy, many of whom were the leaders of the reform movements of the day.

The Canadian Cabinet met on the 27th and decided to justify their non-violent actions over the preceding thirty-six hours and, as it turns out, to justify their non-violent actions of the next several months. When I say decided, I mean consciously, intellectually, decided to adopt an extremely unusual approach. There it is, carefully transcribed in the Cabinet minutes, which to my astonishment I've never seen quoted in any book of Canadian history. I just don't know why. This is the sort of document which indicates the trajectory of a very unusual civilization. It contains such phrases as: "the proper mode of preserving order is by strengthening the civil authorities." This is a remarkable statement for a government to make in the middle of the 19th century; this is not what the British Government was doing at that time; in fact, the British Government sent angry messages over the next few months to the Prime Minister through the Governor, furious that he had not sent troops into the streets in order to do what was done in London, which was to shoot down the people who were causing trouble. It's very interesting to go back and read that correspondence. The great western historian W. L. Morton said that "the Canadian leaders had decided not to answer defiance with defiance but to have moderate combat shame arrogant violence."

What they had done was introduce a clear notion of how any government should behave in a constituted Canadian nation-state. What I am suggesting is that our present constitution was actually born between 1848 and 1849, and that afterwards we fiddled with it as we went along. Indeed we continue to fiddle with it. What do I mean? Well, each civilization defines how it will imagine citizenship. They conceive of a notion which encapsulates their society. Our notion was built around restraint. In other words, restraint was the element which would allow a place as complicated and as unusual as this to survive the catastrophes which were striking the nation-states of Europe and our neighbour to the South.

Our relatively successful addiction to restraint is tied to a shared sense of ourselves as a profoundly egalitarian civilization, one could say a profoundly middle class civilization. It doesn't really matter what the class is if everybody imagines themselves belonging to it. The concept of this structure is that as many people as possible should belong to that single group, in our case, the middle class.

You will find these egalitarian assumptions built into the fundamental structures of this NOT new country. This old country.

I keep saying ours is an old country in the hope that ministerial speech writers will notice and drop their almost automatic use of that terrible phrase: "in this new country where all is possible." The truth is we are in an old country where a certain number of things are possible precisely because we have at least 400 years of experience of working together here; at least 400 years of operating inside what I would call the fundamental triangle, the fundamental three-part foundation of the country: the Aboriginals, the Francophones, and the Anglophones. If you convert that triangle into modern terms, it means that long before anybody conceived of Upper or Lower Canada or the Dominion of Canada, this place was already functioning as a society of minorities. There has never been a majority in this country. It has always been a country made up of minorities. Even the concept of English Canada is a preposterous idea because it was essentially Scottish and Irish. And when you look at the Loyalists, who are usually thought of as English Loyalists, you discover that the percentage of English was very small. There were probably as many if not more Germans. And there were Jews, a sizeable group of blacks, large groups of Irish and Scots and so on. So from the very beginning, the reality of even the English minority was an unusual grouping of smaller minorities.

Think of the country in architectural terms: a foundation of three pillars, Aboriginal, Francophone, and Anglophone, cemented together if you like by the Métis – which is in a sense the only original thing the three groups did together, to our great and good fortune. Why good fortune? Because the Métis were absolutely key in the shaping of enormous parts of the country. They settled, through their military victories, a large part of the southern border of the Prairies for example. And then we constructed on top of that triangular foundation, floor after floor after floor after floor, of additional minorities from around the world.

I'll come back to this architectural image in a moment. But first, I want to point out that the idea that multiculturalism was invented by the Trudeau government – the classic view – is false. This was a multicultural country from the seventeenth century on and has never been anything except a multicultural country. Even if you go back and look at the way in which they conceived a mythological view of Confederation in 1867, you'll see that in their own minds, even if they were trying to wipe out the essential memory of the Aboriginal role, they were nevertheless talking about four major groups, not two major groups. Perhaps the word "multicultural" has been too intensely defined over the last few decades to be recuperated for general historical use. Well then, let's say that Canada has been a country of minorities since the 17th century.

A further point: What I'm describing when I speak of egalitarianism, a minority-based culture and an architectural structure is a very unusual model for a nation-state. A non-monolithic model. Anybody who's here from Europe, or the United States, would agree that the 18th/19th century concept of a nation-state was at its heart monolithic, centralizing, designed to remove, for all sorts of reasons, the power of the barons and the regions. One of the basic assumptions was that a nation-state could only be properly administered by the centre if the civilization was reduced to a single language and if all dialects were eliminated. Often these languages marked for elimination were first denigrated as dialects in order to make such linguistic cleansing seem less shocking.

The result was a mono-linguistic dictatorship of the centre. Throughout the 19th and 20th centuries, until the Second World War, almost all Western nation-states were constructed around that model. That's what built the United States, which is a profoundly 18th and 19th century European monolithic nation.

You could argue that the United States is not monolithic. On the ground that is true. But its conception, its religious texts – the Declaration of Independence, Constitution, Bill of Rights – its mythology are all profoundly monolithic. As an imagined place, it is monolithic. And the way in which it does things is monolithic.

What I'm saying is that in the middle of the nineteenth century, in this marginal, northern, poor, second- or third-rate little group of colonies, which gradually became Canada, we were already in the process of inventing a new concept, an incredibly post-modern concept – almost by mistake – as a way of living together, as a way of dealing with the impossibility of anybody dominating. We – or rather our predecessors – invented a new kind of nation-state. You could call it a country of minorities. You could call it a decentralized country or, as I've often said, a country based on complexity. You can call it anything you want, but the point is it was a rejection, from the 1840s on, of the dominance of the 18th/19th century idea of the monolithic nation-state. All of our subsequent problems – those which have overwhelmed us from time to time over the last 150 years, as they do in every country – can be attributed to attempts by our elites to import ideologies from Europe. That is, by virtue of their own insecurities, they attempted to impose on this country 18th and 19th century European ideas of the monolithic nation-state. This resulted in unpleasantness, violence, discord. In each case the people eventually found a way to restrain their elites, either by throwing them out or by convincing them that complexity, slowness, a lack of clear priorities, obscurity, wasting time, all of these, are essential elements in the success of this country. And that glorious, romantic, heroic leadership may fit just fine into a monolithic nation-state, but it doesn't work here.

Now let me come back to the idea of an architectural image as the best way to describe our civilization. I've thought about this for years. Somehow we have slipped once again into a European approach, a sort of linear view of how the country was created and evolved. This begins with the Manichean idea of two founding peoples. The two are simply the monolithic idea divided into two halves. Immediately, in a world obsessed by measurement – more often than not, artificial measurement – this approach provokes the question – well, how many of each? What are the numbers? Who has the power? How does it all add up statistically? In other words, this is a linear view which leads to a monolithic view. It is a very social science-like view of society. But Canada is not a linear, rational, European monolithic country. It never has been. Which is why I feel an architectural approach is more appropriate, more accurate, being multi-dimensional, spatial. And this country is essentially spatial.

This is an approach which allows us to understand the central role of Francophones without obsessing over birth rates. It also allows us to re-imagine the reality of the Aboriginal role without becoming obsessed by population statistics. This is not, as some cynical people have said whenever I or other people bring this up, an attempt to reintroduce a romantic idea of the past. Nor is it political correctness in any way, shape or form. Remember, out of 400 years of Canadian history – that is since the meeting of the three groups – the first 250 years were dominated by the Aboriginals or they had equal power. Then, for approximately 100 years the European immigrants reneged on their treaty obligations or a large part of them. Then over the last 50 odd years, we have begun trying to act like civilized people again and have begun putting back together the original arrangements. Slowly but surely we've been re-remembering that original triangular foundation.

This last year has been one of the most exciting for a very long time because with the creation of Nunavut and with the Nisga'a Treaty we have managed, in a brand new way, to introduce into what appear to be Western-oriented legal structures two examples of totally non-linear legal and administrative thought. Both Nunavut and Nisga'a are spatial inventions which do not respond to easy questions about the linear nature of power. And that is good. That is very true to the nature of this place.

Let me go a step further. People often say we have British parliamentary democracy. Well, we don't. Our parliament doesn't work anything like the British parliament. It bears little resemblance to that parliament apart from the names of the roles. The way in which it actually works, the way in which it is conceived is not at all British. We talk about having Anglo-Saxon law or English law and the Civil Code. The reality is that our legal codes are a mix of the two as well as being deeply influenced by our first 250 years, that is, by our experience with the Aboriginals. Our social models, even our negotiating models, for example our approach toward constitutional questions, come out of that first 250 years of experience. Even the fact that we invented peace-keeping and have become experts in it is a reminder of the fact that there is another method, and that method in many ways comes out of those first 250 years.

Let me just go back for a second to the idea of egalitarianism. I'm going to quote you one paragraph from Louis LaFontaine's Address to the Electors of Terrebonne, which I quote in every single speech I give, and I'm going to keep on quoting it until people start quoting it back to me.

Because for me this is perhaps the central phrase in the imagining of what Canada would become: [in translation] "To prevent us from enjoying it, the social equality that forms the distinctive character of both the people of Upper Canada and those of Lower Canada would have to be destroyed. Because this social equality must necessarily lead to our political freedom. There can be no privileged caste in Canada outside and above the mass of its people."

This is not a speech by a young student filled with idealism. This is the fundamental declaration of policy from the future first democratic Prime Minister of Canada who, with Robert Baldwin, would set the direction of the country. It isn't surprising that LaFontaine, Baldwin, Macdonald, Cartier, Tupper, McGee, Howe were all obsessed by things such as public education. And their approach toward education did not come out of the British and French traditions. They consciously went and looked for public and egalitarian approaches. They found the basis for Canadian public education in Prussia, Holland, Switzerland, and New York. And the first seeds of our universal health system lie in the egalitarian idea which was formally put in place by Louis LaFontaine.

I'm perfectly conscious of the fact that a percentage of our elites have never accepted this interpretation of Canada. After all, as I mentioned before, they began their explanation of themselves by burning down the Parliament Buildings in 1849. Theirs was and remains the point of view of the classic colonial elite which believes that reality exists elsewhere. Not here. An essay which might help you to understand their point of view is V.S. Naipaul's "The Return of Eva Peron." In his description of what went wrong in Argentina, I think you'll find many echoes of the Canadian situation and of the choices by which we are constantly faced. Let me summarize the argument which they reject. This is an old civilization constructed upon a non-linear, tripartite foundation. This is a minority-based intellectual idea, the opposite of a monolithic society, and has been for 150 years. Canada was the model of the European Union 100 years before anybody thought about the modern idea of Europe.

Let me finish with a few details.

First of all, there is the concept of rivers. In most classic nation-states, including the monolithic nineteenth century nation-state, a river was and is a barrier, a border. It was where wars ended. It was where you separated people. One of the fascinating things about Canada is that rivers have never been barriers. As Harold Innis and many others have explained, rivers were the highways leading to the centre of the country. Until very recently, they were the mode of transportation. They were replaced by other modes of transportation such as railways and now high technology. In our history, rivers were like the hinges of a door – meaning "a joint consisting of two interlocking pieces of metal connected by a common axis around which one or both pieces can turn freely." What is bizarre in Canada's case is that this joint turns in both directions. You can be here in a city, Ottawa, that is a classic example of this idea of a hinge, a river as a hinge in a civilization where, in fact, there are many interlocking pieces turning around one other. This is completely different from the idea of a river as a border.

My second small idea is that, in general, the idea of civilization is taught, especially in the Western tradition, in the following way: it began with nomads – hunters and gatherers – the hunter-gatherer society. And with 'progress' we turned into an agricultural society, and eventually became sedentary. Today, therefore, we have completed this process of 'progress,' because we are urban, sedentary people. I have heard this taught worldwide. It was progress, wasn't it? The Western idea of progress. I would say that, here, with our three foundations, with our architectural structure, with the untameable nature of most of our territory (90 per cent of our territory is untameable in the European/American sense), we have produced a civilization where there is constant tension between movement; you could say nomads or hunter-gatherers or whatever you like, but between movement on one side and sedentarism on the other. Our civilization is therefore built on constant tension between these two things. Any analyst who tries, for example, to describe our novels as products of the first, second, or third stage sadly misunderstands and misconstrues the reality of a civilization. It is permanently founded on this tension between movement and sedentarism. Canada functions as a tension. That is what is interesting.

A third idea: It's not surprising that out of this permanent tension came a school of philosophy. You could call it the Toronto School or the Canadian School, founded by the greatest thinker we have had, Harold Innis. Innis was the first to conceive many of the modern ideas on communications, which were then picked up and developed by people like Marshall McLuhan or, in a completely different way, by Northrop Frye, or in a completely different way by George Woodcock, or in a way by the young Pierre Trudeau when he wrote about balance – his essays on equilibrium were extremely interesting – or by Fernand Dumont or George Grant. Fernand Dumont and George Grant are two very interesting thinkers to put side by side. They were both important thinkers, but they were held back by their attachments to certain earlier European religious ideas, which prevented them from fulfilling their intelligence in the way Innis did. What all of them demonstrated – Innis, McLuhan, Frye, Trudeau, Grant, Dumont – I could add Glenn Gould – is that in this civilization communications is the central theme, communications at every level, even at the most abstract and theoretical levels. Memory is a key element in that concept of communications. Memory has a very important role, here perhaps more important than elsewhere because of the need to communicate. The discussion around the tools of communication, of movement, has always been with us and is still with us. This is in part because of the constant tension between movement and the sedentary. As a result, throughout this century, we have played a central role in the evolution of the philosophy of communications.

I might add that you can tell the country is in crisis when we forget the centrality of communications at every level of our being from the purely philosophical, to the plastic arts, music and the written word; from our mythologies to our practical life. You can tell the country is in crisis when it costs more to fly from Toronto/Montreal to Vancouver than it does from Toronto/Montreal to London/Paris. There you can see, in a very basic sort of way, that Canadians have lost the sense of how absolutely essential the nature of communications is to a place like this. It shows that we have forgotten what Innis said: "that economics must derive its laws from the history of the place rather than deriving the place from a set of all-purpose laws formulated elsewhere."

What have I said so far? This has been a civilization of minorities from the beginning; a three-dimensional, architectural structure; profoundly non-monolithic from the beginning: therefore, outside of the classic American/European nation-state structure even in the mid-19th century; the first of the post-modern nation-states; an old civilization with four centuries of stable evolution inside its complexity; a place where rivers – and therefore other forms of communication – are not borders but hinges; a model which does not 'progress' from movement to sedentarism, but is built on the tension between the two; a civilization which thinks in terms of communications and fails to the extent that it ignores the central role of communications; a poor, northern, marginal society which has intellectually constructed its prosperity through an idea of inclusive egalitarianism. A civilization the very essence of which is its complexity.

All of these ideas are tied in some way to the idea of a spatial non-linear non-rational civilization. The opposite of rational is non-rational, not irrational. A spatial idea of civilization is not in any way, shape or form a European/American concept. This is the least European democracy in the world. When I say European, I am referring to the 18th century model of the nation-state. This is the most

American state in North America. There are only two of us, and the other one is profoundly European.

I'd like to finish with a thought which relates to language. Canadians are extremely comfortable with our own idea of our complexity. Many people in politics, business and academia would like to have a clear view of the place. They would be more comfortable if Canada conformed to a normal model. But Canadians are very comfortable with being incomprehensible by these standards. In a curious way, we know that one of our strongest suits is that half the time the outsiders don't really understand what we're doing. It's a sign of great self-confidence that we can live with this complexity and that we can live on several levels at once. We can be several things at once.

Of course language – or rather, languages –is key to this complexity. Anybody who knows me knows that I believe very strongly in the central role, for example, of the two national languages in Canada. One of our most successful innovations over the last twenty-five years has been the creation of immersion schooling which now educates 317,000 kids, Anglophones in Francophone schools. This would be the equivalent of Germany having about 800,000 kids in French schools, or France about 700,000 kids in German schools. A revolutionary innovation. This and other linguistic innovations are absolutely essential.

But it's also very important not to see our society only through the structures of language. If you do, you are slipping back into the limits of the international structure of English and French. What is the international structure of those languages if not that of the old empires, British, French, American? I'm not criticizing those places *per se*. But why would we want to lead ourselves back into total dependence on a structure which we didn't put in place ourselves, which could only in the end be defined elsewhere as having a meaning; a meaning centred on the ex-empire. Besides, these are structures in which we can't help, whether in English or French, but play a very small role. Such dependence would lead us back into a structure which has built-in assumptions about the monolithic nation-state, about the denial of complexity, about the elimination of minority cultures. Dependence on a monolithic linguistic structure involves a de facto denial of our geographical marginality in the North.

I say this because I know that in some places where Canadian culture is taught, the central way of coming at it is through the language stream or the linguistic stream. And I think that that is not the right way to go about it, because it deforms the interpretation of what we really are. I think it's very important for all of us to be looking for comparisons. Not those which eliminate the linguistic line, but which complement or counterbalance the linguistic line. Otherwise we won't be able to understand our own mythologies.

When we look at Scandinavia, at Latin America, at Middle Europe, at Russia, we find many elements which have a great deal more to do with us, with the reality of how we live in this place, than an approach through linguistics could offer. You find in some of those civilizations a certain sense of melancholy which is not characteristic of either American or Western European cultures. You find a celebration of the provincial – this is very important to us. I always remember Robertson Davies saying to me, not long before his death, that one of the greatest things about his life, one of the things that made him happiest, was to know that he came from the provinces. It was a great strength for a writer. Historically, many of the great writers do not come from the centre. It gives us and these other civilizations a great sense of contrast and difference within society. It's something to celebrate, not something to be embarrassed about. What else? Well you find a sense of nature, out of control, uncontrollable whether it's in Canada, in Northern Europe, or in Latin America. Magic realism is one of the greatest themes of Latin American literature, set in an abiding preoccupation with the nature of time and of historical times. You find the curious contradictions which come from living on the uncontrolled margins of Western democratic civilization. You find countries and civilizations which are able to accept the idea of solitude as a positive, not a negative. As Glenn Gould put it: "the value of life comes from solitude."

What am I saying? I said that the very nature of Canada is complexity. When you go to Montreal – what do you find? A trilingual city. That is to say, language is key, but language cannot necessarily say everything. A European politician visiting Canada said not long ago that all the Francophones in the world, as such, have converging views of the world. That is an interesting idea: people who speak the same language share a set of ethics. It reminds me of the nineteenth century English politicians who used to talk about the duty of empire; it also reminds me of the old joke about the American who says he is happy to be a Christian because the Bible was written in English.

We do not share values because we speak English or French. We share values because our societies are similar. Experience. The situation. History. Geopolitics. Values. Climates. Geographies. Political systems. Attitudes toward violence. And so on and so on. There may also be a language to share. Maybe not. But why think that it is important to share other things if we share a language? I believe that it is important instead to look for differences within the same languages and similarities outside languages. It is extremely important to think that major differences are possible within the same language, that with effort we will find real, philosophical, political, historical, cultural equivalences, friendships, beyond our own linguistic communities.

In Latin America in particular, I find that there are opportunities for absolutely extraordinary intellectual comparisons. Australia is an example of a country where one of Canada's languages is spoken. But that is rather an accident, luck. Elsewhere, there are enormous differences within English and French. People who speak English may come from a democratic environment, just as they may come from a dictatorship. They therefore have very different "real language content." I believe that by finding a balance between the strength that differences within languages give us – languages without centres, languages that are real everywhere they exist – and the strength that similarities outside languages give us, we can find a kind of international modus vivendi that Canadians can adopt.

Passer à l'avenir
Actualiser la canadianité*

Jocelyn Létourneau

C EUX ET CELLES QUI SE VOIENT CONFIER LE MANDAT DE PENSER LE
Canada au tournant du vingt et unième siècle ont une tendance,
normale je crois, à mettre l'accent sur ces problèmes et questions qui
sont au cœur des préoccupations immédiates des gens et de l'actualité.

C'est ainsi que l'on fait grand état des impasses constitutionnelles
et du tarissement de l'esprit et de la pratique démocratiques qui marquent la vie politique au Canada. De même, on ne cesse de revenir sur
la panoplie des problèmes d'ordre sociétal vécus au pays à l'ère de la
mondialisation, le plus important de ces problèmes étant sans conteste
celui de la fragmentation tendancielle de la société canadienne en des
« mondes » bien caractérisés, celui des « gagnants » et celui des « per-
dants », celui des « zones fortes » et celui des « zones faibles », celui des
« migrants haut de gamme » et celui des « classes enracinées », etc.[1].

Loin de moi l'idée de nier ou même de minimiser l'ampleur et la
portée de ces écueils sur lesquels vient souvent s'échouer la gouvernance canadienne, échouements qui constituent autant de naufrages,
petits ou grands, qui assombrissent le futur du pays.

Il est une question cependant sur laquelle on insiste un peu moins,
une question qui renvoie pourtant à l'un des plus grands défis du
Canada à l'aube du vingt et unième siècle, et c'est celle, pour le pays,
de passer à l'avenir.

Passer à l'avenir est ce genre de formule ambivalente que j'aime
bien, à l'instar par exemple de « Penser le Québec dans le paysage
canadien[2] » ou de « Je me souviens d'où je m'en vais » ou encore de

---

*   Ce texte doit être lu comme un essai d'exploration métahistorique et non pas
comme le fruit d'une entreprise de recherche méthodique. L'article garde essentiellement sa forme de présentation orale.

« Honorer ses ancêtres, c'est se responsabiliser devant l'avenir[3] ». Ces formules contiennent en effet une part d'ambiguïté, donc de fluidité, de souplesse, d'ouverture et d'adaptabilité qui, pour moi, ne renvoie absolument pas à de l'hésitation, à du cafouillage ou à de l'incertitude, mais bien plutôt à une disposition sereine, de la part de ceux qui les utilisent ou les trouvent fécondes, pour affronter l'énigme pérenne du politique. Cette énigme, de mon point de vue, n'est autre que celle d'accueillir la complexité de la vie, y compris sa dimension conflictuelle, dans un esprit de médiation, et ce, en s'ouvrant à la possibilité de penser l'impensable jusqu'à soutenir parfois le paradoxe.

On a souvent défini la politique comme étant l'art du possible. Voici une vue plutôt démissionnaire de l'activité suprême du genre humain. Pour ma part, j'associe bien davantage la politique à l'art de négocier l'impossible, une finalité qui exige, de la part de ceux et celles qui exercent cette responsabilité, des vertus et qualités exceptionnelles.

Or, le défi de passer à l'avenir est l'une des facettes cardinales de la politique.

Il n'est jamais simple en effet d'articuler sur un mode porteur le souvenir au devenir de telle manière que les descendants puissent aspirer à une vie dégagée des lourdeurs du passé sans pour cela renier l'héritage des anciens. À plus d'un titre, cette difficulté d'un arrimage heureux du passé à l'avenir est l'un des murs sur lesquels vient se briser toute possibilité de rénovation des représentations symboliques du Canada, rénovation dont on pourrait s'attendre qu'elle contribue à la récupération générale du pays dans un sens avantageux pour l'avenir.

À l'heure actuelle, c'est comme si l'espace politique du Canada était sous l'emprise de trois grands groupements par référence dont deux voulaient, pour se refonder, se rappeler à eux-mêmes dans leurs seules offenses subies (les francophones et les autochtones) alors que l'autre, pour se refonder tout autant et le pays avec lui apparemment, désirait user des pouvoirs délivrants de l'oubli (les anglophones).

Or, à cet égard, mon opinion est pour une fois univoque : ni le rappel impérissable de ce qui fut, ni la pratique de l'oubli, comme modes du souvenir, ne constituent, pour les contemporains désireux d'établir un rapport satisfaisant avec le passé et le futur, un moyen qui se révèle fécond.

Aussi peut-on dire que, du point de vue des conditions pour passer à l'avenir, les Canadiens semblent en ce moment empêtrés dans une impasse dont le dénouement tarde à se manifester.

Faut-il désespérer d'y arriver ? Je ne crois pas. Pourrait-on penser qu'il se trouve, dans l'expérience historique canadienne, un capital mémoriel et factuel par le rappel et les ressources duquel il serait possible de dépasser les insuffisances, les apories parfois, des représentations actuelles du pays ? J'estime que oui.

Il m'apparaît en effet que l'aventure canadienne est une histoire pleine de blessures, certes, mais de possibilités aussi. Il me semble de même que l'aventure canadienne est une histoire d'ambivalences et de dissonances, ce qui, et j'y reviendrai, est une caractéristique globalement positive de l'antériorité du pays de même qu'un fonds, une dot considérable, pour passer à l'avenir.

C'est en effet dans l'ambiguïté de ces blessures et possibilités, de ces ambivalences et dissonances, que s'est élevé le Canada, fragile et fort tout à la fois, c'est-à-dire cherchant continuellement sa voie mais ouvert, pour cette raison précisément, à différentes problématiques lui permettant de se récupérer dans des raccords politiques rendant possible son évolution vers d'autres horizons.

Les mots pour dire le pays

Les mots employés sont importants. Dans un essai récent sur les mots et sur le monde, Alberto Manguel rappelait avec pertinence que les mots donnent à l'expérience sa forme, offrent à la vie la possibilité de vêtir sa nudité [4].

Or quels sont ces mots qui décrivent et révèlent le plus justement le Canada ?

N'attendez pas de moi que je vous parle du pays en vous peignant la beauté du soleil naissant sur l'Atlantique et chatouillant la côte canadienne de ses premiers rayons matinaux. N'espérez pas non plus que je chante ce pays en vous racontant la joie de marcher dans les feuilles d'automne, à Québec, par une journée sans vent et presque pluvieuse ; en vous rappelant à quel point l'on se sent écrasé par le ciel des Prairies ; ou en vous relatant la plénitude ressentie par une traversée des Rocheuses sur la musique de Mahler. Pareilles images et sensations ressortent d'expériences personnelles qui témoignent d'un rapport singulier à la nature universelle, pas au pays. Pareilles images ne sauraient nullement exprimer ce qui me semble être au cœur de l'aventure historique canadienne.

Il est des mots plus subtils, moins racoleurs et moins faux par conséquent, pour dire le Canada. Ces mots ne sont pas très excitants, surtout pour des politiciens, parfois des intellectuels, qui sont en quête de visions simples, univoques, tranchées, assurées, voire joviales, pour vendre ou penser le pays.

J'ai plus tôt mentionné quelques-uns de ces mots par lesquels, me semble-t-il, l'on peut rendre compte de l'expérience historique canadienne. Ces mots sont ceux d'ambivalence et de dissonance, de blessure et de possibilité, de raccord et de récupération. Je pourrais rajouter ceux de tensions et de frictions, de tiraillements et d'interdépendance contrainte, d'ambiguïté et de paradoxe.

Il s'agit de mots qui, au lieu de décrire le Canada sous l'angle d'un corps structuré, puissant, symétrique et stable, bref comme on aime bien qu'un pays soit habituellement présenté ou montré, le rendent dans ses mouvances approximatives, dans ses tâtonnements perpétuels, dans ses indispositions continuelles par rapport à lui-même, dans ses équilibres instables et dans ses proximités distantes; autant de caractéristiques, on l'avouera, qui portent en elles l'idée générale de fluidité, idée qui s'accorde mal avec l'essence supposée des nations et des États, laquelle est réputée exprimer une propriété originelle immuable.

Or, sans verser dans les excès du postmodernisme qui veut, selon la vulgate consacrée, qu'il n'y ait de réalité que textuelle ou coulante, je ne suis pas personnellement partisan de ces visions anhistoriques et téléologiques des nations selon lesquelles il y aurait, à l'origine des touts constitués, une graine contenant en germe l'avenir de ce qui ne pouvait pas ne pas être ou de ce qui aurait dû être mais qui a été empêché ou reste inaccompli[5].

Pour me représenter le Canada dans le mouvement incessant de son ordre ou de son désordre, c'est comme on veut, j'aime bien imaginer le pays sur le mode des fameuses structures mobiles inventées par Alexander Calder, structures dont les éléments palpables, en continuel balancement les uns par rapport aux autres, les uns avec les autres et les uns contre les autres, produisent une sorte de composition dissonante de figures réelles et virtuelles où l'harmonie est toujours en construction.

Cette expression, composition dissonante, me semble particulièrement juste pour rendre et offrir l'expérience historique canadienne dans sa complexité irréductible.

On sait ce qu'est une dissonance : en composition musicale, la dissonance renvoie à l'intervalle incongru et désagréable entre deux sons qui appelle une résolution par un accord harmonique. Paradoxe intéressant, la dissonance comprend aussi les notes responsables d'un tel réarrangement mélodieux. En d'autres termes, la dissonance est tout à la fois la réunion déplaisante de sons *et* l'accord consolant cet effet contrariant ou ennuyeux.

L'image de la dissonance est utile pour aborder le cas du Canada qui, tout en générant continuellement des conflits, sait précisément se récupérer grâce aux frictions et tensions qui scandent sa mouvance.

À maints égards, en effet, l'expérience canadienne fut et reste l'expression de tensions et de frictions incessantes entre forces centripètes et forces centrifuges, tantôt partenaires et tantôt antagoniques, tantôt complémentaires et tantôt contradictoires. Elle fut aussi et demeure encore, par le jeu réfléchi et tâtonnant d'acteurs en concurrence, l'expression d'un dépassement de ces tensions et frictions dans des raccords rendant possible le passage à un ou à d'autres états politiques.

Particularité intéressante mais en même temps frustrante pour bien des observateurs, s'ils se veulent enchaînements par rapport à un ou à des états politiques antérieurs, ces raccords ne furent jamais, et ne sont toujours pas résolution définitive de l'équation canadienne, laquelle ne comporte pas un seul dénominateur commun mais plusieurs dénominateurs conjoints parmi lesquels, assurément et de manière incontournable, il y a le Québec[6].

C'est ainsi qu'en pratique le Canada évolue entre les possibilités continuelles que lui offrent ses acteurs en cherchant à dépasser ses dissonances constitutives, celles qui découlent de sa dualité structurelle en particulier, et l'aporie sur laquelle vient s'échouer toute tentative de résorber ces dissonances en chantant le pays sur le mode de l'harmonie ou de l'unité nationale.

Autrement dit, la possibilité du Canada réside précisément dans l'accueil des tensions et frictions qui lui sont constitutives et dans leur transformation en compromis provisoires, compromis ne levant toutefois jamais la perspective des oppositions et des conflits animant l'évolution du pays.

Là se love, je pense, la singularité canadienne. Une singularité qui n'est la manifestation d'aucun essentialisme transcendantal, mais qui procède de l'histoire et se comprend par elle; une singularité à la donne globalement heureuse plutôt que malheureuse, mais qui n'est pas sans accroc; une singularité dont la mémoire est cependant faiblissante dans l'imaginaire de la classe politique et intellectuelle qui gouverne et inspire actuellement le pays.

Il est une conséquence politique qu'il faut tirer de pareille vision de l'aventure historique canadienne. C'est que toute tentative qui vise à en finir avec la dissonance structurelle et structurante du pays en fixant une fois pour toutes son évolution dans des matrices invariables, une telle tentative, dis-je, est la façon la plus probante de diminuer les possibilités d'avenir pour le Canada[7].

Une ambiguïté féconde

À plus d'un égard, l'expérience historique canadienne fut et reste largement marquée du sceau de l'ambiguïté. J'entends par là que, pour des raisons tenant à l'histoire et non pas à une essence première, l'élan, la trajectoire et la dynamique du pays n'ont jamais été univoques. Je parle ainsi non pour reprendre à mon compte le paradigme encore à la mode, mais daté comme concept métahistorique fondant une vision d'avenir du Canada, des identités limitées, parcellisées et atomisées – ce que certains continuent de traduire, dans le langage courant, par la formule vieillie de « mosaïque canadienne ».

Je dis que l'expérience historique canadienne fut ambiguë parce que les épisodes catalyseurs du devenir canadien ont toujours débouché sur l'ambivalence plutôt que sur l'univocité, c'est-à-dire sur une certaine infinitude, ouverture et imprécision de destin plutôt que sur une inflexibilité de parcours. Cela est vrai de 1759, de 1837-38, de 1840, de 1867, voire de 1982.

En d'autres termes, malgré bien des tentatives en ce sens de la part de petits et de grands acteurs et penseurs, il n'a jamais été possible de focaliser le devenir du pays sur l'axe des ordonnées d'un seul principe structurant. De même, il n'a jamais été possible de séparer l'avenir du pays de son passé, c'est-à-dire de refonder le Canada en faisant fi des présences antérieures qui l'avaient façonné. Il n'a jamais été possible non plus d'imposer aux habitants du pays une seule pratique et vision du Canada, ni d'ailleurs d'éliminer ou de faire abstraction de la volonté des groupements constitutifs du pays de s'affirmer coûte que coûte, *avec et contre* les autres groupements, dans le paysage canadien.

On aurait tort de voir dans l'ambiguïté canadienne la manifestation d'une faillite « nationale », celle d'une incapacité à être collectivement ou celle d'une digression déplorable de destin par rapport à l'idéal type de l'État-nation. Dans mon esprit, l'ambiguïté de l'expérience historique canadienne n'est pas l'expression d'une impuissance à imposer un projet intégrateur. Elle est un *parcours* qu'il faut reconnaître et assumer, une trajectoire dont il faut exploiter les ressources pour activer la suite des choses. À plus d'un titre et à maintes occasions, l'ambiguïté constitutive de l'expérience historique canadienne s'est en effet révélée porteuse d'avenir pour le pays dans la mesure où elle est apparue, simultanément, comme le mode de condensation des blessures et comme le mode d'expression des possibilités formant depuis toujours la matière du passé du Canada.

Autrement dit, plutôt que de déboucher sur l'équivoque paralysante ou de favoriser l'hégémonie d'un seul pouvoir dominateur, l'ambiguïté canadienne a rendu possible et sanctionné en même temps, l'expression des contraires. Il ne s'agit pas de voir dans cette situation la preuve d'une tolérance ou d'une aptitude à la conciliation uniques au monde de la part des habitants du Canada les uns envers les autres. Pour être juste, cette tolérance et cette aptitude apparente à la conciliation ont été maintes fois démenties par les faits. L'ambiguïté canadienne découle plutôt de ce qu'aucun pouvoir latent ou constitué à l'intérieur de cet espace d'interrelations sociales et politiques qu'on appelle le Canada n'a pu imposer sa seule raison aux pouvoirs concurrents, bien que de nombreuses asymétries de réciprocité se soient manifestées entre ces pouvoirs s'exprimant, se rencontrant et se disputant dans l'arène publique.

Si ma vision des choses est exacte, l'ambiguïté d'êtres du Canada témoignerait donc tout à la fois de la pérennité des tensions marquant l'expérience canadienne *et* de l'incapacité manifeste des pouvoirs dominants d'imposer leur logique politique jusqu'au bout, et ce, par suite de la détermination inébranlable de forces concurrentes à s'affirmer et à s'épanouir, c'est-à-dire à être et à obtenir reconnaissance au cœur de l'espace politique institué du pays.

On ne saurait en aucun cas minimiser l'importance de ces forces concurrentes dans la destinée canadienne. À maints égards, on pourrait d'ailleurs soutenir que le Canada s'est historiquement forgé comme un ensemble de paris perdus par la raison intransigeante des pouvoirs dominants ou des majorités contre l'insistance des acteurs ou des minorités à perdurer dans le temps en ne cessant jamais de s'affirmer et en cherchant à faire avec la réalité des choses et celle des autres plutôt que de la refuser ou de s'exiler dans des lieux d'être exigus.

Raconter l'histoire de cette insistance à s'affirmer, à perdurer et à s'ouvrir à l'autre et à l'ailleurs, c'est précisément se donner les moyens de reconnaître le potentiel de récupération propre à l'expérience canadienne. C'est s'attaquer de front à l'opération de transformation des blessures en possibilités. C'est pénétrer au cœur de ce qui a fait la singularité canadienne hier et de ce qui pourrait peut-être la reconduire demain.

Une mémoire d'avenir

La question qui est au cœur de mon propos depuis le début est au fond la suivante : quelle mémoire, quelle histoire d'avenir pour le Canada ? En d'autres termes, quel récit qui rende et offre le plus justement possible l'expérience historique canadienne du double point de vue inséparable de la science et du politique, et ce, dans la conscience de demain ?

On comprendra que je refuse d'endosser ces récits hypocrites qui subliment la réalité passée de l'expérience canadienne pour faire bêtement du Canada le « meilleur pays du monde » et ce, depuis toujours. Je répète ce qui est lapalissade éculée : le rôle de l'historien n'est pas d'occulter la matière de l'histoire, mais de faire face à l'ayant-été dans un souci élevé de rigueur scientifique et d'éthique mémorielle[8]. Or, je l'ai dit, l'expérience historique canadienne est faite de blessures que l'on ne peut pas taire. La marginalisation tantôt délibérée tantôt involontaire, en partie réussie et en partie avortée du fait français, du fait autochtone et du fait métis, dans l'opération de construction de l'État-nation canadien et de canadianisation du pays compte parmi l'une de ces blessures qui, à l'évidence, n'arrive pas à se cicatriser. Il s'agit, je pense, d'une donnée imprescriptible de l'expérience historique canadienne. Cela dit, et j'y reviendrai, on ne peut pas vivre exclusivement dans l'hypothèse où dans l'hypothèque du passé.

Force est d'admettre par ailleurs que je ne suis pas partisan non plus de ces entreprises de reconstitution historique qui, insistant sur la puissance structurante de l'idée et de la pratique de la coopération dans l'expérience historique canadienne, diminuent par là, nécessairement, la puissance tout autant décisive de l'idée et de la pratique de l'affirmation de soi, et donc du conflit identitaire, dans la destinée du pays.

De mon point de vue, il n'est pas possible de faire l'histoire du Canada en ne mettant l'accent que sur les consonances et les convergences qui ont marqué le passé du pays.

Pour ne prendre qu'un exemple, significatif toutefois, la lutte des Canadiens français hier, et celle des Québécois francophones maintenant, pour inscrire leur historicité, leur identité et leur devenir dans la *problématique canadienne*, est tout aussi importante que leurs tentatives et opérations continuelles de conciliation et de collaboration avec les autres habitants du Canada pour bâtir et rebâtir le pays.

Autrement dit, l'histoire du Canada n'est pas l'accomplissement de l'unité dans la diversité ni la victoire des forces de la coopération sur celles de la discordance. Cette histoire est celle de dissonances toujours reconduites et produisant, par le jeu et les décisions avisés et impromptus d'acteurs cherchant à vivre avec et contre la complexité du monde, des voies de passage vers demain, voies de passage, toutefois, jamais parfaites et toujours partielles.

L'équilibre du Canada – c'est, me semble-t-il, ce qui ressort principalement de son passé – est celui de ses déséquilibres et asymétries continuellement contestées, négociées et finalement accueillies, de gré ou de force, par la majorité des décideurs, de même que par la population, et ce, pour qu'advienne *nolens volens* un avenir.

Voilà pourquoi il me semble que la meilleure histoire qui soit du Canada est celle qui, tout en n'oblitérant pas la réalité et la gravité des blessures causées, insiste sur les possibilités qu'ont su donner au pays ces habitants et décideurs qui, plutôt que de refuser ou de contrarier les dissonances constitutives de l'expérience historique canadienne, les ont reçues et traduites politiquement, par esprit visionnaire ou par la force des choses, c'est selon, mais en créant *ipso facto* un mouvement favorable à l'apparition de consonances provisoires.

L'expérience canadienne comme parcours de possibilités : voici une représentation du pays qui me semble historiquement juste par rapport au passé et politiquement porteuse pour l'avenir ; une représentation qui, sans nier les malheurs survenus hier dans le pays, n'y consume pourtant pas l'horizon de demain ; une représentation qui amène les habitants du pays non pas à se rappeler seulement ou oublier uniquement, mais, de manière paradoxalement heureuse – et j'insiste sur cette formule – à se souvenir d'où ils s'en vont.

Un concept clé : celui de canadianité

Pour penser et qualifier la dimension la plus féconde de l'expérience historique canadienne, j'ai, dans d'autres textes et notamment dans celui que j'ai fait paraître dans les pages du journal *Le Devoir* à l'été 1999[9], proposé le concept de canadianité, concept que je distingue de celui de canadianisation, voire de canadienneté[10]. Inutile de dire que cette initiative, audacieuse pour un intellectuel québécois, voire pour un intellectuel tout court, m'a valu bien des reproches[11].

En usant du concept de canadianité, mon objectif n'a pourtant jamais été – et n'est toujours pas, du reste – de fonder une vision radieuse ou naïve du pays. Il faut par ailleurs mal me connaître pour penser que, employant pareil concept, j'aie cherché à me faire artisan organique d'une cause, celle de la promotion du Canada, et ce, au détriment de la reconnaissance d'une identité québécoise distincte.

En tant qu'intellectuel, je crois qu'il importe d'être sincère envers ceux à qui l'on s'adresse. Personnellement, j'avouerai n'avoir qu'une patrie : celle de la pensée responsable, de la démarche éthique et de la conscience aiguë du monde. Et j'admettrai avoir une ambition unique : celle de chercher, en n'étant jamais épuisé ni désespéré par l'échec, ces mots qui rendent aussi justement que possible le passé et l'offrent en héritage aux descendants.

En usant du concept de canadianité, mon intention était de penser l'expérience canadienne, au cœur de laquelle n'a jamais cessé d'être l'aventure québécoise, sous l'angle tout à la fois valide, valable et souhaitable d'une histoire de dissonances, c'est-à-dire d'une histoire de blessures *et* de possibilités.

Mon but était également de m'insérer au cœur des tensions et ambiguïtés porteuses sur lesquelles s'est élevé le pays en les accueillant plutôt qu'en les condamnant ou les décriant, en les révélant plutôt qu'en les subsumant, les distillant ou les omettant.

Usant du concept de canadianité, mon objectif était encore d'ouvrir un espace argumentatif et interprétatif où l'expérience canadienne n'était pas restituée à l'aune du mantra de la conciliation ou de l'inhibition, mais dans ses réciprocités asymétriques et ses équilibres oscillants, dans ses maillages discordants et ses dissonances structurantes, dans ses convergences dissidentes et ses dissidences convergentes, dans ses interdépendances instables et dans la tendre (in)différence réciproque de ses habitants... – pour reprendre le répertoire d'oxymorons employés plus tôt et y ajouter.

Contrairement à bien des observateurs de la scène canadienne qui refusent de s'ouvrir aux possibilités du paradoxe, c'est au cœur de cette fragilité d'êtres du Canada – qui est possiblement l'expression d'une vigueur insoupçonnée – que je perçois et trouve la réalité historique du pays, si ce n'est son utopie, en tout cas son indéniable force de récupération.

On comprendra dans ce contexte qu'un projet comme celui de la souveraineté-partenariat ne me surprend pas ni ne m'importune. J'interprète en effet pareil projet comme un pari *pour* l'avenir du pays et non pas *contre* le futur du Canada[12]. La souveraineté-partenariat, entendue comme elle l'est par la majorité de ses supporteurs québécois, c'est-à-dire comme un moyen de relancer et d'actualiser l'expérience canadienne sur la base de ses spécificités régionales, est l'une de ces ambiguïtés propres à l'aventure du pays qui ont fondé sa destinée jusqu'à maintenant.

Étonnant comme perspective? C'est que penser l'impensable exige d'adopter des postures d'observation et des positions interprétatives non conventionnelles. Pour revenir aux sculptures d'Alexander Calder, n'est-ce pas le paradoxe non aporétique de ces mobiles que de ne pas se laisser piéger dans l'espace circonscrit par le tracé des formes et des figures composant la structure morphologique des œuvres?

En termes moins « académico-poétiques » peut-être, il est bien possible que, pour saisir le sens d'une œuvre de Calder, il faille l'observer en ayant la tête en bas, en se faisant soi-même élément mobile au sein de la sculpture, en fumant du cannabis et en s'éclatant dans des orgies… de mots, ou en décrétant tout simplement qu'il s'agit là d'une œuvre sans bon sens et que c'est dans ce caractère apparemment insensé de l'œuvre que se loge son sens le plus heureux.

Je nous le demande : est-il toujours nécessaire d'imposer un sens définitif, fixe ou forcé à ce qui s'offre au monde dans une certaine ambiguïté d'êtres? Est-il par exemple obligatoire d'enchâsser les Canadiens dans un seul méta-mantra, de focaliser leur donne sur un seul plan identitaire pour les rendre heureux et les sauver de leur dérive apparente dans une veine impensée, et dès lors réputée inimaginable, de l'expérience nationale?

Approfondir la singularité canadienne

À mon avis, il est, en ce qui a trait à l'avenir du Canada, une question plus importante que n'importe quelle autre. Je la formule de manière un peu innocente, sans vouloir donner par là l'impression d'être inconscient par rapport aux problèmes qui marquent le pays. Cette question est la suivante : vaut-il la peine, en dépit de toutes les blessures qui en ont marqué et scandé le parcours, de poursuivre l'expérience historique qui s'est déroulée au sein de cet espace d'inter-relations sociales et politiques qu'on appelle le Canada?

Si la réponse à cette question est négative, le débat est clos. Dans la mesure où l'expérience historique canadienne serait celle d'un échec sur le plan économique, social et politique, la persistance du Canada n'aurait de sens que par rapport à la perpétuation de pouvoirs sectaires. Il serait évidemment absurde d'encourager semblable destin.

Si la réponse à la question de poursuivre l'expérience historique s'étant déroulée au Canada est globalement positive, le défi qui s'offre dès lors aux héritiers de cette expérience, c'est-à-dire à nous, consiste à enrichir le parcours antérieur balisé par les anciens et, pour ce qui est des blessures, à les reconnaître lucidement dans toutes leurs dimensions et extensions en ayant pour objectif de les transformer en possibilités *pour* l'avenir.

Selon cette perspective, ni le souvenir impérissable des malheurs d'hier ni l'avenir délivré des héritages du passé ne sauraient constituer de voies de passage pour ouvrir à demain. Ce passage serait plutôt percé, opéré, pratiqué sur la base d'une reconnaissance et d'une distance critique des contemporains à l'égard de l'action des ancêtres, et ce, dans la conscience du bonheur des descendants.

Au fond, le défi des habitants du Canada n'est pas de préserver le pays coûte que coûte. À plusieurs égards, j'ai pourtant l'impression que c'est cette quête aveugle d'un Canada à édifier et à maintenir envers et contre tous qui anime un grand nombre de décideurs et d'acteurs à l'heure actuelle. Pour eux, le label Canada est pratiquement devenu une fin en soi, l'*alpha* et l'*omega* de la grandeur indiscutable d'un État pourvu d'une population servant d'abord à prétexter son existence et à nourrir sa cause. C'est comme si la déclaration du « meilleur pays du monde » était devenue la déclamation axiomatique du Canada en même temps que la formule magique dédouanant les acteurs du pays de leurs errances passées, présentes et prochaines.

Or, mon sentiment est que l'on ne devrait jamais vivre ni mourir ni lutter pour la face, pour le nom, ou pour l'honneur d'un pays. L'emblème d'un pays n'est pas grand-chose. C'est le « contenu » de ce pays, soit son histoire, sa problématique et ses gens qui sont tout. La différence entre l'amour du pays et l'amour des gens est immense. L'amour du pays entraîne en effet l'obstination, la fermeture et l'intransigeance alors que l'amour des gens appelle le compromis, l'ouverture et le discernement.

Dans ce contexte, le défi qui est le nôtre, tout en étant fort difficile à réaliser, est on ne peut plus clair à définir : il s'agit, tablant sur ce que fut jusqu'ici l'expérience historique canadienne, soit un parcours marqué par les ambiguïtés et les ambivalences, d'écarter les discours et représentations entêtées du pays qui visent à imposer de l'univocité là où il ne peut y avoir que de la diversité, tant sur le plan de la représentation symbolique du Canada que sur le plan du mode de gouvernance le plus souhaitable pour orchestrer les dissonances du pays.

Cette diversité, qui n'a jamais cessé de s'exprimer, voire de s'imposer, à défaut d'être reconnue au diapason de ses volontés et prétentions, est ce qui est au cœur de la problématique canadienne. Elle est aussi ce qui fait la spécificité du pays.

Je ne parle évidemment pas de cette diversité à la mode dans les cercles intellectuels de bon aloi où l'on tend à donner, des collectivités, une image les présentant sous l'angle de la multiplicité des singularités individuelles les composant. On le constate pourtant de plus en plus, la politique de la reconnaissance tous azimuts a ses limites et produit ses effets pervers sur le plan politique.

Je ne parle pas non plus de cette diversité que, au Canada, on appelle multiculturalité et qui a constitué, admettons-le, une tentative avortée pour sortir le pays de sa donnée historique centrale en le refondant dans une idée déshistoricisée de canadienneté.

Je parle de cette diversité structurelle et structurante du pays, diversité indépassée jusqu'à maintenant et peut-être indépassable bien qu'en travail sur elle-même, et qui renvoie à l'existence de trois grands groupements par référence, vivant en situation d'interdépendance contrainte dans un espace institué de proximité distante, soit le Canada.

Ces trois grands groupements par référence, qui peuplent et forment des mondes en tension et en réciprocité les uns *avec et contre* les autres, se définissent certes par rapport à des dynamismes d'ordre linguistico-culturels que rendent bien les concepts d'anglicité, de francité, et d'autochtonité. Mais ces groupements se définissent aussi de plus en plus par rapport à des dynamismes d'ordre politique, civique et identitaire, voire territoriaux, qui renforcent plutôt qu'ils ne gomment, par exemple, la distinction historique qui n'a jamais cessé d'exister entre le Québec, d'une part, et les autres provinces du Canada et le gouvernement fédéral, d'autre part.

Si bien qu'au tournant du vingt et unième siècle, et ce, malgré la volonté de bien des décideurs et acteurs d'empêcher cette mouvance apparemment néfaste au pays, le Canada évolue empiriquement dans le sens d'une dualisation accentuée de son « corps » et dans le sens aussi de l'apparition de deux « majorités » effectives en son sein, « majorités » continuellement confrontées à l'existence d'un troisième groupement constitué et revendicateur de ses spécificités et de ses droits, à savoir les autochtones.

Reconnaissant la présence irréductible et indéfectible de ces trois groupements, d'une part, et de ces dynamismes structurants de dualisation, d'autre part, dans le paysage canadien, que faire pour permettre au pays de passer à l'avenir ?

En évitant de justifier cette proposition par une argumentation qui risquerait d'être fort longue[13], je dirai que le défi actuel des habitants du Canada est d'accueillir l'autochtonité et la québécité dans une idée généreuse et imaginative de canadianité, et ce, sans chercher à noyer ces identités fortes dans une espèce de canadienneté homogénéisante et sans chercher non plus à les enrober dans le novlangue de la rectitude politique de manière à les liquider comme problème et à les réifier comme monument d'apothéose à un passé révolu.

Pour ne prendre qu'un exemple, il m'apparaît ridicule que l'on veuille *a posteriori*, et sous le coup du remords universel fleurissant à une époque où, d'évidence, toutes les collectivités se font pardon à elles-mêmes dans un étalage de contrition vaporeuse, il m'apparaît ridicule, dis-je, de vouloir considérer les autochtones comme étant les « Premiers Canadiens » alors même que le pays s'est élevé sur leur relégation dans les marges de son parcours.

S'agissant des autochtones, le défi qui est le nôtre n'est pas de les réinscrire artificiellement dans une histoire embellie et suave du pays où chaque communauté aurait sa vitrine spécifique au Musée canadien des civilisations. Sur le plan historiographique, ce défi est plutôt de reconnaître les blessures qui ont été infligées aux autochtones dans le temps[14]. Sur le plan politique, le défi est d'inscrire l'autochtonité comme dimension structurante de la canadianité, c'est-à-dire d'insérer la présence et l'identité autochtones au cœur des dynamismes politiques et de la mouvance actuelle du pays – pays dont les autochtones, de leur côté, ne peuvent éliminer ni la présence ni la prégnance dans toute vision de leur devenir[15].

En clair, ce qui doit être au centre des préoccupations des habitants actuels du Canada, ce n'est pas de rapailler l'emblématique du pays, mais d'approfondir sa problématique.

De la perspective dans la prospective

Mon pari comme intellectuel est de croire qu'il existe, dans l'expérience présente du Canada, un espace de possibilité pour aménager un futur viable au pays, et ce, sans qu'il soit nécessaire de répudier, d'oublier ou de désassumer le passé canadien.

La fuite en avant, il est utile de le rappeler, n'est pas la marque d'un dialogue fructueux avec les ancêtres. Elle n'est pas non plus le témoignage d'une attitude responsable à l'égard des héritiers.

Il est au pays trop de décideurs et d'acteurs désabusés ou démissionnaires devant le défi cardinal du politique de transformer les problèmes en projets. Il est également trop de décideurs et d'acteurs déterminés à imposer leur solution tranchée à un pays dont l'expérience est irréductible à l'univocité.

Tout le propos de ce texte a consisté à rappeler à quel point le pays s'était construit, avec et contre l'ambition de ses décideurs et acteurs, dans une ambiguïté d'êtres qui transpirait de ses dissonances inextinguibles.

Si, pour nombre d'habitants du pays, le moyen de passer à l'avenir est à l'évidence de se souvenir d'où ils s'en vont, c'est-à-dire de pratiquer l'histoire dans un rapport de reconnaissance *et* de distance avec les ancêtres, celui de plusieurs autres habitants du Canada est sans nul doute de cheminer en considérant le passé comme une dot et non pas comme un fardeau, c'est-à-dire d'assumer ce qui, dans le passé du pays, a fait sa distinction la plus porteuse pour l'avenir, ce que j'appelle pour ma part *canadianité* – mais le terme choisi a ici bien peu d'importance par rapport à l'idée qu'il recouvre.

On ne saurait dans tous les cas hypothéquer l'avenir par un surcroît de mémoire ni renier le passé par un excès d'oubli. Entre le passé et l'avenir, il peut en effet y avoir, à l'occasion, confluences qui soient fécondes pour le présent. C'est un truisme de le rappeler : la perspective est solidaire de la prospective.

Notes

1. À ce sujet, voir J. Létourneau, *Les Années sans guide. Le Canada à l'ère de l'économie migrante,* Montréal, Boréal, 1996.
2. Voir *id.*, « Penser le Québec dans le paysage canadien », Michel Venne, dir., *Penser la nation québécoise,* 103-122, Montréal, Québec-Amérique, 2000.
3. J'ai longuement argumenté sur pareilles formules *Passer à l'avenir. Histoire, mémoire, identité dans le Québec d'aujourd'hui,* Montréal, Boréal, 2000.
4. Alberto Manguel, *Dans la forêt du miroir. Essais sur les mots et sur le monde,* Paris/Montréal, Actes Sud/Leméac, 2000.
5. À ce sujet, voir J. Létourneau, « Le lieu (dit) de la nation : essai d'argumentation à partir d'exemples puisés au cas québécois », *Revue canadienne de science politique,* 30, 1 (1997) : 55-87 [avec la participation d'Anne Trépanier].
6. Je parle ici du Québec comme espace politique comprenant tous ses habitants et non pas du Québec français seulement.
7. Pour une position semblable, découverte après la rédaction de ce texte, voir Graham Fraser, « In Praise of Ambiguity », *Policy Options politiques,* 21, 1 (janvier-février 2000) : 21-26.
8. Par éthique mémorielle, je me réfère à cette disposition du narrateur qui, dans son récit, cherche à restituer la matière du passé dans son extension la plus large, et ce, par souci de justice envers les anciens.
9. « Assumons l'identité québécoise dans sa complexité », *Le Devoir,* 7-8 août 1999.
10. La « canadianisation » désigne l'entreprise historique de construction d'un espace symbolique, identitaire et culturel – soit un espace de références – proprement canadien, c'est-à-dire étroitement inféodé à l'existence du Canada comme État-nation institué. La « canadienneté » réfère à l'identité nationale canadienne. Le concept de « canadianité » n'est ni précipité identitaire ni principe d'allégeance ou d'appartenance nationalitaire. Il renvoie à un *mode d'être ensemble* propre à différents groupements vivant en situation d'interdépendance contrainte au sein d'un espace institué de proximité, soit le Canada, groupements ayant développé, au fil des temps, des rapports de réciprocité empreints de conflits mais aussi de convergences. Par le concept de « canadianité », j'entends penser la dissonance canadienne dans le sens des possibilités qu'elle ouvre pour l'avenir, sans pour autant oblitérer les blessures qui ne cessent d'animer l'expérience canadienne.

11. On pourra prendre connaissance des remarques « obligeantes » de bien des commentateurs en consultant le site <www.ledevoir.com/ago/1999a/ nletourneau_c.html>.

12. J. Létourneau. J. « L'affirmationnisme québécois à l'ère de la mondialisation », *Revue de l'Université de Moncton*, 30, 2 (1997) : 19-36.

13. Mais dont on trouvera certains éléments clés dans deux textes récemment publiés, soit « Penser le Québec dans le paysage canadien », *loc. cit.*, et « L'avenir du Canada : par rapport à quelle histoire ? », *Canadian Historical Review*, 81, 2 (été 2000) : 230-259.

14. C'est le travail auquel s'est notamment livrée la Commission royale sur les peuples autochtones. Voir le vol. 1 du *Rapport : Un passé, un avenir*, Ottawa, 1996.

15. Pour une position semblable, voir Louis-Edmond Hamelin, *Passer près d'une perdrix sans la voir, ou attitudes à l'égard des Autochtones*, Montréal, Université McGill/Programme d'études sur le Québec, 1999.

Survival Then and Now

Margaret Atwood[*]

I WAS IN ENGLAND RECENTLY GIVING SOME LECTURES, AND I WAS asked, "Do you identify as a woman or as a Canadian?" This is a new sort of question because it contains the phrase "identify as," which not so long ago would have been incomprehensible.

"Well, to tell the truth," I replied, "I identify as a writer. That is what I am – a writer – and what I do is writing. The other things are features that can be used to modify the basic model – think of it as Mr. and Mrs. Potato Head, in which the basic potato is "writer" and the other things – female, Canadian, short, of a certain age – can be stuck onto it, like the plastic lips and ears and so forth in the Potato Family do-it-yourself kit."

My young questioner was not entirely satisfied – she wanted there to be something intrinsic to my gender or my nationality that had caused these reams of marked-up paper to issue from me – so I tried a syllogism. "All women writers are women," I said, "but not all women are writers. And the same goes for Canadians." She was still not mollified, so I resorted to a cheap trick. "Let's face it," I said. "If the poster announcing the lectures had claimed simply, 'Woman to speak,' or even 'Canadian to speak,' would you have come to listen? I doubt it." Everyone laughed, so I suspected I was right.

I started thinking about writing quite a few years before I started thinking about gendering or nationalizing; and so it is with most writers. They are writers first, just as a person running a race is a racer first. And whatever I have had to say about the state of being a Canadian, a woman, a short person with curly hair, etc., has always been predi-

---

[*] Elements of this presentation appeared in an article published in 1 July 1999 issue of *Maclean's*, entitled "Survival, Now and Then."

cated on this primary fact – my membership in that country without borders or passport or government, the centre of which is every writer and every reader and the circumference of which is as far as you can imagine; a country which has its own history and its own aristocracy, but which is neither a monarchy where some reign by virtue of birth, nor a dystopia where all citizens must be exactly the same, but is instead the republic of letters, where desire is the key to the gateway, and where all who wish may enter.

That having been said, we may now go on to consider what I may call the tectonics of Canadian writing – those places where the fault lines are situated and the friction occurs. More specifically, I would like to tell you how I came to write a rather controversial book called *Survival: A Thematic Guide to Canadian Literature*, back in the early 70s, when a conference like this would have been unthinkable. It was controversial partly because many people at the time of its publication denied that there was any such thing as Canadian literature, at all, period.

The English writer Wyndam Lewis, sitting out World War 2 in Toronto, was asked by a wealthy matron where he was living. "Jarvis Street," he told her. "Mr. Lewis," she said, "That is not a very fashionable address!" "Madam," he replied, "*Toronto* is not a very fashionable address." Nor was it then.

The poet Earle Birney, writing in 1939 – a piece entitled, "Canadians Can Read – But Do They?" – said that if you entered the average literate home in Canada at that time, you'd be likely to find only three books in it – the Bible, a collected Shakespeare, and *The Rubaiyat of Omar Khyyam*. The novelist Morley Callaghan, writing in 1938, said that a young Canadian writer should cut his teeth in American magazines and then seek an American publisher, as the chances of making a living in Canada by writing were nil. They decreased to less than nil during the war, due to paper shortages, and right after the war things were much the same. In 1949, Gwethalyn Graham, who'd published what would now be called an international success – a novel entitled *Earth and High Heaven* – criticized the awful distribution and high prices of books in Canada, and said that was why most people read only magazines. And, with some very slight improvements, that's the way things still were when I began to write, in the late fifties.

I wrote and published *Survival* in 1972. It ignited a ferocious debate and became, as they say, a runaway bestseller. This was a shock to everyone, including me. Canadian writing, *interesting*? Among the bulk of Canadian readers at that time such writing was largely unknown, except for Stephen Leacock, and among the cognoscenti it was frequently treated as a dreary joke, an oxymoron, a big yawn, or the hole in a non-existent doughnut.

At the beginning of the 60s, sales of poetry books had numbered in the hundreds, and a novel was doing well if it hit a thousand copies. There were signs of change. Public readings were beginning, at first in coffee-houses, then at universities, but only for poetry. In 1961 there was a total of five Canadian novels published in the country, in English, for the entire year. Mordecai Richler's first novel, published in England, sold two copies in Canada, or so the rumour goes. But over that decade, things changed rapidly. The Canada Council began its grants to individual writers in 1965. In Quebec, the Quiet Revolution had generated an outburst of literary activity; in the ROC (the Rest Of Canada), many poets had emerged, more novelists and short-story writers were becoming known, and Expo '67, the World's Fair, held in Montreal, created a fresh national self-confidence. Audiences had been building steadily, and by 1972 there was a critical mass of readers who wanted to hear more; and thus, through a combination of good luck, good timing, and good reviews, *Survival* became an "overnight publishing sensation," and I myself became an instant sacred monster. "Now you're a target," Farley Mowat said to me, "and they will shoot at you."

How prescient he was. Who could have suspected that this modest cultural artifact would have got so thoroughly up the noses of my elders and betters? If the book had sold the 3,000 copies initially projected, nobody would have bothered their heads much about it, but in the first year alone it sold ten times that number, and suddenly Canlit was everybody's business. The few dedicated academic souls who had cultivated this neglected pumpkin patch over the meagre years were affronted because a mere chit of a girl had appropriated a pumpkin they regarded as theirs, and the rest were affronted because I had obnoxiously pointed out that there was in fact a pumpkin to appropriate. Even now, after twenty-seven years, some Jack or Jackess emerges with seasonal regularity to take one more crack at *moi*, the supposed Giant, in a never-ending game of Let Us Now Blame Famous Women. You get to feel like the mechanical duck at the funfair shooting gallery, though no one has won the oversized panda yet, because I still seem to be quacking.

Over the years, I've been accused of just about everything, from bourgeois superstition to communist rabble-rousing to not being Marshall McLuhan. (I would have liked to have been Marshall McLuhan, but he seemed to have the job pretty much cornered.) Yet when I was writing this book – or rather when I was putting it together, for it was more an act of synthesis than one of authorship, and drew on the ideas of many besides myself – I attached no particular importance to it. I was, after all, a poet and novelist, wasn't I? I did not consider myself a real critic – just a kind of bake-sale muffin lady, doing a little cottage-industry fund-raising in a worthy cause.

The worthy cause was The House of Anansi Press, a small literary publisher formed in 1966 by writers Dennis Lee and David Godfrey as a response to the dearth of publishing opportunities for new writing at that time. Anansi had already made quite a few waves by 1971, when Dennis, an old college friend, button-hooked me onto its board. So there we were one grey November day, a tiny, intrepid, overworked, underpaid band, glumly contemplating the balance sheet, which showed an alarming amount of red ink. Publishing Rule Number One is that it's hard to keep small literary publishers afloat unless you have the equivalent of gardening books to support them.

To pay the bills, Anansi had begun a line of user-friendly self-help guides, the precursors to those popular *Dummies* books, which had done moderately well: *Law Law Law*, by Clayton Ruby and Paul Copeland, which set forth how to disinherit your relatives, avoid being bled dry by your estranged spouse, and so forth; and *VD*, one of the first venereal disease books, which explained about unwanted goo and warts and such, though AIDS was still a decade into the future.

Thus was born *Survival*. As I'd travelled the country's byways, giving poetry readings and toting cardboard boxes of my own books to sell afterwards because often enough there was no bookstore, the absence of views on the subject of Canadian literature was spectacular. The two questions I was asked most frequently about it by audience members were "Is there any?" and, "Supposing there is, isn't it just a second-rate copy of *real* literature, which comes from England and the United States?" In Australia they called this attitude the Cultural Cringe; in Canada it was the Colonial Mentality. In both – and in many smaller countries around the world, as it turned out – it was part of a tendency to believe that the Great Good Place was, culturally speaking, elsewhere.

Through no fault of my own, I happened to be doing a one-year teaching stint at York University. Canadian Literature formed part of the course-load, so I'd had to come up with some easily-grasped approaches to it. Previous thinkers on the subject had been pithy enough, but few in number: there was not exactly a wealth of existing lore.

Back to the Anansi board meeting. "Hey, I know," I cried, in my Mickey Roonyish way. "Let's do a *VD* of Canadian Literature!" What I meant, I explained, was a sort of handbook for the average reader – for all those people I'd met on my tours who'd wanted to read more of this Canadian literature stuff but didn't know where to start. Such a book would not be for academics. It would have no footnotes, and would not employ the phrase "on the other hand," or at least not much. It would also contain lists of other books that people could actually go into a bookstore and *buy*. This was a fairly revolutionary concept, because most Canlit of the past was, at that time, out of print, and that of the present was kept well hidden at the back of the store, in among the Beautiful Canadiana fall foliage calendars.

We now take it for granted that Canadian literature exists as a category – we seem to spend our time squabbling about its sub-categories, and its sub-sub-categories and its sub-sub-sub categories, and about some mythical weapon or religious leader called The Canon – but this proposition was not always self-evident. To have any excuse for being, the kind of book I had in mind in 1972 would have to prove several points. First, that, yes, there was a Canadian literature – that such a thing did indeed exist. (This turned out to be a radical proposition at the time, and was disputed by many when the book appeared.) Second, that this body of work was not just a shoddy version of English or American, or, in the case of Francophone books, of French literature, but that it had different preoccupations that were specific to its own history and geography and geopolitics. This too was a radical proposition at the time, although common sense ought to have indicated that it was, well, just common sense: if you were a rocky, watery northern country, cool in climate, large in expanse, small but diverse in population, multilingual from the very beginning, and with a huge aggressive neighbour to the south, why wouldn't you have concerns that varied from those of the huge aggressive neighbour? Or indeed from those of the crowded, history-packed, tight little island, recently but no longer an imperial power, that had once ruled the waves? Well, you'd think they'd be different, wouldn't you? To justify the teaching of Canadian literature as such, you'd still have to start from the same axioms: i) it exists, and ii) it's distinct.

Back, again, to the Anansi board meeting. The desperate will try anything, so the board agreed that this idea of mine should be given a whirl. Over the next four or five months, after I'd finished my day job, I wrote away at the proposed book, and as I finished each section Dennis Lee edited it, and under Dennis's pencil the book grew from the proposed hundred-page handbook to a length – for the main text – of 246 pages. It also took on a more coherent shape and direction. The book's subtitle – *A Thematic Guide to Canadian Literature* – meant that we were aiming, not at an all-inclusive cross-indexed survey such as the 1,199-page *Oxford Companion to Canadian Literature* – which of course did not exist then – nor at a series of studies of this author or that, nor at a collection of New-critical close readings or *explications du texte*, or even at some deconstructionist presto-chango. (Not that this latter had yet been invented.) Instead we were doing the sort of thing that art historian Nicholas Pevsner had done in *The Englishness of English Art*, or that the American literary critics Perry Miller and Leslie Fiedler were doing in their examinations of American literature: the identification of a series of characteristics and leitmotifs, and a comparison of the varying treatments of them in different national and cultural environments.

For example: money as a sign of divine grace or providence is present in the American tradition from the Puritans through Benjamin Franklin through *Moby-Dick* through Henry James through *The Great Gatsby*. The theme is treated now seriously, now cynically, now tragically, now ironically, just as a leitmotif in a symphony may be played in different keys and in different tempos. It varies as time unrolls and circumstances change, of course: the eighteenth century is not the twentieth. Yet the leitmotif persists as a dominating concern – a persistent cultural obsession, if you like.

The persistent cultural obsession of Canadian literature, said *Survival*, was survival. In actual life, and in both the Anglophone and the Francophone sectors, this concern is often enough a factor of the weather, as when the ice storm cuts off the electrical power. *La survivance* has long been an overt theme in Quebec political life, currently manifesting itself as anxiety about the survival of French. In the ROC, it's more like a nervous tic: what'cher gonner do when Free Trade trashes your ability to control your water supply, or when your government says that the magazines from the huge, aggressive neighbour to the south are the same as yours really, or whether, in the next Quebec referendum, that part of the country will no longer be that part of the country? And so on and so forth.

Survival therefore began with this dominant note. It then postulated a number of other motifs in Canadian literature – motifs that either did not exist at all in one of the literatures with which they were being compared (for instance, there are almost no so-called "Red Indians" in English novels), or did exist, but were not handled in the same way. The Canadian "immigrant story," from fleeing Loyalists, to Scots kicked off their land, to starving potato-famine Irish, to Jews fleeing pogroms in the early twentieth Century, to Latvians emigrating after WW2, to Austin Clarke's Barbadians, to the economic refugees of the 70s and 80s, tends to be very different when told in the United States: none of their stories is likely to say that the immigrants were really trying to get into Canada but ended up in the United States *faut de mieux*. Canada has rarely been the Promised Land, except for those fleeing slavery via the Underground Railway. About the closest we've come to that idea is the title of Wayne Johnson's 1998 novel, *The Colony of Unrequited Dreams*.

The tradition identified in *Survival* was not a bundle of uplifting Pollyanna cheer: quite the reverse. Canlit, at least up until 1970, was on balance a somewhat dour concoction. Some critics who couldn't read – a widespread occupational hazard, it seems – thought I was somehow *advocating* this state of affairs. *Au contraire*: if my book has attitude, it's more like *you are here, you really do exist and this is where, so pull up your socks and quit whining*. As Alice Munro says, "Do what you want and live with the consequences." Or as *Survival* itself says in its last chapter, "Having bleak ground under your feet is better than having no ground at all … a tradition doesn't necessarily exist to bury you: it can also be used as material for new departures."

Many things have happened in the twenty-eight years since *Survival* was published. In politics, the Quebec cliff-hanger and the U.S. domination and the environmental degeneration and the loss of national control brought about by Free Trade have become, not the tentative warning notes they were in *Survival*, but everyday realities. In literary criticism, Regionalism, Feminism, Deconstructionism, Political Correctness, Appropriation of Voice, and Identity Politics have all swept across the scene, leaving their traces. Mordecai Richler's well-known jest, "world-famous in Canada," has ceased to be such a laugh – many Canadian writers are now world-famous, period, insofar as writers can be considered famous. "Postmodern" – in the 70s a cutting-edge literary adjective – is now used if at all to describe kicky little handbags. *Survival*, the book, seemed quainter and more out-of-date as these various years went by, and as – incidentally – some of its wishes were granted and some of its predictions were realized. Yet its central concerns remain with us, and must still be confronted. Are Canadians really all that different from anybody else? If so, how? And is that *how* something worth exploring and – possibly – preserving? In 1972, *Survival* concluded with two questions: *Have we survived? And if so, what happens after Survival?* We're still posing the same questions.

People often ask me what I would change about *Survival* if I were writing it today. The obvious answer is that I wouldn't write it today because I wouldn't need to. The thing I set out to prove has been proven beyond a doubt: no one would seriously argue, any more, that there is no Canadian literature. The other answer is that I wouldn't be able to, not only because of my own hardening brain but because the quantity, range and diversity of books now published would defeat any such effort.

In Canadian culture, however, there's always a negative. At present we have cuts to grants, threats to magazines, publishers in peril through withdrawal of funding, writers struggling with the effects upon their royalties of book-chain deep discounting, and so forth. *Have we survived?*

But this is Canada, land of contrasts. Indeed it is Canada, land of rugs: no sooner has a rug been placed beneath the nation's artistic feet than it is pulled out, but no sooner has it been pulled out in one place than it is inserted in another. Last year, in an astonishing but gratifying development, Quebec announced that the first $15,000 of income from copyrights – from songs to books to computer software – will now be tax exempt. (By no great coincidence, $15,000 is roughly the average income from writing in this country.) Will there be unforeseen consequences? Will Quebec become the Ireland of Canada, tax haven for writers, and the Prague of Europe, the latest chic destination? Will every young, mean and lean creator from all over the country stampede to Montreal, where the rent is cheap and the edible food ditto, so that they can actually have a hope of earning a living from their work?

Experience has shown that where bohemia goes, real estate development is sure to follow. First the artists, then the cafés, then the designers, then the lawyers. M. Bouchard must know this: he's been called many things, but rarely stupid. Could it be that this crafty tax move will revitalize downtown Montreal, which for some years has been bleeding at every pore? And revitalize it by means of – *choc, horreur!* – Anglophone Canadian writers! – who will stream there in their thousands, incongruous exiles from the Rest Of Canada? Meanwhile, there are serious plans afoot to have Toronto separate, not from Canada, but from Ontario, and seek status as the eleventh province. Why not? Toronto has to do something. Those of us who live in that reviled city are treated as cash cows, pariahs and serfs, while being denied the power of our own votes. Why is that? Could it be because Toronto is now – it's official – the most multicultural city in the world?

All M. Bouchard has to do is extend his tax largesse to the publishing industry, and Montreal may once again become the vital centre of Anglophone Canadian literary activity – insofar as such existed – that it was from the twenties to the fifties. Not perhaps what M. Bouchard had in mind – more like his worst nightmare, really. But in that case, the twenty-first century answer to the question posed in *Survival* may be both bizarre and deeply ironic:

> *Have we survived?*
> *Yes. But only in Quebec.*

INDIVIDUALS, COLLECTIVITIES, AND THE STATE
INDIVIDUS, COLLECTIVITÉS ET ÉTAT

Toward a Baroque Governance in Twenty-first Century Canada

Gilles Paquet[*]

> Our natural mode is therefore not compromise
> but 'irony' – the inescapable response
> to the presence and pressures of *opposites in tension*.
> Irony is the key to our identity.
>
> Malcolm Ross (1954)

C ANADA MUST MEET THE TEST OF LIVING WITH THREE FUNDAMENTAL challenges of twenty-first century society: complexity, new forms of collaboration, and citizen engagement. The new information and communication technologies, and the greater connectedness they have generated, constitute only one of the families of forces – albeit an important one – that has increased the level of relevant complexity, uncertainty, and turbulence in the Canadian system. Over the last thirty years, Canada has also become, partly by design and partly due to circumstances, dramatically more demographically variegated, culturally diverse, socially diversified, and politically complicated. Canada has also evolved into a country of citizens who are better informed and better able to express their dissent; better equipped to assert their multiple identities and to demand participation in governing their affairs. As a result, the co-ordination problems that Canada has confronted and has had to resolve have become increasingly daunting.

This quantum of additional variety and complexity has been denied or downplayed significantly by ideologues from the left and the right – *ces terribles simplificateurs* whose purpose is to propose a flat-earth view of reality in order to rationalize the choice of "the solution"

---

*   The assistance of Anne Burgess and Danna Campbell and the comments of Robin Higham have been most helpful.

(more state intervention, lower taxes, etc.) they are propounding. These calls by solutionists for univocal responses, whether the solution is meant to rely on the powers of the invisible hand of the market or of the hidden – or hiding – hand of government, have only compounded the difficulties.

Fortunately, ordinary Canadians have been more pragmatic. Acknowledging the greater variety in the environment as *incontournable*, they have built on this premise a more pluralistic set of reactions better able to deal with that diversity. In other words, they have embraced the old Ashby law of requisite variety (Ashby 1970). Such an approach has required more of a bottom-up, muddling-through, distributed, and collaborative governance – one based on the more or less successful efforts of co-ordinating a large number of actors and participants – in lieu of the simple top-down, hierarchical process of governing that was in good currency in earlier and less complex times.

This paper proceeds through four stages. Firstly, it defines Canadian distinctiveness as *habitus* characterized by irony and *bricolage*. Secondly, it explains why Canada has been rather slow in adapting its governance to cope with the challenges of its disconcerted, learning socio-economy. Thirdly, it suggests that repairs for the many different forms of disconcertion here noted require a more vibrant *bricolage communautaire* – dealing with disconcertion differently from place to place, using different assets, skills, and capabilities, and doing so in a low key. Fourthly, it illustrates, through vignettes of what is happening on three construction sites, how the Canadian governance system of the twenty-first century is evolving.

From Bonding to Loose Intermediation

While much has been written about the decline of social cohesion and the transformation of Canadian sociality over the last few decades (Helliwell 1996; Paquet 1996, 1997a, 1998), most of it has been couched in terms of the erosion of the old social capital bonding, once so good at undergirding reciprocity and mobilizing solidarity (Coleman 1988; Putnam 2000). This erosion of the superglue of family, church, community, hierarchies, etc., can be ascribed to the fact that these institutions were not nimble enough to fit the requirements of the new, knowledge-based learning economy. Much less work has been done, however, on what would appear to be required to construct a new sociality, one based on much weaker ties and more loosely-coupled networks (Granovetter 1973; Paquet 1999a).

In Canada, the transition from bonding to loose coupling has been less smooth and rapid than it should have been because of a significant resistance to this sort of *virage* by a portion of the federal elites. This has led to the mounting of a vigorous counter-argument in favour of 'bridging social capital' – the need to maintain a fairly high degree of centralization in order to bolster redistribution and thereby save the country from falling apart. This has been presented as "the Canadian way" (Paquet 1995a; Chrétien 2000).

Fueling this rear-guard action has been the degree of diffraction of Canadian society, generated by its greater complexity and heterogeneity and the demand for greater citizen participation. It was wrongly presumed by Pierre Elliott Trudeau (among other leaders in Canada) that a response to these challenges could be found in overarching principles, abstract norms, or grand designs and narratives. One of the most prominent of these intellectual devices has been the focus on human rights and the judiciarization of governance via charters, courts, commissions, etc. This has acted as an extraordinary support for a more centralized and hierarchical system. Such schemes, however are most often intellectually disingenuous, practically unhelpful, and perhaps even dangerous for democracy.

More recently, attempts have been made in Canada to hide such centralizing schemes behind efforts at 'branding' Canada – a language falling halfway between the lingoes of business and rodeo – or efforts at creating new devices aimed at 'bridging' divisions. These novel ways of redistributing income and wealth across regions, social groups, and organizations seek to equalize their circumstances and thereby reduce social tensions and envy. Many people involved in public discourse now even declare these redistributive schemes to be the social cement that binds Canadians and constitutes their "distinctiveness."

But distinctiveness is a matter neither of branding nor bridging. Distinctiveness connotes a dynamic *habitus* or *manière d'être* whereas branding refers to static 'markers' and 'identifiers.' As for the seemingly innocuous language of bridging "across big divisions in a society" or "across what are potentially big fractures in a society between rich and poor, between language groups," – the language used by the Senate Standing Committee on Social Affairs, Science, and Technology (Canada 1999) – this is an equally misleading way of trivializing a *manière d'être* by reducing it to fiscal plumbing.

Bonding, with its exclusiveness, is an echo of the traditional society; it does not fit the realities of modern Canada. Nor does bridging, with its emphasis on mechanical, redistributive schemes. Though circumstances would appear to call for looser and more temporary coupling – *cohabitation avec commutation* (i.e., a system in which anyone can claim or deny attachment) – these weak ties can nonetheless provide much strength (Granovetter 1973; Guillaume 1999; Putnam 2000). This last statement is the paradoxical result of a number of reflections on Canadian perplexities generated by Canada's experience in creating a new "multiculture" (Paquet 1999d: chap. 7; Iyer 2000: Part 4).

Fortunately, these subtleties have not been lost on Canadian citizens. Their response *qua* citizens – both to the new circumstances and to the 'magnificent' efforts to deal with them grandiosely – has been much irony vis-à-vis grand schemes and a plea for *bricolage*, first and foremost to effect the needed repair to the institutional order.

The drift from bonding to loose intermediation has, however, been slowed down by various efforts to impose either-or choices on Canadians when the new realities confronting them called for choices of the 'more-or-less' variety – less centralization, more subsidiarity in the name of efficiency, etc. The drift has also been slowed by redistributive bridging schemes when better insurance schemes were required to facilitate risk-taking and to ease transition in a high-risk society. As a result, Canadians have, over the last decades, defined their distinctiveness almost despite their leaders. In fact, they have been quite effective at it. It is worthy of note that this distinctiveness as *habitus* has been characterized by expressions such as "a passion for bronze" (Valaskakis 1990) or "slow adrenaline" (Iyer 2000).

At times, the rejection of grand schemes by the majority of Canadians has been deplored as *occasions manquées*. But Canadians, with their hefty dose of tolerance and apathy, are *ironistes*, "never quite able to take themselves seriously because [they are] always aware that the terms in which they describe themselves are subject to change," and they spend much time worrying about the possibility of having been initiated into the wrong tribe and taught to play the wrong language game (Rorty 1989:73-75). Thus Canadians prefer understatement, irony, and self-mockery in their rhetoric and they most certainly resist being "branded" like cattle or "bridged" in a crippling way in the face of liquid modernity (Bauman 2000). They also prefer to practise a sort of pragmatism and *ad hoc bricolage* and to gamble on a combination of plural, partial, and limited identities, even though this often actually increases the distances between groups of Canadians. This, then, is the Canadian distinctiveness.

Malcolm Ross put it very aptly almost fifty years ago when he said that "we are inescapably, and almost from the first ... the people of the second thought. To remain a people at all, we have had to think before we speak, even to think before we think. Our characteristic prudence is ... this necessity for taking second thought" (Ross 1954, ix). In 2000, an outside observer (Iyer 2000) has come to almost the same conclusion, using almost the same words.

This pragmatic liberalism, couched in a prudent pluralistic and ironic language, has often led to discourses that are difficult for outsiders to decode and understand. Canadians will often pretend ignorance and a willingness to learn from others for the sake of making the others' errors conspicuous through adroit questioning. They will even slide into a manner of discourse in which what is literally said is meant to express its opposite.

Canada as a Disconcerted Learning Socio-economy

The transition from an industrial age to a knowledge-based economy of the last few decades has revealed a separation between the world of physical objects and the world of ideas. These two worlds live according to quite different rules. The world of physical objects, characterized by scarcity and diminishing returns, focuses mainly on allocative efficiency in a static world. The world of ideas is essentially scarcity-free, inhabited by increasing returns, and focused on Schumpeterian efficiency – i.e. the discontinuities in the knowledge base over time and in the dynamic learning ability of the new evolving arrangements these entail (Boisot 1995). Canada is still deeply-rooted in the old economy; it is, however, shifting more and more toward a world dominated by the logic of the new learning economy.

The Learning Socio-economy

In the new economy, individuals, firms, regions, and national economies seeking success have come to depend upon their capacity to learn to a much greater extent than ever before. In such a context, responsive or passive flexibility cannot suffice. What is required is *innovative flexibility* – learning and not simply adapting (Killick 1995).

The emergence of the learning economy has transformed both the division of labour in Canada and the Canadian social fabric. In the industrial world a technical division of labour based on hyper-specialization was efficient; such *travail en miettes* did not promote learning. In order for learning to proceed, one must build on conversations, communities of interpretation, and communities of practice. Specialization must proceed to a greater extent on the basis of *craft* or competencies. To effect this requires a cognitive division of labour (Moati et Mouhoud 1994) – a division of labour based on learning blocks (innovation systems, skill-based production fragments, etc.) – that entails a very different mode of co-ordination.

In the old system, co-ordination meant standardization and economic integration was a way to effect standardization. As a result, hierarchical co-ordination prospered. But in the new system, where the challenge is to harmonize the *capacity to learn and to progress together*, the organization (private, public, or civic) must focus on its core competencies, consciously recognizing that it operates in an ecosystem and must mobilize its community of allies (Moore 1996).

The challenge to foster collective learning calls for the development among all the stakeholders of a much more horizontal, looser co-ordination. And since relationships with stakeholders (suppliers, customers, partners, etc.) cannot be built on simple market relations (because these may not promote efficient co-learning), *networks of relational exchanges* have emerged. In such arrangements, long-term relations based on trust are negotiated. Forms of co-operation that would never have otherwise materialized evolve as a result of the emerging, important, positive feedback and self-reinforcing mechanisms – each generated by external economies or neighbourhood effects – and learning curves yielding increasing returns (Goldberg 1989).

These dynamic processes, involving the interrelationships of groups of actors, generate a variety of *conventions of identity and participation* among these different agents. Proximity (in the different senses of that word – spatial, technological, social, etc.) plays a not insignificant role in the learning process. Co-learning entails co-evolution in an ecosystem that evolves by finding ways to "charter" cross-functional teams from which no important power players are left out and, if feasible, in which "all major players have some stake in the success of the strategy" (Moore 1998:177; Arthur 1994; Krugman 1996; Durlauf 1998).

Such are the trends as Canada drifts into the twenty-first century.

Slouching Toward the Learning Economy

These challenges facing Canada are well known. Yet little in the present structure and functioning of the Canadian economy, be it in the private, public, or civic sectors, would appear to indicate that Canada is progressing as well as it might in this transition.

As a matter of fact, while Canada does score well in terms of certain indicators in international comparisons, when other indicators are used (gross domestic product per capita, Tobin's measure of economic welfare, the so-called Genuine Progress Indicator, or Fordham's index of social health), Canada's relative performance seems to be deteriorating (Paquet 1997b). This deterioration is also reflected in the relative measures of productivity growth, in the coefficient of attraction of foreign capital by Canada, and so on.

One broad hypothesis has been suggested to explain the loss of ground by the Canadian political socio-economy: the general failure of the Canadian system not only to adjust its governance to the new requirements of the learning economy but also to abandon its antiquated, hierarchical, and confrontational governance structures. According to this diagnosis, the Canadian socio-economy is suffering from *disconcertion*. That is, there is a disconnection between its governance and its circumstances (Baumard 1996) which, because it has not been noticed, has not been repaired. Indeed, as R.D. Laing would have put it, Canadians have failed to notice that they have failed to notice this discrepancy.

Many observers have noted that the Canadian socio-economy remains marred by important cleavages and torn by adversarial systems (federal-provincial, public-private, labour-management, small firm against small firm, etc.) that have prevented it from developing into an effective learning economy (Valaskakis 1990). Indeed, the major conclusion of a recent study by the Public Policy Forum is that the most important source of Canada's relatively lacklustre performance on the productivity front is the lack of a culture of co-operation, especially between government and business (Public Policy Forum 1993). Burelle (1995) has shown clearly that the federal-provincial quagmire is not far behind as the major source of friction that prevents the development of an effective co-ordination/governance system.

States as Catalysts

Some have argued, quite rightly, that tension and disconcertion may not be all bad. They can serve as a fount of novelty and a source of enhanced learning. Indeed, heterogeneity and somewhat weaker interpersonal ties – less groupthink – may yield more innovation than a very homogeneous order. But excessively confrontational patterns of interaction do slow down learning. Thus, the central challenge is ensuring the requisite flexibility of the institutional system so as to bring "the skills, experience and knowledge of different people, organizations and government agencies together, and get them to interact in new ways" (Johnson 1992:43). But this requires an important social capital of trust. In Canada, the social capital needed for such co-operation is eroding.

The World Values Surveys provides a very rough gauge of the evolution, over the past few decades, of the degree of interpersonal trust and associative behaviour. Despite the jelly-like character of the available data, some important trends have emerged:

1) the degree of confidence and trust in one's neighbours has remained higher in Canada than in the United States;
2) a significant erosion of social capital has occurred in the United States;
3) the gap between the two countries has declined, meaning a more rapid decline in Canada than in the United States; and
4) the decline of trust and associative behaviour has been even more rapid in French Canada than in the rest of Canada over the post-Quiet Revolution period (Paquet 1996, 1997a; Helliwell 1996).

Given this significant, relative erosion of the social capital of trust in Canada (and even more in Québec), one should not be surprised by the failure of various initiatives, *à la* Gérald Tremblay, to stimulate networks or industrial clusters in Québec. The requisite social glue was not there and there is little evidence that public policies have been at work to develop the requisite new type of social capital that would allow learning networks to thrive (Paquet 1999a).

The state has to rethink its action in the learning economy. As Dalum et al. suggest (1992), this means intervening to improve the *means to learn* (education and training systems), the *incentive to learn* (government programs supporting co-operation projects and networks), the *capability to learn* (promoting organizations supporting interactive learning – more decentralized organizations), the *access to relevant knowledge* (through relationships between agents and sources of knowledge, both through infrastructure and mediating structures), and lastly, fostering the requisite amount of *remembering and forgetting* (acting to preserve competencies and capabilities but also helping groups to move ahead and to let go of older ways). This, in turn, requires a well-aligned nexus of relations, networks, and regimes.

States can be important catalysts in constructing the new "loose intermediation" social capital in several ways, such as improving relationships here, fostering networks there, and developing more or less encompassing formal or informal regimes in other places. This is the central role of what some have called the *catalytic state* or the *resurgent state* (Lind 1992; Drezner 1998). Currently, this catalytic action is not too vibrant. Canadian governments appear to remain characterized both by a certain centralizing mindset and by a chronic neglect of governance issues (Paquet 1995a; Canada 2000). This does not mean that the Canadian governance system is not evolving nor that it is not inventing innovative ways to meet the present challenges (Paquet 1999b). But fiscal imperatives do seem to have mesmerized our governments to such an extent in the last decade that those in a position to act as a catalyst have missed key opportunities (program review, for instance) to effect the sort of repairs to the governance system that might have gone a long way toward providing the Canadian political socio-economy with the non-centralized guidance regime it requires (Paquet and Roy 1995; Paquet and Shepherd 1996).

If one had to characterize Canada retroactively, one might describe it as: 1) a disconcerted socio-economy caught in a tectonic transition between an old, somewhat centralized, political economy and a new, somewhat more decentralized and subsidiarity-driven one, and 2) experiencing a relative lull in its socio-economic performance and a mild form of midlife identity crisis. Moreover, in the face of these circumstances, Canadians are perplexed yet believe not only that 1) there is no simple fix to their predicament and, 2) their "passion for bronze" (Valaskakis 1990) – in other words their belief that *le mieux est l'ennemi du bien* – may not be such a bad thing after all.

New Capabilities and Bricolage Communautaire

There are times when the evolution of the institutional order is such that one can really speak of a change of kind and not simply a change of degree. Such a tectonic but silent change has been under way in Canada over the last few decades (Paquet 1999c). To cope with an ever more turbulent global environment, Canadian organizations have had to evolve and to learn to use their environment more and more strategically, in much the same way that the real surfer catches the big wave.

Managers in the private, public, and civic sectors have had to exploit not only favourable environmental circumstances but also the full complement of imagination and resourcefulness of each team player. They had to become team leaders of a variety of task force-type projects, quasi-entrepreneurs capable of cautious suboptimizing in the face of turbulent environments (Paquet 1996–7, 1998, 1999d). This dual sort of challenge has pressed public, private, and civic organizations to design lighter, more horizontal, and modular structures, to create networks and informal clanlike rapports, and to develop new rules for the game. In general, this has generated some pressure for *non-centralization*, for an expropriation of the power to steer that was once held by the top managers.

Distributed Governance

As globalization proceeds, international economic integration increases and the component parts of the system become more numerous, the central driving force is the pressure to organize for faster learning and more innovation, and this occurs when the actors, confronted with different local realities, are empowered to take decisions on the spot. In this way, international integration has led to some erosion of the relevance of the nation-state – globalization has led to localization of decision-making, to the dispersion of power, and to a more distributed governance process.

These new, modularized organizations cannot impose their views on their clients or members. Indeed, there has been a significant decline in deference to authority in all sectors. To compete effectively, firms, in much the same way as state or civic organizations, must consult: they are moving toward a greater use of the distributed intelligence and ingenuity of their members. A good example is Linux. The strategic organization is becoming a broker, an *animateur*; and, in this network, a consultative and participative mode obtains among firms, states, and communities. The reason for this is that the best learning experience appears to be effected through flexible, intersectoral teams, woven by moral contracts and reciprocal obligations negotiated in the context of evolving partnerships (Paquet 1992, 1994a, 1995b, 1996-7, 1997c).

This entails a major qualitative change. It introduces the network paradigm within the governance process (Cooke and Morgan 1993; Castells 1996, 1997, 1998). This paradigm not only dominates the transactions of the civic sector, but permeates the operations of both the state and market sectors. The network is not, as is usually assumed, a mixed form of organization existing halfway along a continuum ranging from market to hierarchy. Rather, it is a generic name for a third type of arrangement, built on very different integrating mechanisms: networks are consensus/inducement-oriented organizations and institutions (Kumon 1992; Amin and Thrift 1995; Acs, de la Mothe, and Paquet 1996).

Three Learning Capabilities: Relations, Networks, Regimes

In the best of all possible worlds, learning relationships, networks, and regimes would materialize organically as a response to the need for nimbleness in the face of accelerating change, and would become a new form of co-ordination capable of promoting and fostering effective learning in a society of flows, where commutation is omnipresent. Moreover, in such a world, when linkages among actors can be modified and interrupted at any time, culture would become an important bond that would make these networks and regimes operative and effective at collective learning.

Culture refers to those unwritten values and principles that generate a relatively high level of co-ordination, at low cost, by bestowing identity and membership through stories of flexible generality about events of practice that act as repositories of accumulated wisdom. The evolution of these stories constitutes collective learning: a way to interpret conflicting and often confusing data and serves as a social construction of a community.

De Geus uses an analogy from evolutionary biology both to explain the foundations and different stages of such collective learning and to identify the loci for action in correcting learning failures. He addresses the ability of individuals to move around and to be exposed to different challenges (new relations), the capacity of individuals to invent new ways to cope creatively in the face of new circumstances (new networks), and the process of communicating these new ways from the individual to the entire community (new regimes) (de Geus 1997).

First, as noted earlier, a certain heterogeneity is an important source of learning since a community composed of identical individuals with similar histories or experiences is less likely to extract much new insight from a given environment. However, there must be a sufficient degree of trust to sustain learning. This in turn requires a 'cultural' basis of differences that members recognize and share (Drummond 1981-82). The cultural basis of heterogeneity and trust, the mastery of weak ties (i.e., the capacity to build strong relations on weak ties) – these are all obviously dimensions that can be nurtured and represent a critical capability (Laurent and Paquet 1998).

Second, learning is not about the transmission of abstract knowledge from one person's head to another's. It is about the "embodied ability to behave as community members." It is fostered by contacts with the outside, by facilitating access to and membership in the community of practice. Trust is at the core of the fabric of such networks and communities of practice that transform "labourers into members," an employment contract into a membership contract (Handy 1995).

Third, belonging is one of the most powerful agents of mobilization. Therefore, what is required is an important "moral" component to the new membership contract, to make it less contractual and more relational. This *new refurbished moral contract* is "a network of civic engagement ... which can serve as a cultural template for future collaboration ... and broaden the participants' sense of self ... enhancing the participants' 'taste' for collective benefits" (Putnam 1995). These loose arrangements, or regimes, require a certain degree of interaction and proximity; both of these are important features of the learning process.

Relations, networks, and regimes constitute layers of capability in the process of governance. They evolve as the Canadian socio-economy is transubstantiated. But many observers believe that this is happening neither fast enough nor in a sufficiently integrated way: the process is evolving *lentement et par morceau*. As a result, the emerging governance process resembles a patchwork quilt, becoming evermore complex as the environment evolves from placid (Type 1) to turbulent (Type 4) (Emery and Trist 1965).

In our new high-risk and turbulent environment, strategic, hierarchical management is no longer sufficient. We need to develop capacities for collaborative action in managing large scale reorganizations and structural changes at the macro level. The ground is in motion; acting independently may not only compromise effectiveness but may even make things worse and amplify disintegrative tendencies. What is required is collective action by dissimilar organizations whose fates are, basically, positively correlated. This requires trust-enhancing mechanisms such as stronger relationships, networks, and regimes.

Metcalfe (1998:28) has synthesized these sorts of predicaments and the challenges underpinning them, in a catastrophe theory type graph depicting the major aspects of the issue in three dimensions: the degree of complexity of the environment, the quality of management/governance capacities, and the level of governance effectiveness. He shows that as complexity increases (from Type 3 to 4), management capacities must improve to avoid the disintegration of the system. If these capacities already exist, they must be brought into use; if they do not exist, they must be developed. If they do not exist and no development effort is made, or if the capacity-building is inadequate, disintegration ensues.

Deficits on the Capabilities Front

The decline of trust and the erosion of social capital are easy to document. So too is the weakening pattern of networks that defines the old Canada, as well as the consequent relative unhelpfulness of the governance structures. This situation has not been improved by the Canadian tradition of self-doubt which is so difficult to shake off.

And yet, as Jan Morris would put it (quoted in Iyer 2000:122), while Toronto is "a capital of the unabsolute," it is also an extraordinary, successful experiment in multiculturalism and one of the most peaceful cities of its size in North America. Organically, Canada appears to be able to distill a way of life capable of accommodating this growing diversity and to do it somewhat unconsciously. This does not necessarily provide the basis for a satisfactory strategy for improvement in other realms; it simply indicates a general direction for action. The only apparently desirable approach then, is to encourage Canadians to use those local processes as catalysts to improve the situation on all three fronts: trust relations, networks, and regimes.

On the civil society front, repairs are needed to help to generate new forms of loose solidarity at the very time that diversity is growing exponentially and shared values appear to have diminished. Boutique multiculturalism and the reliance on symbolic recognition devices do not appear to be satisfactory strategies (Fish 1999). Nevertheless, since Canadians are hypersensitive to any form of intolerance, such new weak ties cannot be constructed on a basis of a retribalization that carries with it any sort of exclusion.

On the political front, we in Canada now live in a world of plural, limited, and partial identities in which multiple citizenships are common currency. A rethinking of the notion of citizenship is necessary to accommodate these new realities (Paquet 1989, 1994b). We must also reconsider the existing political structures and modify them to permit a greater decentralization in order to provide maximum leverage for the strategic/catalytic state (Lind 1992; Paquet 1996-97).

On the economic front, the development of a stronger basis for stakeholder capitalism and the transformation of the property-rights regime is needed. That will require a shift from the absolute property rights doctrine of the English-speaking legal tradition, wherein shareholders own absolutely all the enterprise, and the formality of market contracting, toward a pluralistic and more encompassing view of property rights and a greater reliance on relational, trust-based, and moral contracts (Paquet and Roy 2000).

Assets, Skills, and Styles behind These Capabilities

To ascertain what might be required to improve the present situation in the private, public, and civic sectors, one must look behind these capabilities, probing into the assets, skills, and styles of co-ordination that currently underpin governance capabilities and shape the Canadian *habitus*.

First, in order to create and maintain these capabilities (relationships, networks, and regimes), there are certain requirements. These include a mix of 1) rights and authorities enshrined in rules; 2) resources (i.e., an array of assets such as money, time, information, and facilities made available both to individuals and institutions; 3) competencies and knowledge (i.e., education, training, experience, and expertise) and 4) organizational capital (i.e., the capacity to mobilize attention and to make effective use of the first three types of resources) (March and Olsen 1995).

Second, Spinosa, Flores, and Dreyfus (1997) have shown that the engines of entrepreneurship (private sector), democratic action (public sphere), and cultivation of solidarity (civil society) are quite similar. They are based on a particular skill that Spinosa, et al. call "history-making," that can be decomposed into three sub-skills: 1) acts of articulation – attempts at *définition de situation* or new ways to make sense of the situation; 2) acts of cross-appropriation – to bring new practices into a context that would not naturally generate them; and 3) acts of reconfiguration – to reframe the whole perception of the way of life. Such individual actions are necessary but insufficient – either to generate new capabilities or to trigger the required *bricolage* in the different worlds. As Putnam (2000) puts it, the renewal of the stock of social capital (relationships, networks, and regimes) is a task that requires the mobilization of communities. This in turn means that we must be able to ensure that these actions resonate with communities of interpretation and practice – what Spinosa et al. call "worlds."

Third, there is no way one can hope to transform these 'worlds' (in the private, public, and civic spheres) unless one can first disclose these 'worlds' (in the sense we use when we speak of the 'world of business' or the 'world of medicine'). By 'world,' we mean a "totality of interrelated pieces of *equipment*, each used to carry out a specific task, such as hammering a nail. These *tasks* are undertaken to achieve certain *purposes*, such as building a house. This activity enables those performing it to have *identities*, such as being a carpenter." Finally, one may refer to the way in which this world is organized and co-ordinated as its *style* (Spinosa et al. 1997:17–19).

Articulation, cross-appropriation, and reconfiguration constitute kinds of style changes (making explicit what was implicit or lost, gaining wider horizons, reframing). In a turbulent environment, the styles of the different worlds are modified as are also the very nature of the equipment, tasks, and identities. This transforms not only the organizational capital but also the rest of the asset base of the system, stimulating a different degree of re-articulation and reconfiguration and enriching the possibilities of cross-appropriation.

The distinctiveness of the Canadian system is this ensemble of components: the way the Canadian system adopts certain patterns of assets and skills, distills capabilities, and constitutes its particular sort of world.

This dynamic has been synthesized in the graph below. It depicts the Canadian political socio-economy as an 'instituted process,' characterized by a particular amalgam of assets, adroitly used and enriched by political, economic, and civic entrepreneurs, through skillful articulation, cross-appropriation, and reframing activities. These are then woven into a fabric of relations, networks, and regimes defining the distinctive *habitus* of Canada as a complex adaptive system.

Such a complex world is disclosed by the examination of its equipment, tasks, and identities, which are organized and co-ordinated in a particular way with a particular style. Modification of the structure of assets, skills, and capabilities is echoed in a transformation of the Canadian world; such a transformation exerts a reverse impact on the pattern of assets, skills, and capabilities.

Radiography of the Governance Process

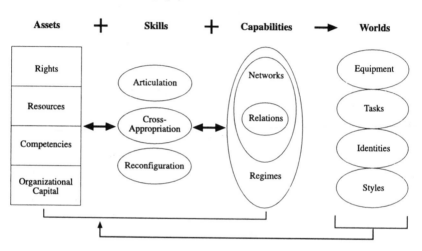

It is quite tempting to highlight one dimension or aspect of this nexus of forces and to suggest that it has a defining impact on the whole structure. Many commentators have elevated certain patterns of rights to this role; others have suggested that the whole system revolves around certain identities. In fact, this misses the central point: that this broad ranging canvas has an overall dynamic, the sort of dynamic that underpins all social systems. In the words of Donald Schön, a social system "contains structure, technology and theory. The structure is the set of roles and relations among individual members. The theory consists of the views held within the social system about its purposes, its operations, its environment, and its future. Both reflect, and in turn influence, the prevailing technology of the system. These dimensions all hang together, so that any change in one produces change in the others" (Schön 1971).

What defines the "Canadian way" is the transversal manner in which these assets, skills, and capabilities are integrated into a social technology; how they constitute an interpretative scheme and a stylization of the world; and how they translate into co-ordinating governance structures and schemes of intervention. Such schemes are inspired by a root framework, but take different forms *hic et nunc*, because the circumstances call for *ad hoc* action. Indeed, as was mentioned earlier, this is the very nature of the Canadian style.

One may observe the "Canadian way" at work in various spheres – in key cauldrons where Canadian distinctiveness is being shaped (schools, workplaces, cities, arts and culture, politics and government, etc.). Each of these loci is a laboratory in which Canada has tackled, with greater or lesser success, the challenges of complexity, collaboration, and citizen engagement in designing an ensemble of assets, skills, and capabilities that gives shape to the Canadian *habitus*.

While no such local vignettes can pretend to exhaust the Canadian distinctiveness, they may act as powerful *révélateurs* not only of the nature of this distinctly Canadian *manière de voir et de faire* but also of some features of this distinctiveness that may be *en émergence*. Such illustrations are useful in understanding the ways in which the Canadian style may serve the country less effectively than it should and in disclosing where catalytic action might be required as a matter of priority.

But what may be most fundamental to the characterization of the Canadian style is the notion that Canada is the "capital of the unabsolute;" that Canadians are uncomfortable with any form of distinctiveness that excludes. This, in turn, generates a phenomenal degree of tolerance for diversity, and a robust rejection of any form of *embrigadement* that binds.

In certain circumstances, aloofness may become complacency, irony may lead to denial, tolerance to diffraction, openness to the erosion of the differences between the outside and the inside, and political correctness to greater social distance between groups. This particular *manière de voir et d'être* is not without a dark side that has sometimes been exploited by shrewd manipulators to manufacture denial and complacency.

Three Problematic Cauldrons

Three loci have been chosen to illustrate this Canadian distinctiveness *en acte*: workplace and enterprise, education and health, and the national multilogue about patriotism and social cohesion.

Workplace and Enterprise

Lately, Canada's productivity growth has been relatively lacklustre. This is linked to co-ordination failures in the workplace and enterprise and to a lack of effective co-ordination among the different sectors (private, public, and civic). Yet there is a systematic denial of the seriousness of this situation. Moreover, feats of analytics attempt to demonstrate that, despite the stagnation of the material standard of living of Canadians, everything is all right with our total well-being.

Canadians have an uncanny capacity to occlude their macro-organizational problems. John Porter (1965) had considerable difficulty in persuading the equality-conscious Canadian population of the 1960s that Canada was a vertical mosaic of classes and elites. In the same way, in the face of ample evidence, Canadians currently are in denial that the Canadian governance apparatus is marred by hierarchy and confrontations. They also do not see that this situation translates into a relative lag in adopting new technologies, an immense lag in the productivity of our service sector, and a certain slowness in its capacity to transform.

Many of these difficulties result from a misalignment of Canada's *structural capital*: its *systems* (processes and outputs), *structure* (the arrangement of responsibilities and accountabilities among the stakeholders), *strategy* (the goals of organizations and the ways sought to achieve them), and *culture* (the sum of individual opinions, shared mindsets, values, and norms within the organizations) (Saint-Onge 1996:13). The major barrier to good performance is the misalignment among these four elements and, in particular, the disconnections between strategy and culture.

In Canada, the 'culture' in which both enterprise and workplace are embedded and which also shapes them, is problematic: 1) the framework of corporate law is dominated by the shadow of the shareholders and does not provide much place for stakeholders (de la Mothe and Paquet 1996) and, 2) the culture of the workplace (which is a significant source of social capital) is not a culture of learning and innovation, and is not geared to taking full advantage of alliances, partnerships, and network externalities (de la Mothe and Paquet 1997).

While in dozens of U.S. states, corporate law allows boards of directors to allocate portions of the net operating surplus to stakeholders other than the shareholders (through amenities, better conditions, etc.), in Canada, any shareholder has the power to sue the board if it were to adopt such a policy. This considerably cramps the style of the board in generating the requisite commitment of these other stakeholders.

The same sort of dysfunction can be seen in the workplace, where a discourse of confrontation is still prevalent, along with the centrality of job action as a method of conflict resolution. As a result, the sort of collaborative governance that might ensure better dynamic (Schumpeterian) performance fails to materialize. This has resulted in Canada's relatively poor showing in a number of areas in comparison to other countries of the Organization for Economic Co-operation and Development.

And yet the rhetoric of competition and confrontation continues to prevail at stage front, while new forms of co-operation, partnering, and joint venturing materialize every day *en catimini* in all sorts of quarters throughout the land. So it is not that there is no progress, rather that the progress is local and informal (as it should be), but without the benefit of a supporting infrastructure.

This is the Canadian way!

Education and Health

Canada spends immense resources on both education and healthcare. Both these systems are national icons and a source of national pride. This explains Canadians' sense of accomplishment with Canada's gold medal in the United Nations international ranking of nations in terms of 'human development.'

But Canadians also turn a blind eye to the critical signs of dysfunction to which experts – in Canada and elsewhere – point in both our educational and healthcare systems. Gross lapses in efficiency and effectiveness, counterproductive silo-type organizations, confrontational policy developments entailing important blind spots, no voice or role for the users, and so on – are all factors acknowledged by experts (Keating 1995; Angus and Bégin 2000; World Health Organization 2000) yet are deliberately suppressed in public debates in Canada. There is an amazing chasm, for instance, between the grim reality that

Canada spends 50 per cent more per capita on healthcare than the United Kingdom does with results that are inferior to theirs and the public display of sacramental denial that there might be any need for repairs in the governance of Canada's 'superior' healthcare system.

This has led to much damning of the two-tiered American system in both education and health. And yet all this occurs with many winks and nods acknowledging some degree of disarray in both Canadian systems. What is resented is radical, in-your-face criticism of the Canadian systems. This is regarded as most unhelpful (if not unpatriotic) and as likely to discourage action *à petits pas* meant to repair those systems.

As an example, young Canadians spend significantly fewer days in class each year than their colleagues in other advanced countries; a recent report suggested that up to 40 per cent of high school students in Ottawa were dysfunctional as learners (Keating 1995:82); our commitment to life-long learning is minimal; the resources dedicated to formal workforce development and training remain a fraction of the sums spent by Canada's industrialized competitors in Europe and Asia (one-third of Germany's commitment and one tenth of Japan's commitment). And the same critical diagnosis might be made about our healthcare system – a highly chaotic system that generates indices of morbidity and mortality well above what one might expect and at quite a high cost (Angus and Bégin 2000).

Obviously, in the face of suppressed criticism, a major overhaul of both systems is most unlikely. What is more likely will be a magnificent and uncompromising rhetorical defense of the status quo, with a concomitant selection, by certain establishments, of particular reforms, selected piecemeal and somewhat covertly implemented in a quasi-underground approach. Any radical challenge will continue to be denounced as a betrayal of Canada's 'perfect' institutions. This is the way 'universality' was assassinated in Canada: piecemeal, covertly, without a national debate, while on the hustings the political classes pretended that they were staunchly defending it.

This might explain what Harold Innis meant when he said "a social scientist in Canada can only survive by virtue of a sense of humour" (quoted in Neill 1972:93).

National Multilogue about Patriotism and Social Cohesion

As global integration proceeds, the nation-state is transformed. Its territoriality becomes problematic to the extent that its borders become porous. Its sovereignty begins to become unbundled and this leads the citizen to re-assess *what belonging means*. The problem of *belonging* echoes the new situation where Canadians increasingly find themselves of mixed origins and authority is dispersed in a multiplicity of sites. A multiplicity of allegiances ensues. Thus, while citizens have traditionally associated their main loyalty with the nation-state, the state has lost its privileged position as the main anchor of belonging as non-territorial modes of organization become increasingly important (Elkins 1995:74–75).

New principles of social cohesion are *en émergence*. We know that they are likely both to evolve at the local level and to echo a non-centralizing philosophy, but the timing of the actual moment of tipping into a new sociality continues to be largely unpredictable.

Not all observers agree on the reality of this tectonic change. Many continue both to believe that 'bridging capital' was the basis of the Canadian 'social glue' that bound us together in the past and to build arguments that it should remain the central adhesive in the years to come.

This is the position of the Senate Standing Committee on Social Affairs, Science, and Technology (Canada 1999) which has suggested that the three pillars on which the sense of social cohesion of Canadians rested, in the post-World War II era, were: the federal programs of redistribution of income; the shared-costs programs through which the federal government provided federal grants to support health care, post-secondary education, and social assistance; and the grants system to equalize the average quality of public services throughout the country. Thus the Committee suggests that nothing short of a new wave of federal institutions can provide the requisite degree of security to Canadians through redistribution.

This is the central theme used by those who argue that medicare is what makes Canada hang together and that anything that threatens the present interregional process of money laundering is bound to put the Canadian edifice in peril.

This 'bridging social capital' interpretation may be nothing more than a slogan in order to aid rationalizing compulsive centralism (because it is necessary for redistribution). It has been propounded, however, by certain groups in English Canada as a founding national myth. The same people who defend this view of income and wealth redistribution as supplying the essential Canadian social glue have also found evidence of a latent demand for such glue, not to mention evidence of latent patriotism in the Molson beer commercial "My name is Joe and I am Canadian." This is surprising.

Indeed, in such a bizarre piece, Canadians are viewed as a people who defiantly harbour limited and multiple identities, all of which are characterized, almost in the same breath, as both crassly opportunistic (in defining themselves through some federal-provincial fiscal plumbing arrangement) and naively sentimental.

There is another interpretation, one rooted in our national irony and our taste for *bricolage*.

Medicare is a prime example of a popular federal redistributive scheme. It is a collectively expensive scheme in which healthcare is presented to the population as a free good, through the hiding hand of the state. It is hardly surprising that the population is favourably disposed toward such a scheme. The fact that elected officials have wished to be seen as providers of a valuable free good is also hardly surprising. This manufactured win-win situation (in which the population pretends that it receives free and universal healthcare and the politicians pretend that they provide that care for free) is, at best, sleight of hand. But only in government-sponsored polls or political harangues does this ever get confused with national identity and citizenship.

In the real world of healthcare, Canadians live by the principle that it is unhelpful to rock the boat. *Bricolage*, nevertheless, has already begun to effect the required repairs to the system through appropriation of whatever techniques appear to be most effective, including those emerging from the United States. This movement of silent reform will slowly replace the existing emphasis on redistribution (which is costly and ineffective) with more effective and cheaper insurance schemes (Mandel 1996). The same may be said about education: the staunch defense of our public education system has never been stronger than at the very moment when Canada is *sotto voce* creating both private schools and universities galore.

Canadian distinctiveness does not, therefore, lie with the safety net. And, because the safety net is under strain, this may be good news. Rather, Canadian distinctiveness rests with Canadian ability to master weak ties; with Canadian capacity to build on loose, casual social connections; and with Canadian facility to elaborate a *modus vivendi* of heterogeneous and diverse groups. Hence, the *leitmotiv* is likely to be appropriate insurance for our high-risk society, rather than income and wealth redistribution.

This emphasis on weak ties in the new social arrangements reminds one of Schopenhauer's parable about porcupines: in the cold of winter, these creatures find ways to come close enough to bring each other some warmth, but not close enough to hurt each other. This means a new form of civic engagement, one that should not be confused with the sort of social cohesion and pacification that is supposed to ensue from massive redistribution of income and wealth (Paquet 2000).

As for the success of recent commercials about 'Canadianness:' it is an interesting illustration of Canadians' general taste for self-depre-cation and irony. The success of the Molson commercial is less evi-dence of suppressed patriotism than evidence of our immense taste for an ironic view of ourselves, for self-mockery. This is the same expla-nation for the popularity of *La petite vie* or *This Hour Has 22 Minutes*.

Conclusion

Let us clearly restate our main point. Canadian distinctiveness is not a set of static and arrested traits, but a certain *habitus* – that is, a certain set of propensities or proclivities which becomes the dominant logic in the face of challenges and pressures. This dynamic *'réactique'* defines the characteristics of the socio-economic system in its dual process of *adapting* to its environment and *adopting* (i.e., bestowing a greater probability of success on) certain types of behaviour by actors or orga-nizations in the system. This is what we mean when we refer to the 'Canadian world,' a distinctive world rooted in special equipment (physical, organizational, legal, etc.), tasks, and identities – all inte-grated into a certain style. This dynamic is in turn anchored in an inte-grated ensemble of assets, skills, and capabilities which are also evolving as a result of pressures both from the external environment and from the evolving internal 'Canadian world' itself.

It is not possible to define this dynamic Canadian distinctiveness in all its complexity in a few paragraphs. But one can identify the main features of the worldview underpinning it and the ways in which this distinctiveness has crystallized in reaction to anomalies and pressures in different sites.

Our hypothesis is that this *habitus* has been characterized by irony plus *bricolage* – that is, a certain denial and disingenuousness at the rhetorical level and a certain *ad hoc* characteristic at the level of prac-tice. This approach, by avoiding grand narratives and grand designs, generates an aloofness *de bon aloi* at the level of discourse, as well as the sort of practicality in action that is capable of generating piecemeal reform in a country that is relatively averse to change.

One major benefit of this approach – devoid of ideology, except perhaps for some latent, soft egalitarianism – is that it dedramatizes even the most ambitious endeavours, making adjustment appear less painful than it really is. Some side malefits of this vision-less approach are that it enables Canadians to avoid fully participating in a number of major modern debates (the appropriate mix of liberalism, democracy, and republicanism; centralization vs. decentralization; egalitarianism vs. subsidiarity; redistribution vs. insurance, etc.) and to surf over change during major periods of transformation without a full awareness of the depth of the reforms underway, or even an adequate appreciation of the auxiliary precautions that might be required.

The other essays in this work illustrate very well the canonical Canadian capacity for ironic denial and *ad hocery*. In all cases (the policy vis-à-vis Aboriginals, the multiculturalist strategy, and the ways in which Canadians deal with the emergence of an ever more important civic sector), evidence can be found to support my hypothesis.

Yet it should not be presumed that Canadian distinctiveness is somewhat "arrested." Indeed, ours is a form of "dynamic irony" (Ross 1954:xii), with the institutional order an emergent phenomenon. Though it is adaptable, evolvable, resilient, boundless, and it breeds of novelty, our distinctiveness is also non-optimal, uncontrollable, unpredictable, and fundamentally not understandable (Kelly 1994:22–23). This explains why the discourses about social transformation of the institutional order are so vague and non-committal (Drucker 1994). We have to be ironic because we must be satisfied with observing the "emergent properties" of the new order as they materialize.

In the transition period to the new millenium, we may expect a strong affirmation of "limited identities," considerable disconnection, and challenges to most of the rigid and centralized institutions. There will also be a growing tendency for the emergent order to become anchored at the meso-level and to be couched in informal rules of the game agreed to by persons who share a "web of trust." One may even expect that, at some point, key signposts or standards will mutate – the minting and issuing of currency, for instance. The main challenge will not be to master the switch from one dominant logic to another but rather to learn to cope with multiple dominant logics and, therefore, with concurrent, distributed, institutional orders (Paquet 1995b, 1997d).

The new so-called co-ordination *en chantier* will loosely intermediate the spectral and distributed network world generated by the information age. In the network age, fluidity is the foundation of dynamism and survival where institutional stability imposes constraints on relational fluidity. Many predict the emergence of an "imperial age" reminiscent of the Roman empire under Hadrian, where the "institutional order" will aspire to being no more than a loose web of agreements that ensures compatibility among open networks (Guéhenno 1993; Paquet 1994b). A baroque governance!

Obviously, this is not an ideal situation. But the optimal may not be the ideal either. There is much to be deplored about the Canadian way degenerating into denial and complacency and revealing a vulnerability to lethargy. Such a method of governing Canada will be costly in the long run. But there is also much to be said for a country that has decided not to take itself too seriously; one that takes to heart the counsel of John Maynard Keynes to economists: avoid dealing with big problems, emulate the dentists, and deal with the small holes (Gordon 1975).

For those who welcome more passion, I suggest the cure of an afternoon at a soccer game in Rome. There, they can experience passion about trivia: armed guards body-searching those coming into the stadium, vigilantly guarding the safety of the visiting team's music band, and ready for the most gratuitous violence at any time.

Meanwhile, back in our aloof country, one can find on the editorial page of the national newspaper – *The Globe & Mail* of 15 June 2000 – an editorial not calling the population to arms, but one entitled "a call to irony."

Qui dit mieux!

On another occasion, in 1999 (Paquet 1999a), I suggested, rather modestly, that when constructing the requisite new sociality in keeping with the Canadian/Québec "spirit" – and Québec's spirit is much more akin to the Canadian spirit than Québecers like to admit – it might not be unreasonable to start with tact and civility. Many ridiculed such a modest start. It looked too much like a celebration of a Band-Aid solution: "solving a problem with a minimum amount of effort and time and cost" (Gladwell 2000:256).

This sort of approach always generates disdain in Canada – at least at the rhetorical level – for it conveys a sense of dogged and indiscriminate effort. This is missing the point. It is really meant to connote the most effective way of responding to the central challenge – finding ways to partition big, intractable problems into small, tractable ones. This is why the Canadian way is *une foule de petites choses*.

References

Acs, Z., J. de la Mothe, and G. Paquet. 1996. "Local Systems of Innovation." In *The Implications of Knowledge-Based Growth for Micro-Economic Policies*, ed. P. Howitt, 339–59. Calgary: University of Calgary Press.

Amin, A. and N. Thrift. 1995. "Institutional Issues for the European Regions: From Markets and Plans to Socio-economics and Powers of Association." *Economy and Society* 24 (1): 43–66.

Angus, D.E. and M. Bégin. 2000. "Governance in Health Care: Dysfunctions and Challenges." *Transactions of the Royal Society of Canada*, 6th ser., vol. 10.

Arthur, W.B. 1994. *Increasing Returns and Path Dependence in the Economy.* Ann Arbor: University of Michigan Press.

Ashby, W.R. 1970. *An Introduction to Cybernetics.* London: Chapman & Hall.

Bauman, Z. 2000. *Liquid Modernity.* Cambridge: Polity Press.

Baumard, P. 1996. *Organisations déconcertées.* Paris: Masson.

Boisot, M. 1995. *Information Space: A Framework for Learning in Organizations, Institutions and Culture.* London: Routledge.

Burelle, A. 1995. *Le mal canadien.* Montréal: Fides.

Canada. 1999. Senate. Standing Committee on Social Affairs, Science, and Technology. *On Social Cohesion.* Ottawa.

_____. 2000. Advisory Council on Science and Technology. Expert Panel on Skills. *Stepping Up: Skills and Opportunities in the Knowledge Economy.* Ottawa.

Castells, M. 1996. *The Rise of the Network Society.* Oxford: Blackwell.

_____. 1997. *The Power of Identity.* Oxford: Blackwell.

_____. 1998. *End of Millenium.* Oxford: Blackwell.

Chrétien, J. 2000. "The Canadian Way in the 21st Century." Speech at the Conference on *Progressive Governance in the 21st Century.* Berlin, June 2–3.

Coleman, J.S. 1988. "Social Capital in the Creation of Human Capital." *American Journal of Sociology* (Supplement): 94, S–95–S–120.

Cooke, P. and K. Morgan. 1993. "The Network Paradigm: New Departures in Corporate and Regional Development." *Environment and Planning D: Society and Space* 11: 543–64.

Dahrendorf, R. 1995. "A Precarious Balance: Economic Opportunity, Civil Society and Political Liberty." *The Responsive Society* 5 (3): 13–39.

Dalum, B., et al. 1992. "Public Policy in the Learning Society." In *National Systems of Innovation*, ed. B. Lundvall, 296–317. London: Pinter.
Drezner, D. 1998. "The Resurgent State." *The Washington Quarterly* 21 (1): 209–225.
Drucker, P.F. 1994. "The Age of Social Transformation." *The Atlantic Monthly* 274 (5): 53–80 (November).
Drummond, L. 1981–2. « Analyse sémiotique de l'ethnicité au Québec. » *Question de culture* 2: 139–153.
Durlauf, S.N. 1998. "What Should Policymakers Know about Economic Complexity?" *The Washington Quarterly* 21 (1): 157–165.
Elkins, D.J. 1995. *Beyond Sovereignty: Territory and Political Economy in the 21st Century*. Toronto: The University of Toronto Press.
Emery, F.E. and E.L. Trist. 1965. "The Causal Texture of Organizational Environments." *Human Relations* 18: 21–32.
Fish, S. 1999. *The Trouble with Principle*. Cambridge: Harvard University Press.
Geus, A. de. 1997. "The Living Company." *Harvard Business Review* 75 (2): 51–59.
Gladwell, M. 2000. *The Tipping Point*. Boston: Little, Brown and Company.
Goldberg, V.P. 1989. *Readings in the Economics of Contract Law*. Cambridge: Cambridge University Press.
Gordon, H.S. 1975. "The Political Economy of Big Questions and Small Ones." *Canadian Public Policy* 1 (1): 97–106.
Granovetter, M.S. 1973. "The Strength of Weak Ties." *American Journal of Sociology* 78: 360–80.
Guéhenno, J.M. 1993. *La fin de la démocratie*. Paris: Flammarion.
Guillaume, M. 1999. *L'empire des réseaux*. Paris: Descartes & Cie.
Handy, C. 1995. "Trust and the Virtual Organization." *Harvard Business Review* 73 (3): 40–50.
Helliwell, J.F. 1996. *Trust and Social Capital in the United States and Canadian Provinces: An Exploratory Empirical Survey*. Mimeo.
Iyer, P. 2000. *The Global Soul*. New York: Alfred A. Knopf.
Johnson, B. 1992. "Institutional Learning." In *National Systems of Innovation*, ed. B. Lundvall, 23–44. London: Pinter.
Keating, D.P. 1995. "The Learning Society in the Information Age." In *Changing Maps: Governing in a World of Rapid Change*, ed. S.A. Rosell, et al., 205–229. Ottawa: Carleton University Press.
Kelly, K. 1994. *Out of Order*. Reading, MA: Addison-Wesley.
Killick, T. 1995. *The Flexible Economy*. London: Routledge.
Krugman, P. 1996. *The Self-Organizing Economy*. Oxford: Blackwell.

Kumon, S. 1992. "Japan as a Network Society." In *The Political Economy of Japan*, ed. S. Kumon & H. Rosovsky, vol. 3: 109–141. Stanford: Stanford University Press.

Laurent, P. et G. Paquet. 1998. *Epistémologie et économie de la relation.* Paris/Lyon: Vrin.

Lind M. 1992. "The Catalytic State." *The National Interest* 27 (Spring): 3–12.

Mandel, M.J. 1996. *The High-risk Society.* NewYork: Random House.

March, J.G. and J.P. Olsen. 1995. *Democratic Governance.* New York: The Free Press.

Metcalfe, L. 1998. "Flexible Integration in and after the Amsterdam Treaty." In *Coping with Flexibility and Legitimacy after Amsterdam*, ed. M. den Boer, A. Guggenbühl, and S. Vanhoonacker, 11–30. Maastricht: European Institute of Public Administration.

Moati, P. et E.M. Mouhoud. 1994. « Information et organisation de la production: vers une division cognitive du travail. » *Economie appliquée* 46 (1): 47–73.

Moore, J.F. 1996. *The Death of Competition.* New York: Harper Collins.

_____. 1998. "The Rise of a New Corporate Form." *The Washington Quarterly* 21 (1): 167–81.

de la Mothe, J. and G. Paquet, eds. 1996. *Corporate Governance and the New Competition.* Ottawa: PRIME.

_____. eds. 1997. *Challenges Unmet in the New Production of Knowledge.* Ottawa: PRIME.

Neill, R.F. 1972. *A New Theory of Value – The Canadian Economics of H.A. Innis.* Toronto: University of Toronto Press.

Paquet, G. 1989. « Pour une notion renouvelée de citoyenneté ». *Transactions of the Royal Society of Canada*, 4th ser., vol. 27: 83–100.

_____. 1992. "The Strategic State." In *Finding Common Ground*, ed. J. Chrétien, 85–101. Hull: Voyageur Publishing.

_____. 1994a. "Reinventing Governance." *Opinion Canada* 2 (2): 1–5.

_____. 1994b. « La citoyenneté dans la société d'information: une réalité transversale et paradoxale ». Dans *Mémoires de la Société royale du Canada*, 6e sér., tome 5: 59–78.

_____. 1995a. « Gouvernance distribuée et *habitus* centralisateur ». Dans *Mémoires de la Société royale du Canada*, 6e sér., tome 6: 93–107.

_____. 1995b. "Institutional Evolution in an Information Age." In *Technology, Information and Public Policy – The Bell Canada Papers on Economic and Public Policy 3*, ed. T.J. Courchene, 197–229. Kingston: John Deustch Institute for the Study of Economic Policy.

_____. 1996. « La grisaille institutionnelle ». Dans *La ré-invention des institutions et le rôle de l'état*, dir. S. Coulombe et G. Paquet, 393–421. Montréal: Association des économistes québécois.

_____. 1996–97. "The Strategic State." *Ciencia Ergo Sum* 3 (3), pt. 1: 257–61; 4 (1), pt. 2: 28–34; 4 (2), pt. 3: 148–54.

_____. 1997a. « Et si la Révolution tranquille n'avait pas eu lieu ». *L'Agora* 4 (2): 35–6.

_____. 1997b. "Canada as a Disconcerted Learning Economy: A Governance Challenge." In *Transactions of the Royal Society of Canada*, 6th ser. vol. 8: 69–98.

_____. 1997c. "States, Communities and Markets: The Distributed Governance Scenario." In *The Nation State in a Global/Information Era: Policy Challenges – The Bell Canada Papers on Economic and Public Policy*, ed. T.J. Courchene, 5:25–46. Kingston: John Deutsch Institute for the Study of Economic Policy.

_____. 1997d. "Slouching Toward a New Governance." *Optimum* 27 (3): 44–50.

_____. 1998. "Governance and Social Cohesion: Survivability in the 21st Century." In *Transactions of the Royal Society of Canada*, 6th ser., vol. 9: 85–116.

_____. 1999a. *Oublier la Révolution Tranquille*. Montréal: Liber.

_____. 1999b. "Innovations in Governance in Canada," *Optimum* 29 (2/3): 71–81.

_____. 1999c. "Tectonic Changes in Canadian Governance." In *How Ottawa Spends 1999-2000*, ed. L.S. Pal, 75–111. Toronto: Oxford University Press.

_____. 1999d. *Governance Through Social Learning*. Ottawa: University of Ottawa Press.

_____. 2000. « Gouvernance distribuée, socialité et engagement civique. » *Gouvernance* 1 (1): 52–66.

_____. and J. Roy. 1995. "Prosperity Through Networks: The Small Business Strategy That Might Have Been." In *How Ottawa Spends – Midlife Crises*, ed. S. Phillips, 137–58. Ottawa: Carleton University Press.

_____. and J. Roy. 2000. *Governance in Canada*. Ottawa: Centre on Governance.

_____. and R. Shepherd. 1996. "The Program Review Process: A Deconstruction." In *How Ottawa Spends – Life Under the Knife*, ed. G. Swimmer, 39–72. Ottawa: Carleton University Press.

Porter, J.E. 1965. *The Vertical Mosaic*. Toronto: University of Toronto Press.

Public Policy Forum. 1993. *Private-Public Sector Co-operation as a Means of Improving a Country's Economic Performance: A Survey of Practices in Canada, the U.S., Europe, and Japan*. Ottawa: Public Policy Forum.

Putnam, R.D. 2000. *Bowling Alone: The Collapse and Revival of American Community.* New York: Simon & Schuster.

_____. 1995. "Bowling Alone: America's Declining Social Capital." *Journal of Democracy* 6 (1): 65–78.

Rorty, R. 1989. *Contingency, Irony and Solidarity.* Cambridge: Cambridge University Press.

Ross, M., ed. 1954. *Our Sense of Identity.* Toronto: The Ryerson Press.

Saint-Onge, H. 1996. "Tacit Knowledge: The Key to the Strategic Alignment of Intellectual Capital." *Strategy and Leadership* (March–April): 10–14.

Schön, D.A. 1971. *Beyond the Stable State.* New York: Norton.

Spinosa, C., F. Flores, and H.L. Dreyfus. 1997. *Disclosing New Worlds.* Cambridge: The MIT Press.

Valaskakis, K. 1990. *Canada in the Nineties: Meltdown or Renaissance?* Montreal: The Gamma Institute Press.

World Health Organization 2000. *World Health Report 2000.*

Evolving State – Civil Society Relationships: The Beginning of a New Era?

Susan D. Phillips

THE RELATIONSHIP BETWEEN THE VOLUNTARY SECTOR AND THE STATE is undergoing fundamental change in Canada, as elsewhere. This is a result of a transformation in both the nature of governance and the character of the voluntary sector. Financial exigencies and neo-liberal preferences for a smaller state have propelled radical restructuring which has resulted in the downloading of services and dramatic cutbacks to program funding. Public sector restructuring has not been driven by financial concerns alone, however. It also reflects a transition from a paradigm of 'government' – of government departments unilaterally setting policy and producing services – to one of 'governance' in which governments work collaboratively and horizontally with other governments and with voluntary and private sector partners. Related to this, governments of both the left and right are taking a renewed interest in active citizenship, manifest by their attempts to encourage volunteerism and promote social cohesion. The result has been a realization on the part of governments that they need the voluntary sector more than ever, not only as partners in service delivery, but in building social capital and a strong civil society. At the same time, the voluntary sector has been rapidly evolving from a model based on charity to one based on civil society – that is, from a model premised on helping those less fortunate to one in which communities have the resources and are empowered to represent and help themselves. This has sparked the emergence of much stronger national leadership aimed at providing strategic direction to the sector and the demand for new policy tools and citizen engagement processes.

As a result, considerable innovation is taking place worldwide in regulatory reform and in the development of new institutions, framework agreements, and other mechanisms for building and sustaining more constructive relationships between governments and the voluntary sector.[1] Canada, too, has initiated sweeping reform aimed at increasing the capacity of the voluntary sector and at building better relationships to allow the sector to fulfil its unique roles in civil society and as a governing partner. The first concrete action toward implementing such reform came in early June 2000 with the federal government's announcement of the Voluntary Sector Initiative, a framework policy supported by almost $95 million over five years and a novel Joint Table process for its implementation. The magnitude and implications of this unfolding change should not be underestimated. Not only will the product of this reform have a major impact on both government and the sector, but the innovative process of collaboration used to produce a strategy for change has already begun to reshape how the federal government works with the sector.

Canada has a strong tradition of volunteerism and a vibrant and diverse voluntary sector of more than 175,000 organizations.[2] So, why does the existing relationship between the voluntary sector and the federal government need to change at all? What would it take to create a strong and enduring relationship, one designed to carry both the voluntary sector and government well into the twenty-first century? Does the federal government's Voluntary Sector Initiative go far enough in creating this kind of relationship? This paper analyzes both the process that led to the announcement of the federal government's Voluntary Sector Initiative and its content. I begin by presenting a conceptual framework for understanding relationships between the voluntary sector and the state. Next, I explore how this relationship has evolved over the years in Canada and outline its primary deficiencies. In the third section, Canada's experiment in relationship reform is examined with a view to understanding the agenda setting and change process. I conclude by arguing that the Voluntary Sector Initiative is a vital first step, but that it faces some distinctively Canadian contradictions that need to be resolved.

Conceptualizing Voluntary Sector–State Relationships

Relationships between the state and the voluntary sector are necessarily complex. They vary enormously across countries and over time, either because they evolve in response to changing circumstances or because they are consciously redesigned. The specific configurations of such a relationship depend on both the nature of government's interests and institutions for structuring expectations and interaction with voluntary organizations, and on the structure and capacity of the voluntary sector.

To varying degrees and in different ways, five distinct dimensions are part of all government–voluntary sector relationships:

1) PUBLIC POLICY ADVOCACY AND DIALOGUE: Above all, voluntary organizations represent citizens. In this role, they advocate, uninvited, on behalf of their constituencies. But, they are also frequently encouraged by governments to participate in dialogue around public policy issues that affect their communities and in which they have expertise. A relationship also affords, to varying degrees, mutual understanding about the nature of the relationship itself: it provides an opportunity for both government and the voluntary sector to understand better the challenges and limitations of the other and to determine, through dialogue, common interests and goals.

2) ACCOUNTABILITY: A relationship entails for both sides a requirement to explain and accept responsibility for carrying out assigned mandates in light of agreed upon expectations.[3]

3) SUPPORT: To varying degrees, a relationship contributes to the development of capacity in the voluntary sector and complements the resources and infrastructure of government. Capacity can be defined as "the human and financial resources, technology, skills, knowledge and understanding required to permit organizations to do their work and fulfil what is expected of them by stakeholders."[4]

4) TRANSPARENCY: In addition to promotion of appropriate conduct and acceptance of responsibility, a sector–state relationship should provide an opportunity for the public to ascertain whether both sides have lived up to commitments made and to understand how, and how well, the relationship is working. Transparency helps to ensure that the relationship is perceived as legitimate – by the sector, by government, and by the public at large.

5) SERVICE DELIVERY: The final dimension of a relationship is the provision of services to citizens, whether on contract, in partnership, or in the absence of government.

In addition to recognizing the multidimensionality of the relationship, it is important to note that relationships between the sector and the state occur at different levels – at the micro, meso or macro levels. The micro level involves one-on-one interaction – an individual department with a particular voluntary organization on a specific policy or programme issue. The meso level delimits relationships between a government department(s) and a subsector or constituency of groups, such as the many organizations representing the disability community or international development. The macro level, involving government as an entity dealing with the voluntary sector as a *sector*, is just beginning to emerge in many countries. In most cases, macro level relationships have been historically underdeveloped or non-existent, so that principles and broad frameworks need to be established as a first step. Although the meso and micro levels may be where organizations and governments live the relationship on a daily basis, the focus of this paper is on the macro level, which in policy terms is *the* contemporary challenge for both the sector and the state.

The Voluntary Sector–State Relationship in Canada

In the past decade or so, the voluntary–state sector relationship in Canada has undergone two deliberate transformations. The first, which began in the late 1980s, was an attempt to impose greater regulation on the sector and was prompted by neo-liberal restructuring of the state and a rise in populist ideas about democracy. The second transition which began in 1997 and is still in progress, is intended to create a more constructive, balanced relationship.

Constructing a Relationship

The Canadian government first began a direct relationship with the voluntary sector in the early 1900s, a period when churches and charities largely controlled welfare, health, and education services. Small grants were given to a few charitable organizations, such as the Canadian Lung Association and the Victorian Order of Nurses, to buy supplies and provide services, especially to vulnerable populations, that governments of the time could not reach.[5] The relationship expanded considerably in the 1940s when the federal government recognized the potential of voluntary organizations in nation building and in constructing a distinctively Canadian citizenship regime. At the time, Canada was developing its own legal framework and administrative practices by which its citizens would be Canadians, in terms of both legislation and identity, not merely British subjects. During the war years, when that legal concept and those desired practices of citizenship were being formulated, concerns about the loyalty of citizens, particularly immigrants from the combatant countries, predominated. These concerns laid the groundwork for a citizenship training programme housed in the federal Department of the Secretary of State.[6] It was felt that citizenship could be learned and practised through participation in voluntary organizations. In addition, collective action was seen as a way for the disadvantaged to help themselves and to achieve equality. The federal government, recognizing that it had a responsibility to support collective action to "help groups weld together individuals in a common community cognizant of its duty to support responsible, democratic government," provided funding to voluntary organizations for programmes related to citizenship.[7]

During the postwar years, concerns about loyalty gave way to concerns about constructing a Canadian identity – which is not surprising given the growing force of both Québec nationalism and economic Canadian nationalism. In the 1970s, operational funding to voluntary organizations engaged in promoting particular aspects of Canadian identity was expanded and institutionalized with programmes that funded official minority language associations, women, multicultural communities, Aboriginal political organizations, and (in the 1980s) disabled persons. At the meso level, operational departments cultivated relationships with their own constituencies by offering operational and project support for organizations, thereby supporting environmental groups and health and welfare organizations, to name but a few.

In addition to its role in enhancing the support dimension of the relationship, the federal government established institutionalized mechanisms for facilitating policy dialogue with voluntary organizations. This was done in two ways. First, the federal government developed a practice of holding consultations on major policy initiatives in which citizen groups were not only invited to participate but were also given research and intervenor funding to do so effectively. Even around the annual budget process, a traditionally secretive affair in parliamentary systems, the minister of Finance held sectoral meetings with leaders of social policy, anti-poverty, and women's groups, as well as with business leaders. The second way of enhancing policy dialogue centred on including representatives of social constituencies within the state. During the 1980s the size of the federal Cabinet grew to over 40 as a result of the creation of ministers responsible for women, multiculturalism, seniors, and youth, among others. Although no single minister was responsible for the voluntary sector *per se*, many of its key subsectors were represented at the Cabinet table.

The regulatory dimension of the relationship, also laid down during this period, was attached almost exclusively to the use of the tax system as a means of indirect support for the sector. In 1967, the *Income Tax Act* was amended to allow deductions for charitable donations and to provide for the tax exempt status of registered charitable organizations.[8] In addition to enhancing incentives for individuals to donate, these new provisions of the tax system created the first comprehensive, national system of registration and supervision of Canada's charities. In exchange for the ability to issue tax deductible receipts, qualified organizations were required to register, report annually, and adhere to certain restrictions on their financial, operational, and political activities.

The result of this process of nation building, combined with the construction of a regulatory framework around the tax system, has been to assign responsibility for the voluntary sector–state relationship to the national state. This is ironic given that, as appropriate to all civil matters, jurisdiction over voluntary organizations actually rests with provincial governments. Although provincial governments have extensive contacts with voluntary organizations in the context of service delivery in a wide variety of areas, the federal government has claimed the dominant role in the relationship with the voluntary sector through use of its spending power and control over the national tax system. The stance of most provincial governments to the voluntary sector has been non-interventionist – indeed, some might say, benignly neglectful.[9] Even Québec, which operates under the civil code of law and maintains its own tax system (and thus requires separate registration for charities), has been largely laissez-faire in regulating the sector, although it is naturally the focal point for the relationship in most other respects.[10]

Deconstructing the Relationship

The supportive elements of the long-standing relationship between the federal government and the voluntary sector were largely dismantled in the late 1980s and early 1990s as a result of the rise of neo-liberalism and populism. The inherent balance, by which the state recognized both a benefit from and a responsibility to the sector, was reduced to a government-dominated contracting and regulatory regime. Calls for even more regulation marked this transition. A philosophy of neo-liberalism that emphasized a smaller state and competitive markets characterized both the Mulroney Conservatives, in power from 1984 to 1993, and the first mandate of the Chrétien Liberals. When neo-liberalism met the very real financial pressures for deficit reduction, the results were significant cutbacks in government spending, particularly to social programs, and a choice by the federal government to get out of many areas of activity not considered 'core business,' by downloading or offloading to the private and voluntary sectors. Financial assistance to voluntary organizations was cut dramatically, sometimes as much as 50 to 100 per cent in a single year, often without warning. The groups that were hardest hit were advocacy and umbrella organizations – those not directly engaged in service delivery. Where financial support remained, project or contract funding usually replaced operational support, thus forcing voluntary organizations to seek out projects to support their daily operations, sometimes diverting them from their core missions, and generally speeding up the tempo of the "dance of contract management."[11] As the federal government cut intergovernmental transfers and downloaded costs onto provincial governments, they, in turn, downloaded to municipalities and voluntary organizations. Although Ottawa was usually blamed, many provincial governments had strong neo-liberal ideas of their own and were delighted to shrink the size of the provincial state. For example, in many service areas, such as homecare, which had been provided almost exclusively by the voluntary sector, private sector competition was deliberately introduced by some provincial governments; consequently, private sector firms saw the opportunities in these new 'markets' and began to go head-to-head with voluntary sector providers, often driving the latter out.[12]

Restructuring of the voluntary sector–state relationship was not just about money, however. The rise of populist ideas reinforced a backlash against voluntary organizations engaged in public policy debates because populism saw no need for intermediaries in the relationship between citizen and elected official. The notion of the 1940s that organizations were grounds for citizenship training was antithetical to a populist politician of the 1990s. In particular, one backbench member of Parliament, John Bryden, became a vocal critic of the lack of accountability and efficiency of voluntary organizations and, on the basis of his own analysis of annual tax returns of selected voluntary organizations, released a series of reports that called for much stronger regulation. The motive underlying these criticisms, by his own admission, was a concern that parliamentarians were in competition with civil society groups to be heard. Although Bryden did not succeed in creating a cadre of supporters among the Liberal party, his work captured the attention of the media whose members had long ignored the sector, but who now recognized the potential for scandal. The response from government was to add more auditors to Revenue Canada staff and to order the review of executive salaries in the sector by a parliamentary committee (which found no evidence to support Bryden's claim of exorbitant staff salaries and quickly lost interest in pursuing the issue). At the same time, Revenue Canada apparently became more conservative in its decisions to register new charities and more vigilant in policing the advocacy activities of registered organizations, particularly smaller groups.

Two other developments in the early 1990s caused significant deterioration in the public dialogue aspect of the voluntary sector–state relationship. The first was that consultation processes were deliberately redesigned to focus on representation by individuals participating as individual citizens, rather than by organized groups of citizens. Sectoral consultations were replaced by multistakeholder sessions, which may have enhanced cross-sectoral learning but diluted the voice of the voluntary sector. Sector advocates within the state were also removed by a major organizational restructuring beginning in 1993 that jettisoned many of the representatives of social interests from the Cabinet and abolished government advisory councils, such as the Canadian Advisory Council on the Status of Women.[13] By the mid-1990s, not only was it harder for the voluntary sector to be represented *within* the state, but it was more difficult to make representation *to* the state. The cumulative effect of these changes was that the credibility of the voluntary sector was purposely undermined, as it became painted with the derogatory brush of 'special interest groups.' In spite of this, opinion polls show that public trust in the voluntary sector has remained high.[14]

The Need for Change

This downloading and state restructuring, laid on a tax-based regulatory system largely unreformed since its establishment in the late 1960s, have generated a number of serious problems in each of the five dimensions of the sector - state relationship. Here, we examine the current strengths and basic weaknesses in each aspect of the relationship with a view to demonstrating the need for particular kinds of reform.

Public Policy Dialogue

Policy advocacy by voluntary organizations has become unduly restricted, although many parliamentarians and public servants probably still feel it is not restricted enough. Government regulates advocacy activity in two ways: by controlling which kinds of organizations are permitted to register as 'charities' and thereby be able to issue tax receipts for donations and by regulating the advocacy activities of registered organizations. Canada, which uses a common law definition of charities (emanating from the Elizabethan *Statute of Charitable Uses*, 1601), has one of the most restrictive systems of registration among developed countries, notably more restrictive than the US or the UK.[15] In the US, as in many other countries, the definition of 'charity' is expanded beyond the traditional common law interpretation by the specification in the tax code of a number of additional categories of organizations that qualify for registration. The UK has expanded and kept the common law definition of charity appropriately flexible by institutional means: acting in its quasi-judicial capacity, the Charity Commission of England and Wales annually hears hundreds of cases about the kinds of purposes that ought to be considered charitable, so the existing definition is continually open to renewal. In contrast, Canadian groups that are denied registration by the tax agency must take their case to the Federal Court of Appeal – a very expensive court of first instance. Hence, only about twenty cases have ever proceeded through the courts and only one has reached the Supreme Court.[16] As a result, groups engaged in educating about environmental protection, promoting multiculturalism or harmonious race relations, and supporting patriotism (including better relations between Anglophones and Francophones) are excluded from registration in Canada, but not in the US or UK. Although the evidence is sketchy, this limited interpretation of the common law is probably most detrimental to multicultural communities that approach philanthropy and community help in different ways than other communities.

Once registered, political activity is limited to an arbitrary level, defined in a manner that the tax system can regulate. The current rule is that resources spent on political activity cannot exceed 10 per cent of the total of an organization's resources in any given year. The definition of political is vague, but refers to a broad band of activity between partisan (which is banned completely) and consultation invited by governments (which is unfettered). In the atmosphere of the 1990s, the application of the '10 per cent' rule reinforced perceptions that the federal government wished to curtail advocacy by critics of state restructuring. In addition, apparently stricter enforcement of the rule during this period by Revenue Canada, now the Canada Customs and Revenue Agency (CCRA), contributed to a sense of unfairness in the regulatory system: that small, newer groups are treated differently than large, traditional charities. For instance, while the large and respected Canadian Cancer Society might get away with an anti-smoking campaign, small and more vocal groups, such as the Non-Smokers Rights Association, might be (and, indeed, have been) audited for similar political activities.[17] The problem was compounded by timing, since the restrictions on advocacy came at the very time when voluntary organizations felt a growing responsibility to speak out against the impact of social program cuts and other effects of state restructuring.

ACCOUNTABILITY

Accountability in the voluntary sector necessarily involves both self- and government regulation, given the public trust held by the sector. The Canadian system has deficiencies in both. On the one hand, self-regulation at a broad sector or sub-sector level has been underdeveloped. This is a result of the historical absence of strong cross-sectoral national or provincial organizations and of sector-based watchdog agencies (such as the National Charities Information Bureau in the United States). This is starting to change, however, with the leadership role assumed by the Canadian Centre for Philanthropy which is mobilizing sector-wide voluntary compliance with its Code of Ethical Fundraising and Financial Management, and by other intermediary organizations with requirements for member accreditation.

On the other hand, the governmental regulatory system is simultaneously cumbersome and disappointing.[18] The disappointment stems from the inherent contradiction in tying the regulatory regime so closely to the *Income Tax Act*, 1985. As a recent review of Canadian charity law notes, "The dominant legislative motive, naturally, has been either to protect the public treasury against abuse and fraud, or to 'subsidize' the sector through 'tax expenditures.' The integrity and efficiency of the sector, although important to these objectives, remain only instrumental goals."[19] The CCRA, as first and foremost a tax collection agency, can neither regulate the sector effectively nor equip it with the tools to govern and regulate itself successfully.

The framework is cumbersome in several ways. The first is a product of its uniformity, which means that all registered organizations, from the small group run entirely by volunteers to the largest university or teaching hospital in the country, must annually report exactly the same information. Not surprisingly, most of the problems related to failure to report or inaccuracies in reporting encountered by the Charities Directorate of the CCRA emanate from very small organizations in which the volunteer treasurer did not fully understand or have the time to fill out the thirteen-page form. The only sanction for noncompliance or for failure to report that is available to the CCRA is de-registration. To paraphrase Marilyn Taylor, this uses a sledgehammer to crack a walnut.[20] Thus, it comes as no surprise that very few organizations are ever fully sanctioned.

A second problem is that the regulatory guidelines are vague, or simply unhelpful, in several areas. This applies particularly to the regulations governing business activities that do not provide adequate guidance to voluntary organizations in shaping their own conduct at a time when business activity is increasingly undertaken in a desperate search for new sources of revenue. Finally, the regulatory regime has been increasingly politicized – or, at least, perceived to be politicized. Due to the limited resources assigned to the CCRA Charities Directorate, audits in recent years have been done rarely at random, and only on a complaints basis. This has created a growing unease that those organizations that are overly critical of government policy or disliked by certain politicians are more likely to be the target of investigation.

TRANSPARENCY
Transparency has also suffered as a result of the nature of the regulator. As a tax department, the CCRA operates under rules of confidentiality that extend to its Charities Directorate. Consequently, neither the applications for registration, nor the reasons for approval

or rejection of such applications, nor (until recently) other information about an organization's annual return are made public. Thus, the public has no easily accessible, reliable, independent source of information about the sector as a whole or about a specific organization that may be soliciting donations. The list of registered charities, however, is now available on the CCRA website – a major step forward in providing a basic measure of transparency.

SUPPORT

As outlined above, support entails not only assistance with 'hard' infrastructure, such as funding, human resources, and technology, but also shared understanding and knowledge. By the 1990s, the sector had reached a crisis of capacity. Support in the form of financial assistance had been severely cut back and, since the sector was poorly understood, there was never a significant transfer of human resources or other expertise between governments and voluntary organizations. And by this time, understanding and shared expectations were at an all-time low because many Canadian governments presumed that voluntary organizations could and would simply pick up the load resulting from cuts in government programming.

To a large extent, the lacuna of support and understanding stems from institutional design. In contrast to both the UK and the US, the Canadian relationship lacks institutional support for capacity building and for better self-governance within the sector. There is no federal or provincial equivalent to the Charity Commission of England and Wales which, as an arms-length government body, backed by legislation, both regulates and supports the sector. Nor does the tax department play the intrusive but instructive role of the US Internal Revenue Service which uses its expertise to educate as well as supervise the sector. Although the CCRA often attempts to be supportive as well as act as a watchdog, many organizations are reluctant to ask for assistance or information for fear of being bitten by an auditor. Moreover, the Charities Directorate is so limited in resources that there are few opportunities to be proactively helpful in providing good governance tools. Moreover, without another voice at the Cabinet table, the needs of the sector were being largely overlooked by the federal government.

One aspect of support that is of particular importance to voluntary organizations is funding. Most voluntary organizations have been detrimentally affected by the public sector restructuring of the past decade. The result has been that voluntary organizations face a triple whammy. First, having seen their government funding cut substantially and their core funding withdrawn in favour of short-term project funding, they are left with fewer resources and less ability to undertake long-term planning due to the uncertainty of funding. Second, as governments cut or withdrew from the provision of many services, client demand for services provided by voluntary organizations has increased. Third, because the entire sector is facing the same funding dilemma, competition for funds has increased, making it more difficult to diversify sources of funding. From the sector's perspective, the issues that must be addressed are not simply or even primarily about *levels* of funding, but the need for stable, multi-year funding commitments in order to facilitate planning; for recognition of the costs of administration and evaluation that are associated with projects and contracts; and for consistency of practices across departments.

SERVICE DELIVERY
By the mid-1990s, the Canadian sector was under extreme pressure to provide more services with fewer resources. Most organizations have responded as best they could by searching out new funding sources, recruiting more volunteers, and cutting operational costs in ever more innovative ways. For example, they moved to cheaper spaces, shared administrative, back-office functions with other organizations, and even merged. In some cases, however, programmes have had to be cut, certain clients left unserved or, in extreme cases, organizations allowed to go under.[21] At the same time, voluntary organizations have come under pressure by government and other funders – themselves faced with difficult choices and scarce funds – to undertake outcome-based performance evaluation of their work. Although many organizations see evaluation as inherently useful, they often lack the resources, time and expertise to conduct effectively such evaluations. The point is that issues of service delivery are intimately linked to capacity-building and to dialogue with governments.

The Process of Change

Despite mounting problems in the sector–state relationship, the Liberal government had neither a clear diagnosis nor specific remedies. It did see, however, that an increasingly strained relationship with the voluntary sector would make smaller government and new forms of horizontal governance difficult to sustain in the long run. Not only was government relying on the sector more than ever to deliver services that had been offloaded, but it needed the sector's ideas and expertise as a substitute for the internal policy capacity that had been cut so dramatically in the early 1990s. Like so many governments of both the right and left, the Chrétien Liberals felt the need to express a fuzzy, warm feeling about the inherent value of the voluntary sector and to make promises that the sector would be an equal partner. The first positive step was taken in the 1996 (and repeated in the 1997) budget: the tax provisions for charitable donations were improved as a result of very effective lobbying by the sector. The important benchmark for the sector, however, was the 1997 election. In its election platform, published as the policy book popularly known as *Red Book 2*, the federal Liberals committed to building a stronger voluntary sector and, in particular, to enhancing its capacity. The significance of this event lay in the commitment itself, not in the content. Indeed, the *Red Book* promises were vague and the Liberals probably had few, if any, concrete ideas about how to fulfil them. In a sense, this was fortunate for the voluntary sector as it created an opportunity for it to sketch in some specifics, which it did not hesitate to do.

The structure, resources, and leadership of the voluntary sector are as important in shaping the nature of the relationship with the state as are the institutions of government. In the Canadian context, the structure of the sector reflects the federal system: local organizations are generally organized into regional or provincial bodies, and those provincial units into national umbrella organizations. Although this generally facilitates the exercise of a voice simultaneously at the provincial and national levels, organization is by subsector (eg., child-care, homecare, parks and wilderness groups, and so on). What has been missing in Canada is a strong cross-sectoral organization at the national level, equivalent to the Independent Sector in the United States or to the National Council of Voluntary Organizations in England, to speak for the sector more or less as a whole. Recognizing this gap and the need for national leadership in the face of the extreme pressures created by government restructuring, a group of key sector leaders came together in 1995 to form a loose association, without legal organizational form, called the Voluntary Sector Roundtable. With funding from the J.W. McConnell Family Foundation, the Voluntary Sector Roundtable identified four priorities for its work over the next few years, one of which was enhancing accountability. Although polls indicated that the Canadian public still had a high level of trust in the voluntary sector, the Voluntary Sector Roundtable understood clearly that without enduring public trust, the financial foundation, volunteer support, and programme credibility of the sector would be in serious peril. Concerns about maintaining public confidence were heightened in the mid-1990s. Not only was the climate permeated with calls for more regulation, but the backlash from American scandals had been imported and a major, homegrown scandal over the conduct of the Canadian Red Cross in handling the country's blood system had emerged. If the sector had not coalesced in this critical period and undertaken a major initiative in changing the nature of the sector–state relationship, it is very probable that the federal government's electoral promises would have remained empty ones for lack of ideas or it would have caved in to the calls for much greater regulation.

As the Voluntary Sector Roundtable knew, it would have appeared extraordinarily self-serving for it to undertake the task of investigating accountability in the sector, particularly if it concluded, 'no problem.' The Voluntary Sector Roundtable therefore chose to appoint an arms-length panel of experts to research the issues, consult with Canadians, and report back with specific recommendations to improve accountability and governance in the sector. The panel, loosely modelled after the Deakin Commission on the Future of the Voluntary Sector in England, would give legitimacy through distance, while nonetheless allowing the sector to maintain ownership of the process.[22] Possibly for the first time, the Canadian voluntary sector, *as a sector*, was doing something very public for its own good. Shortly after, the federal government initiated its own process, first internally, then collaboratively, with the sector to determine how to meet its electoral commitments. In content, both drew extensively on the recommendations made by the Panel on Accountability and Governance of the Voluntary Sector Roundtable.

The Panel on Accountability and Governance in the Voluntary Sector

The Panel on Accountability and Governance in the Voluntary Sector, launched by the Voluntary Sector Roundtable in October 1997, was given a mandate to produce a discussion paper for consultation in eight months and a final report at the beginning of 1999.[23] The Voluntary Sector Roundtable carefully chose the six panel members to bring not only knowledge of the sector, but expertise in business and government as well, and, in the Canadian style, to include members from different parts of the country and, coincidentally, with quite different political views or affiliations.[24] The choice of Ed Broadbent to chair the Panel gave it instant visibility and its nickname. All members of the Panel on Accountability and Governance in the Voluntary Sector, including the chair, served as volunteers; none were token participants; all chose to be actively involved in crafting the discussion paper and in leading public consultations.

Unquestionably, many observers, including some members of the Voluntary Sector Roundtable, believed at first that the panel would stick primarily to the narrower aspects of accountability – board governance, ethical fundraising, and management – that are internal to the sector. But the Panel on Accountability and Governance in the Voluntary Sector chose to interpret its mandate broadly, to encompass relations with government and the corporate sector and saw its work as an opportunity to reshape the neo-liberal/populist discourse that had portrayed the sector as little more than a collection of special interest groups. In addition, the panel stapled the idea of capacity building to that of enhancing governance and accountability: the idea that governments have some responsibility toward the sector if it is to fulfil its potential as the "third pillar of society," to use the language of *Red Book 2*. Thus the mandate, as interpreted by the panel, was to reshape relationships in fundamental ways, not simply to tinker with intra-organizational mechanisms of accountability. Sometimes in the public policy process, 'ripeness' is all. Luckily for the Panel, its time was ripe. Not only did the sector galvanize around the work of the Panel on Accountability and Governance in the Voluntary Sector, but the federal government had to figure out how to meet its *Red Book* policy commitments and was thus open to new ideas.

The work of the Panel on Accountability and Governance in the Voluntary Sector was organized as three tasks: research, consultation, and reporting. The first stage of its work involved research into existing practices and models of accountability. These included not only best practices within the sector, but also an examination of the regulatory and relationship models of many other countries, particularly England, where the Charity Commission represented a more customer-service model of regulation and where the Deakin Commission had laid out many of the issues, and the United States, where sector self-regulation and state supervision are much more extensive. The recommendations of the panel reflect the cross-Atlantic influence and the explicit rejection of the American model as inappropriate to the Canadian context.

The result of this research was an interim discussion paper, released in May 1998, that formed the basis for an engagement process involving roundtable meetings in fifteen centres across the country, an online questionnaire, and the opportunity to submit briefs, of which more than 100 were received. The intention was not only to gather information from voluntary organizations across the country, but to leave a 'footprint' of heightened local interest and mobilization around issues of accountability.[25] All of this information was synthesized into a final report, entitled *Building on Strength: Improving Governance and Accountability in Canada's Voluntary Sector*, released in early February 1999.

The Joint Table Process

In mid-1998, the federal government began its own internal process for determining how it would fulfill its electoral commitments. The multidepartmental committee of senior officials that was formed made rather slow progress, as do so many of these committees. Its work was advanced by the creation of a secretariat, the Voluntary Sector Task Force, which has full-time staff and is housed in the Privy Council Office, giving it considerable stature. Since the task force was formulating its own recommendations to Cabinet at the very time that the Broadbent Panel report was released, it was considerably influenced by the panel's recommendations. To its credit, the federal government recognized that the issues were complex, that the way ahead was a major social experiment inasmuch as no model could simply be imported from another country, and that process mattered. Instead of moving forward unilaterally, the federal government established a joint process with equal participation by the voluntary sector.

This process took the form of three 'Joint Tables,' created in March 1999 (still served by the Voluntary Sector Task Force) that focused on: building a new relationship, strengthening capacity, and improving the regulatory framework. This was a unique experiment. The tables functioned in a truly collaborative manner in that each was co-chaired by a representative from the sector and by a senior public servant, and the membership (of about twelve per table) was chosen in equal proportion by each partner. In this, the Voluntary Sector

Roundtable chose wisely and convinced good people representing national, regional, and local perspectives and experience to participate. The Joint Table process marks the beginning of a new relationship whose success largely depends on two critical factors. The first is the trust that developed through joint ownership of the process and open, candid discussions. The second is that the politicians were involved early on when about twenty ministers met with members of the Joint Tables soon after the tables were formed and again later to discuss preliminary recommendations. For all three tables, the process was a learning experience both for the voluntary sector members and public servants – not simply in terms of the issues, but also in terms of the culture of the other sector.[26]

The Joint Tables worked within a very short time frame, a mere six months from beginning to end. The short time period was due both to a desire to move recommendations forward to Cabinet for the fall of 1999 so that any budget implications could be included for the next fiscal year, and to a realization that the tables could work on the issues for years and still leave many things unresolved, given the complexity of the task. In mid-September 1999, a single report was released that synthesized the recommendations of the three tables. The fact that this report was publicly released is itself a significant change in government procedure: normally such a report would have been viewed as advice to Cabinet and kept secret, at least until ministers had had a chance to consider it.

A Shared Blueprint for Action

The diagnosis of the difficulties in the existing voluntary sector–state relationship and the recommendations for its renewal made by Broadbent's external panel of experts and by the sector and government representatives at the Joint Tables are nearly identical. This suggests that the nature of the problems are obvious and that there is considerable consensus on the solutions.

As a starting point, both reviews stressed the importance of capacity building in the voluntary sector if it is to realize its potential and both identify similar responsibilities for the federal government in helping to build this capacity. These measures include enhancing skills development, possibly through secondments to voluntary organizations; assisting with information management and technology (IM-IT); and clarifying government funding policies. Concerning the last issue, the triumph for the sector members of the Joint Capacity Table was that they convinced the government officials that the table had to address financial issues, despite the preliminary reluctance of the officials to do so. It took some reiteration to make it clear that the sector was not saying simply, "give us more money," but were concerned with the way money flows (e.g., project/contract vs. operational; short term vs. long term), considering it critical. In addition, as part of its options for creating an 'enabling environment,' the Joint Tables recommended creating a task force to study funding, a new initiative on volunteerism, and increasing knowledge about the sector both by stimulating research and creating a satellite account related to the economic value of the sector as a subset of the Statistics Canada system of national data gathering.

A second task related directly to building a new voluntary sector–state relationship. On this matter, both the Broadbent Panel and the Joint Tables argued that a relationship needs to evolve and suggested a number of institutional and procedural mechanisms to encourage it to evolve in a strategic manner. Perhaps the most visible and symbolic of these was the development of an 'accord,' modelled after the British compacts, between government and the sector. In addition, both supported the ideas of creating a ministry responsible for the sector or some other permanent political voice at the Cabinet table and establishing an ongoing administrative secretariat.

Third, the need for institutional change emerged as a shared priority. The Broadbent Panel was in favour of developing a new institution to oversee and support the sector from two perspectives. First, the Panel argued that one of the best ways to enhance accountability in the sector is through a process of self-accreditation closely coupled with public transparency. Organizations should report annually on a number of key aspects of their work and this information should be easily accessible by the public, thus providing the reporting organizations with an incentive to provide accurate information (of course, there remained the need for some direct government regulation as well). The second argument stemmed from a recognition that most of the organizations in the sector are very small, run entirely by volunteers. As a result, many of the problems of non-compliance encountered by the CCRA are a result of lack of knowledge or capacity, not intent. The CCRA, as the main institution of the state for interaction with the broad diversity of the sector, is neither transparent nor capable of supporting organizations to build better practices related to governance and accountability. The panel proposed a new Voluntary Sector Commission, a variant of the Charity Commission of England and Wales, to supplement the more narrowly regulatory functions of the CCRA. The Joint Regulatory Table concurred with the importance of institutional change and proposed three alternative models for an oversight agency – an enhanced Charities Directorate of the CCRA; an advisory body; and a quasi-judicial commission – that should be developed further through broader consultation.[27]

Fourth, the need to expand access to the tax system by a broader range of public benefit organizations was emphasized as an essential aspect of capacity building and of creating an enabling environment. Since governments increasingly expect communities to assume greater responsibility for their own well-being, it is essential to equip these communities with the appropriate policy tools to attract supporters and donors. A tax incentive is one way of doing so. Both reviews proposed a mechanism for gaining greater access to the tax system through the development of a list of public benefit organizations that are 'deemed' to be charities for purposes of the tax system, much the same way as national arts service organizations and amateur athletic associations are currently granted the same status as common law charities under the *Income Tax Act*, 1985.[28] Opposition to this idea came from both the Department of Finance which feared that it would be costly in lost taxes and from Cabinet which saw it as stirring up controversy without much immediate political gain.[29]

The government's ability to determine which organizations get access to the tax system is one way in which it limits the advocacy and political activity of voluntary organizations. The second way it does so is by placing direct limits on such activities by registered organizations. Both reports affirmed the legitimacy of public policy advocacy by voluntary organizations, including those registered as charities, although the Joint Tables went further than the Broadbent Panel in their recommendations related to creating space for such activity. Indeed, the Regulatory Table considered this to be one of the most pressing issues of all.[30] The underlying problem is that governments have always seen advocacy as illegitimate because its connection to the charitable mission is not appreciated; in reality, advocacy occurs in the context of educating and informing on matters related to the central mission and can thus be considered a public benefit. In addition, there is a double standard in how the federal government treats advocacy by the charitable and the private sector. While advocacy by registered charities is severely limited by the '10 percent' rule, businesses are allowed to write off the cost of lobbying against their income, thereby potentially reducing the amount paid in taxes. Although neither the panel nor the members of the Joint Tables suggested permitting unlimited or partisan advocacy activity by registered organizations, both argued in favour of more permissive regulations.

Finally, significant regulatory reform was understood to be essential by both reviews in providing an appropriate, facilitating environment that would enable the voluntary sector to do what it does best and provide a foundation for a more constructive relationship. This includes limiting the enormous burden of personal liability borne by directors of voluntary organizations that is, according to at least anecdotal reports, starting to discourage professionals and other volunteers from sitting on boards of directors.[31] Although this falls partly within provincial jurisdiction, the federal government could play an important role as convenor or leader of a review of directors' liability. Other proposed regulatory reforms focused on: simplifying reporting requirements, especially for small organizations; introducing intermediate sanctions short of deregistration for non-compliance with CCRA regulations; and providing better guidelines for related business activities.

The Voluntary Sector Initiative

The federal government's initial response to the work of the Joint Tables was made in early June 2000. It announced the Voluntary Sector Initiative to institutionalize an ongoing joint process and provide $94.6 million in funding for a package of reforms. In terms of process, the Voluntary Sector Initiative is enormously complex, with the bulk of the work of elaboration of details and implementation directed by six Joint Tables modelled directly after the 1999 experiment, assisted by a Joint Co-ordinating Committee that manages cross-cutting matters related to consultation and communications strategies.[32] A reference group of eight senior ministers has been formalized to provide political leadership, with a core group of assistant deputy ministers working as an executive committee constituted to provide strategic direction within the public service (a counterpart steering committee of Voluntary Sector Roundtable members provides direction on the voluntary sector side). Within government, the Voluntary Sector Task

Force in the Privy Council Office continues to provide staff support, and a similar secretariat has been funded by the Voluntary Sector Initiative to provide support for voluntary sector participation. The Tables were thus designed to lead the biggest engagement process that has ever been undertaken with a broad diversity of the sector, from the national to grassroots level.

In terms of content, the government has taken an important step toward establishing a more constructive and balanced relationship with the sector, generally following the advice of the Joint Tables. These reforms include:

- development of an accord between the federal government and the voluntary sector;
- support of almost $10 million for celebration of the International Year of Volunteers; and development of an ongoing initiative to promote volunteerism;
- various capacity building measures, including skills development, research, and increased knowledge of the sector; a Satellite Account within the System of National Accounts on the economic value of voluntary activity; routinization on a three-year cycle of the National Survey of Giving, Volunteering, and Participation; and policy internships and academic fellowships;
- assistance with IM-IT to promote both connectivity to the Internet and better online tools; and
- some regulatory reform and increased transparency including greater public access to the information on charities filed annually with the CCRA; a simplified tax form for registered charities with annual incomes under $100,000; and the introduction of clearer guidelines on the conduct of related business activities.

In addition, further study is being undertaken regarding the design of a new oversight institution, funding policies, directors' liability, intermediate sanctions, and a less expensive appeals process for those organizations refused registration by the CCRA.

This initiative is clearly a major step by the federal government toward building a more positive relationship with Canada's voluntary sector. Its significance should in no way be diminished. To date, however, the initiative does not address the top priorities of either the

Broadbent Panel or the Joint Tables. There is no commitment to institutional change; no mention of expanding access to the tax system; no significant regulatory reform regarding public policy advocacy; nor joint discussion of funding regimes. There is much to be said for careful analysis before launching a major policy or institutional change. But in this case, a necessary element of social experimentation will be involved: no amount of study will work out beforehand all the kinks in the implementation of a new regulatory commission or of new approaches to advocacy – inevitably, a certain degree of ongoing tinkering will be required.

The innovative process of genuine collaboration that characterizes the Joint Tables has already increased trust between federal public servants and sector leaders. But it also raises expectations that real change is possible and that the government is interested in pursuing such change. The federal government has too much at stake to allow reform on the top priorities to be stalled indefinitely or, worse, abandoned on the so far unconvincing premise that it would be too expensive.

Conclusion:
Canadian Distinctiveness, Distinctive Contradictions

The reasons why and the way in which the relationship between the federal government and the voluntary sector is being reshaped shares much with other developed countries. Many of the same issues are on the agendas of other countries, and some of the same instruments, such as accords, are being tried out in a variety of jurisdictions. In many respects, however, the reform process of the Voluntary Sector Initiative is distinctively Canadian and, as a result, has generated a number of contradictions that will need to be resolved before a more constructive relationship can truly come into being. Not surprisingly, these distinctive patterns and their attendant contradictions reflect age-old tensions in the Canadian political system – the role of the state, the complexities of federalism, and the nature of democracy.

One intriguing characteristic of the contemporary interest in building a stronger, more engaged civil society is that the reform process looks largely to the state to achieve this. In Canada, in contrast to the US for example, social movements and the voluntary sector have long looked to the state not only to provide legitimacy as part of a citizenship regime, but also to offer financial and other types of support.[33] This state-centred approach is partly a matter of philosophy – that the state remains a relevant and central institution despite less public trust and confidence – but it is also practical. In the absence of a strong philanthropic community or corporate support for the voluntary sector, the resources for capacity building are not going to emerge spontaneously from other sources. The underlying contradiction is that, although the federal government has accepted a responsibility for capacity building, it is caught between a neo-liberal and an enabling model of the state. This is evidenced by its unwillingness to review funding regimes in a joint manner as part of the Voluntary Sector Initiative. To some degree, this unwillingness reflects a reluctance to get locked into operational funding for certain categories of groups – that is, to begin another version of the abandoned Secretary of State programmes, thus tying up resources and privileging the recognition of some groups over others. The dilemma, however, is that the current funding regime, with its inherent uncertainty caused by short-term project funding, limits the ability of voluntary organizations to undertake strategic planning – one of the major barriers to strengthening capacity in the sector. To be clear, voluntary sector leaders are not simply asking for more money but for more effective, stable funding regimes. If governments are truly interested in enhancing the capacity of the sector to fulfil its potential, funding regimes will eventually need to be addressed.

A second, characteristically Canadian feature is that the weight of state–voluntary sector relationship-building has been borne primarily by the *national* state, even though the regulation of the voluntary sector is constitutionally provincial jurisdiction. A particularly Canadian twist to this relationship-building is its link to promoting national unity, from the federal perspective. By building stronger, more direct relationships with citizens, the federal government hopes to increase its visibility and credibility, both of which have been diminished as direct transfers to individuals have given way to indirect transfers through provinces and tax credits. One intended benefit of a stronger relationship with more active citizens and voluntary organizations is that it may provide a welcome foil to provincial interests in times of difficult federal-provincial relations. The federal initiative derives its legitimacy not only from the fact that the federal government does have a direct relationship with voluntary organizations and citizens, but from the fact that it became the *de facto* regulator through a charitable registration system tied to the national tax system. The contradiction is that, for fear of stepping on provincial jurisdiction, the federal government will be neither eager to wear its acquired role of regulator in an obvious manner, nor to get on with the vital need to reform regulatory institutions, either on its own or in collaboration with the provinces.

The final, distinctively Canadian aspect is that the reconstruction of a new and stronger relationship between the federal government and the voluntary sector is caught between two different models of democracy. These can be characterized as traditional representative democracy that focuses on elected officials as the primary vehicle for representing and responding to the views of constituents, and participatory democracy that puts a premium on engagement and participation of citizens between elections, whether representing themselves directly or participating through their civic organizations.[34] Caught between these two approaches to democracy, the Voluntary Sector Initiative faces a contradiction. Though an explicit goal is to encourage active citizenship, the federal government has so far been unwilling to acknowledge the legitimacy of or permit greater public policy advocacy by citizen groups if they receive a public benefit through the tax system as registered charities. It has also curtailed any discussion of expansion of access to official registration for community organizations that may be more likely to engage in advocacy. This concern over advocacy by registered charities is a Canadian quirk and is simply not an issue in other countries that are engaged in similar processes of renewing sector–state relationships.[35] It is both a fiction and a danger to cleave to traditional models of representative democracy in a era in which more collaborative governance and a stronger, civil society-based model of the voluntary sector are needed and encouraged.

It would not be an exaggeration to say that the Voluntary Sector Initiative may well mark the beginning of a new era between the federal government and the voluntary sector. The federal government's reluctance to move forward on the top priorities identified by both the Broadbent Panel and the Joint Tables, however, suggests that it still has difficulty working out some peculiarly Canadian contradictions. It appears to be stuck on the old image of the sector as primarily a service provider, rather than as a community builder. Perhaps, in the ongoing Joint Tables, movement toward addressing the key aspects of a renewed relationship will be forthcoming. Until this happens, a genuine partnership, able to accommodate both more collaborative forms of governance and more active civil society will not be complete.

Notes

1. A few examples illustrate the extent of innovation taking place. In 1998, the Blair government negotiated a "compact" (what Canada is calling an accord) with the voluntary sectors in each of England, Scotland, Wales and Northern Ireland – an experiment that is now being taken up by New Zealand, among others. See N. Deakin, *"Putting Narrow-Mindedness out of Countenance": The UK Voluntary Sector in the New Millennium* (London: Centre for Civil Society Studies, London School of Economics, January 2000). Following a three-year consultation process, Ireland has recently developed a White Paper on relationships between the community/voluntary sector and the state that is intended to form the basis for long-term strategic planning aimed at supporting the sector's contribution in building a more inclusive society. Government of the Republic of Ireland, National Anti-Poverty Strategy, *A White Paper on a Framework for Supporting Voluntary Activity and for Developing the Relationship between the State and the Community and Voluntary Sector* (Dublin: The Stationery Office, 2000). In South Africa, new legislation and the creation of a Directorate for Nonprofit Organizations have attempted to create an environment in which civil society organizations can flourish. See B. Streek, "State Bid to Engage NGO Sector," *Daily Mail and Guardian* (15 February 2001).
2. For a discussion of the nature of the sector in Canada, see M. Hall and K.G. Banting, "The Nonprofit Sector in Canada: An Introduction," in *The Nonprofit Sector in Canada: Roles and Relationships*, ed. K.G. Banting (Montréal and Kingston: McGill-Queen's University Press, 2000).
3. Panel on Accountability and Governance in the Voluntary Sector, *Building on Strength: Improving Governance and Accountability in Canada's Voluntary Sector*, (Ottawa: Voluntary Sector Roundtable) 1999: 11.
4. Government of Canada/Voluntary Sector Joint Tables [hereafter Joint Tables], *Working Together: Report of the Joint Tables* (Ottawa: Voluntary Sector Task Force, Privy Council Office, 1999): 29, available at <http://www.vsr-trsb.net/publications/pco.e.pdf>; see also G.R. Ramsey and R. Reynolds, *The Social Reconnaissance Project: Discovering Philanthropic Leadership Opportunities* (Vancouver: Vancouver Foundation, 1997): 14.

5. Joint Tables, *Working Together*, 19.
6. L.A. Pal, *Interests of State: The Politics of Language, Multiculturalism and Feminism in Canada* (Montréal and Kingston: McGill-Queen's University Press, 1993): 75–6; J. Jenson and S.D. Phillips, "Regime Shift: New Citizenship Practices in Canada," *International Journal of Canadian Studies* 14 (Fall 1996): 111–36.
7. Pal, *Interests of State*, 85–6.
8. Ontario Law Reform Commission, *Report on the Law of Charities* (Toronto: Ontario Law Reform Commission, 1997): 262–71.
9. Exceptions are Alberta which has tried, half-heartedly, to regulate fundraising; Ontario whose Office of the Public Guardian and Trustee has some, rarely used, supervisory role over the conduct of charities; and British Columbia which has created a ministry responsible for the voluntary sector. Beginning in 2000, several provinces have taken a more active interest in the health of and provincial relationship with the voluntary sector. The government of Newfoundland and Labrador has developed a Strategic Social Plan that contains accord-like provisions (available at <http://www.gov.nf.ca/ssp>); Québec has initiated a policy on community action (a description of the policy is available at <http://www.mss.gouv.qc.ca/saca>); and British Columbia announced its intention to develop a framework agreement (or accord) with the sector. In 2000, the Québec government initiated a process to develop a partnership with community organizations.
10. Although Québec has not used its powers to extensively regulate the sector, it has perhaps more constructive relationships in service delivery than most other provinces, largely because Québec has not chosen to cut social programmes to the same extent as other provinces. It has also understood the role of the sector in nation building, although not used the sector as fully as it might in this regard. In recent years, the Québec government has been active in creating an *'économie sociale,'* a hybrid of the voluntary and for-profit sectors, to provide many social services and boost employment. For a comparison of the stance of the Québec and Ontario governments toward the sector in the area of homecare, see J. Jenson and S.D. Phillips. "Distinctive Trajectories: Homecare and the Voluntary Sector in Québec and Ontario," in *The Nonprofit Sector in Canada: Roles and Relationships,* ed. K.G. Banting (Montréal and Kingston: McGill-Queen's University Press, 2000).
11. S.R. Smith and M. Lipsky, *Nonprofits for Hire: The Welfare State in the Age of Contracting* (Cambridge: Harvard University Press, 1993).
12. Jenson and Phillips, "Distinctive Trajectories."

13. Jenson and Phillips, "Regime Shift," 121–3.
14. M. Berm, "In the Dark: Role and Value of Charitable Sector Little Known Among Public," *Inter Sector: A Newsletter for Imagine Community Partners* 4 (3) (March/April, 1998): 2.
15. A. Drache with F.K. Boyle, *Charities, Public Benefit and the Canadian Income Tax System: A Proposal for Reform* (Toronto: Kahanoff NonProfit Research Initiative, 1998); D.J. Bourgeois, *The Law of Charitable and Nonprofit Organizations,* 2nd ed. (Toronto: Butterworths, 1995); and R. Hirshhorn and D. Stevens, *Organizational and Supervisory Law in the Nonprofit Sector* (Ottawa: Canadian Policy Research Networks, 1997).
16. In early 1999, the Supreme Court rendered its decision in the case of the Vancouver Society of Immigrant and Visible Minority Women, a group that was denied registration by Revenue Canada on the basis that its educational goals do not fit the traditional heading of education and that the community it intended to benefit was not sufficiently broad to fit under the community benefit heading. The decision was a loss for the group. In a split decision, the Court ruled in favour of Revenue Canada, noting that the common law definition could not be stretched that far. The victory of the case for the sector is that the Court explicitly invited Parliament to rework the definition of charity, arguing that this should be done by the legislature not the courts. For a brief discussion, see A. Drache, "Canadian Developments," *International Journal of Nonprofit Law* 1 (3) 1999. Available at <http://www.icnl.org/journal>.
17. Such were the perceptions of many in the sector. The differential enforcement of regulations and more conservative approach to registration by the CCRA is difficult to assess empirically, however, due to the confidentiality regulations under which the department operates.
18. Ontario Law Reform Commission, *Report*, 250.
19. Ontario Law Reform Commission, *Report*, 262.
20. M. Taylor, "Between Public and Private: Accountability in Voluntary Organizations," *Policy and Politics* 21 (1) (1996): 69.
21. Municipality of Metropolitan Toronto, City of Toronto and Social Planning Council of Metropolitan Toronto, *Profile of a Changing World: 1996 Community Agency Survey* (Toronto: Municipality of Toronto, 1997).
22. Commission on the Future of the Voluntary Sector, *Meeting the Challenge of Change: Voluntary Action into the 21st Century* (London: National Council of Voluntary Organizations, 1996).
23. I cannot claim that the following is a dispassionate or objective analysis because I served as the Research Director for the Panel.

24. The members were: the Honourable Ed Broadbent, Robert Brown, Dale Godsoe, Angela Kan, Arthur Kroeger, and the Honourable Monique Vézina.

25. A discussion guide could be downloaded for use by any organization that wanted to facilitate its own session, the results of which could be forwarded to the panel if desired, although the goal was as much to get community organizations thinking about sectoral issues as it was to obtain feedback. Anecdotal reports are that this engagement process was highly successful and that groups still use the discussion guide to animate strategic planning discussions. It is a telling sign of contemporary pressures in the sector that, in many locales, these sessions were the first time that staff and directors from different subsectors (e.g. social services, arts, faith communities, women's organizations) had ever been in the same room at the same time to discuss issues of sectoral importance. Most are so busy fighting daily fires that they have little time to think about policy issues of sectoral importance or take the time to attend meetings. In this case, not only did local leaders attend, but virtually all had read the discussion paper thoroughly and had thoughtful comments to make on it. It is also telling of Canadian political culture that the Broadbent Panel often had a hard time convincing participants that it was *not* a government-sponsored body.

26. Individually, the Joint Tables worked in different ways: some commissioned research, some invited speakers, and some relied on the expertise of those at the table.

27. Although no preference among these three models was officially endorsed in the report of the Joint Tables, it was made clear that the voluntary sectors of the Regulatory Table favour a quasi-judicial commission. See Joint Tables, *Working Together*, 56.

28. The argument that extending access to the tax system in this manner would open the door to radical fringe groups, such as neo-nazis, is unfounded in my view. As the Joint Table rightly noted, additional criteria for acceptance as a deemed charity might be adherence to the *Canadian Charter of Rights and Freedoms* and international conventions. For some thoughtful discussion on this point, see Government of Canada/ Voluntary Sector Joint Tables, *Working Together: Supplementary Paper A: Education, Advocacy and Political Activity* (Ottawa: Voluntary Sector Task Force, Privy Council Office, 1999)

29. It is unlikely, however, that the relationship between the number of organizations registered under the tax system and the amount of individual

giving is a linear one. For instance, if there were an additional 10 per cent of organizations to which you could make a tax receipted donation, would you necessarily increase your charitable giving by 10 per cent, or might you simply distribute your current level of giving differently?

30. Joint Tables, *Working Together*.
31. The June 1999 Supreme Court decision in the case of *Bazley vs. Curry* found the board of a voluntary organization vicariously liable for sexual abuse by an employee many years earlier. This has considerably expanded the scope of liability for directors and naturally made many boards very nervous.
32. The six substantive Joint Tables deal with the accord, regulatory, capacity, national volunteerism initiative, awareness, and information management-information technology. In addition to the Joint Tables, there are a number of specialized working groups dealing with issues such as directors' liability. Although the Voluntary Sector Initiative does not address advocacy or funding in a joint manner, there are sector-only working groups on both and a government-only study on federal funding practices.
33. This point is made perhaps most clearly in relation to the women's movement. See S. Burt, "Women's Issues and the Women's Movement since 1970," in A. Cairns and C. Williams, eds., *The Politics of Gender, Ethnicity and Language in Canada* (Toronto: University of Toronto Press, 1996) and S. Bashevkin, *Women on the Defensive: Living through Conservative Times* (Chicago: University of Chicago Press, 1998).
34. For a discussion of participatory democracy, see J.J. Mansbridge, *Beyond Adversary Democracy* (Chicago: University of Chicago Press, 1983) and B. Barber, *Strong Democracy: Participatory Politics for a New Age* (Berkeley and Los Angeles: University of California Press, 1984).
35. In interviews with government officials in England, Scotland, and Ireland, even those working in the tax departments, described advocacy to me as the life blood of democracy and an expected, respected role of charities. (Personal communication, 2000). See S.D. Phillips, "Voluntary Sector-Government Relationships in Transition: Learning from International Experience for the Canadian Context," in *The Nonprofit Sector in Interesting Times: Case Studies in a Changing Sector*, ed K. Brock and K.G. Banting (Montréal and Kingston: McGill-Queen's University Press, 2003).

Malentendus multiculturels : France, États-Unis, Canada

Denis Lacorne

L A CHOSE EST SUFFISAMMENT RARE POUR ÊTRE SOULIGNÉE : UN Français qui a une opinion favorable du multiculturalisme, et pas n'importe quel Français, le premier ministre Lionel Jospin, lors d'une visite officielle à Ottawa, en décembre 1998 – pensant peut-être flatter ses hôtes – vanta les mérites du multiculturalisme canadien. Ce faisant, il créait un malentendu pour les futurs interlocuteurs qu'il devait rencontrer quelques jours plus tard au siège du Gouvernement du Québec[1]. Lionel Jospin n'avait pas saisi qu'au Canada, il y a multiculturalisme et multiculturalisme, et que la conception fédérale n'était pas compatible avec la conception québécoise d'une singularité ethno-politico-culturelle qui ne devait, à aucun prix, être noyée dans un vaste ensemble pluriel. Jospin ne connaissait pas l'histoire du multiculturalisme canadien; il ne savait pas que, du point de vue québécois, la conception moderne du « multiculturalisme » tuait son ancêtre, le « biculturalisme anglo-québécois ».

La notion de multiculturalisme n'est pas, malgré les apparences, une catégorie universelle. Les variantes du multiculturalisme français, américain, canadien, ne peuvent être comprises que si elles sont remises en leur contexte. Penser le multiculturalisme en contexte, c'est d'abord penser aux « formes primitives » du multiculturalisme, c'est-à-dire à ce qui exprimait une pluralité de cultures ou une différence culturelle, avant même que le mot soit inventé et popularisé par les médias.

Concrètement, aux États-Unis, cela veut dire penser la tolérance religieuse et le pluralisme culturel; au Canada, cela signifie penser le biculturalisme et le fédéralisme; en France, la chose est nettement plus délicate, car il y a là une difficulté intrinsèque de notre histoire politique. On a du mal à raisonner en termes multiculturels, parce que le « multiculturalisme » relève de l'impensable politique.

Je m'explique : notre tradition centraliste, anti-pluraliste, est liée au triomphe de l'absolutisme monarchique, c'est-à-dire à la destruction des régions autonomes, du pouvoir des villes, des communes et des parlements provinciaux. La Révolution, dans sa phase jacobine, exagérait encore plus ces tendances en abolissant les privilèges et en effaçant de la carte de la France les vieilles provinces. La Révolution ôtait toute légitimité à la notion de pluralisme en idéologisant son contenu : désormais « le pluralisme n'était pensable que sous les catégories infamantes du privilège et de l'intérêt[2] ». La décentralisation, le partage de la souveraineté, le fédéralisme étaient donc des notions contraires à l'esprit jacobin, au point même de constituer un « crime » inédit, le « crime de fédéralisme ». Voilà ce que disait Robespierre, à propos de ses adversaires girondins :

> [...] Nos accusateurs voulaient nous donner un gouvernement étranger à nos mœurs, étranger à nos principes d'égalité ; nous avons soupçonné qu'on voulait faire de la République française un amas de Républiques fédératives qui seraient sans cesse la proie des guerres civiles[3].

Une impossibilité française : penser le multiculturalisme

Revenons à l'époque moderne, au voyage de notre premier ministre au Canada. Qu'on ne s'y trompe pas, l'objet d'admiration, pour Jospin, était le « multiculturalisme des autres » ; il n'était pas question pour lui de défendre un type universel d'identité multiculturelle dont la France serait le modèle. Et comment l'aurait-il pu ? Car la France était, jusqu'à une période récente, le pays réfractaire par excellence aux idées multiculturelles. La conception française de l'identité nationale reste éminemment rousseauiste, centraliste, unitaire, jacobine. Notre Constitution et nos juges constitutionnels nous interdisent de penser la pluralité des peuples constitutifs de la nation française. Nos sociologues, et je parle des meilleurs, ne pouvaient, jusqu'à une date récente, concevoir une France qui soit autre chose qu'une communauté abstraite de citoyens, tous égaux devant la loi, tous capables de transcender leurs « appartenances particulières », tous « arrachés » à leurs identités d'origine par un acte de pure volonté politique[4]. Dominique Schnapper, dans *La communauté des citoyens*, écrivait ainsi, en 1994 : « C'est *l'effort d'arrachement* aux identités et aux appartenances vécues comme naturelles par l'abstraction de la citoyenneté qui caractérise en propre le projet national. Il existe *une seule* idée de la nation[5]. »

La nation, dans cette perspective, serait donc politiquement et culturellement neutre. On est loin des conceptions tayloriennes de la nation, fondées sur le refus de la neutralité culturelle de l'État, sur *l'authentification* d'une pluralité de cultures, et surtout sur la *reconnaissance* que ces cultures doivent s'épanouir pleinement, car elles exprimeraient, chacune à leur façon, des valeurs ou des mérites égaux. L'idéal français de l'intégration républicaine, quelles qu'en soient les variantes, s'oppose à l'idéal taylorien d'une « politique de la différence » fondée sur la dénonciation de « toutes les discriminations » et le refus de « toute citoyenneté de seconde classe[6] ».

En France, derrière le discours savant des sociologues, se profile un autre discours plus simpliste et réductionniste : le « jacobinisme réflexe » de nos intellectuels et de nos hommes politiques qui restent persuadés que la France est vraiment une *République une et indivisible* et qui ne peuvent concevoir le multiculturalisme comme autre chose qu'un complot visant à l'éclatement de la société française, une survivance sournoise du « crime fédéraliste », jadis dénoncé par les Jacobins.

Les exemples abondent. Ils expriment parfois des considérations philosophiques et plus souvent des peurs, des craintes, des anxiétés liées à un autre phénomène qui n'a rien à voir avec notre passé jacobin, à savoir la découverte que la France est, comme les États-Unis ou le Canada, un pays d'immigrés. Il faut ici rappeler que la France a toujours été un pays d'immigrés, puisqu'environ un Français sur cinq a au moins un grand-parent qui n'est pas né en France. Mais peu de Français le savent : c'est dire la force des courants assimilationnistes dans notre imaginaire national.

Ainsi, l'essayiste et journaliste Christian Jelen, le fils d'un modeste artisan polonais immigré à Paris, qui devait son ascension sociale à son seul mérite et aux vertus du système d'enseignement public français, s'inquiétait en 1997 des dangers d'un multiculturalisme importé des États-Unis et mal adapté aux besoins de la France moderne. Il dénonçait, dans un pamphlet provocateur, la « régression multiculturelle », et la « lugubre perspective d'une société fragmentée en groupes ethniques » qui ne pourrait, à terme, que défaire « le lien national », pour aboutir, peut-être, à « la mort de la République[7] ».

La dénonciation du multiculturalisme n'est pas, en France, un phénomène qui se limiterait à la droite de l'échiquier politique. À droite, on craint le multiculturalisme, parce qu'on voit en lui un cheval de Troie : une philosophie perverse qui donnerait trop de pouvoir aux immigrés, à commencer par les Nord-Africains, qui seraient, si l'on en croit les partisans du Front National, « inassimilables ». La critique de l'extrême droite n'est pas surprenante : elle correspond à la persistance des vieux schémas de pensée racistes hérités de Gobineau, de Barrès, et de Maurras. La critique de la gauche est plus étonnante ; elle mérite une explication.

Les critiques de gauche proviennent de trois groupes différents : de l'intelligentsia ultra jacobine – représentée par des politiques comme Jean-Pierre Chevènement ou encore Régis Debray – des enseignants de l'école publique et enfin de certains groupes ou écoles sociologiques. Le premier courant est illustré dans un petit livre de Debray intitulé *La République enseignée à ma fille*. Dans cet opuscule, Debray exprime une forte inquiétude vis-à-vis de ce débat multiculturel qui nous vient d'Amérique, et il se demande si la transposition du débat en France ne risque pas, « exactement comme en Amérique », de détruire notre vie publique en y introduisant de dangereuses « passions identitaires[8] ».

Plus intéressante, parce que plus originale, est la démarche des partisans d'une école républicaine rénovée. Pour ceux-ci, la nouvelle mode de la pédagogie multiculturelle n'est qu'une régression démocratique qui s'inspire, pas toujours consciemment, des pires poncifs de la pensée contre-révolutionnaire d'un Burke, d'un Bonald ou d'un Maistre. Maistre, rappelons-le, était radicalement réfractaire à l'esprit des lumières, et l'humanisme universel n'était pour lui qu'une absurdité philosophique :

> Il n'y a point d'homme dans le monde. J'ai vu, dans ma vie, des Français, des Italiens, des Russes, etc. ; je sais même grâce à Montesquieu, qu'on peut être persan ; mais quant à l'homme, je déclare ne l'avoir rencontré de ma vie ; s'il existe, c'est bien à mon insu[9].

Or le rôle de l'éducateur est d'enseigner les « valeurs communes » de la République. L'école n'est pas seulement un lieu de savoir et d'acquisition des connaissances, c'est aussi un instrument de promotion social[10]. La pédagogie multiculturelle est dénoncée en des termes qui rappellent les écrits de Neil Bissoondath au Canada[11]. Ainsi Alain Pierrot dénonce cette curieuse méthode d'apprentissage de la lecture utilisée dans certaines écoles de l'Est parisien, qui consistait à inviter des percussionnistes africains dans les classes de lecture, pour motiver les élèves, sous prétexte que ce qui était « bon pour l'identité » était nécessairement utile à la maîtrise de l'alphabet[12].

D'autres éducateurs, comme le philosophe Pierre Statius, dénoncèrent le Centre d'Analyse et d'Intervention Sociologiques (CADIS) – l'équipe sociologique fondée par Alain Touraine et dirigée par Michel Wieviorka – en accusant ses membres de « reprendre et de transposer en France le débat anglo-saxon sur le multiculturalisme », tout en prétendant qu'il s'agirait là d'un « nouvel âge de la modernité[13] ». Or qu'est-ce que la modernité selon Statius? C'est l'idée de citoyenneté héritée de la philosophie des lumières, – une citoyenneté désincarnée qui se fonde sur « la possibilité d'une communication rationnelle entre les hommes » et qui pose « *l'unité*, au moins en droit, de l'humanité, par opposition à la *barbarie* qui, quelque forme qu'elle prenne, revient toujours à penser l'humanité comme essentiellement divisée (que ce soit en classes, ou même en cultures hétérogènes)[14] ». Les grands mots sont lâchés : les partisans d'une sociologie multiculturelle ne seraient que des barbares.

Enfin, Pierre Bourdieu et son disciple Loïc Wacquant ont développé un discours critique original qui dénonce les trois sophismes du multiculturalisme :

1) Le « groupisme », c'est-à-dire la « réification de divisions sociales privilégiées canonisées par la bureaucratie étatique »;
2) Le « populisme », qui remplace l'analyse des structures de pouvoir par la « célébration de la culture des dominés », élevée au rang de « proto-théorie en acte »;
3) Le « moralisme », qui conduit à ignorer les réalités socio-économiques et à disserter *ad infinitum* sur la « reconnaissance des identités », alors que la « triste réalité » se situe à un tout autre niveau : seulement un jeune sur dix issu d'une famille pauvre (un ménage gagnant moins de 15 000 dollars US) accédera à l'université, contre 94 pour cent des jeunes issus de familles disposant d'un revenu égal ou supérieur à 100 000 dollars US.

L'enjeu, en définitive, selon Bourdieu et Wacquant, n'est ni « ethnique », comme on le prétend, ni limité au « microcosme universitaire » et à la question « de la reconnaissance des cultures marginalisées par les canons académiques ». Il est d'une autre nature : il renvoie à l'« exclusion continuée des Noirs », tout en masquant la banqueroute du système américain d'enseignement public. La « triste réalité » est fondamentalement sociologique dans le sens le plus classique du terme : celle de l'accroissement des inégalités de classe. Dans cette perspective, le multiculturalisme est tout sauf un concept universel. Il ne serait que la manifestation spécifique du drame américain – celui de la discrimination raciale, des inégalités de classes et des inégalités d'accès au « capital culturel des classes supérieures[15] ».

Derrière le débat des éducateurs et des sociologues se profile une forte tradition jacobine admirablement pensée et théorisée par les juges constitutionnels français. L'exemple du « statut de la Corse », tel qu'il fut traité en 1991 par le Conseil Constitutionnel est révélateur. Le point de départ est une loi qui prétend innover à peu de frais en affirmant, pour satisfaire les revendications des nationalistes corses, que le « peuple corse » est une « composante du peuple français », et qu'il mérite un traitement territorial particulier de la part de l'État central. Cette redéfinition des composantes du peuple français est inacceptable pour les juges français, parce que contraire à la Constitution et à la Déclaration des droits de l'homme et du citoyen de 1789. « Le peuple de France », affirment-ils, est « *une catégorie unitaire insusceptible de toute division*[16] ».

Les juges du Conseil Constitutionnel légitimaient l'argument qui leur avait été présenté par les députés requérants, en ces termes d'un jacobinisme irréprochable :

> Admettre la consécration législative du peuple corse c'est admettre à plus ou moins brève échéance celle de 'peuple réunionnais', de 'peuple martiniquais', de 'peuple canaque', etc. Or, ceci est directement contraire à l'article 2 de la Constitution qui interdit toute distinction à raison de l'origine ou de la race. Comment, en effet, distinguer le peuple corse des autres composantes du peuple français, sinon par l'origine ethnique ? Si le gouvernement a d'autres critères, qu'il les donne[17].

Le Conseil Constitutionnel n'a donc pas pris le risque d'ouvrir la boîte de Pandore.

À défaut de s'affirmer comme un « peuple » autonome, les Corses peuvent-ils pratiquer leur langue comme ils l'entendent ? Les juges du Conseil Constitutionnel donnent ici une réponse positive puisqu'ils acceptent l'article 53 de la loi qui prévoit « l'insertion dans le temps scolaire de l'enseignement de la langue et de la culture corses ». Ils précisent bien que « cet enseignement n'est pas contraire au principe d'égalité dès lors qu'il ne revêt pas un caractère obligatoire[18] ». La langue corse a donc statut de langue à option, comme le latin, l'anglais, ou l'espagnol.

Mais cet encouragement au pluralisme culturel est ténu. Il n'est en effet pas question que les Corses (ou les Basques et les Bretons) utilisent leur langue dans leurs rapports avec les fonctionnaires de l'État central et les juges des tribunaux locaux. La langue de la République reste bien le français (art. 2 de la Constitution), et la signature proposée par le premier ministre, de la *Charte européenne des langues régionales ou minoritaires* n'est pas, selon les juges, conforme à la Constitution française. Celle-ci, précisent-ils dans une décision de 1999, défend le « principe d'unicité du peuple français » ; elle interdit, par conséquent, que « soient reconnus des droits collectifs à quelque groupe que ce soit, défini par une communauté d'origine, de culture, de langue ou de croyance ». La Charte européenne des langues régionales, concluent les juges, est contraire à la Constitution puisqu'elle « confère des droits spécifiques à des 'groupes' de locuteurs de langues régionales ou minoritaires, à l'intérieur de 'territoires' dans lesquels ces langues sont pratiquées ». La Charte « porte [donc] atteinte aux principes constitutionnels d'indivisibilité de la République, d'égalité devant la loi et d'unicité du peuple français[19] ».

Le biculturalisme canadien

Existe-t-il un multiculturalisme canadien avant la création d'une politique multiculturelle fédérale ? La réponse est oui, à l'évidence. Mais il s'agit d'une forme particulière de multiculturalisme propre au Canada et qui a pour nom « biculturalisme ». Il n'est pas nécessaire de relire les écrits de Henri Bourassa pour saisir la nature d'un Canada « binaire », composé de deux nations fondatrices. Il suffit de se reporter au rapport préliminaire à la mise en place de la *Commission royale sur le bilinguisme et le biculturalisme* pour comprendre l'importance et la persistance d'une telle conception : la Commission devait préciser les étapes qui permettraient de « développer la Confédération canadienne sur la base d'un partenariat égal entre les deux races fondatrices ». Un tel projet était difficilement acceptable pour une nouvelle génération d'immi-

grés qui se sentait exclue du pacte fondateur et qui concevait le
Canada comme une nation d'immigrés, à l'image des États-Unis. C'est
pourquoi, sans doute, les critiques les plus vives contre les recom-
mandations formulées par la « *B and B Commission* » furent exprimées
par les représentants de groupes ethniques peu nombreux, mais bien
structurés et politiquement actifs. Je pense en particulier aux viru-
lentes critiques émises par deux Ukrainiens, le sénateur Paul Yuzyk et
Jaroslav Bohdan Rudnyckyj – membre de la *Commission royale* et
directeur du Département d'études slaves de l'Université du
Manitoba[20]. C'est dans ce contexte critique que se développe la
philosophie multiculturelle des fédéralistes. Manifestement, le multiculturalisme défendu par Pierre Trudeau au début des années 1970
menaçait le point de vue des nationalistes québécois ; il faisait du
Québec une province comme les autres. Le bilinguisme officiel n'était
qu'un moyen habile de déplacer les enjeux et les allégeances pour faire
oublier aux Québécois l'importance d'une tradition authentiquement
biculturelle. Le multiculturalisme fédéral s'inscrivait donc dans un
projet plus large de destruction créatrice et de recomposition de la
nation canadienne[21].

Mais la réalité canadienne est plus complexe qu'il apparaît au premier abord, et il n'est plus possible d'affirmer aujourd'hui, quoiqu'en
pense Louise Beaudoin, que les nationalistes québécois sont réfrac-
taires aux idées multiculturelles[22]. Il y a bien, au Québec, un « nouveau
nationalisme » qui donne toute sa place à la pluralité des appartenances et des cultures des nouveaux immigrés et qui récuse par là
même les tendances autoritaires et ethnocentriques du « vieux nationalisme[23] ». Lionel Jospin n'avait donc pas tout à fait tort de vanter les
mérites du multiculturalisme, mais que savait-il à l'époque du nouveau nationalisme québécois ?

Le pluralisme culturel des États-Unis

Le fédéralisme américain et l'habitude américaine de s'imaginer
comme une « nation de plusieurs peuples » facilitent à l'évidence l'ac-
ceptation d'une pensée multiculturelle. Penser le multiculturalisme
américain, c'est d'abord se référer à ses « formes primitives », avant
même l'usage du mot. Elles sont nombreuses, à commencer par la tradition anglo-hollandaise de la tolérance religieuse, sur laquelle John
Rawls a écrit quelques bonnes pages dans *Libéralisme politique* ainsi que

dans son fameux article consacré à la notion de « *overlapping consensus* ». Mais la définition la plus intéressante d'un « multiculturalisme d'avant la lettre » est sans doute celle du « pluralisme culturel », imaginée en 1924 par Horace Kallen, un disciple de William James, et un ami et contemporain de John Dewey[24].

Le « pluralisme culturel » conçu par Kallen est éminemment polémique. L'auteur de la formule s'inscrit en faux contre une autre tradition américaine : celle du « *melting-pot* », inventée, ou plutôt popularisée (car il s'agit d'une vieille métaphore industrielle), par un écrivain anglais – Israel Zangwill – qui rédigea, pour un public exclusivement américain, une pièce de théâtre intitulée *The Melting-Pot*. L'immense succès de cette pièce symbolisait le triomphe des idées assimilationnistes. Et pourtant la pièce fut très vite l'objet de critiques acerbes de la part de critiques littéraires qui l'estimaient trop « facile », et d'essayistes qui s'inquiétaient des effets nocifs d'une assimilation trop rapide sur les nouveaux immigrants. Kallen offre la plus intéressante des critiques d'une américanisation trop rapide. Son argument est étonnamment moderne car il repose sur la dénonciation de ce qui est déjà une forme de globalisation mondiale : la culture de masse, le rouleau compresseur de la société de consommation, tels qu'ils prenaient naissance sous ses yeux entre 1915 et 1924. Le grand danger pour Kallen était l'uniformité culturelle, c'est-à-dire une culture « américanisée », fondée sur le plus petit commun dénominateur des connaissances humaines ; une culture dominée par l'émergence d'une nouvelle presse « grand public » cherchant le scandale et la facilité pour mieux vendre ses titres. Il y avait donc un immense danger : l'utilisation par la presse des idées racistes à la mode – à commencer par celles d'un Ku Klux Klan en pleine résurgence.

Kallen est le premier témoin critique d'une massification de la culture américaine. Il exprime une vraie nostalgie pour ces nombreux journaux d'immigrés allemands, polonais, juifs et cetera, qui préservaient avec talent des pans entiers de la culture européenne. Et il déplore, au moment de l'engagement américain dans la Première Guerre mondiale, le fait que les étrangers, et surtout les immigrés allemands, doivent oublier leur langue pour éviter l'accusation d'anti-patriotisme. C'est l'époque des grandes campagnes d'américanisation, de la recherche de cet être artificiel, éminemment contrôlable : l'« Américain à cent pour cent ». Tout cela, Kallen le déplore. Pour expliquer sa conception de la nation américaine, il a recours à des métaphores musicales : la *polyphonie*, par opposition au *plain chant*, ou encore l'*orchestration* d'une symphonie où chaque instrument préserve son timbre, sa sonorité, sa personnalité. C'est bien ainsi qu'il voit l'Amérique : une immense orchestration des peuples immigrés, une grandiose polyphonie. Mais sa polyphonie n'exclut pas une forte allégeance à un système politique préexistant, celui de la Constitution fédérale de 1787. Kallen souhaite que les États-Unis, cette « fédération de cultures nationales », maintiennent une véritable « vénération » pour le système créé de toutes pièces par les délégués de la Convention de Philadelphie[25]. Le seul, le vrai danger, pour lui, est le conformisme anglo-saxon et son excroissance monstrueuse : le darwinisme social et sa transposition populiste au sein du KKK. Le citoyen américain est donc placé devant une dramatique alternative. Il lui faut choisir, affirme Kallen, entre « la Kultur Klux Klan et le pluralisme culturel[26] ».

Conclusion : La Corse n'est pas (encore) le Québec

J'ai raisonné jusqu'ici en amont en proposant de m'interroger sur les « formes primitives du multiculturalisme » pour mieux comprendre la portée de ce concept polysémique, les usages, et les malentendus auxquels il a donné lieu. Or c'est bien en France qu'existe la difficulté la plus grande : notre incapacité à concevoir les conditions de possibilité d'un vrai multiculturalisme, notre gêne à penser le multiculturalisme, et notre tendance à ne pas comprendre ce qu'il signifie en Amérique du Nord. Et pourtant les mentalités françaises ne sont pas aussi jacobines ni aussi rigides qu'il apparaît au premier abord. Le débat sur la Corse de l'été 2000 est un bon révélateur des changements de mentalité qui pointent à l'horizon de notre univers politique.

En effet, des événements récents – la mise en place du processus dit « de Matignon » – sur l'initiative du premier ministre, Lionel Jospin, laissent entendre que le vieux jacobinisme français est moribond. Le processus de Matignon correspond à l'élaboration d'un projet de loi sur la Corse, qui fut soumis par le Gouvernement et accepté par l'Assemblée de Corse le 28 juillet 2000. Ce projet devait être soumis pour adoption au Parlement français au début de l'hiver 2001. Le processus a ceci de remarquable : pour la première fois dans l'histoire de la République, il permet à une région française (la Corse) de disposer d'une part de la souveraineté nationale. Il met en place un processus évolutif qui donne le droit à l'Assemblée de Corse d'expérimenter avec la loi nationale pour la modifier, si nécessaire, afin de tenir compte des particularités socio-économiques de la Corse. Or, « modifier une loi », c'est une façon modeste, certes, mais néanmoins réelle de « faire la loi ». Que dit en effet le texte de Matignon ? Il propose que le Parlement national donne « à la collectivité territoriale de la Corse la possibilité de *déroger par ses délibérations à certaines dispositions législatives*, dans des conditions que le Parlement définirait ». Ces « dérogations », ou encore ces « expérimentations », seraient jugées par le Parlement avant d'être généralisées dans une période plus lointaine qui nécessitera une révision de la Constitution en 2004[27].

Ces propositions novatrices firent scandale au point de provoquer la démission du ministre de l'Intérieur, Jean-Pierre Chevènement, au nom des principes mêmes du jacobinisme dont ce dernier s'autoproclamait le meilleur des gardiens. Chevènement justifiait ainsi sa position dans un entretien au journal *Le Monde*, peu de temps avant sa démission :

> Venons-en au fond : depuis la Révolution française, la République s'est définie par le règne de la loi, votée par le Parlement et devant laquelle tous les citoyens, sans distinction d'origine, sont placés en position d'égalité. À partir du moment où la France deviendrait une sorte de patchwork, juxtaposant des lois corses, franc-comtoises, savoyardes, basques, berrichonnes, bretonnes, alsaciennes, nous serions revenus à l'Ancien Régime. La République n'est pas, dans notre histoire, une parenthèse à refermer[28].

Les gardiens de la République ont aujourd'hui perdu la bataille, et le processus de Matignon suit son cours. Or ce processus ne met pas seulement en place une politique de dévolution législative ; il innove dans un autre domaine, lui aussi sans précédent en France, puisqu'il propose pour la Corse une nouvelle politique linguistique. Le projet de réforme annonce ainsi que « l'enseignement de la langue corse prendra place dans l'horaire scolaire normal des écoles maternelles et primaires et pourra ainsi être suivi par tous les élèves sauf volonté contraire des parents[29] ». Apprendre le corse, dans cette optique, n'est plus choisir une matière à option, comme le prévoyait la loi sur le statut de la Corse de 1991. C'est une ardente obligation[30].

Il reste que la Corse n'est pas le Québec et que le peuple corse est toujours constitutionnellement privé du droit de s'ériger en « peuple ».

Mais disposer du pouvoir de « modifier » des lois, c'est déjà posséder une part de la souveraineté. L'évolution politique en cours est donc riche d'enseignements ; elle signale la fin de ce que j'appelais la « difficulté française » à penser le multiculturalisme.

Lionel Jospin n'avait sans doute pas saisi la vraie nature du multiculturalisme canadien, lorsqu'il visita ce pays en 1998. Mais il poursuivit manifestement sa réflexion au point d'inscrire une problématique multiculturelle au cœur du processus de Matignon. Y a-t-il pour lui un bon modèle étranger du multiculturalisme? Il est sans doute trop tôt pour répondre. La France n'est pas encore un pays fédéral même si elle avance timidement dans cette direction. L'utopie jospinienne est celle d'une République qui serait capable de « conjuguer unité et diversité[31] ». La phrase est nouvelle dans le vocabulaire politique français. Elle est familière aux habitants du Nouveau Monde, puisqu'il s'agit au fond de la traduction française d'une vieille devise latine empruntée à un poème de Virgile (*Moretum*) et érigée depuis plus de deux siècles en devise officielle des États-Unis : *E Pluribus Unum*[32]. C'est ainsi, à coups de réformes graduelles et de petites phrases, que l'on met fin en France au fétichisme de la République une et indivisible.

Notes

1. Louise Beaudoin reprochait ainsi à Jospin d'avoir alimenté la cause des fédéralistes anglo-canadiens en vantant le mérite du multiculturalisme. Jospin faisait amende honorable en affirmant que la France était prête à accompagner la « voie politique » du Québec, quelles qu'en soient les conséquences. Voir *Le Soir*, 19 décembre 1998.
2. F. Melonio, *Tocqueville et les Français*, Paris, Aubier, 1993 : 36.
3. M. de Robespierre, discours à la Convention, 24 septembre 1792, cité dans Laurence Cornu, « Fédéralistes ! Et pourquoi ? » Dans *La Gironde et les Girondins*, F. Furet et M. Ozouf, dir. Paris, Payot, 1991 : 270.
4. D. Schnapper, *La communauté des citoyens. Sur l'idée moderne de nation*, Paris, Gallimard, 1994 : 24.
5. *Ibid.*, 49, souligné par l'auteur. Dans son dernier livre, Dominique Schnapper présente une conception plus riche et plus nuancée du même débat. Lieu abstrait de la modernité politique, la citoyenneté est conçue par Schnapper, *en situation*, dans la relation dynamique qu'elle entretient avec les particularismes des « collectivités historiques » qui constituent

la société réelle. Dans cette perspective, la sociologie de la citoyenneté ne peut ignorer les aspects affectifs du lien social. Or celui-ci est bien souvent imaginé comme « ethnique » par les acteurs sociaux. On peut le déplorer, comme on peut déplorer « l'ethnicisation constante » des relations sociales dans la société américaine, mais c'est là un phénomène imparable des sociétés démocratiques modernes. Le sociologue, conclut Schnapper, doit s'efforcer de penser « la dialectique de l'ethnique et du civique » ; il doit aussi réfléchir aux moyens de dépasser cette antinomie et sa décision ne peut être, en dernière instance, que philosophique et politique. Voir D. Schnapper, *La Relation à l'autre. Au cœur de la pensée sociologique*, Paris, Gallimard, coll. Essais, 1998.

6.   C. Taylor, *Multiculturalisme. Différence et démocratie*, Paris, Aubier, 1994 : 57–58, 84–87.

7.   C. Jelen, *Les casseurs de la République*, Paris, Plon, 1997 : 14-5.

8.   R. Debray, *La république expliquée à ma fille*, Paris, Seuil, 1998.

9.   J. de Maistre, cité dans Gérard Gengembre, *La contre-révolution ou l'histoire désespérante*, Paris, Imago, 1989.

10.   O. Cousin, « Les élèves face à l'école républicaine », dans P. Statius dir., *Actualité de l'école républicaine ?* Caen, Centre régional de documentation pédagogique de Basse-Normandie, 1998 : 95-107.

11.   N. Bissoondath, *Selling Illusions: The Cult of Multiculturalism in Canada* (Harmondsworth : Penguin, 1994).

12.   A. Pierrot, « École républicaine et multiculturalisme », *Actualité de l'école républicaine*, op. cit. : 116. Sur ce même type de débats aux États-Unis, voir D. Lacorne, *La Crise de l'identité américaine. Du melting-pot au multiculturalisme*, Paris, Fayard, 1997 : 243-82, ainsi que id., « Des coups de canon dans le vide ? La civilisation occidentale dans les universités américaines », *Vingtième Siècle*, n° 43, juillet 1994 : 4–17.

13.   P. Statius, « La Crise de l'école républicaine : entre le constat vérifié et le fantasme à questionner », *Actualité de l'école républicaine*, op. cit. :135-50. On trouvera une présentation complète des thèses du CADIS dans M. Wieviorka dir., *Une Société fragmentée ? Le multiculturalisme en débat*, Paris, La Découverte, 1996.

14.   L. Ferry et A. Renaut, cités (et réappropriés hors contexte) par P. Statius, *ibid.*: 145.

15.   P. Bourdieu et L. Wacquant, « La nouvelle vulgate planétaire », *Le Monde diplomatique*, mai 2000 : 6-7.

16.   *Décision 91.290 DC*, 9 mai 1991 (Décision sur le statut de la Corse). < www.conseil-constitutionnel.fr >

17.   « Mémoire des députés requérants en réplique aux observations du gouvernement », cité dans L. Favoreu et L. Philip, dir., *Les grandes décisions*

du Conseil Constitutionnel, 7ᵉ édition, Paris, Sirey, 1993 : 764. F. Giacobbi, le président du Conseil Général de haute Corse, réagissait ainsi : « Quand vous reconnaissez le peuple corse à l'intérieur du peuple français, vous faites une distinction raciste. » *Ibid.*

18. *Décision 91.290 DC*, 9 mai 1991. (Décision sur le statut de la Corse). < www.conseil-constitutionnel.fr >

19. Conseil Constitutionnel, *Décision 99-412 DC*, 15 juin 1999.

20. Voir K. McRoberts, *Misconceiving Canada. The Struggle for National Unity* (Toronto : Oxford University Press, 1997) : 117–36.

21. J. Webber, *Reimagining Canada* (Montréal and Kingston : McGill-Queen's University Press, 1994) : 62-66. On trouvera en français une bonne analyse de ce débat dans A. Dieckhoff, *La Nation dans tous ses États. Les identités nationales en mouvement*, Paris, Flammarion, 2000 : 167–90.

22. Voir la note n° 1.

23. Qu'on se reporte ici à l'excellent ouvrage collectif de M. Venne, dir., *Penser la Nation québécoise*, Montréal, Québec-Amérique, 2000.

24. Sur les origines du multiculturalisme américain, l'influence de Zangwill et de Kallen, voir D. Lacorne, *La Crise de l'identité américaine*, 243–282.

25. Sur les formes diverses du « patriotisme constitutionnel » américain, voir D. Lacorne, *L'Invention de la République. Le modèle américain*, Paris, Hachette, coll. Pluriel, 1991.

26. H. Kallen, *Culture and Democracy in the United States* (New York : Boni and Liveright, 1924) : 43.

27. *Propositions du gouvernement soumises aux représentants des élus de la Corse*, Paris, 20 juillet 200.

28. Entretien au *Monde*, 19 juillet 2000. Dans *La République des bien-pensants*, Paris, Plon, 1999, Jean-Pierre Chevènement réaffirme sa philosophie rousseauiste et jacobine et dénonce toute dérive ethniciste. La France, pour lui, est une nation de citoyens égaux, une « création suprêmement politique » qui ne saurait donner place aux considérations d'origine ethnique ou régionale. La communauté des citoyens, affirme-t-il, est « délivrée de la sombre mythologie des origines », c'est ce qui lui a permis d'intégrer sans trop de problème des millions de nouveaux immigrés tout en restant fidèle « à sa langue, à sa culture, à sa manière d'être au monde », (107-108). La forme la plus extrême du jacobinisme français est bien illustrée dans un article récent de Jean-Luc Mélenchon, l'un des dirigeants de la « Gauche socialiste » et le secrétaire d'État à la formation professionnelle à l'époque : « Mieux vaudrait perdre la Corse que la République… L'ethnicisme sous toutes ses formes est un obscurantisme. Il conduit… à l'exclusion, au crime et à la guerre civile. Le dossier corse en est intrinsèquement empuanti. Les habitants de l'île en

paient déjà le coût, dans le silence de la peur », *Marianne*, 28 août 2000.

29. *Propositions du gouvernement soumises aux représentants des élus de la Corse, op. cit.*

30. Sur les difficultés pratiques de cette future obligation, voir S. Le Bars, « Enseignement du corse : les principes de Matignon à l'épreuve du terrain », *Le Monde*, 8 octobre 2000.

31. Lionel Jospin, « Mon pari pour la Corse », *Le Nouvel Observateur*, 17 août 2000.

32. Sur l'origine de cette devise et sa véritable signification, voir D. Lacorne, *La Crise de l'identité américaine*, 278–279.

Aboriginal Peoples in the Twenty-first Century: A Plea for Realism

Alan C. Cairns

I DO NOT EXPECT THE ARGUMENTS IN THIS PAPER, ESPECIALLY THOSE IN the last half, to convince all who read or heard this presentation. In fact, if I fail to convince you, I may have succeeded in the much more important task of contributing to a discussion. The Aboriginal policy field has too many converts and too few discussions in which we listen to each other. Converts and discussion have an uneasy relationship: basically, each is the other's most feared opponent. At the turn of the century, converts and ideologies can look after themselves; discussion, however, needs help. Hence the following pages.

This paper has a single objective – to clarify the debate about how Aboriginal and non-Aboriginal peoples are to live together in the future. We cannot be successfully forward-looking, however, without understanding the past that has shaped us. The first half of the paper, accordingly, focusing as it does largely on the last half of the century, establishes how we got to 'now.' Now is defined as the post-1969 White Paper (Canada 1969) era, in which, I argue, there are two roads to the future – the self-government route based on Aboriginal nations and the urban route.

This is the era of Aboriginal nationalism; of Oka; of the Royal Commission on Aboriginal Peoples (RCAP); of major advances by Aboriginal peoples in the *Constitution Act*, 1982; of a huge increase in the number of Aboriginal post-secondary graduates; of the dramatic growth of the urban Aboriginal population; of the dawning recognition that Aboriginal communities, especially First Nations, are not going to disappear as believers in assimilation once thought; of the birth of Nunavut (1999); and of many other developments, most of which would have been inconceivable fifty years ago. This background underlines the reality that ours is a new era – that indeed we are creating a new Canada – and that we desperately need more understanding if we are to avoid major policy errors.

Of the many issues needing attention, I have selected the coexistence of the two roads to the future mentioned above. The last half of the paper, grandiosely subheaded "a plea for realism," tries to disentangle the issues posed by this apparent choice, to stick-handle through the claims of both the advocates and opponents of each route. I conclude that the debate is poorly conducted and that both roads will be with us for the foreseeable future. We need more information and analysis and less ideology if we are to make progress in one of the most politicized and conflict-filled policy areas on our agenda. (The paper focuses disproportionately on status Indians because neither Inuit nor Métis [with only eight small settlements in northern Alberta] confront the choice between the urban and the self-government route to the same degree.)

From Paternalism to Aboriginal Nationalism

No dialogue between Indians and the federal government preceded the release of that government's 1969 White Paper which proposed ending the separate status of Indian people and their assimilation into Canadian society. This act of paternalism was repudiated by the organized opposition of Indian peoples, led by the Indian Chiefs of Alberta (Indian Chiefs of Alberta 1970). The subsequent withdrawal of the White Paper was more than the defeat of a particular policy initiative. The historic federal policy of assimilation was in ruins. Since then, it has been generally assumed that Indian communities would survive as such – that they would have a distinct, ongoing communal existence in Canada (Weaver 1990). Thirty years after the White Paper's defeat, Canadians are still grappling with that new reality.

Since then, the federal government has lost or given up its leadership role. Initially, it appeared that the policy of assimilation had been cast in the dustbin of discarded experiments. For the first decade after the White Paper's withdrawal, the relevant actors repositioned themselves behind the vague consensus that assimilation, at least as a conscious policy, was dead, and that the emerging policy question was how Indian peoples – as peoples – or, as the terminology evolved, as nations – should be fitted into the Canadian constitutional order. In the period leading up to the *Constitution Act*, 1982, Inuit and Métis emerged and made independent claims for recognition and self-government. This foreshadowed the new constitutional category "Aboriginal Peoples of Canada," defined in the *Constitution Act, 1982*, s. 35(2), as including Indian, Inuit, and Métis.

Increasingly, initiatives in the broad field of Aboriginal policy came from Aboriginal organizations, particularly the National Indian Brotherhood, later renamed the Assembly of First Nations, which spoke for the legal status Indian population living on reserves. Its voice, and that of other Aboriginal organizations, was strengthened by a fortuitous convergence of factors.

The federal government policy of funding the major Aboriginal organizations – which commenced in the early 1970s, on the premise that the poverty, small populations, and geographical diffusion of Aboriginal peoples would otherwise marginalize them in democratic politics – gave them not only a voice but ultimately a unique status among the claimants for government attention. They quickly came to be much more than the standard interest group speaking for a particular clientele or cause. As the major Aboriginal associations acquired confidence, they decisively distanced themselves from the proliferating ethnic associations which represented the ethnocultural communities gathered under the official policy of multiculturalism. They represented not ethnic minorities, but nations.

The nation label gained sustenance from the opening up of the Constitution in response to Francophone nationalism in Québec, particularly following the victory of the Parti Québécois in the 1976 provincial election. This placed the question of Canada's future on the bargaining table. What kind of people were Canadians? What revised institutional arrangements and constitutional reforms were appropriate for a country increasingly separated from Europe, with an immigration policy that was transforming the face of major metropolitan centres, one that confronted a Québec nationalist challenge to its very survival, and one with indigenous peoples no longer willing to accept their marginalization? The opening up of the Constitution was quickly seen as providing an arena in which Aboriginal peoples could advance their claims for recognition, self-government, and an end to their stigmatized marginalization.

Trudeau's assertion "Everything is up for grabs" was a direct response to a reinvigorated, assertive Québec nationalism. Aboriginal peoples successfully inserted themselves into constitutional politics and made major gains in the *Constitution Act, 1982*. Simultaneously, their self-description as nations gathered momentum. The National Indian Brotherhood renamed itself the Assembly of First Nations. The 1983 Penner Committee, with its ringing advocacy of self-government for Indian peoples in its report, systematically employed the term nation in a clear response to the messages of Indian spokespersons who appeared before it (Canada 1983). The language of nationalism clearly added symbolic legitimacy to claims for recognition and special treatment.

This was evident in the four Aboriginal constitutional conferences, 1983 to 1987 (Schwartz 1986), primarily focusing on the inherent right of self-government. The conferences gave additional proof of, and stimulus to, the emerging distinct status of Aboriginal peoples. Aboriginal associations participated almost as bargaining equals of the federal and provincial governments on the other side of the table. Their goal was to carve out a separate category of constitutional space for the implementation of the inherent right of self-government. No other interest group that flourished in democratic, pluralistic politics, whether representing women, disabled persons, Italian Canadians, or others, were given similar recognition.

The rhetoric surrounding the concept of nation became the standard terminology used to identify Aboriginal peoples. Indians became 'First Nations' in a clear attempt to gain historical priority and a stronger legitimacy than that of the two founding nations of French and English newcomers. The Métis also employed the self-identifying, status-raising label of nation as, to a lesser extent, did the Inuit. Perhaps, however, the most decisive indication of the status-enhancing capacity of the nation terminology was the dramatic diffusion of such self-labelling among Indian bands themselves. By 1999, about 30 per cent of over 600 Indian bands had added nation to their official name. Most of them had populations well under one thousand people (Canada 1985, 1990, 1999).

The language of nationalism changes the nature of Aboriginal policy discussions. The term nation easily, almost automatically, leads to a justification for an ongoing future existence, and therefore for the policy tools to achieve that goal. Nation attracts the supportive attention of prominent political theorists – Will Kymlicka, Sam LaSelva, Charles Taylor, Jim Tully – in a way that the term 'villages' would not. They add a certain philosophical legitimacy to Aboriginal nationalism and to the consequences that logically attach to that labelling. Nation, inevitably and desirably in the eyes of its proponents, stresses an internal within-group solidarity, while stressing the 'otherness' of the non-Aboriginal majority.

This otherness is reinforced by the widespread employment of the language of colonialism to describe the history of Aboriginal/non-Aboriginal relations from which an escape is sought. The colonial analogy is a dramatic reminder that the relation of indigenous people to the Canadian majority from the last half of the nineteenth century to the present has *always* been massively influenced by international trends – particularly the world of empire and of its ending. In the former, when a handful of European states ruled much of humanity, the wardship status of Indian peoples – their marginalization – their subjection to the demands of a majority confident of its own cultural superiority – did not have to be argued in terms of first principles – it was simply assumed. Canadian rule over indigenous peoples – most dramatically in the case of status Indians – was simply a spillover from the larger world of empire outside Canada.

The implicit international support in the imperial era for wardship for Indians, for their exclusion from the franchise until 1960, for leaving Inuit (then Eskimo) isolated and forgotten, and for the marginalization of the Métis, evaporated when empire ended. When the British left India, the French handed over power in Senegal, the Dutch lost control of Indonesia, and the Portuguese finally succumbed to exhaustion and retreated from Angola and Mozambique, the message flowing across Canadian borders no longer justified hierarchy with Aboriginal peoples at the base, whether hierarchy was conceived in cultural or racial terms.

The international system was no longer a club of white states. The Commonwealth – now a multicultural, multiracial association – contrasted dramatically with the older view of the white dominions as Britain overseas. The United Nations was transformed into a multiracial institution, with European states in a minority, after the collapse of European empires and the emergence of more than a hundred new states. The United Nations launched a crusade against colonialism and racism that inevitably challenged the legitimacy of white leadership over indigenous peoples in settler colonies – even if that leadership was dressed up in the language of trusteeship and guardianship.

We can argue, therefore, that the emergence of Aboriginal nationalism was overdetermined. It fed on the opening up of the Canadian Constitution; on the demise of European empires and the subsequent transformations in the international system; on the funding of

Aboriginal associations by the federal government; on the defeat of the White Paper; and on the contagious, world-wide diffusion of nationalism among indigenous peoples. The simultaneous emergence of indigenous nationalism in Australia (Aborigines) and New Zealand (Maori) as well as in Canada, underlines the international forces at work. Those wishing to understand Aboriginal nationalism in Canada, accordingly, must look outward beyond domestic, within-Canada causes to embrace changes in the international environment. To look inwardly only at our domestic selves blinds us to the fact that indigenous peoples around the globe learn and borrow from each other. There is, in other words, an indigenous international.

The colonial analogy drawn from the international arena and the widespread diffusion of the label nation were appropriate yet, at the same time, potentially misleading. Colonialism was clearly a reasonable description of the system of alien rule and the displacement of Indian peoples onto reserves, thought of as schools for their civilization. It was somewhat less appropriate for Inuit and Métis, in that they were not subject to a separate administrative system, nor subjected to the same degree of cultural assault as Indians. On the other hand, they too were marginalized, defined as backward, and not considered to be full, ordinary citizens.

Colonialism, however, is also misleading. The end of colonialism in yesterday's world of the demise of the European empires resulted in independence. The new flag of a new country was raised, and the international community acquired a new member. The ending of colonialism in Canada, however, does not usher in independence but requires a rapprochement with the majority – the working out of arrangements that combine self-government where land-based Aboriginal communities exist with membership in the Canadian community of citizens. Colonialism focuses attention on the self-rule dimension, but it positively deflects attention from the rapprochement dimension, which requires a positive collaboration with yesterday's oppressor. Therefore, it contributes to a misunderstanding of the requirements of a workable reconciliation.

Nation is also Janus-faced. It is status-raising for those who employ it. It speaks to a positive sense of belonging and to a people's desire for a continuing future existence. For peoples whose difference has been reinforced by their treatment by the majority society, the attribution of nation is a logical if not inevitable response to their situation, especially for land-based communities. The term nation, however, can be misleading. Nation is a potent word that presupposes population sizes and self-government capacities that are beyond small populations of several hundred or several thousand people. The accompanying nation-to-nation theme, the key concept in the analysis of the RCAP report (Canada 1996), also misleads as it inevitably conjures up an image of Canada as an international system. It suggests autonomous, discrete actors bargaining the terms of their separate coexistence. If, however, "within Canada" means anything, the reality is that a part is rearranging its relationship with the whole of which it is a part. In other words, when federal and provincial governments are bargaining their future relations with an Aboriginal nation in a land-claims/self-government negotiation for example, the members of the latter group are also and simultaneously represented as citizens by the federal and provincial governments. If this is not so, the whole system of voting and elections in federal and provincial politics and the receipt of standard federal and provincial services are based on a misunderstanding – an assertion that would find minimal support.

It is possible, and perhaps probable, that the leading players in public discussions realize that the language of colonialism, of nation, and of nation-to-nation in the Canadian context does not carry the same meaning and consequences in Canada as it did in Algeria or Kenya. There may be a tacit understanding on both sides of the table that these terms – colonialism, nation, and nation-to-nation – have a more limited, restricted meaning than the full sense of the words suggests. Even so, their use adds a potential element of confusion to our attempts to work out our relations with each other. The increasingly common description of Canada as a multinational country normally fails to mention that the Québec nation is some 7,000 times larger than the average Aboriginal nation proposed by the RCAP. Further, the RCAP figures – average nation size of 5,000-7,000 people – are not a current reality, but a goal that can only be achieved by aggregating small bands into larger units, a goal certain to generate considerable resistance. We cannot think clearly if we forget such realities.

Nor can we think clearly if we overlook the constitutional changes and judicial decisions that have provided indigenous peoples with constitutional support for their aspirations. The *Constitution Act, 1982,* declared that "The existing aboriginal and treaty rights of the aboriginal peoples of Canada are hereby recognized and affirmed," and "In this Act 'aboriginal peoples of Canada' includes the Indian, Inuit and Métis peoples of Canada," (s. 35(1) and (2)). This constitutional affirmation was, in effect, a repudiation of the original *British North America Act*, 1867, which in s. 91(24) simply treated Indians as a subject of federal jurisdiction, indicating that their constitutional recognition had nothing to do with their rights, but simply with which government had authority over them. Section 91(24) presupposed wards who, for their own sake, had to be governed by others. Section 35(1), by contrast, identified the rights of peoples that are to be recognized and affirmed. Section 35(2) created a new constitutional category, "aboriginal peoples of Canada," which inevitably generated pressures from the least favoured member of the category – the Métis – who achieved a constitutional recognition in 1982 they had long sought – access to state-provided, positive benefits, available to status Indian peoples. The move from s. 91(24) (1867) to s. 35 (1982), from wards to rights holders, was the domestic equivalent of the end of colonialism in the overseas territories of the former European empires. That domestic equivalent, of course, falls short of independence. The new status to which it leads is to be "within Canada."

The courts, which historically had played a limited role in affirming Aboriginal rights, made important contributions in the post-White Paper decades. Two decisions – Calder (1973) (*Calder* v. *AG BC*, [1973] SCR 313) and Delgamuukw (1997) (*Delgamuukw* v. *BC*, [1997] 3 SCR 1010) – underline the judicial contribution, which can be followed in more detail in any of the standard case books in Canadian constitutional law. In Calder, the Supreme Court dismissed an application by the Nishga (now Nisga'a) Indians of northwestern British Columbia for formal recognition of their Aboriginal title based on their immemorial occupation of the land. Six of the seven judges, however, recognized the concept of Aboriginal title, three of whom suggested that their Aboriginal title had not been extinguished. Subsequently, the Trudeau government announced a land claims policy, which is the origin of the modern land claims settlements already completed and of the many negotiations, especially in British Columbia, that are now underway.

In Delgamuukw, the Supreme Court confirmed that Aboriginal title existed in British Columbia and that it constitutes a right to the land itself, not just to traditional uses such as hunting. The Court also held that oral history should be included in the evidence legitimately before the Court. Both of these strands of Delgamuukw have profoundly transformed the treaty process in British Columbia by dramatically enhancing the bargaining resources of First Nations negotiators.

The Pervasive Impact of Nationalism

The emergence of Aboriginal nationalism and the response to it are highlighted in some of the key events of the past decade and a half listed below. This brief and elementary listing – all that space limitations allow – is neither exhaustive nor faithful to the complexities behind the events, but it will serve to underline the temper of the present era.

- The role of Elijah Harper in preventing debate on the Meech Lake Accord in the Manitoba legislature, just as the three-year ratification clock was running out in 1990, was a crucial factor in the defeat of the accord. Harper's role, backed by enthusiastic First Nations support, symbolized the willingness of First Nations – if their own demands were not met – to defeat a major constitutional effort to bring Québec back into the constitutional family with, in Prime Minister Mulroney's words, honour and enthusiasm.
- The Oka crisis of 1990, as well as other, less dramatic, indicators of frustration and anger expressed in road blocks, occupations, and demonstrations, underlined the growing tension in Aboriginal/non-Aboriginal relations.
- The massive, five-volume report of the Royal Commission on Aboriginal Peoples, released in 1996, its policy recommendations and its governing nation-to-nation theme, confirmed that the status quo was not viable. The RCAP Report is a document of Aboriginal nationalism.
- The establishment of the BC Treaty Commission in 1993, following the century-long denial by British Columbia governments that Aboriginal title was a continuing reality, suggested that even the most obdurate provincial government could not prevail against the combination of politicized First Nations claims and a supportive Supreme Court jurisprudence of Aboriginal and treaty rights.
- The passage of the Nisga'a treaty in 2000, in spite of a deeply divisive debate in British Columbia, including a court challenge, suggested that Aboriginal nationalism could be accommodated within Canadian federalism.
- The emergence of Nunavut in 1999 as a quasi-province with an Inuit majority was an even more symbolic indication of the possibility of finding common ground.

On the other hand, the confrontation between Québec and Aboriginal nationalism, particularly of the northern Cree and Inuit, over the territorial integrity of Québec should it secede from Canada, underlined the limits of compromise, and confirmed that Aboriginal nationalism would be a major player and a major complication if Canada was threatened with a split.

- Nationalism, defined as the unwillingness to forget, and the willingness to pursue claims for redress for past maltreatment was a supportive factor in the emergence into public attention of the history of sexual and physical abuse in residential schools and the pursuit of claims for compensation by thousands of former students. These claims, which threaten devastating financial impacts on the major churches involved in what a recent scholar described as *A National Crime* in his history of residential schools (Milloy 1999), only surfaced when yesterday's paternalism was displaced by assertive nationalism.

The recognition and accommodation of Aboriginal nationalism *within Canada* is one of the most difficult, high-priority tasks confronting Canadian policy-makers. "Within Canada" indicates that the goal is not only to recognize Aboriginal difference but also to generate a positive identification with, and participation in, the Canadian community of citizens. Aboriginal nationalism is not enough. It has to be supplemented by a shared citizenship with other Canadians if our living together is to go beyond a wary coexistence.

The Spirit of the Times – Then and Now

Cumulatively, the preceding suggest a profound transformation in the spirit of the times from the conventional assumptions of forty years ago; in different language, the self-consciousness of the major players has been transformed; their very identities differ; non-Aboriginals no longer assume an unchallenged authority to be in charge, while Aboriginal peoples sense the possibility that this time historical momentum may be on their side. Differently phrased, Aboriginal peoples now occupy the moral high ground once occupied by the majority society that had justified its former leadership role, by virtue of the superior civilization it was assumed to be spreading. These changes in mood, in temperament, in identity, in consciousness, in confidence, and in taken-for-granted assumptions about who was in charge, and about what a desirable future would look like, are not easily pinned down, yet they are fundamental components of where we are.

This profound transformation is best illustrated by the fate of the rhetoric of assimilation. Formerly the trademark of the non-Aboriginal liberal / left progressives in the middle of the twentieth century, it recently re-emerged on the right end of the spectrum in the Reform party and its successor, the Canadian Alliance, as a reaction against the policy thrust toward special treatment and a constitutionalized third order of Aboriginal governments. Now, however, the liberal / left end of the spectrum passionately opposes the assimilation it formerly supported; it now sees that assimilation as an unacceptable expression of cultural arrogance and ethnocentrism.

Assimilation was formerly the policy of the progressives. The Saskatchewan Co-operative Commonwealth Federation (CCF) under Tommy Douglas and Woodrow Lloyd, 1944–64, was a passionate advocate of assimilation well before the 1969 White Paper (Pitsula 1994). Some of this was a spillover from Afro-American pressure to join the mainstream in the United States, a perspective that saw American blacks seeking to 'get in' as anticipating what Canadian Indians would seek when their Martin Luther King belatedly emerged. Assimilation also drew sustenance from the belief that industrial civilization was the great leveller of cultural difference. Anthropologists took it for granted that assimilation was both the inevitable and desirable goal toward which we were heading. (Loram and McIlwraith 1943) Against such a powerful tendency, resistance was seen as futile. More generally, of course, assimilation had been the historic policy of the Canadian state since Canada was founded.

Support for assimilation has now drifted to the right end of the political spectrum. Preston Manning (Manning 1992), Stockwell Day – now succeeded by Stephen Harper – have replaced Tommy Douglas. Mel Smith (Smith 1995), Tom Flanagan (Flanagan 2000), and others now defend in a very different political-intellectual climate the ideas that attracted Trudeau and the team which produced the White Paper (Canada 1969). The tone of contemporary advocates of assimilation is, of necessity, different from the tone of its supporters of thirty to fifty years ago. Yesterday's advocates wrote and spoke with the easy authority that history was on their side. Contemporary advocates are not so sure. They frequently assert that they write against an unsympathetic climate of political correctness that challenges their right to speak. Other authors have noted the inhibitions which attend speaking out against what they detect as a political consensus behind the overall thrust toward recognition and implementation of the inherent right of self-government (Cairns 2000:14–16 for references).[1]

This is another example of the changing spirit of the times: forty years ago, in the Hawthorn report of the mid-sixties (Hawthorn 1966–67) and in the 1969 White Paper, treaties were considered of marginal importance. Trudeau, indeed, found it inconceivable that one section of society could have a treaty with another part of society, declaring that "we must all be equal under the laws and we must not sign treaties amongst ourselves" (Trudeau 1969). Now, the RCAP report informs the reader that treaties are the key, the fundamental instrument for regulating relationships between Aboriginal and non-Aboriginal peoples (Cairns 2000:134–36 for a discussion).

Observing the erosion of yesterday's conventional wisdom too easily leads to a complacent arrogance among the supporters of today's conventional wisdom, convinced that they have arrived at truth. A much better lesson would be a reminder that we, too, will be seen, in hindsight, as yesterday's conventional wisdom.

Some Characteristics of the Present Debate

The present dialogue or debate has the following characteristics. First, there is now a burgeoning literature. Any reasonably-sized bookstore currently stocks a sizeable collection of books under the rubric of Native studies. The media now devote considerable attention to Aboriginal issues. The *National Post*, which gives extensive coverage to Aboriginal issues, vigorously and recurrently attacks special status and espouses assimilation. Aboriginal issues are one of the staples of Jeffrey Simpson, the leading national affairs columnist for the *Globe and Mail* (Simpson 1998; 1999; 2000). Polar positions are now expressed in the national party system. The Reform and the Canadian Alliance analysis of the Aboriginal policy area closely mirror the assumptions behind the 1969 White Paper (Reform Party of Canada 1995; Cairns 2000:72).

Second, there are prominent Aboriginal participants in the public dialogue. They include the major national and provincial Aboriginal associations whose leaders are often skilled in getting media coverage. They conduct research and publish major position papers. They are joined by a small but growing cadre of Aboriginal scholars in law and other disciplines. Their work receives practical sustenance from Native studies departments, Native studies associations, and specialized journals of Native Studies. They have already made major contributions to our collective search for improved understanding. Their numbers and importance will increase with the dramatic increase in number of Aboriginal graduates of post-secondary institutions.

Third, there is now an extensive university-based community of scholars whose focus is Aboriginal issues. Research is not monolithic – contrast, for example, on the non-Aboriginal side the work of Jim Tully (Tully 1995) and Tom Flanagan (Flanagan 2000), or on the Aboriginal side John Borrows (Borrows 1999), Taiaiake Alfred (Alfred 1999), and Mary Ellen Turpel-Lafond who now sits on the bench of the Provincial Court of Saskatchewan (Turpel 1989–90).

Given the above welcome diversity, it remains true that the major contemporary academic contributions to the debate come from an influential cadre of university law professors, who have taken on the task of enlarging the constitutional space for Aboriginal self-government. Their goal is to provide a legal rationale for the maximum jurisdictional autonomy for the Aboriginal governments of the future. They are unquestionably the major academic contributors to public discourse. Their importance is magnified by the role of the courts in the evolution of Aboriginal rights. Their contributions are supplemented by political scientists, anthropologists, and historians. Each of these disciplines brings different strengths and weaknesses to Aboriginal studies and to Aboriginal policy.

The conclusion is irresistible that the dominant role of legal scholars in defining the issues at stake, in fleshing out a rights-based discourse, and in contributing to a leading role for the courts has contributed to Aboriginal gains. On the other hand, academic legal contributors in this policy area show little concern for Canadian citizenship as a uniting bond, or more generally, for what will hold us together, and show much less interest in the 50 per cent of the Aboriginal population in urban areas, whose concerns are less amenable to the language of rights.[2]

A Plea for Realism

It is perhaps inevitable that Canadians – be they Aboriginal and non-Aboriginal, citizens and scholars – disagree on where we should go.

We still hear the voices of assimilators and their antithesis – those who describe our future as coexisting solitudes maintaining a possibly friendly possibly cool distance from one another. There is another slightly different divide between advocates of a nation-to-nation relationship – competing solidarities who engage in a domestic version of international relations – and others who stress the necessity, at least at one level of our relationship, of a common citizenship as the contemporary source of the empathy that makes us feel responsible for each other. Each of these divides and the rhetoric that sustains them could easily consume the remainder of these pages. It would be a worthwhile task to explore the plausibilities, the exaggerations, the kernels of truth, and the simplifications that attend each side of the above divides. Each divide, in its own way, is at the very centre of our present search for understanding.

I have decided to focus on a different divide, or contrast, in the remaining pages – one which deserves more attention than it has received. This discussion will turn on two roads to the future: that of Aboriginal peoples in landed communities on the path to self-government and that of urban Aboriginals. The pressure and temptation when confronting two roads is to assume the necessity of choosing one, to set the two roads as rivals, to imply that those who have not chosen 'our' road can only have done so because of some false consciousness which clouds their reasoning, to suggest that the urban Aboriginal is somehow betraying Aboriginality by subjecting him/herself to the perils of cultural contagion that will eat away at Aboriginal difference that should be cherished and protected, or to intimate that the travellers on the self-government road overestimate the possibility of cultural renewal and economic viability for small nations distanced from urban centres.

I prefer not to take sides, but rather to try to think my way through both of these routes to the future, on the premise that there are advantages and disadvantages to each. To condemn one or the other I view as an unhelpful ideological position at this stage of our understanding and evolution.

Two Roads to the Future

We have more information and analysis now than ever before to inform our policy decisions. Formerly, non-Aboriginals dominated the policy discussions of Aboriginal issues. This was especially true for status Indians. By definition wards are, after all, objects of policy determined by paternal authorities, not participants in its making. For the last thirty years, in contrast, we have had a dialogue with extensive and growing Aboriginal participation. The scholarly community studying Aboriginal issues is now dramatically larger than even a quarter of a century ago. Non-Aboriginals still dominate the field, but scholarly contributions from Aboriginal academics are on the increase. Further, non-Aboriginal academics are aware that their scholarly authority no longer flows automatically from their skin colour. These are all positive developments. Nevertheless, I argue that our understanding is imperfect, that there are immense gaps in our knowledge, that ideology plays too prominent a role, and that the inevitable politicization of a field in which nationalism and the response to it is the dominant focus often gets in the way of realism.

Whether we speak of Aboriginal policy writ large to include Indians, Inuit, and Métis or focus only on the status Indian population – the largest of the constitutionally recognized "Aboriginal peoples" – the reality is that there are two roads to the future – the self-government road and the urban route. This is obvious from even a casual acquaintance with elementary demographic data – half of the Aboriginal people live in urban centres.[3]

Amazingly, the coexistence of these alternative futures, which should be thought of as complementary, is consistently, if not almost systematically, overlooked or deprecated by those who have cast their votes either for the nation-government route and who see urban life as a distraction or a threat, or by those who see self-government as slowing down the desirable migration to the job opportunities of the city. I argue for acceptance of the coexistence of these two roads to the future, coupled with the belief that each road merits the attention of policy-makers and analysts.

My reasons are elementary. Both roads exist and, as noted above, have about the same number of travellers. Of the status Indian population 42 per cent live off reserve, and 58 per cent live either on reserve (54 per cent) or on crown (4 per cent) land (1996 figures, Canada 1997b:xiv). When Métis and Inuit are included, about half of the Aboriginal population overall is urban. Generally speaking, these two roads lead to different goals. The self-government option, especially when it is practised with competence and integrity, can be a valuable instrument for cultural retention and renewal. The urban option, by its very nature, is more attuned to participation in non-Aboriginal society, with the resultant probability of higher income, less unemployment, and so on. Neither of these goals deserves to be deprecated as such – to be defined as unworthy, as representing an irrational choice. To opt for urban life is not an act of betrayal. To remain in an Aboriginal community, in part because that is where 'home' is, is not to opt for the past.

The fact that both routes exist and that they serve different purposes suggests that they should not be judged by the same criteria. Cultural survival and the modernization of tradition may be the appropriate and priority criteria for judging self-governing nations. Economic opportunities and higher incomes and other pursuits congenial to urban living are the appropriate criteria for assessing Aboriginal urban life. When the RCAP Report foresaw a future in which Aboriginal peoples would be proportionally represented in such prestigious professions as "doctors ... biotechnologists ... computer specialists ... professors, archaeologists and ... other careers" (Canada 1996, 3:501) it was not referring to options available in small rural nations. To compare small rural nations with urban settings in terms of their respective capacities to sustain such professions would be to cook the books in favour of urban life. Equally, however, to make cultural renewal the prime criterion for judging the relative merits of urban living and self-governing nations is to predetermine the outcome against the urban setting. Each road to the future should be judged in terms of criteria appropriate to its virtues. This does not mean that economic criteria are irrelevant to judging self-government, nor that cultural criteria have no place in judging the urban situation, but that their relative significance varies according to the setting.

Clarity is not helped by attaching scare words to one or the other route. 'Assimilation,' brandished as an aggressive description of the consequences of urban living – sometimes of course by its non-Aboriginal supporters – stigmatizes Aboriginals in the city. Assimilation implies losing oneself in someone else's culture. Further, since assimilation was the official, historical policy of the Canadian state, to be accused of having been assimilated suggests succumbing to a policy initially premised on the inferiority of Indian cultures. Of course, assimilation rhetoric often presupposes that an Aboriginal identity can only survive if it manifests itself in vastly different behaviours and beliefs from those of the non-Aboriginal majority. This is simply simplistic social psychology. Identity divergence and cultural convergence are obviously compatible. Is this not what has happened among the Québec Francophone majority? Culturally, convergence of values with Anglophone Canada is well advanced compared to half a century ago. On the other hand, a nationalist identity is unquestionably stronger. This, however, is not to suggest that identity loss never occurs, or to deny that after several generations of intermarriage in urban settings, individuals may retain only a sliver of Aboriginal culture and be happy with what and who they have become. To say that this could never happen is a form of blindness. To assert that it not be allowed to happen is to deny individual choice. However, my larger point remains – a modernizing, urban Aboriginality is perfectly compatible with the retention of a strong Aboriginal identity.

Equally unhelpful are scare words attached to the separate existence of Indian communities. In the assimilation era, reserves were pejoratively referred to as the Gulag Archipelago, as representative of apartheid, and as equivalent to displaced persons camps. More recently, given the drive to self-government, they have been criticized as making "race the constitutive factor of the political order" and as "based on a closed racial principle" (Flanagan 2000:194). These are all rhetorical devices to foreclose debate. Indian communities, unlike provincial communities, will be closed communities in the minimum sense of controlling their own membership. To describe them as "race based" (Gibson 2000), however, is not helpful, given the high rate of intermarriage. Further, at the present time, only about 5 per cent of Indian bands employ "blood quantum" criteria for membership and they were reproved by RCAP (Canada 1996, 2 (1):237–40).

The existence of two roads to the future constitutes the fundamental reality against which should be judged the adequacy of the distribution of attention, of research, and in general, of all attempts to throw light on where we are and might go. From nearly every perspective, the urban dimension of Aboriginality is relegated to secondary importance, when it is not completely ignored. The recurrent use of the colonial analogy contributes to the neglect of the urban situation. The language of nation fits poorly with urban Aboriginals; the possibilities for self-government are limited. Accordingly, since neither nation (as the actor to battle colonialism) nor significant powers of self-government (the purpose of the struggle) make as much sense in the urban setting, urban Aboriginals remain largely outside the purview of one of the most potent organizing labels in contemporary discourse. They are, therefore, naturally overlooked. The leading role of the academic legal community includes paying scant attention to the urban situation, which, in truth, does not lend itself as readily to analysis in terms of Aboriginal rights. Further, the urban setting lacks a compelling, simplifying focus equal to the appeal of nationalism and self-government as self-evident good causes for scholars to support. The urban scene presents a host of discrete practical problems that resist consolidation under a single rubric.

Indeed, when the heady language of nationalism, of treaties, of inherent rights to self-government, and of nation-to-nation relations casts its aura over one route to the future – self-government and cultural renewal – the second, urban route, which can easily be portrayed negatively in terms of youth gangs, Aboriginal ghettos in the urban core, language loss, and high rates of intermarriage, can be seen as an embarrassment. Indeed, it may even be seen as the road that obviously should not have been taken.

The nation and self-government focus of academics simply duplicates the historical operational bias of the federal department of Indian Affairs which, in administering the *Indian Act*, 1985, concentrated overwhelmingly on reserve-based Indian communities. The focus on Indian land-based communities is reinforced by the fact that the strongest and most visible national Aboriginal organization, the Assembly of First Nations (AFN), rests squarely on the Indian bands/nations, whose status is governed by the *Indian Act*, 1985. For nearly twenty years, the most visible Aboriginal leader has been the Grand Chief of the AFN.

The favourable bias toward Aboriginal (especially Indian) nations and their self-government is graphically underlined by the RCAP Report, that is dominated by the nation-to-nation theme, contrasted with what it portrays as a "rootless urban existence"(Canada 1996, 2 (2):1023). This negative judgment of the urban situation supports the focus on nation and on self-government as its servant for the task of cultural renewal. Alternatively, the nation preference, supported by a global ethnic revival and by a colonial analysis that sees self-government as the culmination of the anti-colonial struggle, requires a negative view of urban Aboriginal life, seen as getting in the way of the movement of history.

From these perspectives, urban Aboriginal life is distinctly unpromising. Urban Aboriginals come from too many diverse nations to coalesce into a sharing, self-governing group even if they had a coherent land base, which they do not. Further, urban Aboriginal life is, by definition, the setting for increased cultural contact leading both to cultural erosion and the diminishing use of native languages and traditional customs. From the cultural perspective, therefore, urban living is easily viewed as a threat, not as a promise, and those who choose it are seen by its critics as, in a sense, lost to the cause.

Further, especially in the major cities of western Canada, but not confined to them, the Aboriginal concentration in urban core areas has depressing ghetto characteristics. Crime, drug abuse, youth gangs, violence, and prostitution are widespread (LaPrairie 1995). Recent reports speak of normlessness; of a fractured social fabric; and "the emergence of Canada's first US-style slum" in Winnipeg, evident to even a "casual visitor," and becoming evident in "other Prairie cities" (Mendelson and Battle 1999:25; National Association of Friendship Centres and the Law Commission of Canada 1999:63-5).

In the absence of some countervailing evidence, the preceding passages would constitute an almost unanswerable condemnation of the urban route. There is, however, another side. The RCAP outlined numerous positive features of urban life. The employment situation is superior; incomes are markedly higher; urban Indian people have the highest life expectancy among Aboriginal peoples; various indicators of social breakdown are much higher for the on reserve compared to the non-reserve population (Cairns 2000: chap. 4). As well, preliminary findings of the Department of Indian Affairs Research and Analysis Directorate, based on 1991 data, reported a marked advantage for off-reserve status Indians in terms of life expectancy, educational attainment, and per capita income. Life expectancy was 4.6 years longer and per capita income 50 per cent higher (Beavon and Cooke 1998). Evelyn Peters reported "a significant urban Aboriginal population earning a good income" of $40,000 or more in 1990 (Peters 1994: 28 and Table 15).

These trends feed on the truly dramatic increase in the number of Aboriginal post-secondary graduates. In the late 1950s, there were only a handful of Indian university students. In 1969, there were fewer than 800 Aboriginal post-secondary graduates. Now, more than 150,000 Aboriginal people have completed or are in post-secondary education (Borrows 1999:75). There was an increase in the number of Inuit and Indian students enrolled in post-secondary institutions of nearly 750 per cent from the numbers in 1977–1978 to the more than 27,000 reported in 1999–2000 (Canada 1997a:36 and 2001:33).

This dramatic educational expansion, and the urbanization to which it will contribute, will almost certainly increase the out-marriage rate (see also Clatworthy and Smith 1992:36). In a recent study employing five-year data ending in December 1995, the overall out-marriage rate was 33 per cent, ranging from 22.8 per cent out-marriage on reserve to 57.4 per cent off-reserve. In general, the smaller the reserve population, the higher the out-marriage rate (Canada 1997b:21–3).

It is implausible to assume not only that this educational explosion can be contained but also that most graduates can have satisfying lives and find meaningful employment in small, self-governing nations with a weak private sector. This remains largely true even if, by a process of consolidation, the average population of self-governing nations is raised to the viable level of 5,000–7,000, as advocated by the RCAP.

Further, as John Borrows argues, Aboriginal peoples should seek to influence the overall structure of the larger society through vigorous participation. For Borrows, to think of Indianness, or more broadly Aboriginality, as restricted to self-governing, small national communities is to be condemned to a limited and partial existence. Borrows argues, in effect, that the expression of a modernizing Aboriginality should be diffused throughout society in politics, culture, the professions, and so on. He denies that Aboriginality is a fixed thing; he is obviously open to a selective incorporation of values and practices of non-Aboriginal society. As he says "Identity is constantly undergoing renegotiation. We are traditional, modern, and post-modern people" (Borrows 1999:77). Accordingly, the self-governing component of Aboriginal futures, while important, is by itself not enough. Neither, however, is the urban route.

Hundreds (sixty to eighty if RCAP hopes for consolidation are realized – more if they are not) of small, self-governing native communities will be scattered across the land, wielding jurisdictions proportionate to their capacity and desire. They are not about to disappear in any foreseeable future. Aboriginal and treaty rights "recognized and affirmed" in the *Constitution Act, 1982* s. 35(1), cannot be removed by anything short of a constitutional amendment, the pursuit of which would be an unthinkable act of constitutional aggression. The relocation of communities is not possible. Dispossession of lands and setting band members adrift is not a policy choice. A ruthless cutting of benefits to encourage exodus is neither humane nor an available option. Any expeditious attempt to wind down the existence of small, self-governing nations would arouse an opposition that could not be overcome in a democratic society. Such a policy cannot be implemented; even if it could, to do so would be undesirable. The result would be a rapid exodus to the city that would add many more individuals to the dark side of urban life and would exacerbate the developing Aboriginal urban crisis while adding few success stories.

If we eliminate the pipe dreams of assimilation advocates from the spectrum of available policies, we are left with about half the Aboriginal population living in small, self-governing communities: these communities are not going to go away. They are sustained not only by inertia and by the fact that they are home, but their survival is buttressed by Aboriginal and treaty rights. The powerful force of nationalism can be mobilized on their behalf. Although limited by small populations, the availability of self-government provides some leverage for Aboriginal peoples to shape the terms of interaction with the majority society.

Further, Canadians through their governments are now engaged in major efforts to respond to Indian land claims where Aboriginal title still exists – most visibly in British Columbia, but also in Québec and Atlantic Canada. Discussions are underway to enlarge the land and resource base of many First Nations. When the preceding efforts are coupled with various attempts to increase economic activity on Indian reserves, the continuing significance and presence of self-governing Aboriginal communities is one of the taken-for-granteds of the Canadian future.

Neither the self-government route nor the urban route is an easy road to an unblemished, positive future for Aboriginal peoples or for their relations with their non-Aboriginal neighbours. The urban route, as already indicated, holds out the disturbing possibility in several metropolitan centres of becoming a Canadian version of those American cities that have a black middle class coexisting with a black ghetto. The Canadian parallel of an urban Aboriginal middle class and an Aboriginal ghetto could undermine the civility and social stability of a number of Canada's major metropolitan centres.

There is no easy answer to this unhappy prospect. The present relative inattention to the chequered reality of urban Aboriginal life is, however, obviously damaging. Since it would be arrogant of me to make specific recommendations, that would almost inevitably be either obvious, platitudinous, or superficial, I will restrict myself to the observation that we have studies and a literature that is helpful. *Seen But Not Heard: Native People in the Inner City*, by LaPrairie, is an excellent analysis, replete with policy suggestions and references to the pertinent literature (LaPrairie 1994).

The route of self-governing nations, even if there were no more outstanding claims and if existing lands and resources were significantly supplemented, will not produce across-the-board successes – healthy, Aboriginal communities, functioning democratically, whose members have standards of living comparable with neighbouring non-Aboriginal communities. Most communities are small; many are isolated; and the politics of which are often dominated by kinship relations in circumstances where the public sector is large and the private sector weak. Conditions are therefore often not propitious for victories over poverty, anomie, and existing inequalities.

The RCAP Report launched a comprehensive package of proposals, too detailed to be listed here, to improve the quality of Aboriginal life in every major dimension. Achievement of these goals, the report argued, required an extensive reallocation of lands and resources, economic opportunity expenditures, major improvements in housing and community infrastructure, dramatically enhanced educational opportunities and attainments, including training 10,000 Aboriginal professionals in health and social services within ten years, and much more (Canada 1996, 5:213).

The RCAP Report proposed a massive increase in annual public spending, rising to an additional $1.5 to $2 billion in year five, to be sustained over a number of years (Canada 1996, 5:56). Elsewhere the report wrote of an investment of up two billion a year for twenty years (Canada 1996, 5:60). This was defined as a "good investment for all Canadians" (Canada 1996, 5:55), as after fifteen to twenty years the positive benefits of these expenditures would generate a net gain, that would benefit both Aboriginal people and other Canadians and their governments (Canada 1996, 5:57). This cost-benefit analysis is surely at best somewhere between an educated guess and a leap of faith. Even assuming the translation of RCAP proposals into government policy, many Aboriginal nations will remain impoverished, welfare dependent, and anomic.

Canada does not have a clean slate. The legacy of history cannot be wished away. The present distribution of Aboriginal peoples in towns, cities, reserves, in Nunavut, and elsewhere is not going to be transformed by depopulating the reserves, or Nunavut, or Métis settlements in Alberta by a massive migration to urban settings. But it is equally the case that the urban Aboriginal presence is not a passing phase to be repudiated by a massive return to various homelands. Many Aboriginals in the city have no homelands or, if they do, have no desire to return. Both these realities will confront Canadians in any middle range future we care to visualize. There will always be movements of individuals back and forth for a multitude of reasons. Where self-government successes occur, those nations may receive a net inflow, if the would-be returnees are welcomed (Canada 1997b:5). Conversely, if positive urban Aboriginal role models become more frequent, urban life may become more of a beacon – seen as a plausible choice to make.

The coexistence of alternative futures should be viewed positively. Since the two routes do not have the same advantages – cultural renewal may be more likely in self-governing contexts and economic gains for individuals more predictable in urban settings – each route acts as a check against the other. They are complementary rivals, especially for those who have homelands to which they can return.

In these circumstances, the task of the state is to encourage both successful adaptation of individuals to urban life and community success stories in self-governing nations.

Policy for the Future

Sound future policy requires an evolving understanding of what is developing in two different contexts. A series of natural experiments is unfolding at this very moment. There are hundreds of nation-renewing experiments already, or soon to be, underway. What works and what does not, and why? Multiple experiments are underway in urban settings too, and their significance will surely deepen and more innovations will occur as more urban governments and politicians are seized of the complexities, the dangers, and the possibilities created by the urban Aboriginal population.

If, by constant monitoring, we were made aware of what works and what does not, we could facilitate the diffusion of successful practices among both Aboriginal and non-Aboriginal governments. Achievement of this goal will require independent monitoring bodies to examine and report on both roads to the future. Similar proposals have surfaced in previous inquiries. The Hawthorn Report of 1966–67 proposed an Indian Progress Agency with the task of "preparing an annual progress report on the condition of the Indian people of

Canada" to include, *inter alia*, educational, legal, economic, and social data and analysis (Hawthorn 1966, 1:402–3). The purpose was to improve the quality of policy-making and public discussion and hence, in general, to act as a constant reminder of what remains to be done.

Thirty years later, the RCAP proposed an independent Aboriginal Peoples Review Commission headed by an Aboriginal chief commissioner, with most of the other commissioners and staff also to be Aboriginal. The Commission's task would be to monitor and report annually on progress being made "to honour and implement existing treaties ... in achieving self-government and providing an adequate lands and resource base for Aboriginal peoples ... in improving the social and economic well-being of Aboriginal people; and ... in honouring governments' commitments and implementing" RCAP recommendations (Canada 1996, 5:19–20). The Commission's focus would be broad. It would include "the activities of provincial and territorial governments within its review" (Canada 1996, 5:19). The essential task would be to act as a watchdog to see that non-Aboriginal governments do not slacken in their endeavours. Judging the performance of Aboriginal governments does not appear as part of its mandate, however, though some monitoring might indirectly be undertaken by RCAP's proposed Aboriginal Government Transition Centre, which would be assigned various tasks to facilitate successful transitions to self-government (Canada 1996, 5:167–69). The Transition Centre would presumably have only minimal, if any, interest in Aboriginal peoples in urban settings.

The proposal offered here is more complex than that proposed in either Hawthorn or the RCAP. The recommendation is for two monitoring agencies. Implicitly they would be providing annual material to facilitate the comparison between an urban route and a self-government route. Explicitly, they will provide ongoing commentary and analysis – in the one case on the probably hundreds of self-government experiments underway and in the other on the developing indicators of achievements and shortfalls in urban Aboriginal life.

Surely such an ongoing set of monitoring and analyzing reports would reduce the ideology that dominates contemporary discussion. How these agencies should be institutionalized and how their analyses should be disseminated to have maximum effect would have to be worked out. The proposal may seem threatening, even paternalistic, especially to self-governing nations. Relatively soon, and possibly even immediately, however, the staffs of these agencies will have Aboriginal majorities. This is not the time for specifics, but rather for throwing out an idea for public discussion. Those who resist the proposal should suggest alternative means by which we can profitably learn from the fact that we are in the early stages of major policy experiments in areas where our ignorance is vast. To reduce that ignorance is to reduce the cost it imposes on Aboriginal peoples. Some will deny that these are experiments and thus there is nothing to learn, but such claims are not believable. Others might argue that if self-government is an inherent right, the manner of its exercise should be immune from public scrutiny. Such a claim will only survive if evidence of misgovernment is rare or sporadic, which is implausible given the number of small nations potentially involved and the immense problems and temptations they will encounter.

Both routes – the self-government and the urban – place the Aboriginal future directly within Canada. Even the largest unit of self-government, Nunavut, is clearly fully within Canada and deeply dependent on external funding. This will be overwhelmingly true for First Nations. They cannot realistically isolate themselves from the provincial, territorial, and Canadian contexts in which they live. Only 5 per cent of Indian bands – 30 out of 623 – have on reserve populations of more than 2,000; 405 of 623 bands have on reserve populations of less than 500. There are 111 bands with on reserve populations of less than one hundred (Indian and Northern Affairs Canada 1997:xvi). The RCAP reports that a "disproportionate number of Aboriginal people live in small, remote, and northern communities" (Canada 1996, 5:39). The RCAP recognized that the jurisdictions they are capable of wielding are severely limited, so the commissioners recommended aggregating bands to produce an average size of 5,000 to 7,000 for the sixty to eighty nations they hoped would emerge. These are still small populations, with a limited capacity to deliver services. Their populations, therefore, will be heavily dependent on federal and provincial governments for many services; the services they will receive from their own governments can only be provided if their governments are recipients of large infusions of outside monies. This double dependence makes it imperative that individual members of self-governing nations be thought of as full Canadian citizens in the psychological and sociological sense of the term. It is for this reason that the Hawthorn Report of the mid-1960s coined the phrase "Citizens plus" as an appropriate description of the place of Indian peoples in

Canadian society. (Inuit and Métis were outside Hawthorn's terms of reference.) If Aboriginal individuals and the communities where they live are seen as strangers proclaiming "we are not you," the danger arises that the majority will agree that "they are not us." We must constantly work towards a common citizenship to support the "we" group that sustains our responsibility for each other. This will provide the secure basis for pursuing the "plus" dimension of Aboriginal Canadians.

Recognition as members of the Canadian community of citizens is equally necessary for Aboriginals in the city. Intermingled with non-Aboriginal neighbours, with at best only limited self-government possibilities, their links to municipal, provincial, and the federal government will be crucial to their quality of life.

In both cases, therefore, it is essential that Aboriginal people be thought of as fellow citizens. In contemporary, democratic Western societies, citizenship provides the bonds of solidarity. Empathy weakens when citizenship erodes. At a certain point in the erosion, we see each other as strangers, owing little to each other.

If this thesis is accepted, one responsibility of our governors and of the major Aboriginal organizations will be to work constantly for a reconciliation between Aboriginal nationalism and Canadian citizenship. This is also an appropriate, indeed urgent, responsibility for scholars who wish to influence the course of events. The RCAP, the most elaborate inquiry into indigenous peoples and their relation to the majority society ever undertaken, failed in this task. The idea and reality of Aboriginal nations and nationalism crowded out that of Canadian citizenship. Discussion of the former was fulsome, passionate, and repeated. Discussion of the latter – mention is perhaps more accurate – was infrequent and typically lukewarm, except when claims for equality apropos the receipt of services were made. Thus, the shared rule dimension of Canadian federalism – participation in the Canadian practice of self-government via elections and Parliament – was little more than an afterthought. Access of Aboriginal governments to section 36 equalization payments did not receive the standard justification that it is a response to our common shared citizenship; instead it was justified on the weak claim that we share an economy.

In other words, the RCAP, the most exhaustive inquiry ever undertaken of Aboriginal and non-Aboriginal relations in Canada, failed to ask the elementary question "What will hold us together?"

and thus the RCAP failed to answer it. This is a mistake that should not be repeated.

Conclusion

Realism suggests the following:

- There are two roads to the future: the nation or self-government road and the urban route; both require the attention of policy-makers.

- Both roads can be thought of as natural experiments that need to be carefully monitored so we can learn from success and avoid the needless repetition of policy errors. Accordingly, two monitoring, analyzing, reporting agencies should be established to reduce the number of gaps in our knowledge.

- Both roads are clearly within Canada. Canada is not just a box or container, but a political community bound together by a solidarity based on citizenship. Aboriginal peoples must be part of, not outside, that community. A nation-to-nation description of who we are is insufficient. Aboriginal nationhood and Canadian citizenship should not be seen as rivals, but as complementary patterns of belonging to a complex political order. If we recognize only our diversities, "we" will become an uncaring aggregation of solitudes.

Notes

1. The politicization of this policy area generates unusually polemical scholarly debates, as well as exchanges between authors and reviewers that threaten civility.
2. An important research project remains to be undertaken to 1) identify the changing relation between Aboriginal peoples and those who study them, and 2) assess the shifting relative influence of various disciplines. The hegemony of law is less than a quarter of a century old. Such a study should also track the emergent, growing role of indigenous scholars in the major disciplines. In doing so, it should also note their

distribution among the three categories of Aboriginal people – Indian, Inuit, and Métis.

3. As always, there are exceptions to a simple contrast between self-governing nations and urban life, where nation has limited salience. There are urban reserves and urban nations. Further, some, albeit limited options for self-government can be made available to urban Aboriginals. Nevertheless, the contrast between self-government for Aboriginal nations and an urban existence is sufficiently real to focus discussion around these two alternative visions of the future.

4. Aboriginal students in post-secondary programs are much more likely than other Canadians to select trade and non-university programmes than university programs – 76 per cent to 24 per cent for registered Indians; 70 per cent to 30 per cent for other Aboriginal students, compared to 58 per cent to 42 per cent for other Canadians (1991 figures) (Santiago 1997:14–16).

References

Alfred, T. 1999. *Peace, Power, Righteousness*. Don Mills: Oxford University Press.

Beavon, D. and M. Cooke. 1998. *Measuring the Well-Being of First Nation Peoples*. Mimeo, (October).

Borrows, J. 1999. "'Landed' Citizenship: Narratives of Aboriginal Political Participation." In *Citizenship, Diversity and Pluralism: Canadian and Comparative Perspectives*, ed. Alan C. Cairns, et al. Montréal and Kingston: McGill-Queen's University Press.

Cairns, A.C. 2000. *Citizens Plus: Aboriginal Peoples and the Canadian State*. Vancouver: University of British Columbia Press.

Canada. 1969. *Statement of the Government of Canada on Indian Policy*. Presented to the First Session of the Twenty-eighth Parliament by the Honourable Jean Chrétien, Minister of Indian Affairs and Northern Development. Ottawa: Department of Indian Affairs and Northern Development.

_____. 1983. House of Commons. Special Committee on Indian Self-Government. "The Penner Report." *Minutes and Proceedings*, no. 40, 12 and 20 October.

_____. 1985, 1990, 1999. Department of Indian Affairs and Northern Development. *Schedule of Indian Bands, Reserves and Settlements including*

Membership and Population Location and Acreage in Hectares, 1 June 1985; December 1990; 22 January 1999. Ottawa.

_____. 1996. *Report of the Royal Commission on Aboriginal Peoples*. 5 vols. Ottawa: Canada Communication Group Publication.

_____. 1997a. Department of Indian Affairs and Northern Development. *Basic Departmental Data 1996*. Ottawa: Indian and Northern Affairs Canada.

_____. 1997b. Department of Indian Affairs and Northern Development. *Indian Register Population by Sex and Residence 1996*. Ottawa: Indian and Northern Affairs Canada.

_____. 1997c. Research and Analysis Directorate: Indian and Northern Affairs Canada. *Implications of First Nations Demography: Final Report, August*. Four Directions Consulting Group

_____. 2001. Department of Indian Affairs and Northern Development. *Basic Departmental Data 2000*. Ottawa: Indian and Northern Affairs Canada.

Clatworthy, S. and A.H. Smith. 1992. *Population Implications of the 1985 Amendments to the Indian Act: Final Report*. Perth, ON: Living Dimensions.

Flanagan, T. 2000. *First Nations? Second Thoughts*. Montréal and Kingston: McGill-Queen's University Press.

Gibson, G. 2000. "A Separate Political Class." *National Post*. 27 July.

Hawthorn, H.B. ed. 1966 and 1967. *A Survey of the Contemporary Indians of Canada*. 2 vols. Ottawa: Queen's Printer.

Indian Chiefs of Alberta. 1970. *Citizens Plus: A Presentation by the Indian Chiefs of Alberta to Right Honourable P.E. Trudeau, June 1970*. Edmonton: Indian Association of Alberta.

LaPrairie, C. 1994. *Seen But Not Heard: Native People in the Inner City*. Ottawa: Department of Justice Canada.

Loram, C.T. and T.F. McIlwraith, eds. 1943. *The North American Indian Today*. Toronto: University of Toronto Press.

Manning, P. 1992. *The New Canada*. Toronto: Macmillan.

Mendelson, M. and K. Battle. 1999. *Aboriginal People in Canada's Labour Market*. Ottawa: Caledon Institute of Social Policy.

Milloy, J.S. 1999. *"A National Crime:" The Canadian Government and the Residential School System, 1879 to 1986*. Winnipeg: University of Manitoba Press.

National Association of Friendship Centres and the Law Commission of Canada. 1999. *Urban Aboriginal Governance in Canada: Re-fashioning the Dialogue*. Ottawa.

Peters, E. 1994. *Demographics of Aboriginal People in Urban Areas in Relation to Self-Government: A Report Prepared for Policy and Strategic Direction,*

Department of Indian Affairs and Northern Development. Ottawa: Indian
    and Northern Affairs Canada.
Pitsula, J.M. 1994. "The Saskatchewan CCF Government and Treaty Indians,
    1944–64." *Canadian Historical Review* 75 (1) (March).
Reform Party of Canada. 1995. *Aboriginal Affairs Task Force Report.*
    15 September.
Santiago, M. 1997. Research and Analysis Directorate. *Post-Secondary
    Education and Labour Market Outcomes for Registered Indians.* Indian and
    Northern Affairs Canada.
Schwartz, B. 1986. *First Principles, Second Thoughts: Aboriginal Peoples,
    Constitutional Reform and Canadian Statecraft.* Montréal: Institute for
    Research on Public Policy.
Simpson, J. 1998. "Aboriginal Conundrum." *Globe and Mail.* 15 October.
_____. 1999. "Why Aboriginals Must Keep Running." *Globe and Mail.*
    24 June.
_____. 2000. "Crossing the Aboriginal Divide." *Globe and Mail.*
    20 September.
Smith, M.H. 1995. *Our Home or Native Land?* Victoria: Crown Western.
Trudeau, P.E. 1969. *Remarks on Indian, Aboriginal, and Treaty Rights.* Speech
    given in Vancouver, BC. 8 August.
Tully, J. 1995. *Strange Multiplicity: Constitutionalism in an Age of Diversity.*
    Cambridge, NY: Cambridge University Press.
Turpel, M.E. 1989–90. "Aboriginal Peoples and the Canadian Charter:
    Interpretive Monopolies, Cultural Differences." *Canadian Human Rights
    Yearbook* 6.
Weaver, S. 1990. "A New Paradigm in Canadian Indian Policy for the 1990s."
    Canadian Ethnic Studies 22 (3).

The Texture of Canadian Society
Le caractère de la société canadienne

Canadian Business:
'No, I'm from Canada'

W. Michael Wilson*

T HOUGH IT WAS TEMPTING – AND PROBABLY WOULD HAVE BEEN MORE entertaining – to do a parody of the recent very popular beer commercial, this essay will address Canadian distinctiveness in business. Having said that, however, there are a few business images to reflect upon:

- It is possible to establish a world class business based upon the snowmobile.
- Canadians were destined to lead in telecommunications because it was cold outside. Better to stay inside and talk on the phone.
- We had to do something with all the rocks, trees, and beavers.

Instead, because at a tender stage in my professional life I was counseled only to speak about those subjects of which I at least had a passing knowledge, I am going to talk about the exciting subject of the financial services industry and consider whether there is a distinct Canadian view of it. There are a few caveats I would like to make before beginning.

First, in regard to the use of terms such as 'Canadian' and 'American,' I am aware that, leaving aside matters of race and gender, there are differences between individuals from Québec, the East Coast, Alberta, and the West Coast and that the term 'Canadian' means more than simply the Torontonian view. I would also like to emphasize,

---

*   The views expressed are those of the author and should not be attributed, directly or indirectly, to his employer, Royal Bank of Canada, or any other organization.

though it may seem otherwise at times, that there are differences between people of Atlanta, New York, and Los Angeles. The use of 'American' is for ease of reference only.

I have had the good fortune to work for the last decade for two extremely large financial institutions. One is based in the United States, with Canadian operations that were sold a few years ago. The other one is based in Canada with U.S. operations and aspirations of expanding them. In the first case, I seemed to spend significant time explaining that things were different in Canada. Recently, I seem to have made the same effort to consider whether there are differences between Americans and Canadians.

This paper has its genesis in two short stories that I should like to relate. The first one has to do with the negotiation of a potential joint venture with a South American businessman. He strongly preferred working with us because, as he put it, "Canadians actually listen." The second story concerns a friend who had been sent to Europe to run a somewhat mediocre operation. This friend had been successful in improving the business over a two-year period, or as he put it, "two years less a day," and was looking forward to his return to Canada, notwithstanding the vastly different business culture that he had learned to function within. When he explained to his successor that the culture was different and would require adjustments, his successor, who happened to be from the U.S., explained that my friend would not have to worry because he would – as he put it – "whip these people into shape."

What I have learned, though it is impossible to define, is that a distinct Canadian approach to business can be attributed, I will argue, to the role of government regulation in business and the need to preserve distinctiveness in the face of globalization. The subject of financial services reform over the last five years provides an unusual opportunity to compare American and Canadian approaches to similar issues. The United States government passed in late 1999 the *Gramm-Leach-Bliley Act* on financial privacy and pretexting, also referred to as the *Financial Services Modernization Act*. This legislation repealed the *Glass-Steagall Act*, which had been in place since the 1930s and had significantly restricted and compartmentalized financial services in the United States. The new legislation removed almost all barriers contained in the old legislation. In Canada, after adopting a new regulatory framework in 1992, reviewing two proposed bank mergers, and holding several inquiries into the state of the Canadian financial services industry, the Canadian federal government released, in 1999, the White Paper entitled *Reforming Canada's Financial Services Sector – A Framework for the Future*, to serve as the basis for new legislation that is expected in the near future.

The two documents are noteworthy because they deal with several identical matters. For example, they both deal with ownership restrictions, regulatory approvals, and business powers. In the area of ownership restrictions, the Canadian White Paper would limit the ownership to 20 per cent of the voting equity. This would effectively preclude large institutions from either acquiring or merging with each other. The U.S. legislation contains no equivalent restrictions. Indeed, the U.S. legislation encourages ownership of virtually any 'financial' business, regardless of size, provided no anti-trust matters arise. In Canada, the approval process for mergers or investments or acquisitions of financial institutions are subject to the prior approval of the Minister of Finance and a long process of regulatory scrutiny involving public consultations, the Competition Bureau, and Office of the Superintendent of Financial Institutions [OSFI]. The regulatory process obliges the Minister to consider the public interest and, if appropriate, impose conditions on the proposed transaction. The U.S. legislation, on the other hand, effectively contains a deemed approval requirement. The Canadian proposals will preserve the long standing restrictions against banks selling insurance in bank branches or participating in the auto-leasing business. There are no similar restrictions under the *Gramm-Leach-Bliley Act*. There are of course many other components in the two regulatory schemes, but I suggest that the subjects I have noted are sufficient to make the point that the regimes are different.

The shape of the financial services industry that could emerge in the two countries has been, and will continue to be, a source of keen debate. The Canadian proposals are likely to perpetuate the status quo – that relatively large banks that compete in a relatively small, fragmented market will find it increasingly difficult to compete against much larger competitors. The market capitalization of Royal Bank is about two times larger than the largest non-bank financial institutions. On the other hand, the largest U.S. bank is eight times larger, by market capitalization, than Royal Bank. Under the U.S. legislation, further consolidation among financial institutions is likely, with the result that already large institutions will become larger and more efficient. If one is concerned about the competitiveness of Canadian institutions compared to international ones, these trends could be disturbing.

But the point here is not to speculate about the future of the financial services industry. Instead, the issues worth pursuing are both to recognize that the Canadian and American regulatory regimes are dramatically different and then to consider what these differences suggest about Canadian attitudes towards business.

According to the Canadian proposals, changes to the financial services sector were needed to:

- Enhance competition thus making the sector more vibrant;
- Empower consumers in order to provide an important discipline to competition and make the sector more responsible to their needs;
- Strengthen the relationship between financial institutions and the communities they serve in order to make the sector healthier;
- Increase flexibility so that the regulatory framework would more effectively balance the need for safety and soundness with the need to facilitate competition and innovation.

All these changes were driven by, among other things, technological and demographic changes.

When the *Gramm-Leach-Bliley Act* became law, a number of comments were made by various commentators and politicians:

- "This day we can celebrate as an American day."
- "Eliminating barriers to financial services competition will allow American companies to better compete in the global economy."
- "The Act will help the American financial services system play a leading role in propelling our economy into the 21st , continuing the longest peacetime economic expansion in our history."
- "When *Glass-Steagall* became law, it was believed that stability and growth came from government overriding the function of free markets."
- "We are here to repeal *Glass-Steagall* because we have learned government is not the answer. We have learned that freedom and competition are."
- "The world changes and Congress and the laws have to change with it."
- "Voters believe that reform is vital to America's ability to maintain its position as a financial superpower in the global markets."

The differences between the two approaches are apparent. For example:

a) In the area of competition:
   Canada – competition must be balanced against other needs of the community
   US – competition will benefit all stakeholders
b) In connection with consumers:
   Canada – consumers must be 'empowered' to foster competition.
   US – consumers will benefit from competition
c) The view of the market:
   Canada – community based
   US – global

The purpose for describing these differences is to show that the Canadian regulatory environment, at least in connection with financial services, has led Canadians to develop a particular skill set in business. As an aside, I concede that there may well be a 'chicken and egg' dimension with respect to the causal relationship.

In my experience, at least in financial services, to function in the Canadian market, several skills and strategies are required:

- a consultative approach to negotiations driven by the need to function in a regulatory environment characterized by discretion as opposed to explicit rules;
- a focus on business problem-solving;
- a broad approach to issues that reflects the need to address broader community concerns; and
- a view that business arrangements are an exercise in building something.

These skills emerge from the necessity of having to work in a small, relatively closed market that is heavily influenced by government intervention and economic trends emerging from outside the country. The extent of interdependence that arises from these relationships obliges business people to look at issues in a broad sense. It also limits the scope of initiatives for any individual organization in terms of solving a business problem.

Within Canada, at least in terms of financial services, these skills have led to the creation of a strong and vibrant financial services industry. And that is a critical element in the Canadian economy. The pressing question, then, is whether these skills will allow Canadians to continue to prosper in the context of globalization. For my purposes here, I can offer these thoughts. If globalization – if it is capable of definition – implies a free, open market, then this will be different from the Canadian experience. On the other hand, if globalization leads to a market of interdependent competitors, then the skill set that I described before will probably be useful. The larger issue is whether the Canadian economy can generate sufficient wealth, in a timely way, to retain talented business people.

"I Am Canadian!" From Beer Commercials to Medicare: In Search of Identity

Monique Bégin

W HEN PREPARING FOR THIS PRESENTATION, I MENTIONED THIS conference to Michael Marzolini, president of Pollara Inc., the biggest Canadian polling company, who immediately retorted that "Canada had a culture of envy while the Americans had a culture of greed." This took me aback, I admit. Although not the terms of my own view of ourselves in comparison to our neighbours to the south – how do we know who we are if not in comparison with the Other? – I suspect that this perception of Canadians has some truth to it. This, however, is a topic for another conference.

Today's Canadians, at least Canadians of older immigration stock – Scots, English, Irish – mentally compare themselves constantly with the United States. As Stephen Graubard wrote in his introduction to a *Daedalus* issue on Canada: "Canada, compelled to live cheek by jowl with a more populous society, itself supremely self-confident and more than occasionally aggressive, particularly in respect to its economic and cultural power, has never found the experience easy. No Canadian is ever able to ignore or forget the United States."[1] And the Americans do not help them – or do they? – in their search for identity with the *"Blame Canada!"* song that figured prominently at the 2000 Oscars ceremony! French Canadians, however, do not participate in that exercise as much. On the one hand, they are busy opposing 'the English' i.e. the rest of Canada; on the other hand, they rather like the Americans and do not feel threatened by them on any level.

But how do recent newcomers to Canada, first from Europe, then from Asia, South America, or Africa, think and act at that level? Do they adopt our legendary lack of national self-esteem or do they rather focus on the immense potential of global connectedness that their presence among us offers their new country? I would suspect the latter is closer to reality. When co-chairing the Ontario Royal Commission on Learning (1993–1995), I heard repeated demands from parents and ethnic cultural associations, but more importantly from high school students themselves, for the inclusion in the curriculum of international languages in addition to the standard English and French. Some were most interested in the cultural benefits of learning another language; they argued that learning another language and about the culture from which it springs helps students appreciate other people, here and in other countries. Others saw foreign language acquisition in terms of travel and personal enrichment. Still others emphasized the importance of knowing other languages in this era of global business. As a trading nation, being able to speak the language of our trading partners is an advantage, teenage students told us. Our rich variety of linguistic abilities resulting from the number and diversity of new immigrants can make the difference between a deal and no deal, they added, confident that the sky is the limit.

Actually, Canada is made up of three broad demographic groups: the 'French,' the 'English,' and the others – the 'ethnic' Canadians. Adding the Native people, the country is made up of four groups. Each of these groups, in turn, subdivides into two, three, or more categories. The French, for instance, meaning the Quebecers, now consist of the old stock of Francophone *Québecois pure laine*, as well as relatively recent Haitian immigrants, Asian Francophones, Jewish, Christian, and Muslim Francophones from North Africa and the Middle East, as well as more recent immigrants from all over the world who have to learn French to settle in *la belle province*. With them also lives a decreasing but still important group of Anglophones who are either these 'newly arrived future citizens' or descendants of earlier settlers. Outside Québec are the Acadians and the other Francophone minorities. Each of the other nine provinces and the three territories show distinctive regional characteristics in their social make-up, not just in their physical environment. The Aboriginals, seen by other Canadians as a clearly homogeneous entity, are – and have been kept – an even more fragmented population. According to the *Report of the Royal Commission on Aboriginal Peoples* (1992), they form forty-five linguistic-cultural groups in Canada, the Crees and the Ojibways being the largest.

Consequently, any attempt to find a common denominator among all Canadians in order to define the texture of our society is a very daring and risky proposal. The elusive concept of 'political culture' may help us best to capture some elements of what Canadians are all about, or think they are all about. The political culture consists of shared beliefs and values that inform our collective behaviour. This necessarily also includes the perceptions and images we have of ourselves, as well as the icons with which we identify.

Toward the end of the eighties, writing on this same topic of our identity for the above-mentioned issue of *Daedalus*, I identified two domains of public debate and two domains of public silence that distinguish us from the Americans and define us as different. The two great Canadian silences in public life were religion and big business, while two great debates were the status of women and issues of world peace and development.

Americans easily define themselves in terms of particular religious denominations and, as all the past primaries show, bring the issue upfront in their electoral campaigns; Canadians seem to recognize instinctively the potential divisiveness of religion in the public sphere. All public figures consent to a wise silence, despite a voice here and there expressing the moral values of the New Right. It is not always a serene silence, but rather a voluntarily imposed one. Not a tormented one either, but a silence that at times feels like talking. Yet – a silence. Some may argue that the mid-eighties' acrimonious debate in Ontario about full public funding of the Catholic school system disproves my thesis. This was probably not so much a case of open religious bigotry as an example of barely disguised resistance to the rights of Francophones. In my eight years in the federal Cabinet, religion was never discussed. Trudeau, who shaped Canadian public philosophy for some seventeen years, felt very strongly – as did his predecessors – that religion and politics, church and state, ought to be and be seen as, completely separate. Yet, contrary to the American Constitution, which provides for a clear separation between church and state, Trudeau did not seek to include such a provision in our 1982 renewed Constitution.

If big business is also a silence in our public life, except when we decry it, I think it is because we feel more comfortable thinking of ourselves as a nation of small entrepreneurs and family businesses. Canadians like to believe they are a hard-working people who may at times be daring in business ventures but who have nothing in common with the risk, abuse, and violence of big business. Peter C. Newman's *The Canadian Establishment* seems more appropriate as a coffee table art book of the rich and the famous than as the rigorous analysis of a

Canadian reality that it is. Maybe we are, as American social scientist Francis Fukuyama would say, a "low-trust society," a fertile ground for family businesses, but one that has difficulty adapting to successful globalization, compared to "high-trust societies" such as Japan, Germany, or the United States.[2] But this view of ourselves may be undergoing profound transformation with the mastery, by many more Canadians, of mutual funds and stock markets, the phenomenon of company mergers, and globalization.

That defining the status of women is a great Canadian debate should not surprise anyone. For a good thirty years now, Canada has shared with the Scandinavian countries the remarkable distinction of being among the few Western nations that have been officially discussing, and acting on, feminist issues at all levels of government. This does not mean that Canada is the ideal feminist environment even if the public debate does include women and women's issues. This debate is about reforms, not radical changes, and this marks the difference between Canada and the Nordic countries. Here, the debate must remain sensible, for only then do all people feel comfortable and reassured that social change will not take place at their expense. Modern feminism has truly been a social movement in Canada and has remained one at least in Québec, with the anti-poverty march of the Fédération des Femmes du Québec under Françoise David's leadership, that resulted in the Fall 2000 World March of Women. In 1982, the equality clause was enshrined in Section 28 of the Constitution and Charter of Rights. This makes our American neighbours envious, for its equivalent, the Equal Rights Amendment, was never passed as the 27th amendment to the US Constitution.

The other debate is one that takes place among the citizenry, one that many politicians and senior officials do not seem to see and hear, or are ashamed of: world peace and development. As Margaret Catley-Carlson, former president of the Canadian International Development Agency (CIDA) put it: "Whatever our motivation – religious, humanitarian, ethical, idealistic – it is powerful. It is the bedrock of public support for an official aid program ... the level of public support [for aid and development over the decades] has stayed high in Canada, in the 70 to 85 percent range." And, referring to a 1987 survey, she added that "nine out of ten [Canadians] wanted Canada to be among the more generous donors or a world leader in development assistance."[3] We have no reason to doubt that this sentiment has changed, even if many Canadians are sceptical about whether development and aid actually work. In the same way that Canadians think of themselves as egalitarian at home, they feel comfortable with a foreign policy based on an equal partnership among all nations and have never had any expansionist desires. Being the northern neighbour of the wealthiest and only superpower, they are very much aware of the interdependence of nations. Even if their once strong support of American foreign policy has slipped seriously over the last decade, they remain loyal partners, while their officials try to impress Canadian viewpoints and nuances on their Washington counterparts, not always with success. Three topics particularly interest them: famine and poverty; the plight of refugees; and peace and security, including denuclearization of the world. It is as if the national conversation on these issues progresses along an informal network that covers the country. But it is not a national debate, for official Canada wants to dissociate itself from these 'soft' issues so close to the population.

These Canadian 'silences' and 'debates,' although controversial, like so many reflections published about ourselves in comparison to our neighbours to the South – for example, Staines's edition of *The Forty-Ninth and Other Parallels*, or Malcolm's *The Canadians* – do not seem to meet once and for all our unending quest for identity.[4] No discussion of what kind of a society we are can avoid speaking to who we are.

And discussing who we are in the year 2000 cannot be done without mentioning the stupefying phenomenon of current TV commercials that choose to do just that: selling goods by asserting, not their products, but who we are, and who we are in relation to the Americans. Canadians will remember the Molson beer ads and the mythical "Joe Canadian."

> Hey, I'm not a lumberjack or a fur trader.
> I don't live in an igloo, or eat blubber or own a dog sled,
> And I don't know Jimmy, Sally or Suzie from Canada, although I'm
> certain they're really, really nice.
> I have a prime minister, not a president.
> I speak English and French, not American, and I pronounce it
> 'about' not 'a boot'.
> I can proudly sew my country's flag on my backpack.
> I believe in peace keeping not policing, diversity not assimilation,
> and that the beaver is a truly proud and noble animal.
> A toque is a hat, a chesterfield is a couch and it is pronounced 'zed',
> not 'zee' – 'zed'.

Canada is the second-largest land mass, the first nation of hockey,
and the best part of North America.
My name is Joe and I am Canadian.
Thank you.[5]

But another TV commercial also ran concurrently that I saw repeatedly
on the CBC – this time promoting Purex Advanced, a detergent. It
stated that "We, Canadians, we work more [implied: than the
Americans], play more, sweat more and eat more, and our clothes
show it," hence the need for a super powerful detergent. Another ad,
appealing to nationalistic gut feelings, had Burger King saying: "And
we have it your way, Canada!"

CBOT (CBC-TV) *Newsday* had a special interview with the creator
of the Molson ad, during which he confirmed it as an unprecedented
success. Everyone wants to use the ad. We know he is not bragging.
Conservative leader Joe Clark paraphrased it at his party's national
convention in Québec City. Heritage Minister Sheila Copps showed it
in Boston at an official conference. I was at Canada House in London
when our High Commission received a video copy of the ad and
enthusiastically announced that it will be used in their future presentations promoting Canada. We watch it, ranted by the actor, in live
performances at theatres and hockey games. *The Ottawa Citizen* of
19 April 2000, in its coverage of the Stanley Cup playoffs, reported
that: "After his live recitation before 18,500 fans at the Corel Centre
Monday night [April 17], actor Jeff Douglas, 28, was rewarded with a
standing ovation. The same has happened in arenas from Toronto to
Vancouver." And it seems that there is now a website for "The Rant."

The commercial was written by thirty-five-year-old Glen Hunt of
the Bensimon Byrne D'Arcy agency in Toronto. When interviewed, he
referred to several street interviews of young people, aged nineteen to
twenty-five, during which he had elicited their feelings about a number of topics, including their views about Canada. "It was really like a
boiling volcano waiting to boil up and erupt," he said, adding that he
composed the 136 words in about fifteen minutes – with some polish-
ing afterwards – for they were things he'd always wanted to say.

The sociologist in me noted the cultural phenomenon, but I will let
the audience draw its own conclusions. Three commercial ads at the
same time – and there may be more – exploiting crude nationalism
'against' the Americans means that market studies have told the
advertising business that it sells. There may be a more profound mean-

ing to it but I do not think so. "The Rant" (Joe Canadian) should be taken at face value: a collective shout, no more, aimed at people who do not hear us. More interesting are the recent focus groups conducted by Environics Research Group for the Bank of Canada that sought to identify a popular consensus on Canadian icons for our new currency bank notes. Well, the only icon that met with some degree of agreement was ... the Famous Five, the women who obtained from the British Privy Council the judgment that women were "persons"! So we have a problem; we define ourselves by the negative and when the time comes for positive identification of who we are, we do not easily recognize heroes and we are weary of icons.

Let us move from images of ourselves to common values to see if we can find more agreement there. Medicare, our universal health care system, would appear to meet the test. The most loved government programme over the decades, all Canadians, including Québecers, are quite proud of it, even when they worry about its future as they do right now. Only thirty years old, Medicare has become deeply entrenched in the Canadian identity.[6] But we are not talking here of the quality or range of medical care, the way we train our nurses, how our hospitals are organized, or who pays what to whom and how. What interests us in a discussion of the texture of our society is the collective belief that our health care system makes us different than others, especially the Americans, by virtue of some intrinsic moral superiority that we attach to our Medicare. As a piece of legislation, the *Canada Health Act*, 1984, which spells out the five basic conditions or principles of the system, has now reached icon status – so loaded with emotions that it is impossible for any politician to risk reopening the Act, even to improve it.

Public figures like to repeat that while Americans consider health care as a market commodity, we, Canadians, are proud to see it as a public good, "a common citizenship right – something that all Canadians will need at some point in their lives, and something which is available to them because they share a Canadian identity." [7] In the words of health economist Bob Evans, "the Canadian health care system, precisely because it *is* different, responds to and reflects significant, if perhaps subtle, features of 'Canadianness.' It is one of the most convincing forms of evidence, perhaps *the* most convincing, that we are not Americans after all. ... At the most basic level, the public funding system embodies a view of the relationship between the individual and the environment. Nature is, at best, rather hostile and difficult to control. With no regard for virtue or vice, illness or injury can strike anyone. There is no moral reason why the victim should be exposed to financial insult on top of physical injury. Health care in Canada is free, because to charge the patient is to tax the sick." [8]

Health care systems are the product of specific historical and socio-economic circumstances; they evolve, rooted in each country's political culture, in its value system. In that sense, health care systems are not easily exportable. As far back as post-World War I, we can document historically why and how the Canadian health care system developed as a universal and comprehensive programme, and why and how the American initiatives to that effect failed miserably, ending up in two restricted and targeted programmes – Medicaid and Medicare. We can show how European immigrants of a socialist tradition influenced Canadian political parties and politics, while the same immigration remained a marginal factor in American politics – a Milwaukee, Wisconsin, local political culture. We can explain how the Canadian parliamentary system makes it easier to pass government legislation in the House of Commons than does the American presidential system in Congress and Senate. It is harder, however, to explain how an ethic of shared responsibility comes about. As Bob Rae, one of the rare public figures to speak about values these days, says in his discussion of Rabbi Hillel's three questions: "Social democracy is about reciprocal rights and responsibilities. It is about what we owe each other. ... The extension of public, tax-based support for health care and education are rightly seen as the bedrock of modern solidarity. ... Public health insurance is a key expression of the principle of solidarity."[9]

Some will argue, rightly so, that the principle of solidarity and the value of sharing do not appear to be very high on the public agenda these days. For twenty years in the United States, fifteen in Canada, excessive individualism and self-fulfilment – 'me-ism' – has been the rule. The Reagan administration, rooted in neo-conservative economics and the supremacy of the market, preached public budget reductions, tax cuts, deregulation, and general economic renewal through less government, to the detriment of any other public agenda. This ideology swept across North America and, in general, the Western world. Questions of fairness and equity were no longer heard. The "blame the victim" doctrine freed individuals from any collective responsibility. If I succeed, and if my neighbour, separately, also succeeds, there will of necessity be a "trickle down" effect for those at the bottom, the theory goes. Galbraith, talking to America of its political complacency, ridiculed the situation, saying that "Americans were being rewarded as they so richly deserved. If some did not participate, it was because of their inability or by their choice '... [Reagan's] appeal was widespread; it allowed Americans to escape their consciences and their social concerns and thus to feel a glow of self-approval." [10] Ten years earlier, the sociologist Etzioni pleaded with fellow Americans for the need for renewed "mutuality" on the eve of the new millennium – for an enhanced commitment to others and to shared concerns.[11] How different from the Americans are we really?

Notes

1. S.R. Graubard, ed., *In Search of Canada* (New Brunswick, USA and London, UK: Transaction Publishers. Originally published as a special issue of *Daedalus* (Fall 1988), by the American Academy of Arts and Sciences, 1989): vii.
2. F. Fukuyama, *Trust: The Social Virtues and the Creation of Prosperity* (New York: Free Press, 1995).
3. M. Catley-Carlson, "Aid: A Canadian Vocation," *Daedalus* 17 (4) (Fall 1988): 322.
4. D. Staines, ed., *The Forty-ninth and Other Parallels* (Amherst: University of Massachusetts, 1986); A. Malcolm, *The Canadians* (Markham: Fitzhenry & Whiteside, 1985).
5. Used with permission of Molson Canada. ©2000 Molson Canada.
6. As a complete programme including both the coverage for hospital stays and doctors visits.
7. L. Osberg, *The Equity, Efficiency and Symbolism of National Standards in an Era of Provincialism* (Toronto: Caledon Institute of Social Policy, 1996): 5.
8. R.G. Evans, "We'll Take Care of It for You: Health Care in the Canadian Community," *Daedalus* 17 (4) (Fall 1998): 157, 163.
9. R. (Bob) Rae, *The Three Questions: Prosperity and the Public Good* (Toronto: Penguin Books, 1998): 101, 111, 112.
10. J.K. Galbraith, *The Culture of Contentment* (Boston, New York, London: Houghton, Mifflin 1992): 28.
11. A. Etzioni, *An Immodest Agenda: Rebuilding America Before the 21st Century* (New York: McGraw-Hill, 1983).

The Multicultural Wheel: The Texture of Canadian Society and Literature in the Twenty-first Century

Maya Dutt*

M ULTICULTURAL QUESTIONS HAVE PERVADED ART, LITERATURE, and sociopolitical and economic studies for several decades now. The questions reflect the wide spectrum of concerns central to any discussion of multiculturalism. They critically examine problematic areas like canonization of specific cultures, affirmation of a mainstream 'we' as distinct from a marginal 'other,' and foregrounding of ethnicity and literary response. They point out, curiously enough, that dual currents coexist – a community consciousness and an ethnic awareness together with a desire for a supra-ethnic national identity which will forge national consciousness.

Canada has a rich and varied multicultural population profile. Ethnically heterogeneous, it has about 36 per cent white British Canadians, 32 per cent French Canadians, 2 per cent Natives; the remainder made up of diverse ethnic origins such as Asian, African, European, and Jewish. Immigrants from all parts of the world have contributed to its demographic evolution. Whereas at the turn of the twentieth century the influx of immigrants came from Europe and Eastern Russia, during the last thirty years, the major source of immigrants to Canada has been from the Asia-Pacific region. This ethnic diversity shows all signs of broadening still further in the twenty-first century. The evolving global, demographic, and economic trends seem to suggest that Canada's future immigrants will come from non-traditional countries in Asia, Africa, and Latin America (Canada 1985:668).

*   The research on which this article is based was funded with the assistance of the government of Canada through the Canadian Studies Programme of the Shastri Indo-Canadian Institute (SICI). Neither the government of Canada nor SICI necessarily endorses the views expressed herein.

Many programs have been initiated to create an awareness of multiculturalism in Canada. The multicultural policy of 1971 as well as programs implemented to date, however, do not seem to have met the needs of the minority. "To a large extent multiculturalism has been treated as a folkloric extravaganza, a social handicap and a political football" (Passaris 1989:3). Many works of literature reflect the cultural and political bitterness of immigrant communities. As Passaris affirms, "it would seem that the federal government's original policy has run its course and is no longer an adequate foundation for visionary and creative programs and initiatives that will pave the way for a vibrant, dynamic and harmonious Canadian society by the turn of the century" (1989:3). A new approach needs to be devised that will ensure and guarantee the full and equal co-operation of all Canadians in the various spheres of nation building. The 1987 bill entitled *An Act for the Preservation and Enhancement of Multiculturalism in Canada* has laid a legislative foundation for a new vision of multiculturalism. This bill may well become the springboard for a positive and creative multiculturalism, where the priceless asset of multiracial human resources in Canada can be used to its full potential to evolve a great nation.

Literature reflects the times, and immigrant literary texts serve as major points of reference for the dual purpose of exploring and evaluating the different racial, cultural, religious, and value orientations that are in the process of evolving and merging with one another and with the mainstream culture. The texts are in fact authoritative cultural studies that "cut across diverse social and political interests and address many of the struggles within the current scene" (Grossberg et al. 1992:1-3). They are politically engaged since they question inequalities within power structures and seek to restructure relationships among dominant and subordinated cultures. They examine the entire range of a society's belief and institutions, the means of production of texts and other paraliterary questions such as publication, distribution, and marketing. Much of the immigrant and Native Canadian literatures produced in the recent past deals with multicultural issues that either posit unity in diversity or seek a merger of the various racial and cultural groups in Canada. The texts seem to suggest that both of these are myths where the core symbols are distance and difference. The literary construction of such myths can explain, justify, or even undermine an existing reality. Just as British colonizers justified their presence in the colonies on the basis of the myth of the racial inferiority of the colonized peoples, so runs a counter myth of a heroic past and a rich cultural heritage. It then becomes a celebration of difference rather than of unity.

Native and immigrant literary texts often seem to support the idea of a genuine aspiration to recognize and appreciate diversities, despite the differences among tens of thousands of Asians, Latin Americans, Mexicans, West Indians, not to mention the Native Canadians themselves. Newly empowered voices ask for their narratives to be heard. A few selected texts by some representative writers of both minority cultures are examined here with a view to prove that "the culture of the next century will put a premium on people's ability to deal productively with conflict and cultural differences," as Graff and Phelan observe, for "learning by controversy is sound training for citizenship in that future" (Graff and Phelan 1995:v). Works of fiction by writers such as M.G. Vassanji and Bharati Mukherjee are evaluated as examples of the South Asian diaspora in Canada, while selected works of the Native Canadian writers Jeannette Armstrong and Basil Johnston provide the basis for studying the cultural differences inherent in yet another cog in the Canadian multicultural wheel. These cogs, as their works reveal, are engaged in the process of learning to participate meaningfully in all the issues critically important to society, culture, and government. This empowerment of the so-called marginal groups – retaining rather than submerging their distinctive identities – effects itself through the utilization of language as strategy and weapon. The problematic of cultural difference is linguistically embedded in the texts produced by immigrant writers in their attempts to vocalize the anxiety provoked by the hybridization of lifestyle and of language itself. As Bhabha asks: "Where do you draw the line between languages? Between cultures? Between disciplines? Between peoples?" (1994:59). The immigrant as well as Native Canadian writers have chosen to give voice to their psychic, cultural, and territorial anguish in an alien language that they have made as much a part of themselves as their mother tongues.

The term 'South Asia' has acquired numerous imaginative identities for Europeans and others – in its various guises as the Subcontinent and its association with the isle of Serendip and the glories of the Raj. It has been both the cradle of Gandhism and a tourist's dream of uncountable riches and/or nightmares of teeming poverty. Although many Canadian writers have participated in this sort of conceptualization (from Sara Jeannette Duncan to Sharon Pollock), the literature written by the South Asians themselves has been less widely appreciated. At the outset, it must be admitted that an inherent weakness in the literature by South Asians in Canada is these authors' excessive concern with their countries of origin and not enough with Canada, their new land by adoption. Except for one slender novel, *No New Land*, the majority of Vassanji's novels are set in Tanzania, his country of origin, Rohinton Mistry's novels are set in India, and all except the latest of Michael Ondaatje's offerings are placed anywhere but in Canada. This leads to a certain degree of decontextualization or rather dual contextualization. An answer to this may perhaps be sought in the fact that so many South Asian Canadians are caught between two cultural worlds, and any understanding of their actions presupposes this type of dual contextualization. Immigrants carry with them the cultural baggage of old traditions, familiar forms of ritual practices, and aspects of culture such as dress, lifestyle, songs, stories, and folklore. Their immigration constrains their *ability* to live a tradition-based lifestyle, but not their overwhelming *need*. Encountering the challenges of the new traditions in their new homeland, they become part of the challenge merely by their presence in the environment. South Asian immigrants belong to different racial, cultural, religious, and value orientations and have found it difficult to adjust to the new and complex mix of peoples and cultures in their changed environment. This is obvious from the wide variety of South Asian Canadian writing that cannot be treated as one cohesive unit. The term "South Asian writing" includes more than it excludes. It implies not only immigrants who have come to Canada directly from Sri Lanka, India, Pakistan, or Bangladesh, but also those generations of Caribbeans and Africans whose roots can be traced to India. Many first-generation writers communicate the tensions of psyches that have been doubly displaced, portraying not only the physical and economic deprivations that drove them from their native lands, but also the hostility, racism, and neglect they had to face in their new homeland. There is evidence, among most South Asian Canadian writers, of a consistent pattern of dealing with the countries of origin in their earlier works, and then moving on to Canadian subjects and themes.

Vassanji's *No New Land* (1991) is an example of the writing of a South Asian Canadian writer taking on Canadian subjects in his work as he develops a greater affinity with his new homeland. Yet his latest work, *The Book of Secrets* (1994), goes back to his racial past, as did his earlier works, *The Gunny Sack* (1989) and *Uhuru Street* (1992). This evinces a felt need on the part of the immigrant writer to rediscover the shared communal/cultural past that will function as a frame of reference for the uprooted community to know who it is in relation to what it was and thereby acquire self-knowledge and self-pride. Vassanji, in his writings, endeavours to provide such a map for his people. So great was his urge to assume the role of transmitter and preserver of his cultural inheritance that he took to fiction writing as a full-time job. He says: "I write about my own people because we are a people without any sense of history and place ... We know the name of the place we stay, we know our immediate surroundings, but we tend to look towards a future – of a better future maybe. But where is our past? Where are our roots?" (Quoted in Gill.)

Salim Kala's quest for his roots, for his self, for the traces of his past in *The Gunny Sack* becomes writer Vassanji's quest as well. Where *The Gunny Sack* is an assertion of the historical presence of African Indians in Africa, *The Book of Secrets* is part generational history, part social chronicle, part detective story, a living tapestry joining the past to the present. Sandwiched between these novels is *No New Land* – a novel which Vassanji says he wrote "purely for fun" (Nasta 1991:21). *No New Land* illustrates the writer's continuing preoccupation to write his community into existence in Toronto; it centres on the lives of some of the Asians who emigrated from Dar-es-Salaam to Canada, and how they re-defined themselves in an alien land. He gives a voice and a being to his people who are silent and, by the same token, "absent from or invisible" in the dominant discourse in Canada. Vassanji re-presents Toronto with its superstores, high-rises, and CN Tower blinking a message that these Asian immigrants cannot decode. It is a Toronto seen through the eyes of an 'othered' Asian – a world of wonders and concealed booby-traps where every step is a mystery "fraught with belittling embarrassments, and people waiting to show you up" (*No New Land*:32). These Asians had left Africa – their home for several generations – and come to Canada "with a deep sense that they had to try to determine [their future], meet it part-way and wrest a respectable niche in this new society" (*No New Land*:43). To their dismay they find that the new society is not so eager to open its doors to them. Jobs are scarcer to come by than hen's teeth. Nurdin Lalani realizes that subtle racial prejudices work against him in the arena of job-hunting – "Canadian experience" being the trump card they always call:

> The first few rejected job applications he took in stride: a few disappointments only to enhance the sweetness of eventual success. But

the pattern persisted, and slowly in his mind the barest shadow became discernible, of impending despair, the merest possibility of a jobless vista ahead, but nonetheless frightening (*No New Land*:43-4).

This is Canada. The Lalanis uncover a new meaning of this oft-repeated phrase – one altogether different from that obtaining in white Canadian discourse. Vassanji's concern is to show how Asian immigrants adjust to the new reality. The past in which the immigrants are firmly rooted becomes a deadly quicksand in a changed environment. They have to come to terms with their past: not escape from it but acknowledge it in order to face the present reality and move toward the future. "Before, the past tried to fix you from a distance, and you looked away ... Now it was all over you. And with this past before you, all around you, you take on the future more evenly matched" (*No New Land*:207).

Jamal, as well as Fatima, shows the pragmatism that is essential for survival. Jamal emerges as the most vibrant of all the personages in the novel. There is no doubt that *No New Land* is more clearly identifiable as Canadian, dealing as it does with the harsh realities of the immigrants' experiences, and of the angst of the human spirit caught between two worlds. However, it is ironic that this novel, which is about exile, does not have the scope, grandeur, or significance of Vassanji's earlier works, such as *The Gunny Sack, Uhuru Street*, or *The Book of Secrets*, which seem to be works of exile. As another immigrant writer, A.H. Itwaru, claims, "To be in exile is considerably more than being in another country. It is to live with myself knowing my estrangement" (1989:202). *No New Land* is all about this sense of alienation experienced by a displaced community as its life intersects with the larger population. It is paradoxical that this more ostensibly Canadian work takes second place to *The Gunny Sack*. Texts such as *No New Land* fit more precisely into the debate about multiculturalism while not representing immigrant writing in Canada.

The most impressive novels of the South Asian fiction writers are set outside Canada, have nothing to do with "Canadian experience" or the Canadian landscape, and cause a Frank Davey to marginalize them by offering the excuse that they "contain few if any significations of Canada or of Canadian polity" (Davey 1993:97). Such an exclusion is paradoxical, considering the claim inherent in the title of Davey's book, *Post-national Arguments*, and the ideals enshrined in the *Canadian Multiculturalism Act*, 1985, that seek to dismantle the danger of any one group asserting its influence and hegemony over another. The bottom-line is that writers perceived as 'ethnic' are offered, at best, the promise of inclusion without assimilation in the much-publicized trope of the 'mosaic.' The divisiveness within the term 'South Asian' is itself too vast and entrenched, allowing the danger of not finding a common ground for discussion. The concepts of colour, ethnicity, and race cannot be subsumed within the comforting pieties of an inclusivist theorizing. The notions of pluralism and multiculturalism offer various options. While pluralism maintains that human beings should be viewed as unique persons, race being their least important attribute, multiculturalism holds that people should be seen first and foremost as representatives of their groups, race being crucial to the argument. Such simplifications cannot do justice to the cause of the immigrant writer in Canada. Although many have been published by leading publishers, they are not received in the same manner as white writers.

An immigrant woman writer perhaps is doubly marginalized as is evident from an examination of Bharati Mukherjee's work. Her writings tend to be treated as part of South Asian Canadiana despite her having changed her country of domicile – they deal with specifically Canadian experiences. Some satirize the federal Department of Citizenship and Immigration, some encapsulate the insularity of Indians in Canada, some reveal the abyss between the races despite good intentions. Mukherjee is a controversial writer in that she has managed to alienate the Indian audience while endearing herself to non-Indian readers and critics. Perhaps this is attributable to the "Indian-bashing" evident in such novels as *The Tiger's Daughter*, *Wife*, or *Jasmine*, which is a trivialization of the Khalistan issue interspersed with shallow delineations of stereotyped characters. However, her short stories, collected in *Darkness* (1985) as well as *The Middleman and Other Stories* (1988), draw on her immigrant experience in Canada. Perhaps one can detect shades of paranoia or a persecution complex when Mukherjee says:

> In the years that I spent in Canada – 1966 to 1980 – I discovered that the country is hostile to its citizens who had been born in hot, moist continents like Asia; that the country proudly boasts of its opposition to the whole concept of cultural assimilation ... in Canada I was frequently taken for a prostitute or a shoplifter, frequently assumed to be a domestic, praised by astonished auditors that I didn't have a "sing-song" accent. The society itself, or important elements in that

society, routinely made crippling assumptions about me, and about
my 'kind' (*Darkness*:2).

If a well-educated, even Westernized Asian, can be traumatized by such
experiences, one need not wonder about the shattering agony and growing insecurity experienced by others less fortunately circumstanced.

Many of the Indo-Canadian protagonists of Mukherjee's stories
are innocents abroad, lost souls in an alien environment, trapped by
forces they cannot hope to control. Their quest for love, friendship,
communion, security, and identity are systemically blocked by overt
as well as covert racism. Their transplantation on alien soil has generated ills that cannot be cursed by old-world mores. Mukherjee's
"uneasy stories about expatriation" in Canada (*Darkness*:1985:2-3) as
well as her more exuberant and confident stories about slow-but-sure
assimilation into the melting pot of the US – effactually underscore the
helplessness of the immigrant in the no-man's land between two cultures – the one they have left behind and the other they have yet to
gain. Mukherjee clothes the travails of her disenchanted characters in
the garb of self-conscious parody that assumes an ironical dimension:

> Like V.S. Naipaul ... I tried to explore state-of-the-art expatriation.
> Like Naipaul, I used a mordant and self-protective irony in describ-
> ing my character's pain. Irony promised both detachment from, and
> superiority over, those well-bred post-colonials much like myself,
> adrift in the new world, wondering if they would ever belong
> (*Darkness*:2).

The question to be pondered is whether old-world beliefs can offer
some measure of relief in the climate of "new-world reasonableness"
(*Darkness*:64). Learning by controversy is sound training for the citizen
of the future. Learning to participate meaningfully in all the issues pertinent to the new society's culture and government seems to be an
uphill task for the average immigrant. Yet it must be done. The two
distinctive cultures between which the immigrants and their progeny
find themselves need not necessarily be in conflict if one is seen as a
support to the other. No Asian can hope to ignore his roots – the 'visible' nature of his ethnicity disallows it. Old World tradition and
culture, like religion, are best seen in the nature of moral and spiritual
support. The writer's cultural-cum-spiritual contribution to the process of nation building takes shape in empowerment through

language, utilization of the word as strategy and weapon. As Cyril Dabydeen remarks, "The collective Canadian spirit is enhanced and enriched by the varied cultural streams and in the fusion of old and new traditions towards a vital celebration of the oneness of the evolving Canadian consciousness" (1987:10).

The situation in Canada is rendered more complex because of the presence of Native Canadian writing that is always about Canada, unlike South Asian Canadian writing which sometimes occupies a slightly different spatiotemporal region. There is no more a homogeneous identity to Native Canadian writing than there is to South Asian immigrant writing. The differences in culture and tradition, and even more so in language, are equally vast and apparently insurmountable. There are fundamental rifts between the Native peoples of Canada and those who colonized them centuries ago. An ongoing internal colonialism affects the multiple layers of their relations in Canada, including art and literature. The rifts are manifest in the inequality of economic, social, and cultural power between the two groups, rifts that can perhaps be traced to the ambivalent attitude toward Natives that has prevailed since the white man first set foot on Canadian soil. Native Canadians were long imprisoned within the twin stereotypical formulations of 'noble savage' and 'implacable foe.' Today, the image encountered is more often one of poor victims of circumstances beyond their control.

Contrary to expectations, Canada's Natives have not become extinct, although much of their religions, languages, and entire tribal cultures have been submerged in the attempt to 'civilize' them through Western education and the Christian religion. History has proved the falsehood of the doomed culture theory. Far from disappearing, Canada's Native population is now increasing at a faster rate than the general population. There is also a strong indication that an erstwhile oral tradition is emerging into a highly articulate and formal literature. "We have not faded into the earth like snow before the summer sun of 'progress' nor have we stagnated in some sort of retrograde time capsule. We have survived and will continue to survive because of, and in spite of, the changes," asserts Kateri Damm, Native Canadian critic and poet (Armstrong 1993:16).

Critics and writers like Maria Campbell and Lee Maracle strongly affirm that indigenous cultures and languages have survived because of Native peoples' strong links to the land, the 'Mother' despite the onslaught of Euro-Canadian culture on their resources and their lands.

Deep-seated resentment exists among many Native Canadian writers towards the paternalistic, colonial policies that were initiated supposedly to civilize and Christianize indigenous peoples, towards the residential schools and missionaries who conspired to remove the gynocratic influence from the spiritual, political, economic, and social realms of the indigenous peoples' lives. Nonetheless, these peoples' very numerous and distinct cultures have continued to be transmitted from one generation to another through language, song, dance, traditional economic practice, and governing structure. These specific indigenous ways continue to provide a spiritual, social, political, and economic context that distinguishes Native peoples from non-Native peoples and contributes to the formulation of self.

The issue of identity seems to affect all layers of existence of the indigenous peoples. In the past, their 'Nativeness' had so often been defined by others, and to such an extent, that at times their awareness and knowledge of themselves had been obliterated. A multiplicity of definitions – status, non-status, treaty, urban, on reserve, off-reserve, mixed bloods, enfranchised, and the like – has forced Native Canadian writers to reconsider some of the assumptions underpinning their own literature. During the past two decades – despite cynical and skeptical reactions from the domain of mainstream literature – more and more Native Canadians have found their voice and have recorded the multitude of problems that have affected them. Their common aim seems to be "to distinguish once and for all, right from wrong, truth from fiction – to set the record straight … Understanding themselves in this challenging social context is their task" (Petrone 1990:139). Many of these writers are already able to deal with the culture clash and their own identity, with perception, detachment, and control, moving beyond the worst excesses of emotion and diction that marred earlier protest literature.

One of the reasons why Native literature is so interesting is that while it enshrines very old traditions, as a literature it is very young, and so are most of its writers. These writers have learned to draw on their ancient traditions – renewing their bonds with a biospheric world where all manner of things participate in a dynamic cosmic relationship. Many of the recent works of literature incorporate the significance of ancient ceremonies and rituals, the special role of elders as wise counsellors and custodians of cultural and spiritual beliefs, the importance of community life, the bonding between the young and the elderly, the voice of vision and prophecy. This, then, is their answer to the deadening, strangling effects of a modern civilization that denies the societal instincts of man. The so-called mainstream culture has much to imbibe from these traditional influences, instead of relegating Native literature to the margins as a ghettoized literature and a historical curiosity. As Daniel David Moses comments: "My image of that mainstream is that it is pretty wide but it's spiritually shallow. I don't think we are worried about being 'subsumed.' If we become part of that mainstream, we're going to be the deep currents" (Moses and Goldie 1992:xiv).

If literature provides an avenue into the perceptions of reality by other people across cultures and generations, then it behoves non-Natives to stop and listen, to try to understand what it means to be Native. For Natives have access to cultural traditions that have enabled them to survive under extreme conditions; they have ways of perceiving and dealing with life and literature that derive from an ecosystemic, non-anthropomorphic perspective on the world which we are all in dire need of.

If Jeannette Armstrong has dealt with the brutal themes of colonialism, cultural and physical deprivation, and racial genocide, she has ameliorated these by attempting to find a way out through spiritual reaffirmation and active political struggle. The protagonist of *Slash* realizes that he has to rebuild the life of his people:

> I had to find out what things were left of the old ways in my own Tribe and make it usable in our modern Indian lives ... Like our language. We couldn't preserve it by having a linguist come and record it ... We could only preserve it by using it. It was the same with our values and our rights (*Slash*:210-11).

Issues of assimilation and integration have continued to remain problematic for Native Canadians, as much as for the South Asian immigrants. A fresh answer to the question, "What does it mean to be Canadian?" has to be sought; the basic philosophies inherent in this discussion have to be re-examined in the interests of nation building. Most Native Canadians unequivocally feel that adjustments must be made on both sides. As Basil Johnston explains in his foreword to Rupert Ross's book, *Dancing with a Ghost*:

> as long as the governments and the agencies of this country fail to recognize that many original peoples of this country still cling to their

different values and institutions, and so long as they insist that the original peoples abandon their ancestral heritage and embrace European culture, so long will penalties be unconsciously imposed upon the Natives and injustices and injuries be committed. And so long as the government and the officials of this country continue to act as if the original peoples are the only ones in need of instruction and improvement, so long will suspicion and distrust persist (1992:ix).

Native Canadian literature has in recent years given the lie to the criticism that it is all about the agony of a segregated and marginalized existence. The horror stories are offset by works, such as Johnston's *Moose Meat and Wild Rice,* that bear testimony to the fact that a rollicking sense of humour underpins the Native temperament. The exhilarating stories in this collection depict present-day Indians and Indian-white relations, with the gentle satire cutting both ways. Light, but nevertheless realistic, narrated as fiction but based on fact, the escapades undertaken by the populace of Moose Meat Reserve encompass havoc and hilarity, prejudice and pretense. The impression these stories leave behind is that all is not lost – that bridges of understanding can be built between two worlds (red and white) that exist now as separate realities. The predicament of the Native Canadian is one of non-existent choices: to assimilate or not to assimilate. It seems, ironically enough, that they are damned if they do, damned if they don't. But there is a glow of optimism here in these stories – the spirit of indomitable courage and resourcefulness in the face of a multitude of social and psychological problems that seem grim to an outsider. As Edward Said remarks, "narratives of emancipation and enlightenment in their strongest form were also narratives of integration not separation, the stories of people who had been excluded from the main group but who were now fighting for a place in it" (1993:xxx). The mainstream culture has to be flexible enough to admit new groups since basically all cultures are involved in one another and no single culture is pure.

I would like to conclude with a quote from one of the most powerful voices among Native Canadians – that of Jeannette Armstrong:

In my quest for empowerment of my people through writing, there are two things of which I must steadfastly remind myself. The first is that ... although severe ... damage has been wrought, healing can take place through cultural affirmation ... The second ... is that the dominating culture's reality is that it seeks to affirm itself continuously and must be taught that *numbers* are not the basis of democracy, *people* are ... It must be pushed, in Canada, to understand and accept that this country is multi-racial and multi-cultural now ... It is this promotion of an ideal which will ... make possible the relearning of co-operation and sharing in place of domination (Armstrong 1992:209-10).

References

Armstrong, J., ed. 1993. *Looking at the Words of Our People: First Nations Analysis of Literature*. Penticton, BC: Theytus.

_____. 1992. "The Disempowerment of First North American Peoples and Empowerment Through Their Writing." In *An Anthropology of Canadian Native Literature in English*, ed. D.D. Moses and T. Goldie, 207-11. Toronto: Oxford University Press.

_____. *Slash*. 1985. Penticton, BC: Theytus.

Begum, J. and M. Dutt, eds. 1996. *South Asian Canadiana*. Madras: Anu Chithra.

Bhabha, H.K. 1994. *The Location of Culture*. London: Routledge.

Canada. Royal Commission on the Economic Union and Development Prospects for Canada. 1985. *Report*.

Dabydeen, C., ed. 1987. *A Shapely Fire: Changing the Literary Landscape*. Oakville, ON: Mosaic Press.

Davey, F. 1993. *Post-national Arguments: The Politics of the Anglophone Canadian Novel since 1967*. Toronto: University of Toronto Press.

Gill, H.K. 1992. "Discovering the Past in *Uhuru Street*." *Sunday Observer*. 29 February.

Graff, G. and J. Phelan, eds. 1995. *Adventures of Huckleberry Finn: A Case Study In Critical Controversy*. Boston: St. Martins Press.

Grossberg, Lawrence, et al., eds. 1992. *Cultural Studies*. New York: Routledge.

Guerin, W.L. et al. 1992. *A Handbook of Critical Approaches to Literature*, 4th ed. New York: Oxford University Press.

Itwaru, A.H. 1989. "Exile and Commemoration." In *Indenture and Exile: The Indo-Caribbean Experience*, ed. F. Birbalsingh. Toronto: TSAR Publications.

Moses, D.D. and T. Goldie, eds. 1992. *An Anthology of Canadian Native Literature in English*. Toronto: Oxford University Press.

Mukherjee, B. 1985. *Darkness*. Markham, ON: Penguin Canada.

Nasta, S. 1991. "Interview with Moyez Vassanji." *Wasafiri* (16): 19-21.

Passaris, C. 1989. "Canadian Multiculturalism: The Wealth of a Nation." In *Multicultural and Intercultural Education: Building Canada*. Calgary, AB: Detselig.

Petrone, P. 1990. *Native Literature in Canada*. Toronto: Oxford University Press.

Ross, R. 1992. *Dancing with a Ghost: Exploring Indian Reality*. Markham, ON: Reed Books.

Said, E.W. 1993. *Culture and Imperialism*. London: Chatto & Windus.

Vassanji, M.G. 1991. *No New Land*. Toronto: McClelland Stewart.

_____. *The Gunny Sack*. 1989. New Delhi: Viking-Penguin India.

Culture, Identity, and the Market
Culture, identité et marché

Packaging Canada/Packaging Places: Tourism, Culture, and Identity in the Twenty-first Century

C. Michael Hall

THE LANDSCAPE – WHICH INCLUDES THE BUILT ENVIRONMENT AND its material and social practices, as well as their symbolic representation (Zukin 1991:16) – may be read as a text (McBride 1999). Based on the premise that "landscapes are communicative devices that encode and transmit information" (Duncan 1990:4), researchers examine both the 'tropes' that communicate this information and how they are read by those who come into contact with them. Tropes are signs and symbols into which various meanings are condensed. They include items in, and of, the built and physical environment – such as buildings, monuments, public spaces, trees, and parks – and also signs, slogans, relationships, brands, and even language(s) associated with the landscape under study. This last includes the languages of consumption associated with specific places and spaces (Jackson and Taylor 1996; Hall 1997). As a 'text', therefore, landscape is multidimensional, lending itself to many interpretations. As a conceptual tool, reading the landscape not only illustrates the ideology of the landscape (Cosgrove 1984:15), but it can also illuminate the way it may "reproduce social and political practices" (Duncan 1990:18). For example, King (1990:53–4) explained how the ideological context of the garden-city movement is "expressive of an implicit environmental determinism." Similarly, Kearns, and Philo (1993) identified the many ways in which the identity of the city can be constructed and reveal its different associations to space in the contemporary city. More recently, attention has also focused on the way in which places may be imaged in order to attract and retain people and capital.

Issues of ideology, identity, and representation have become central to many of the analyses of the manner in which places have come to be packaged as a product to be sold (e.g., Kearns and Philo 1993).

Contemporary imaging strategies are typically policy responses to the social and economic problems associated with deindustrialization and globalization, and associated economic restructuring, urban renewal, multiculturalism, social integration, and control (Roche 1992, 1994). The principal aims of imaging strategies are to:

- attract tourism expenditure;
- generate employment in the tourist and related industries;
- foster positive images for potential investors in the region, often by 'reimaging' previous negative perceptions;
- provide an environment that will attract and retain the interest of professionals and white-collar workers, particularly in so-called clean service industries such as tourism and communications;
- increase public spirit by making communities feel good about themselves (Hall 1992).

In the urban sphere, imaging processes are characterized by some or all of the following:

- development of a critical mass of visitor attractions and facilities, including new buildings, prestige, flagship centres (e.g., shopping centres, stadia, sports complexes, indoor arenas, convention centres, and casino development);
- hosting hallmark events (e.g., Olympic Games, Commonwealth Games, and the Grand Prix) and/or major league sports teams;
- development of urban tourism strategies and policies often associated with new or renewed organization and development of city marketing (e.g., city promotional campaigns such as St. John's "The City of Legends" [Stewart 1991]);
- development of leisure and cultural services and projects to support marketing and tourism efforts (e.g., the creation and renewal of museums and art galleries and the hosting of art festivals, often as part of a comprehensive cultural tourism strategy for a region or city).

Imaging strategies are therefore conscious attempts by places to seduce. In particular, they seek not only to develop something which is attractive but also to package specific representations of a particular way of life or lifestyle for consumption. Therefore, representations of culture are intimately connected to place marketing. Whether we use culture in the sense of being indicative of a "particular way of life, whether of a people, a period, a group, or humanity in general" or "as a reference to the works or practices of intellectual and especially artistic activity" (Williams 1983:90), culture is becoming commodified and bought and sold in the global marketplace. Cultural policies are used to generate artistic and 'high' cultural activity in order to attract visitors and to make the city an attractive place to live for the middle-class, white collar workers, and businesses, while wider notions of cultural identity are also being used to attract investment, visitor, and employment ventures. The use of cultural images to attract visitors is not new. It has been around for as long as tourism itself. The effects of place marketing, however, may be pervasive within specific places targeted for consumption; indeed the notion of selling places implies not only trying to affect demand through the representation of cultural images, but also the manipulation and management of the supply-side – those things that make up a community's life – in a package that can be 'sold.' Such actions clearly have implications not only for how the external consumer sees a place but also for how the people who constitute the place are able to participate in making both the collective and individual identity and the structures that sell place (Hall and Hodges 1997).

Imaging and place marketing began to be recognized as significant urban phenomena from the early 1980s, at a time when globalization started to be seen as a significant economic and social phenomenon, and when substantial changes in the nature of consumption and production also occurred. Indeed, it is no coincidence that in this time of dramatic shifts in the character of contemporary capitalism that the 1980s were characterized as the decade in which consumers were taught "how to desire" (Bocock 1993; York and Jennings 1995:44; Pawson 1997:17). For producers, an essential means of achieving this has been by "romancing the product" through the use of brands (Pawson 1997). Branding is a way of seeking to add value to commodities including services and places. A successful brand creates distinctiveness in the marketplace. As Pawson notes: "It is an investment in product quality at the same time as seeking to create more illusory associations to appeal to specific groups of consumers in the local spaces of globalized capitalism. Both branding and advertizing are inherently spatial practices, used by producers in the expansion and differentiation of markets" (1997:17). In the case of urban reimaging, marketing practices, such as branding, rely upon the commodification of particular aspects of place, exploiting, reinventing, or creating place images in order to sell the place as a destination product for tourists or investment. Through this process, the ways of living particular to a place may become commodified in order to transform them into a commercial product or a specific dimension of place promotion that can be experienced by the consumer.

Given the shifts in the nature of production noted above, it should not be surprising that in the same way that the nature of production is regarded as having changed, so has the nature of consumption (Glennie and Thrift 1992). For example, Hall reported "greater fragmentation and pluralism, the weakening of older collective solidarities and block identities and the emergence of new identities associated with greater work flexibility [and] the maximization of individual choice through personal consumption" (1988:24). In this context, it therefore became apparent to those who were seeking to reimage the city that the desires of those who consume have to be accorded far greater prominence. Such desires must be actively catered to when urban places and spaces are created for them to consume (e.g., see Kotler et al. 1993). Hence, production has moved towards even greater degrees of flexibility. But in a world of consumers differentiated by social segments and lifestyle niches, it is the symbolic meanings of products that matter as well as their inherent qualities (Pawson 1997). These attributes are encapsulated in successful brands "which, through careful management, skillful promotion and wide use, come in the minds of consumers, to embrace a particular and appealing set of values ... both tangible and intangible" (Interbrand 1990:6). Brands therefore demonstrate the falseness of trying to separate production from consumption (Bell and Valentine 1997). As Laurier observed: "To build binary opposites is to make one dependent on the other, and so there cannot be consumption without production ... it is apparent that they merge in many places and that each process certainly does have effects on the other ... even if they are causal or may never ever be explicable" (1993:272). We therefore come full circle: places are increasingly trying to seduce; if the argument regarding the relationship between consumption and production is correct, people also want to be seduced when they consider their destination options.

The following discussion examines some aspects of the processes of urban imaging in Canada. It attempts to uncover some of the ideological messages and forces encoded in the landscape and to examine how they are read by those who inhabit and visit Canada (Duncan

1990; Duncan and Duncan 1988). Such a position is also idiosyncratic. As Daniels and Lee observed, "the geographies we inhabit are multi-centred; there is no grand central place or single, privileged vantage point" (1996:12). The position is thus my own.

Cultural Settings: Cities Do Not Just Exist in the Present. They Are Products of the Accumulated Past(s)

As noted above, throughout the Western world, cities which were affected by deindustrialization in the 1970s and early 1980s have responded with the development of imaging strategies in an attempt to attract new investment and create employment. Canadian cities have also adopted these strategies in order to position themselves as 'world class' or 'international' sites. Tourism, and cultural tourism in particular, has been an integral component of the imaging strategies of Canadian cities. Yet the success of cultural tourism strategies that focus on arts and heritage attractions is somewhat problematic. As Ekos Research Associates reported in a review of urban cultural tourism projects in Canada, "high culture does not appear to be a major magnet for tourists. ... [but] there is recurring and consistent evidence that shows that once tourists reach major Canadian destinations (for whatever motivating factors) many will consume large amounts of culture. This is true even for those who did not consider culture in their original travel destinations." Therefore, they continue, "there may be a more profound payoff in considering how to encourage tourists to consume more arts and culture once they make a travel decision rather than trying to attract tourists with arts and culture" (Ekos Research Associates Inc. 1988:25).

Despite the evidence surrounding the relatively poor direct attractiveness of arts and culture to tourists, cities have persisted in using art galleries, museums, and festivals as tools for urban redevelopment and for changing the image of destinations. Unfortunately, most urban regimes have failed to recognize that "very few tourists perceive these cultural domains as isolated entities. Culture, as the symbolic environment of the destination, is often viewed as a meaningful whole" (Ekos Research Associates Inc. 1988:22). Greater attention should therefore be given to integrating all of the various aspects of cultural life in a destination in a manner which benefits the community, rather than the commodification of certain elements for the perceived satisfaction and conspicuous consumption of the visitor.

Tourism can stimulate culture through the development of urban imaging strategies. However, such stimulation is limited, as the cultural policies developed to support such strategies focus only on cultural elements that can be commodified through the creation of a cultural industry for the consumer of culture. Furthermore, the economic implications of developing a tourist economy may be somewhat problematic given that the shift from a goods- to a service-producing economy does not occur evenly. For example, Pollock (1991) noted that the benefits of tourism growth in Greater Vancouver and Victoria are poorly distributed throughout the economy. Nevertheless, despite concerns over the real benefits of pursuing the tourist dollar and the real long-term returns of place marketing, Canadian cities continue to attempt to image themselves as international cultural tourism destinations.

"Influencing travellers to visit a particular city destination comes through conveying the essence or image of that city as well as the specifics of what there is to see and do" (David-Peterson Associates Inc. 1992:15). That said, "product specific advertising is more effective than advertising which attempts to modify images concerning a particular destination" (Ekos Research Associates Inc. 1988:32). Even with the development of new tourism attractions and corresponding alterations to marketing strategies, changing the image of a destination is an extremely difficult exercise given the weight of previous perceptions.

Rather than market a distinct product to the consumer through a combination of appropriate advertising, attractive pricing, and the opportunity for unique visitor experience, urban imaging strategies are creating a stage of "serial monotony" whereby different cities look the same (Boyer 1988; Harvey 1993). As Block commented with respect to the redevelopment of the port of Montreal for the 350th anniversary celebrations: "For Nancy L'Estrange, the Old Port is cleaner and prettier than in her hometown of Toronto. 'I think it's beautiful – and it doesn't smell,' she said. 'There isn't that organic stuff we've got in Toronto. I don't see any ducks, bird faeces, or seaweed and other things floating in the water like we see in our harbour'" (1993:A3). In the competitive new environment surrounding city promotion, many of the imaging strategies designed to gain competitive advantage are sanitizing and commodifying representations of local culture. Moreover, they often fail to be inclusive of the public they are meant to serve.

Summer Olympic Games: "The Biggest and Most Costly Mega-project in the History of Toronto."

Toronto made a bid to host the 2008 Summer Olympic Games. Toronto's bid, much like its previous, unsuccessful bid for the 1996 Games, was built on a waterfront redevelopment strategy that sought to revitalize the harbour area through the development of an integrated sports, leisure, retail, and housing complex. However, as in the case of the Sydney Games, or in any other mega-event with substantial infrastructure requirements, important questions should be asked about both the event's development process and who would actually benefit from hosting the event.

One of the most striking features of this Toronto bid was the extent to which information on the bid was either unavailable or provided only limited detail on the costs associated with hosting the event. However, unlike the Sydney Olympic bid, Toronto was fortunate to have a non-profit public interest coalition, Bread Not Circuses (BNC), actively campaigning for more information on the bid proposal and for government to address social concerns.

BNC argued that given the cost of both bidding for and hosting the Olympics, the bidding process must be subject to public scrutiny. "Any Olympic bid worth its salt will not only withstand public scrutiny, but will be improved by a rigorous and open public process" the organization contended. It went on to assert that Toronto City Council support for an Olympic bid must be conditional on:

- the development and execution of a suitable process to address financial, social, and environmental concerns, ensure an effective public participation process (including intervenor funding), and include a commitment to the development of a detailed series of Olympic standards. A time-frame of one year from the date of the vote to support the bid should be set to ensure that the plans for the participation process are taken seriously;
- full, open, and independent accounting of the financial costs of bidding and staging the Games;
- full, open, and independent social impact assessment of the Games (Bread Not Circuses 1998a).

Other key elements of a public participation process should include:

- full, fair, and democratic processes to involve all of the people of Toronto in the development and review of the Olympic bid;
- an Olympic Intervenor Fund, similar to the fund established by the City of Toronto in 1989, to allow interested groups to participate effectively in the public scrutiny of the Toronto bid;
- development of an independent environmental assessment of the 2008 Games, and strategies to resolve specific concerns;
- development of a series of financial, social, and environmental standards governing the 2008 Games, similar to the Toronto Olympic Commitment adopted by City Council in September of 1989 (Bread Not Circuses 1998a).

In addition to the factors identified by BNC, the city's previous experiences with stadia and events raise substantial questions about the public liability for any development. For example, in 1982, then Metropolitan Toronto Chairman, Paul Godfrey, promised that Toronto's SkyDome, a multipurpose sports complex used for baseball and Canadian football, could be built for 75 million CAD, with no public debt. However, the final price of the development was over 600 million CAD, with taxpayers having to pay more than half. BNC also noted that the previous Toronto bid costs were 60 per cent over budget, "with a great deal of spending coming in the final, overheated days of the bidding war leading up to the International Olympic Committee (IOC) Congress. There was no public control, and little public accountability, over the '96 bid," while "there was virtually no assessment of the social, environmental, and financial impact of the Games until Bread Not Circuses began to raise critical questions. By then, it was too late to influence the bid" (Bread Not Circuses 1998c).

BNC lobbied various city councillors to influence their decision whether or not to support a bid. Only one councillor out of fifty-five voted against the Olympic bid proposal however, even though the only information the councillors had to rely on was a 20-page background document to the proposal. When city councillors voted on the project, they did not have:

- an estimate of the cost of bidding for the Games;
- a list of the names of the backers of 'BidCo,' the private corporation heading up the Olympic bid;

- a reliable estimate of the cost of staging the Games;
- a plan for the public participation process, the environmental review process, or the social impact assessment process;
- a detailed financial strategy for the Games.

Such a situation clearly had public interest organizations, such as BNC, very worried about the economic, environmental, and social costs of a successful bid. Clearly, the history of mega-events such as the Olympic Games indicated that such a situation was not new (Olds 1998). The International Olympic Committee (IOC) already sought to ensure that the Games be environmentally friendly. Perhaps it was now time to see that they be socially and economically friendly and build wider assessment of the social impacts of the Games into the planning process as a mandatory component of bidding. BNC, in a letter to the IOC President, requested "that the IOC, which sets the rules for the bidding process, take an active responsibility in ensuring that the local processes in the bidding stage are effective and democratic" and specifically address concerns regarding the "financial and social costs of the Olympic Games" and proposed that:

- an international network be created to include the Centre for Housing Rights and Evictions (COHRE), the Human and Land Rights Network (HIC) Housing Rights Subcommittee, academics, and non-governmental organizations (including local groups in cities that have bid for and/or hosted the Games);
- a set of standards regarding forced evictions, be developed and adopted by the network;
- a plan be developed and implemented to build international support for the standards, including identification of sympathetic IOC, National Olympic Committee (NOC), and other sports officials;
- the IOC be approached with the request that the standards be incorporated into the Olympic Charter, Host City Contracts, and other documents of the IOC (Bread Not Circuses 1998b).

Such a social charter for the Olympics would undoubtedly greatly assist in making the Games more place friendly and perhaps even improve the image of the IOC. However, at the time this paper was written, the books of the Toronto bid had still not been opened for public scrutiny. Nor has there been adequate response to the proposal to create of a set of social standards for the Olympics. The revitalization of place requires more than just the development of product and image. The re-creation of a sense of place is a process that involves the formulation of urban design strategies based on conceptual models of the city that are, in turn, founded on notions of civic life, the public realm, and the idea of planning as debate and argument (Bianchini and Schwengel 1991). As Smyth recognized: "This needs to be undertaken in a frank way and in a forum where different understandings can be shared, inducing mutual respect, leading to developing trust, and finally conceiving a development which meets mutual needs as well as stewarding resources for future generations ... This proposes a serious challenge to the public sector as well as to the private sector, for authorities have undermined the well-being of their local populations by transferring money away from services to pay for flagship developments" (1994:254).

Unfortunately, such ideas have only limited visibility within the place marketing and imaging realms. Tourism and place planning are often poorly conceptualized with respect to participatory procedures, and the institutional arrangements for many of the so-called partnerships for urban redevelopment actually exclude community participation in decision-making procedures.

Canadian Cities: Commodities for Consumption?

Today, everything seems to be a commodity available for consumption. Of course, it is not. In fact, the commodity has to be a commodity of a certain type with a given symbolic value which reinforces preferred lifestyles and representations of identity. These commodities are not evenly distributed in urban space. They are presently located disproportionately in the inner city areas, with many of the outer suburbs forgotten by those seeking to reimage the city, even though that is where the majority of residents live. Nevertheless, these commodities still seduce. They are produced and/or packaged to seduce the visitor; to attract international capital, albeit for increasingly shorter periods of time; and to seduce the locals. At a time when restructuring and change seems to be the norm and when employment becomes increasingly casual in nature and insecure, political elites need to be seen to be doing something. New brands, new developments, the hosting of events, and the creation of new leisure and retail spaces are all a sign that something has been done. However, those who visit cities on a regular basis see that, even though they are trying to reimage themselves as places that are different, they still look the same. Harvey's (1989) concern over the "serial monotony" of the redeveloped and reimaged city is reinforced. As Zukin observed, the city is a site of spectacle, a "dreamscape of visual consumption" (1991:221). It is, therefore, perhaps not so surprising that at a time when little competitive edge can be gained among cities in terms of the reconstruction of their physical space, then emphasis is placed on the lifestyle opportunities they offer to those who can afford them.

If there are no lasting benefits and no identifiable economic opportunity costs associated with selling the city, then we are left with the Bourdieu proposition that "the most successful ideological effects are those which have no words" (quoted in Harvey 1989:78). If the function of a flagship development such as hosting an Olympic Games, a Commonwealth Games, a Grand Prix, or a major waterfront redevelopment scheme is then "reduced to inducing social stability, assuming the generated experience is sustainable for enough people over a long period and is targeted towards those who are potentially the harbingers of disruption ... what is the purpose of marketing the city?" then asks Smyth (1994:7).

Murphy and Watson (1997) described Sydney as a "city of surfaces." Such a comment may also apply to many Canadian cities and, perhaps, to attempts to image Canada itself. While the spaces are the same, however, the places are different. Place has a distinct location which it defines; place is fixed. Space, in contrast, is composed of intersections of mobile elements with shifting, often indeterminate borders (de Certeau 1984; Larbalestier 1994). Daniels and Lee suggest that "reading human geography ... is a complex and critical act of interpretation and as readers, we are engaged in interpreting writers' interpretations ... of worlds which are already construed, or misconstrued, by meaning or imagery" (1996:5). Fortunately, city places and spaces are continually read "in various ways, by a variety of people pursuing a variety of endeavours, in walking, in working, in reading, in speaking, in all or any of our everyday practices" (Larbalestier 1994:187). While space is being constructed by urban growth coalitions in the desire to reimage the city, places remain open to negotiation and interpretation.

Despite the conscious development of space in a manner that aims to seduce the visitor and the investor, places can still resist commodification. Indeed, the very complexity of place – with its dense networks of social networks – ultimately makes it interesting, though not always easily accessible for the visitor. Hewison observed that "the time has come to argue that commerce is not culture, whether we define culture as the pursuit of music, literature or the fine arts, or whether we adopt Raymond Williams's definition of culture as 'a whole way of life'. You cannot get a whole way of life into a Tesco's trolley or a V & A Enterprises shopping bag" (1991:175). Such arguments are important because they run counter to the notions of commodification of place and culture as product which are intrinsic to place marketing.

In experiencing places I don't want to be seduced in a contrived space, rather I want to be surprised. Despite the efforts of successive provincial and municipal governments, cities still have the capacity to surprise. However, such surprises tend not to occur in the planned spaces of the redeveloped waterfront, but rather in the back streets and the suburbs. These, though, are the 'messy' spaces – the ones that real estate speculators and developers have not yet reached and where successive politicians' grandiose monuments have not yet been realized. In promoting the city to the wider community, including those who live in the suburbs, those who cannot afford inner city living, and those who are seeking more than the casino and the riverside restaurant, it is to be hoped that those places will continue to thrive.

References

Barnes, T. and J. Duncan, eds. 1992. *Writing Worlds: Discourse, Text and Metaphor in the Representation of Landscape.* London: Routledge.

Bell, D. and G. Valentine. 1997. *Consuming Geographies: We Are Where We Eat.* London: Routledge.

Bianchini, F. and H. Schwengel. 1991. "Re-imagining the City." In *Enterprise and Heritage: Crosscurrents of National Culture,* ed. J. Corner and S. Harvey, 212–234. London: Routledge.

Block, I. 1993. "Port Popularity: 3 Million Visitors Can't All Be Wrong." *The Gazette.* Montreal, 31 August, A3.

Bocock, R. 1993. *Consumption.* London: Routledge.

Boyer, C. 1988. "The Return of Aesthetics to City Planning." *Society* 25 (4): 49–56.

Bread Not Circuses. 1998a. *Bread Alert!* (E-mail edition) 2 (2) 20 February.

_____. 1998b. *Bread Alert!* (E-mail edition) 2 (3) 26 February.

_____. 1998c. *Bread Alert!* (E-mail edition) 2 (8) 8 April.

_____. 1999. *The REAL Olympic Scandal: The Financial and Social Costs of the Games.* Media Advisory, 17 March.

Cosgrove, D. 1984. *Social Formation and Symbolic Landscape.* London: Croon Helm.

Cosgrove, D. and S. Daniels, eds. 1988. *The Iconography of Landscape: Essays on the Symbolic Representation, Design and Use of Past Environments.* Cambridge: Cambridge University Press.

Daniels, S. and R. Lee, eds. 1996. *Exploring Human Geography: A Reader.* London: Arnold.

David-Peterson Associates Inc. 1992. *Toronto as a Tourist Destination.* Prepared for KPMG-Peat Marwick Stevenson and Kellogg on behalf of Metropolitan Toronto Convention and Visitors Association, et al. Toronto.

de Certeau, M. 1984. *The Practice of Everyday Life.* Los Angeles and Berkely: University of California Press.

Duncan, J. 1990. *The City as Text: The Politics of Landscape Interpretation in the Kandyan Kingdom.* Cambridge: Cambridge University Press.

Duncan, J. and N. Duncan. 1988. "(Re)reading the Landscape." *Environment and Planning D: Society and Space* 6: 117–26.

Duncan, J. and D. Ley, eds. 1993. *Place / Culture / Representation.* London: Routledge.

Ekos Research Associates Inc. 1988. *Culture, Multiculturalism and Tourism Pilot Projects and Related Studies: A Synthesis.* Prepared for Communications Canada, Secretary of State Tourism Canada, in the context of the Conference on Tourism, Culture, and Multiculturalism.

Glennie, P.D. and N. Thrift. 1992. "Modernity, Urbanism and Modern Consumption." *Environment & Planning D: Society and Space* 10: 423–443.

Greiner, N. 1994. "Inside Running on Olympic Bid." *The Australian* 19 (September): 13.

Hage, G. 1997. "At Home In The Entrails Of The West: Multiculturalism, Ethnic Food And Migrant Home Building." In *home/world: space, community and marginality in Sydney's west*, H. Grace, G. Hage, L. Johnson, J. Langsworth and M. Symonds, 99-153. Annandale: Pluto Press.

Hall, C.M. 1992. *Hallmark Tourist Events: Impacts, Management and Planning.* Chichester: John Wiley.

_____. 1996. "Hallmark Events and Urban Reimaging Strategies: Coercion, Community and the Sydney 2000 Olympics." In *Practicing Responsible Tourism: International Case Studies in Planning, Policy and Development*, ed. L.C. Harrison and W. Husbands, 366-379. New York: John Wiley.

_____. 1997. "Geography, Marketing and the Selling of Places." *Journal of Travel and Tourism Marketing* 6 (3/4): 61-84.

_____. 1998. "The Politics of Decision Making and Top-down Planning: Darling Harbour, Sydney." In *Tourism Management in Cities: Policy, Process and Practice*, ed. D. Tyler, M. Robertson, and Y. Guerrier, 9-24. Chichester: John Wiley & Sons.

Hall, C.M. and C. Hamon. 1996. "Casinos and Urban Redevelopment in Australia." *Journal of Travel Research* 34 (3): 30-36.

Hall, C.M. and J. Hodges. 1997. "Sharing the Spirit of Corporatism and Cultural Capital: the Politics of Place and Identity in the Sydney 2000 Olympics." In *Sport, Popular Culture and Identity*, ed. M. Roche. Chelsea School Research Centre Edition 5: 95-112. Aachen: Meyer & Meyer Verlag.

Hall, S. 1988. *Brave New World: Marxism Today* (October): 24-29.

Harvey, D. 1989. *The Condition of Postmodernity*. Oxford: Blackwell.

Harvey, D. 1993. "From Space to Place and Back Again: Reflections on the Condition of Postmodernity." In *Mapping the Futures: Local Cultures, Global Change*, ed. J. Bird, B. Curtis, T. Putnam, G. Robertson, and L. Tickner. London: Routledge.

Hewison, R. (1991). "Commerce and Culture." In *Enterprise and Heritage: Crosscurrents of National Culture*, ed. J. Corner and S. Harvey, 162-177. London and New York: Routledge.

Jackson, P. and J. Taylor. 1996. "Geography and the Cultural Politics of Advertising." *Progress in Human Geography* 20 (3): 356-71.

Kearns, G. and C. Philo, eds. 1993. *Selling Places: The City as Cultural Capital, Past and Present*. Oxford: Pergamon Press.

King, A. 1990. *Urbanism, Colonialism, and the World Economy: Cultural and Spatial Foundations of the World Urban System*. London: Cambridge University Press.

Kotler, P., D.H. Haider, and I. Rein. 1993. *Marketing Places: Attracting Investment, Industry, and Tourism to Cities, States, and Nations*. New York: The Free Press.

Larbalestier, J. 1994. "Imagining the City: Contradictory Tales of Space and Place." In *Metropolis Now: Planning and the Urban in Contemporary Australia*, ed. K. Gibson and S. Watson, 186-195. Annandale: Pluto Press.

Laurier, E. 1993. "'Tackintosh': Glasgow's Supplementary Gloss." In *Selling Places: The City as Cultural Capital, Past and Present*, ed. G. Kearns and C. Philo, 267-290. Oxford: Pergamon Press.

McBride, B. 1999. "The (Post)colonial Landscape of Cathedral Square: Urban Redevelopment and Representation in the 'Cathedral City.'" *New Zealand Geographer* 55 (1): 3-11.

Murphy, P. and S. Watson, 1997. *Surface City: Sydney at the Millennium.* Annandale: Pluto Press Australia.

Pawson, E. 1997. "Branding Strategies and Languages of Consumption." *New Zealand Geographer* 53 (2): 16-21.

Philo, C. and G. Kearns. 1993. "Culture, History, Capital; a Critical Introduction to the Selling of Places." In *Selling Places: The City as Cultural Capital, Past and Present,* ed. C. Philo and G. Kearns. Oxford: Pergamon Press.

Pollock, A. 1991. "Tourism – The Professional Challenge – A Framework for Action," Appendix 2. *Tourism Trends and their Impact on Training and Education, Interim Report.* Vancouver: n.p.

Roche, M. 1992. "Mega-events and Micro-modernization: On the Sociology of the New Urban Tourism." *British Journal of Sociology* 43 (4): 563-600.

_____. 1994. "Mega-events and Urban Policy." *Annals of Tourism Research* 21 (1): 1-19.

Simson, V. and A. Jennings. 1992. *The Lords of the Rings: Power, Money and Drugs in the Modern Olympics.* London: Simon & Schuster.

Smyth, H. 1994. *Marketing the City: The Role of Flagship Developments in Urban Regeneration.* London: E & FN Spon.

Stewart, J.K. 1991. "Retaining Cultural Values: Case Studies in Heritage Tourism." Workshop notes prepared for Building Community Tourism: Charting a Course for the 1990s. Whistler Centre for Business and the Arts, Canada, 21-24 April.

Stock, B. 1993. "Reading, Community and a Sense of Place." In *Place / Culture / Representation,* ed. J. Duncan and D. Ley, 314-328. London: Routledge.

Washington, S. 1999. "IOC Allegations May Affect Funding." *Australian Financial Review* 19 (January): 5.

Williams, R. 1983. *Keywords.* London: Fontana.

York, P. and C. Jennings. 1995. *Peter York's 80s.* London: BBC Books.

Zukin, S. 1991. *Landscapes of Power: From Detroit to Disney World.* Los Angeles and Berkeley: University of California Press.

_____. 1996. "Space and Symbols in an Age of Decline." In *Re-Presenting the City: Ethnicity, Capital and Culture in the Twenty-First Century Metropolis,* ed. A. King. Houndsmill: Macmillan Press.

Canadian Distinctiveness and Cultural Policy as We Enter the Twenty-first Century

Shirley L. Thomson

I N THE TWENTIETH CENTURY, CANADA CAME TO OCCUPY A SIGNIFICANT place in the world. Our reputation continues to grow: in terms of our technology, our government policy, and, I will argue, our culture. The forces of continentalization continue to increase, yet Canadian culture remains – and, I believe, will remain – distinct and distinctive, the reflection of our unique sensibilities. Canada's cultural agencies play an important role in fostering the expression of this sensibility. We must ensure that they have the resources to continue doing so.

In the past half-century, Canada has accomplished a great deal in the cultural arena. We have built an admirable arts infrastructure within the country and we have produced a significant number of artists and writers whose work is appreciated worldwide. A number of factors have contributed to the success of Canada's artists and to the quality – and qualities – of artistic and cultural endeavour in this country. These rest very largely in the Canadian sense of community and the institutions that stem from it. Canadian art, taken as a whole, reflects a medley of many community voices.

North-South integration is, however, changing the face of Canada. It is important in these circumstances that we have a clear idea of the differences between Canadian and American sensibilities. Equally important to note is the importance of the Crown agencies that sustain our Canadian distinctiveness and the authentic voices of our artists.

Our International Stars

Over the past several decades, Canadian culture has gained an increasingly important profile on the international scene. We have only to think of writers and playwrights such as Michael Ondaatje, Margaret Atwood, and Michel Tremblay; musicians such as Ben Heppner and Diana Krall; filmmakers Atom Egoyan, David Cronenberg, and François Girard; of such popular entertainers as Céline Dion and Shania Twain. In attracting a wide following in many countries, Canada's artists have, each in his/her own way and media, touched on and explored universal human themes. There are Canadian Studies programmes in many countries. Canadian literature is studied in universities all over the world.

Factors in our Success

The success of our artists can to some extent be attributed to ease of travel and the multiplication and speed of communications – another area in which Canada is a leader. I would also attribute it to government cultural policies of the last fifty years, policies that are facing new challenges as we move into the twenty-first century. These, however, are subsidiary factors. The 'Canadian sensibility,' more than anything else, accounts for the international success of our artists. I want, therefore, to begin by looking at the quality of artistic and cultural endeavour in this country and what it reveals about the Canadian sensibility.

One aspect of that sensibility is the acceptance of a plurality of groups. Our culture is a medley of many community voices. Northrop Frye in *The Bush Garden* pointed out that "unity and identity are quite different things ... and ... in Canada they are perhaps more different than they are anywhere else." He went on to explain, "Identity is local and regional, rooted in the imagination and in works of culture; unity is national in reference, international in perspective, and rooted in a political feeling."[1] "Real unity," he continued, "tolerates dissent and rejoices in variety of outlook and tradition" (Frye 1971: ii, vi).

One of the oldest paintings in the Canadian collection of the National Gallery of Canada illustrates this point: that Canada is made up of many communities, pursuing their own cultural expression while sharing the support of a unified political system. I am thinking of the 1807 portrait of Joseph Brant by William Berczy. The subject of the painting, Joseph Brant, was a hereditary chief of the Mohawks. He led the Six Nations in support of the British during the American Revolution and afterwards brought them to Ontario to settle. The Six

Nations have produced an impressive number of outstanding artists. Pauline Johnson, daughter of a Mohawk chief, was the first Aboriginal poet to achieve an international reputation. Last fall, Six Nations photographer Greg Staats won the Council's Duke and Duchess of York Prize in Photography.

William Berczy, the painter, was also an immigrant to the young province of Ontario. Born in Bavaria, in present-day Germany, he led a group of German settlers to New York state in 1792. Finding arrangements there uncongenial, he brought his group to Markham (just north of Toronto), where they settled in 1795. Berczy had received extensive training as a painter in Europe. Once established in Canada, he turned to art again as the source of his livelihood. Both these men represent communities moving into Canada and sharing their cultural heritage.

Over the past two centuries, this pattern of a diverse artistic tradition nurtured by the unceasing contribution of immigrant communities has repeated itself thousands of times. Finding a home and some degree of economic security in Canada, artists have worked comfortably with a foot in each of two cultures – that of their origins and that of their point of settlement. The nineteenth-century Dutch-born artist, Cornelius Krieghoff, was the subject of an exhibition at the National Gallery of Canada (October 2000 to January 2001). He painted what many people see as quintessential scenes of French-Canadian life. Yet, however well the paintings achieve this objective, they also show clearly an indebtedness to the Dutch tradition of winter scenes. From the prairies, in the mid-twentieth century, we have a manifestation of this very pattern of nourishment from immigrant traditions: the deeply Orthodox work of the Ukranian-born artist William Kurelek.

In recent years, Canadian culture has been greatly enriched by the work of artists Asian born or of Asian descent. I think of writers Rohinton Mistry, M.G. Vassanji, and Michael Ondaatje; of filmmakers Paul Wong and Mina Shum; of musicians Adyita Verma and Jon Kimura Parker; and of painter Takao Tanabe. The work of Canada's outstanding artists reflects the qualities of dozens of contributing communities that make up the Canadian cultural landscape. In addition to those just mentioned, we are indebted to the Armenian community (Atom Egoyan), the African community (Djanet Sears), and the Italian community (Nino Ricci).

In French Canada, the cultural tradition is so long and rich, and the names legion, that it is difficult to know where to begin. Keeping to artists widely recognized at the closing of this century, a perusal of the European cultural press will turn up in short order the names of Anne Hébert, Robert Lepage, François Girard, and Michel Tremblay.

No other country, proportionate to its population, produces such a wealth and variety of art as Canada.

North-South Integration

Is the pool of Canadian artistic talent, or the environment that forms that talent, threatened by globalization and international market forces? I am cautiously optimistic. Currently, we have a large pool of talented artists, and our environment of internal and international mobility is a great stimulus to the creative imagination. Canada is also relatively prosperous and there is a significant art audience. To this extent, we can feel quite confident about the vitality of Canadian culture and its expression through the work of practising artists in the immediate future.

The area where I have deep concerns, however, is in the long-term future of the distinctively Canadian cultural institutions that support that talent and market. International stars do not spring forth *sui generis*. All artists require some kind of incubation period, during which they depend for support and encouragement on their families, communities, and countries while they learn their trades and develop their distinctive styles.

This kind of support, even at the simplest family level, is dependent on two major factors: the economy and political will. For Canada, the terms *globalization* and *international market forces* really mean *continentalization*. In the last two decades we have witnessed the gradual integration of the Canadian economy into the American. The recently proposed merger of Canadian National with the giant U.S. railway, Burlington North Santa Fe, is symbolic of the north-south trade axes that are replacing the traditional east-west axes that had their origins in earlier European patterns of exploration and colonization.

One indirect effect of this realignment has been the movement of head offices to the United States. With these head offices go both corporate and private resources: potential sponsorship money, expertise in the voluntary sector of the arts, active community contributors, and audiences. It is clear, furthermore, that for the United States, culture is business. Americans do not take kindly to any country that might try, forcefully or even very tentatively, to protect its own culture or limit the spread of American culture. Although cultural products were exempted from the North American Free Trade Agreement, pressure on the cultural front will not let up, as was evident in the controversy over split-run magazine publications.

In any case, we all know that physical or regulatory barriers, in this age of Internet, satellite dishes, and electronic commerce, will not in themselves be enough to sustain Canadian cultural distinctiveness. Canadian artists and arts organizations need direct, broad-based, institutional support.

American versus Canadian Sensibility

Let me now make a couple of broad generalizations about what it is we are trying to preserve. First, the Canadian sensibility has traditionally shown a greater deference to authority and a greater respect for community than the American. The American sensibility is more individualistic and more prone to view social relations in contractual terms, as agreements between equals that can be broken off at any time.

Seymour Martin Lipset has been a leader in documenting the differences between American and Canadian sensibilities. In *Continental Divide*, he describes the difference between America's classical libertarian sensibilities that emphasize distrust of the state, egalitarianism, and populism, and the conservative British and European sensibilities of Canada, that are "accepting of the need for a strong state, for respect for authority, for deference" (Lipset 1990:2). The divide between Canada and the United States is dwindling, he says, as both sides move toward the middle. The contrast is of degree, not of absolutes. But in its tradition of social and health services, government ownership, and what Lipset calls "constitutional rights to ethnocultural survival," the Canadian sensibility is still very different from that of the American (Lipset 1990:3). In his list of differences Lipset mentions as well the ability of Canadians to maintain healthy, liveable inner cities. This is a factor of some importance in fostering a vibrant cultural life.

The rest of the world is intrigued by the difference in sensibility that shows up in Canada's cultural products. We are North Americans but we have not shed our roots in other parts of the world. In Marshall McLuhan's words, Canada is a "borderline" case. It is borderline in the literal sense of being a population spread out in a thin band along the

U.S. border. It is also borderline in the historic sense of always having been at the periphery of much larger imperial entities: French, British, or American. It is borderline in the sense of being vulnerable: its continuing existence is precarious. McLuhan saw this borderline characteristic as an asset: "Canadians," he wrote, "are the people who learned how to live without the bold accents of the national ego-trippers of other lands" (McLuhan 1977:227). He added a fourth interpretation: in this sense, borders are not barriers so much as openings that create a sense of perspective, making it possible to interpret events and to mediate among diverse groups. Canada's many internal borders – political, religious, ethnic, psychic – act as intervals that make what we say and do resonate for others.

This more thoughtful and attentive attitude toward the world in all its cultural variety is the specific quality informing the Canadian sensibility. As Margaret Atwood put it in "Nationalism, Limbo and the Canadian Club," Americans see themselves as "a huge healthy apple pie, with other countries and cultures sprinkled around the outside, like raisins." We see ourselves, she argues, as a raisin, and the other parts of the universe as "invariably larger and more interesting" (Atwood 1982:87–8).

The Need for Crown Agencies

I have argued that, to preserve the variety of outlook that is a distinguishing feature of the Canadian sensibility, Canadian artists and arts organizations need direct, broad-based institutional support. That support has traditionally been provided through our cultural Crown agencies. Our Crown agencies embody Canada's more thoughtful and respectful attitude towards the wider world. They arose from the recognition that, given a small population spread over a vast area, there would be gaps that society itself could not fill, where the state would have to step in without interfering.

The sensibility that produced our Crown agencies recognized the wisdom of having a political regime that clearly distinguishes between the head of state and the leader of the government. It recognized that there are many important questions that the government leader and his or her elected party colleagues must tend to; but that there are also others that must be dealt with in the public realm, while being kept at arm's length from politicians. For that reason, we now have over thirty major Crown agencies in this country. Among them are some of our most important cultural institutions, including the National Gallery of Canada and the Canada Council for the Arts.

Peter Newman and Angus Reid, among others, have pointed out how Canadians are losing their distinctiveness (Newman 1995). That respectful openness to the world is disappearing. Our turning inward, as Lipset points out, entails some loss of awareness. In making us more American, it may also, however, yield benefits through increased self-confidence, self-reliance, and individualism. The full implications of this transformation of the Canadian psyche will be apparent in the coming decades; we can, however, point out some early effects. The economic integration of Canada with the United States is far more complete than the cultural integration. It has entailed the loss of a large number of Crown agencies operating in the economic sphere: CN, Canada Post, Air Canada, and PetroCanada. These agencies were privatized because of international market forces.

In cultural terms, however, Canadians tend more than ever to define themselves in terms of their difference from the United States; our cultural Crown agencies continue to support those differences. For half a century or more, these agencies have been the sustaining force behind the voices that make up a distinctive Canadian artistic ethos. It is my belief that they will continue to provide the best bulwark against the loss of that distinctiveness.

As Charles Taylor pointed out, art is "a crucial terrain for the ideal of authenticity." Support for Canadian distinctiveness implies support for what is authentic in the work of our artists; and this ideal of authenticity "requires that we discover and articulate our own identity" (Taylor 1991:81–2.). Authenticity may be self-referential in *manner* but the *matter* must serve to articulate something beyond the self. *I do things my way* but not *I do my thing*. What we do must be a response to the larger claims of nature and our world, but the artist, in responding, must do so in his or her own authentic voice. Our cultural agencies give artists an opportunity to develop authentic voices. They give resonance to those voices; they support what is best and most authentic in the work of our writers and artists; they sustain our Canadian distinctiveness, our specific sensibility, and our way of apprehending and evaluating the world. In the United States, the National Endowment for the Arts, for example, is not empowered to make grants to individual artists. Individuals, in the libertarian tradition, are on their own. The Canada Council for the Arts, on the other hand, reserves 20 per cent of its grants budget for grants to individual artists. Individuals in Canada have a place in a civil network.

As the forces of continentalization grow stronger, Canada urgently needs a reaffirmation of the policies that support Crown agencies in the cultural sector, among them the Canada Council for the Arts, the CBC, the National Film Board, the National Gallery, the Canadian Museum of Civilization, and the National Arts Centre. Artists themselves overwhelmingly recognize the importance of these agencies. As Inuit filmmaker Zacharias Kunuk explained: "With Council financing and video as our tool, we have been able to record and save our culture"(Kunuk, in conversation with Canada Council, 1999 August). And as Acadian writer Antonine Maillet wrote: "*Sans doute aurais-je écrit, avec ou sans le Conseil des Arts. Mais aurais-je pu le faire au même rythme, et avec la même liberté ? Le peuple acadien n'avait pas d'antécédents d'écriture avant ma génération. Il avait besoin d'un encouragement inconditionnel et ferme pour croire à son étoile, pour réaliser l'impensable de faire franchir à une culture le passage de l'oral à l'écrit.*" (Maillet, correspondence with the Canada Council, 1999).

In concluding, let me be clear that I do not think there is anything wrong or morally inferior about the U.S.-style libertarian sensibility. We should realize, however, that for Canadians to embrace that sensibility would leave us without the real ground of our distinctiveness and the *raison d'être* of our sovereignty. It is not the fact that an artist or a producer of art was born in Canada or is a Canadian citizen that is going to interest others. It is the distinctiveness and authenticity of that artist's sensibility, of his or her way of perceiving and evaluating the world.

My final note is one of optimism. Whatever the political and economic changes we face, I think that Canada will remain distinct. An irreducible factor making for Canadian cultural distinctiveness is our land. Canadian culture, whatever forms it may take, will always have to shape itself to our demanding geography and landscape. Ontario poet Al Purdy recognized this:

> during the fall plowing a man
> might stop and stand in a brown valley of the furrows
>   and shade his eyes to watch for the same
>   red patch mixed with gold
>   that appears on the same
>   spot on the hills

> year after year
> and grow old
> plowing and plowing a ten-acre field until
> the convolutions run parallel with his own brain –

(Purdy 1972:119).

I sincerely hope that Canada's cultural agencies will be empowered to continue fostering this creative tension in our artists' voices between the places that we come from and the place where we are throughout the twenty-first century.

References

Atwood, M. 1982. *Second Words: Selected Critical Prose.* Toronto: House of Anansi Press Ltd.

Frye, N. 1971. *The Bush Garden.* Toronto: House of Anansi Press Ltd.

Lipset, S.M. 1990. *Continental Divide.* New York and London: Routledge.

McLuhan, M. 1977. "Canada: The Borderline Case." In *The Canadian Imagination,* ed. David Staines. Cambridge, MA: Harvard University Press.

Newman, P. 1995. *The Canadian Revolution: From Deference to Defiance.* Toronto: Viking Penguin.

Purdy, A. 1972. "The Country North of Belleville." *Selected Poems.* Toronto and Montréal: McClelland & Stewart Ltd.

Taylor, C. 1991. *The Malaise of Modernity.* CBC Massey Lectures Series. Toronto: House of Anansi Press Ltd.

Pour une convention multilatérale sur la culture

Jean-Louis Roy

E N DEUX COURTES DÉCENNIES, NOUS SOMMES PASSÉS « DE LA FIN DE
l'histoire » posée comme conséquence inéluctable de la victoire de
l'économie de marché aux exigences plus durables « de la recomposition » de la communauté internationale. Nous sommes passés de
« l'euphorie conquérante » des vainqueurs de la grande bataille
idéologique du siècle précédent aux requêtes multiples visant à
assurer la sécurité et le développement de la famille humaine. Nous
sommes passés de l'énoncé d'un *credo* de certitudes concernant les
finalités à la réalité de la délibération concernant ces finalités.

Considérables, ces bouleversements constituent des révélateurs
précieux. Ils prouvent hors de tout doute que nous vivons une période
exceptionnelle et font apparaître à nouveau les deux dimensions constitutives de la famille humaine : d'une part, son aspiration à l'unité, cette
très ancienne quête toujours déçue ; d'autre part, l'évidence de sa diversité constitutive, positionnement toujours remis en cause.

Pour les uns, l'installation de l'économie de marché comme unique
fiduciaire du développement fournit enfin le cadre unique de référence
et des principes susceptibles d'ordonnancer le monde selon un modèle
unique. Pour les autres, ce qui est advenu dans la dernière décennie du
vingtième siècle, c'est d'abord la mise à jour de tout ce qui a été recou-
vert, dissimulé, empêché par les sédimentations idéologiques
dominantes au siècle dernier, une sorte de libération ou d'irruption des
aspirations, des identités, des cultures, des disparités aussi, si triste-
ment prégnantes dans notre monde.

Ceux-là ne remettent pas nécessairement en cause l'économie de
marché. Ce qu'ils mettent en cause, c'est sa revendication d'autonomie
absolue, sa prétention à animer seule le développement, sa négation
de l'espace public, sa prétention à poser comme « naturelles » des

normes construites par des opérations privées et à les présenter comme des règles, valeurs et objectifs susceptibles de structurer les sociétés, toutes les sociétés ; les activités humaines, toutes les activités humaines. Leur argumentaire occupe désormais une place centrale dans les discussions et négociations en cours visant l'aménagement de la communauté internationale.

Qu'il s'agisse de la réforme des institutions multilatérales, de la négociation du millénaire, de la mise en marché de nouveaux produits découlant de l'application de la science génétique aux espèces végétales et animales, de la mise à jour des politiques sociales, des réformes de l'aide publique au développement, l'économie de marché est soumise à la question récurrente suivante : « Que lui faut-il devenir pour être une voie diversifiée d'organisation du monde, pour prendre en compte le vaste domaine du désir et des besoins humains ? »

En 1993 et 1994 ce sont les producteurs de culture qui, les premiers, ont soumis la logique de l'économie de marché à cette question fondamentale, réclamé et obtenu une première « exception » à son implacable logique. Utile, voire indispensable en son temps, cette politique défensive apparaît obsolète dans la phase actuelle de la mondialisation. Elle a eu cependant l'immense mérite de réhabiliter la délibération et d'imposer la permanence de l'espace public.

Dans la phase actuelle de la mondialisation, il apparaît raisonnable de penser le développement culturel de la famille humaine à partir des quatre assises suivantes :

1. Les conditions de la libre circulation des idées et des œuvres de l'esprit au plan international n'ont jamais été aussi favorables, et ces dernières disposent de moyens technologiques nouveaux de grande portée pour la diffusion, la connaissance et l'appréciation des cultures du monde ;

2. La culture est devenue matière de l'industrie, de l'économie nationale et internationale, et les industries de la culture font désormais partie de l'économie de marché ;

3. L'identification des espaces de création avec les espaces culturels convenus tend à se distancier comme reflet de la mutation des sociétés, de l'accélération de leur recomposition, et de la présence des cultures du monde partout dans celui-ci grâce aux réseaux mondiaux de communication dont Internet ;

4. Les évolutions technologiques annulent en partie les contenus de l'exception culturelle. Ces derniers pourraient être réduits à

une constellation symbolique dans l'avenir prévisible. Les tenants de l'exception culturelle ont justement évalué cette mutation en abandonnant cette appellation en faveur de celle plus juste, plus dynamique aussi, de diversité culturelle, ce grand territoire de l'imprévisible.

Dans un tel contexte, il ne s'agit pas de recomposer autrement les politiques culturelles anciennes, d'en rénover la façade et, d'un secteur à l'autre, d'éteindre les feux. Une autre synthèse, complexe, difficile et indispensable, doit être trouvée. Cette synthèse appelle une véritable révolution copernicienne dans notre appréhension, compréhension et appréciation de la diversité culturelle du monde. Cette recomposition n'est pas évidente, ni les formes susceptibles de l'exprimer et de la traduire en termes opérationnels. Pour ma part, j'estime qu'elle doit se déployer dans une convention multilatérale spécifique exprimant les réalités du monde tel qu'il est en train de se reconstituer.

Aucun texte cependant, aucune perspective de renouvellement ne fera l'économie d'une recomposition radicale qui est d'abord celle de nos esprits habitués à penser le monde à partir des prismes nationaux et occidentaux. Sommes-nous capables d'une hospitalité plus universelle, d'une interprétation de l'histoire des sciences, des arts et du droit qui soit inclusive et non exclusive? Sommes-nous capables de comprendre les ères de civilisation et les cultures du monde comme des fragments susceptibles de complémentarité bien davantage que des totalités qui s'affrontent? Sommes-nous désireux de prendre en compte et de privilégier la fécondation réciproque des cultures dans la longue durée, plutôt que leur appropriation à des fins d'apologie nationale, de puissance ou de domination?

Je travaille présentement à la préparation d'un dictionnaire interculturel. Les enfants qui le consulteront apprendront que le lointain ancêtre de l'ordinateur est un mathématicien chinois dont les inventions ont transité par l'Inde avant d'être assimilées par les Arabes qui les ont transportées en Europe voilà six siècles, puis, deux siècles plus tard, acclimatées à l'Amérique qui en a fait notamment le réseau des réseaux. Ils y apprendront aussi que Matisse disait de l'art contemporain qu'il s'appuie sur les créations de la Renaissance et les images du Moyen-Âge, et plus loin dans le passé, vers l'art hindou et persan. Il existe comme une mondialisation verticale et les métissages sont plus anciens que l'actuelle mondialisation horizontale. « La rivière », disent nos amis africains, « est plus vieille que la route ».

Vous connaissez les travaux magistraux de Joseph Needham, travaux consacrés à la Chine, et les deux questions qui les éclairent :

1. La question de ses amis chinois : « Comment pouvez-vous soutenir que la science moderne origine seulement de l'Europe ? »
2. Et sa propre question : « *How could it be that the Chinese civilization had been much more effective than the European in finding out about nature and using natural knowledge for the benefit of mankind for fourteen centuries or so before the scientific revolution ?* »

La synthèse évoquée plus haut doit bien évidemment déborder les perspectives des lobbies culturels occidentaux et celles des politiques qui leur donnent un prolongement du côté du pouvoir. Elle trouve sens et direction dans cette recomposition radicale de nos esprits et dans nos esprits.

Si les cultures du monde sont diverses, et elles le sont, si cette diversité constitue une valeur radicale, alors il faut en tirer les conséquences et lancer le grand chantier de l'inclusion des cultures dans les programmes scolaires, les œuvres en référence, nos programmes de soutien à la création, la direction prise par les industries de la culture, celles aussi des grandes manifestations culturelles nationales et mondiales actuelles et à venir. Cette approche doit inclure aussi la recherche des convergences éthiques à l'œuvre dans notre monde. Bref, ce qui nous est demandé par l'exceptionnelle mutation politique et technique actuelle et par l'explosion de nos capacités de communication et d'interactivité, c'est de dégager les fondements communs des « identités en flux » évoqués par Charles Taylor, dans un monde où la reconnaissance devient un enjeu de premier plan, dans un temps aussi, pour citer à nouveau le grand philosophe, où il apparaît « déplorable et injustifié de tracer des frontières trop étroites qui n'incluraient pas tout le genre humain. »

Nous plaidons ici pour un changement de nature des conceptions des identités et des cultures comme préalable à l'aménagement de l'espace culturel mondial et des politiques culturelles nationales. Traduites dans des règles communes, ces conceptions doivent, à terme, être consignées dans une convention multilatérale spécifique et traduire notamment les impératifs suivants :

1. Reconnaissance de la singularité et de la centralité du domaine culturel dans l'ensemble de la production humaine;
2. Attachement au pluralisme, l'indispensable adhésion à sa propre culture et à l'existence de toutes les cultures, et engagement de traduire cet attachement dans des politiques inclusives;
3. Consentement à la libre circulation des biens et œuvres culturels ne pouvant être réduits à la production du divertissement;
4. Maintien des conditions de la concurrence et rejet de toute situation de monopole dans la production et la diffusion des œuvres culturelles. Autrement, dans un grand nombre de pays, les entreprises culturelles locales seront balayées et la production propre réduite à l'insignifiance. Dans cet esprit, la recherche d'un niveau équitable de réciprocité assurant « la présence sur un territoire d'œuvres culturelles étrangères et la diffusion à l'étranger d'œuvres culturelles nationales » doit être initiée et conduite à son terme;
5. Possibilité d'un soutien public à la création et aux infrastructures de production, de distribution et de diffusion des œuvres culturelles;
6. Enrichissement substantiel du volet d'appui aux cultures du monde dans la politique de coopération internationale.

Cette synthèse inédite s'impose. Ni le *statu quo* des politiques classiques, ni la reconduction de « l'exception » ne sont susceptibles de produire la sécurité culturelle indispensable à la sécurité spirituelle, sociale et matérielle de la famille humaine dans le siècle qui vient. Cette synthèse s'impose. Cependant elle a peu de chance de réussir si l'exclusion des bénéfices de la mondialisation devait se perpétuer, exclusion qui, selon la Banque mondiale, touche une bonne moitié de l'humanité, ces pays « non-membres de l'économie mondiale » selon la triste expression de l'Organisation de Coopération et de Développement Économiques (l'OCDE).

Telles sont les finalités d'une convention multilatérale spécifique en matière de culture. Certes une telle convention n'est pas susceptible à elle seule d'éponger les inquiétudes et les affrontements actuels. Mais elle y contribuera indiscutablement et substantiellement en les insérant dans un pacte de confiance conjuguant les réalités du monde telles qu'elles deviennent et la volonté des hommes et des sociétés rassemblées, en renouvelant la notion même d'identité et en faisant apparaître la part déterminante et commune qu'elle recèle. Il nous reste à placer au centre de notre réflexion et de nos travaux la réalité du lien entre les cultures en nous rappelant ce court poème de Shinoyasu Anzuki : « J'ai appris quelque chose d'intéressant aujourd'hui, la lumière sans objet réflecteur n'éclaire pas. »

Identity and Otherness in Canadian Foreign Policy

Maria Teresa Gutiérrez-Haces

I N ANALYSES OF CANADA FOR OVER FIVE DECADES, CERTAIN ISSUES ARE recognized as mandatory for any work or research carried out in Canada or abroad. Canadian foreign policy is one of the political topics considered to have become a mandatory issue, competing in importance with the analysis of Canadian federalism. An analogous situation has occurred throughout the cultural and social studies fields, where projects on multiculturalism and Canadian identity have also been the subject of important essays, not only in Canada, but also abroad.

For years, these issues have been particularly attractive to many political scientists from outside Canada who explore the singularity of Canadian foreign policy in relation to their own fields of study. Therefore, analyses related to the self-definition of Canada as a middle power, and the implications of the Third Option as part of Canadian foreign policy under the Trudeau government, has been one of the most recurrent topics in academic activity at the international level. The same applies to multilateralism and internationalism, distinctive features of Canadian international policy.

More recently, the establishment of a foreign policy based on United Nations (UN) proposals that promote the principles of Human Security has also inspired numerous analyses. Such topics are among the most visible examples of interest in Canadian Studies in relation to their political and international aspects, but not to the exclusion of interest, as in the fields of literature and political philosophy, where writers such as Margaret Atwood, George Grant, Charles Taylor, Margaret Lawrence, Northrop Frye, and James Tully have become genuine international Canadian icons.

In spite of the intellectual success of Canadian foreign policy as an object of survey, there are areas for analysis that have not been deeply explored, perhaps because the approach of a foreign writer is not necessarily aimed at answering the same questions of interest to a Canadian scholar. One of the short-term effects resulting from the study of Canadian foreign policy internationally has been the appearance of projects that differ from those carried out in Canada. In many cases, such projects stand out both for their innovative methodology and their use of non-traditional analytical tools from fields such as psychology, literature, and social and cultural studies among others (Badie and Smouts 1999:23–27, 38–64). This digression from traditional approaches prevailing in international studies has diversified and enriched the study of Canada in the field of international relations.

Discourse on 'otherness,' obviously related to identity analysis, both of which have served as tools for the specific analysis of Canadian foreign policy, fits in this perspective. In this essay, discourse on otherness is an analytical resource, expressed on three levels in Canadian foreign policy. On the first level, 'alterity' emerges as a substantial part of a strategy that the Canadian government has often used, since the Second World War, to legitimize several government policies designed to reinforce internally the discourse on Canadian identity.

Similarly, at a second level of analysis, discourse on alterity in Canadian foreign policy has been incorporated for twenty-five years, in one of the international strategies used by the Department of Foreign Affairs and International Trade. This department's promotion of Canadian Studies programmes and culture systematically contributes to the Canadian identity studied and promoted abroad, thus reinforcing from the outside, the image and identity existing in Canada.

A third level of analysis provides an additional variant to the use of alterity within the discourse on Canadian foreign policy. This third path shows that the discourse on alterity also influences the analyses carried out by some foreign writers. This third use consists of examining and using Canadian foreign policy as an explicative resource to study specific aspects of foreign policy of another country. This tendency, though based on the tradition of comparative studies, goes beyond this field in a certain way, as its originality resides much more in the use of the discourse on alterity than in the comparison of political processes.

Plainly speaking, it could be said that analyses by foreign writers display a marked tendency to examine Canadian foreign policy as a means of analyzing a reality that has nothing to do with Canada, thus overstepping the geographic, political, and intellectual boundaries of the initial analysis of Canada.

Thus the analysis of democracy in Canada, the study of multiculturalism, the promotion of human rights, Canada's experience as the United States's neighbour, and its participation in free trade, have all become resources for explaining situations often opposed, such as antidemocratic policy practices, commercial protectionism, violation of human rights, the lack of a sustainable environmental strategy, and the absence of a comprehensive policy on the ethnic minorities in other countries.

This essay has two purposes. On the one hand, it aims to analyse the link between the formulation of Canadian foreign policy and the Canadian government's repeated efforts to build a pan-Canadian identity based mainly on the international promotion of certain universal values. On the other hand, it aims to analyse, based on elements that make up a substantial part of the official discourse on Canadian foreign policy, a discourse on otherness and identity in Canada.

In this sense, three important distinctions that are implicitly but not necessarily exhaustively, analysed in this study, should be made clear from the outset:

- The formulation of a discourse on the Canadian identity, within its own discourse on foreign policy of this country, has been a federal political strategy toward international policy since the forties.
- The province of Québec has also formulated its own *identitaria* discourse on international policy, especially from the sixties on, as a result of changes brought about by the Quiet Revolution. This discourse shares, to a great extent, federal postulates around the international promotion of Canadian values but has, at the same time, issued other postulates to gain acknowledgement of Québec as a political speaker in the international arena. The reflections of Louis Bélanger on the subject widely illustrate the way in which the international policy of Québec formulates the Québécois identity:

En raison à la fois de son statut et de ses objectifs, l'État du Québec doit faire face de façon évidente au défi de se faire reconnaître comme interlocuteur politique à l'étranger. Cette quête d'identité n'est pas aussi singulière qu'il le semble puisque, au-delà de la reconnaissance formelle, chaque État cherche dans ses relations avec l'extérieur la reconnaissance d'une expérience historique particulière (Bélanger 1995:71).

• This means both that foreign policy traditionally formulated by the federal government and that deriving from Québec, express a clear political will to use international policy as a mechanism of *identitaria* affirmation.
• The use of otherness in this strategy is closer to the federal government's attempt to formulate a pan-Canadian identity.

This essay approaches an analysis of Canadian foreign policy mainly from the perspective of identity and otherness, but it does not mean to downplay the validity and importance of the international policy of Québec in examining identity.

The legitimation of postulates inherent in a certain foreign policy depends directly on how closely the interests and values of the society relate to the proposals put forward by the state through its foreign policy. In view of all this, the state needs to build an 'Imaginary,' which any individual could identify with. This Imaginary must be made up of symbols, whether individuals, ideas, principles, or rituals, to transmit a feeling of common identity (Edelman 1983; Elder and Cobb 1983).

National feeling is unquestionably an elusive concept. It evokes both the sense of belonging to a certain territory and of loyalty to certain values and national institutions, which doubtless represent the most useful cohesion resource for any state. It is also a prerequisite for foreign policy to be considered legitimate. Our analysis of Canadian foreign policy and, through it, the formulation of a pan-Canadian identity, has been theoretically enriched by William Bloom's work on identification theory. This theory "is concerned precisely with the deep psychological relationship between an individual and his/her social environment," and the internationalization of these "social attitudes", thus providing "an analytical tool which clarifies the attitudes and the motivation of both the individual and the mass citizenry in relation to their state and their state's international relations" (Bloom 1990:4). In his analysis, Bloom mentions that the connection between internationalization and identification may occur if "(1) symbols of the state present an appropriate attitude in situations of perceived threat, or (2) symbols of the state behave beneficently towards the individual" (1990:61).

Though a specific case survey on Canadian foreign policy is not presented in Bloom's works, his analysis of the need for a state to produce symbols that strengthen the feeling of a national identity and a foreign policy that strengthens such identity through its international actions, offers important lessons for our research.[1] And he adds: "From a power political perspective of internal political control it is advantageous, therefore (a) to evoke a common identification and then (b) to possess a monopoly of power in terms of manipulating the symbols of that identity" (1990:51).

Further on, Bloom insists in his analysis that "the national identity dynamic, therefore, describes the social-psychological dynamic by which a mass national public may be mobilized in relation to its international environment ... the mass national public will mobilize when it perceives either that [its] national identity is threatened, or that there is the opportunity of enhancing national identity" (1990:79).

One of the most interesting characteristics of the Canadian case is precisely the virtual absence of symbols traditionally sought by other states to create or reinforce the national identity. The decision of Prime Minister Lester B. Pearson in 1964 that Canadian society needed its own flag to distinguish it from the United Kingdom is an example of an attempt to build a more tangible identity in Canada. As Pearson stated: "On the evening of Sunday, 17 May 1963, I addressed the National Convention of the Royal Canadian Legion in Winnipeg. Under the steely eyes of a hostile audience, I announced to the assembled war veterans and to the country at large that we were going to have a distinctive Canadian flag. For me, the flag was part of a deliberate design to strengthen national unity" (Pearson 1975, 3:270).

In his works, Bloom insists on the need for the state to be able to create symbols and rituals with which it clearly identifies. Nevertheless, we think that symbols and rituals also tend to reinvent themselves, the way a specific society does. In this sense, the process of globalization has obviously influenced the speed to which traditional symbols and rituals have weakened or disappeared.

Considering all of the above, we think that Canadian foreign policy, formulated on a universal axiological base and not on rituals and symbols, has escaped, to a certain extent, the decay related to certain principles, heroes, deeds, and sagas that nourished the foreign policy of certain countries. An example of this argument would be the international strategy that, in recent years, has been implemented in Canada. This strategy of the Department of Foreign Affairs and International Trade was based on a series of principles known as Human Security and was the main objective of international negotiations undertaken by then Foreign Minister Lloyd Axworthy.[2] It served as a justification for Canada's presence on the international scene.

Within Canadian foreign policy, the international promotion of what is commonly known as human values has traditionally occupied an important place. Practically every Prime Minister, and everyone else responsible for Canadian foreign policy, from W.L. Mackenzie King (1921–1926, 1926–1930 and 1935–1948), Louis Saint-Laurent (1948–1957), Lester B. Pearson (1963–1968) or Pierre Elliott Trudeau (1968–1980), to former Minister of Foreign Affairs and International Trade, Lloyd Axworthy (1993–2000), and current Prime Minister Jean Chrétien (1993–) have always mentioned these values as a key element to explain and justify Canada's position in the world (Pearson 1975; Melakopides 1998; Granatstein and Hillmer 1999).

Since the 1940s, it has often been said, in both national and international forums, that Canadian foreign policy implies responsibility for as well as an answer to the needs of humanity. Louis Saint-Laurent as foreign minister, for one, stated it clearly in 1947: "No foreign policy is consistent nor coherent over a period of years unless it is based upon some conception of human values" (as quoted in Melakopides 1998:3). The inclusion of certain human values in Canadian foreign policy directly reflects the main ideas of the prevailing political culture of the country, which has traditionally favoured moderation, intercession, and cooperation as well as sharing and looking after those less fortunate. In other words, "concern for the welfare of others is one of the central values" (Canada, External Affairs 1970, fascicule "International Development":9.)

Suffice it to say that this political culture, as well as Canadian international policy, has been deeply influenced by religious principles from both Catholicism and Protestantism, mainly through a great number of politicians who have been responsible for formulating and implementing Canadian foreign policy. According to writers such as Costas Melakopides and Denis Stairs, the circle created by the ideas and actions of Pearson on Canadian internationalism, in the Department of External Affairs at the end of the 1940s, and more strongly between 1963 and 1968, was closely related to ethical and religious principles. Like other public officers involved in Canadian diplomacy such as Arnold Heeney and Scott Reid, Pearson was the child of a protestant minister; Walter Ridell was a Methodist minister; Hugh Keenleyside also came from a Methodist background (Stairs 1994; Melakopides 1998:85).

According to this line of analysis, it is important to mention that the main idea behind Pearsonian internationalism was definitely the interdependence of all creatures. Melakopides mentions that the moral values that sustained this discourse were connected to the Canadian and British Protestant tradition. This reflection has also been thoroughly analysed by other writers such as John English who stated that Pearson, throughout his public life: "never spoke of God or called upon him to explain or justify his ways ... Nevertheless, Pearson's thought, language, and ethics bear heavily the weight of the tradition [of British Protestantism]" (as quoted in Melakopides 1998:85).

As of 1945, the values traditionally sustained by Canadian foreign policy were transformed into what is commonly known as 'Canadian Internationalism.' This translated into certain specific international actions by the Canadian government, such as the creation of peacekeepers, promotion of human rights, support for democratization, disarmament and weapons control, and aid to development in economically weak countries. We must not forget that such objectives were promoted by Canadian diplomacy in the midst of the East-West conflict arising from the Cold War.

This internationalism was based on what Pearson considered to be one of Canada's principal defenses: being a mid-power historically inclined towards multilateral style actions (Cooper 1997; Nossal 1985:52–84, 138–164). As Pearson stated in 1948: "modesty or timidity should not be confused with isolationism ... this timidity is a sensible recognition of the fact that middle powers ... can now merely expand their responsibilities and their worries." That meant "a recognition of the internationalist view that countries must come closer together inside a United Nations rather than take over areas and responsibilities outside it" (Pearson 1970:68–69).

In hindsight, Pearson was doubtless one of the prime ministers who most contributed to the creation of the 'Canadian international identity' and to the idea, widely spread over the years, that Canada, speaking politically and internationally, possesses an 'exceptional' and 'different' character. His main worry – amply documented in his memoirs and by his biographers – was not only the need to imprint a clear, pragmatic idealism on his internationalism, but also to create the internal conditions for consolidation of a national identity that would unite Canadians.

Such worry was obvious in the third volume of his autobiography, where he often repeats it in passages such as:

> My passionate interest when I was in government, apart from the ultimate question of peace and war, was in the national unity of our country. In some respects this was the most important issue of my career. National unity is a problem of many facets embracing, among other factors, the constitution, federal provincial relations and the bread and butter issues of tax sharing and equalization grants. But, in the long run, I am convinced that the problems of culture and language are pre-eminent; and I would like to think that our government made a permanent contribution to their solution" (Pearson 1975, 3:236).

At the time, foreign policy was greatly influenced by the findings of the Royal Commission on Bilinguism and Biculturalism (1963), created at his initiative as prime minister, out of determination to have the French language officially recognized in political matters, including diplomacy: "I was convinced from the beginning, as I remain convinced now, that a prime element is the recognition of the French language. Nothing could be more important in my mind than an effort to make our French-speaking people feel that their language is an equal language in Canada." And again: "I was convinced that if Canada were to be strong, independent, and distinct state on this continent, we had to do everything in our power to extend French culture and the French language throughout Canada" (Pearson 1975, 3:236–37).

From the 1970s, during the Trudeau era, the language issues and human values promoted by Canadian foreign policy changed. They came to be identified and mentioned officially as 'Canadian values' within the context of the foreign policy of the country. Canada's emphatic and steady defence and promotion of these values internationally has given rise to a kind of 'international identity.' Paradoxically, this identity has been better accepted and supported domestically than official proposals offered to consolidate a national identity internally. In this regard, Melakopides affirms that, "Canadian foreign policy may, therefore, provide an indirect but compelling answer to the perennial question of Canada's 'identity.' For if

Canada is perceived by non-Canadians as one of the most honourable, enlightened, and civilized international actors which comes mainly from the record and the motives of Canadian foreign policy" (Melakopides 1998:4).

We may therefore deduce that Canadian foreign policy applies its actions and initiatives internationally as a spearhead to promote certain values and principles that are internally reworked and recycled to promote a Canadian identity. In other words, otherness turns into a privileged resource for Canadian foreign policy. As stated by Melakopides, "this is especially paradoxical because, for a country that appears perennially sensitive about its identity, Canadian foreign policy seems, in fact, to contain the most promising answer. If a country's identity hinges on the perceptions of others, Canada's identity could best be captured by the way it is seen, and the reasons it is so seen, by the world" (1998:14). This strategy has worked, to a certain extent, as a permanent 'contrivance' to consolidate 'from the outside,' the set of values, ideals, and principles that constitute the heart of the Canadian identity. This identity, perceived from outside, pretends to recreate an internal identity that will underpin from 'inside' the unfinished project of pan-Canadian unity.

This attempt to create an exogenous *identitaria*, based on Canada's international actions, would not have been possible if an 'imaginary' had not previously been built internally around what would ideally comprise a Canadian identity and Canadian values. Without this imaginary, the creation of exceptionalism in 'Canada's foreign policy (distinction-distinctiveness-unique) would be very hard to maintain.

At this point of our analysis certain questions should be addressed:

- How and who creates an 'imaginary' in foreign policy?
- Is it possible to speak about institutions and minds that feed a specific 'imaginary'?
- What have been and are the perceptions and experiences of Canadians of yesterday and today regarding the construction of a Canadian identity?
- What are the perceptions of foreigners who study Canada and who also build their own 'imaginary' about Canadian 'distinction/distinctiveness'?

Historically, the construction of the imaginary *identitaria* in Canada has faced two great challenges: cultural diversity and the antagonism caused by a politically complex linguistic diversity. How have these two aspects affected foreign policy? Regarding these questions, certain dates offer important clues to the way in which the Canadian imaginary *identitaria* is built:

- Until 1936, every document in the business and financial world was issued in English, even papers to conduct small trade operations.
- In 1938, a reform to the *Civil Service Act* required government officials to "speak the language spoken by most of the people they served."
- In 1947, the *Canadian Citizenship Act* legally acknowledged the people who lived in Canada as Canadians.
- Only after the First World War (1914–1918) was it decided to professionalize the Canadian Army and to take into consideration that most of the troops spoke French while the high-ranking leaders ordered in English.
- In 1947, Prime Minister W. L. Mackenzie King appointed an *ad hoc* commission to investigate the absence of bilingual public services, after discovering that not even police reports acknowledged this situation.
- In 1958, the National Capital was established.
- In 1965, Canada obtained its own flag and stopped using the Union Jack, symbol of the United Kingdom.
- In 1969, the federal government was officially established as bilingual (Francis 1997).

These dates offer a very accurate idea of the facts, experiences, and perceptions on which the inhabitants of Canada were building their imaginary *identitaria*.

It is quite obvious that these aspects must all have influenced Canadian foreign policy, that in turn faced its own identity problems. One of these problems was the unanswerable influence of England on the institutional and bureaucratic order within the operations of Canadian foreign policy (Morton 1962:32–57).

This analysis does not intend to repeat the well-based explanations on the origins of Canadian foreign policy before and after the *Statute of Westminster, 1931*, or the way it marked it, or its functional link to British international policy. However, we can doubtless say that the years after 1930 were especially difficult for a country such as

Canada which began constructing its own diplomacy quite late, while on the same continent, Latin American countries and, of course, the United States had been diplomatically autonomous for over a century (Story 1993; Hilliker 1990). Indeed, prior to the Second World War, every Canadian international relationship, as well as its commercial diplomacy and its safety and espionage systems had to pass through British High Commissioners abroad before arriving in Ottawa.

Obviously, the institutional order established following the Second World War offered Canadians the opportunity to open their own embassies and conduct a foreign policy that was more their own than before 1945.

In the aforementioned paragraphs, I dealt with the postulates that Canadian foreign policy depends on the extent to which the interests and values of society are reflected in the proposals put forward by the Canadian state. With this idea as a guideline, I will now consider certain reflections arising from an analysis of official documents published by the Department of Foreign Affairs and International Trade (DFAIT).

Firstly, I will analyze how foreign policy objectives have evolved in the debate over Canadian identity, based on documents published by the department responsible for foreign affairs between 1970 and 1990. In these documents, I will examine the kind of Canadian identity that is reflected in Canadian foreign policy, which, as I have already mentioned, promotes values that do not have as a conceptual referent either a language or a predominant culture. These values essentially reflect universal interests and worries. This is wherein lies its internal consensus and international success.

From these documents, it can be inferred that the Canadian identity promoted specifically by foreign policy tries to reconcile its relationship with the United States on two levels. On one level, Canadian foreign policy emphasizes its identity and differentiation through internationalism and Canadian values. On another level Canadian foreign policy, more recently, has promoted Canadian identity based on a concept of American-ness or North American-ness, which relates back to a space called North America.

'Americanity' is then the antithesis of an Americanized identity and the answer to the accusations concerning the continentalization of Canadian foreign policy. As Fox explains,

Canada's search for identity led Canadians to stress their North-American-ness when they sought to differentiate themselves and their policy from the British and Britain's policy, while North-American-ness got in the way when differentiation from the United States and American policy was sought ... Australians demonstrate their sense of identity ... by calling the English Pommies; Canadians have no comparable word for demonstrating that they are not Americans; but they too make use of symbols of counteridentification, particularly in foreign policy. 'Independent' for them means not just foreign policies that are freely chosen; it may also mean made-in-Canada policies and even policies deliberately different from those the United States has chosen" (Fox 1985:64, 76).[3]

Canadian values, mostly after 1990, have been promoted within a strategic thrust of Canadian foreign policy which has been called 'Public Diplomacy.' The intended outcome of this strategy was "to create interest and confidence in Canada abroad and an international public environment favourable to Canada's political and economic interests and Canadian values" (Canada, DFAIT, 1999:32). In other words, among the stated objectives of Public Diplomacy is the promotion of Canadian identity abroad and the enhancement of Canadians' attachment to Canada by means of a greater awareness of the international role of this country.

The White Paper entitled *Foreign Policy for Canadians* was issued in 1970 and discussed six diplomatic areas in which Canadian foreign policy intended to concentrate its strategies: economic growth; sovereignty and independence; peace and safety; social justice; improvement of quality of life; and conservation of harmony in the environment. This document has been quoted and analysed to such an extent that thirty-one years after its publication, it remains an 'icon' of Canadian foreign policy (Canada, External Affairs 1970).[4] I will limit comment on it to aspects that reinforce an analysis of the promotion of values and Canadian identity in the international sphere.

One aspect that attracts attention is the idea of Canada as a 'mentor-state.' Melakopides mentions the perception of Trudeau when this document was published: "Trudeau perceived Canada as a 'mentor state' capable of being a model to the world. He repeatedly referred to the need for a 'global ethic'" (Melakopides 1998:9). Clearly, the mechanism of promoting Canadian values through Canadian international policy forms part of a much wider process in which Canadian foreign policy seeks to teach, share, and guide other countries in relation to Canadian values, and even to promote the acceptance of global ethics. This strategy, as already mentioned, combines the ethical-religious tradition of Judeo-Christian ideals, conveyed in such famous phrases by Trudeau as "We are all brothers," or "We are one on this earth" (as quoted in Melakopides 1998:9).

From this point of view, Canadian values must prevail, and what better way than to use established diplomatic channels: "A society able to ignore poverty abroad will find it much easier to ignore it at home; a society concerned with poverty and development abroad will be concerned about poverty and development at home" (Canada, External Affairs 1970, fascicule "International Development":9). On analysis, the document also argues that Canadians, as well as their government, would not be able to create a really fair society, inside Canada "if [they] were not prepared to play [their] part in the creation of a more just world society" (1970:9).

One point that deserves to be mentioned: all of the documents under discussion contain evidence of a deepening economic character of Canadian foreign policy, under two courses of action – commercial diplomacy and aid to development. These two courses complement the strategies used to promote universal values that Canada has adopted as its own. In this sense, it must not be forgotten that the economic historian Donald Creighton defined Canada as a "commercial state;" thus the economic component was always present in the strategies linked to Canadian foreign policy.

The second document on Canadian foreign policy, produced by the Special Joint Committee on International Relations of the Senate and the House of Commons, called *Independence and Internationalism*, was issued as a Green Paper and meant to be a base document to elicit the opinion of Canadians on the new directions of Canadian foreign policy (Canada, Special Joint Committee 1986). These directions had been made public a year earlier by Brian Mulroney's government under the title *Competitiveness and Security: Directions for Canada's International Relations* (Canada, Foreign Affairs 1985). Several observations derive from the Green Paper. The first recognizes that the government established a new precedent: public consultations on foreign policy that gave a more democratic character to the development of Canadian foreign policy. Secondly, it was the first time that

Canadian foreign policy was analysed by a parliamentary *ad hoc* committee and debated both in the House of Commons and in the Senate. A third observation from reading the Green Paper is that the first of the six objectives proposed in it was national unity; the other five objectives were practically the same as those already proposed in *Foreign Policy for Canadians*, published in 1970 by the Liberal government of Trudeau.

A significant observation arising from the Green Paper was the need to create an international image of Canada, based on the values that identify it and make it highly reputable (Canada, Special Joint Committee 1986:27). This proposal is all the more relevant given that it contained the opinion of many Canadians: about 700 individuals, 300 witnesses and 287 organisms appeared before the committee in a first stage of hearings in the summer of 1985. Later, in May 1986, 245 organizations took part in a second round; these citizens agreed that national unity and strengthening the Canadian identity should be the top aim of Canadian foreign policy: "National unity has a grip on the souls of Canadians ... It stands at the head of Canada's objectives as the *sine qua non* for all the other collective goals that Canadians may decide to pursue." This subject is noteworthy for the document clearly mentions that Canadians have "recently been directing foreign policy to the achievement of national unity" (1986:32).

An aspect that stands out in *Independence and Internationalism* is the discourse on 'otherness' constructed around the concept that "the world acts as a mirror for Canadians." Another important point along the same line is the mention of Canada's bicultural and bilingual character followed by a statement that "Canada has to be able to present an image abroad that Canadians recognize as their own" (1986:32).

In contrast to the conciliatory tone of most of the other documents mentioned herein, *Independence and Internationalism* is quite direct about the position Canada is to play in its attempt to promote national unity through the promotion of global ethics: "Canada must be wary of foreign governments that may be tempted for one reason or another to take steps that could damage Canada's national cohesion" (1986:34). Incidentally, it should be noted that Lloyd Axworthy, Liberal member of Parliament for Winnipeg and Jean Chrétien, as Liberal MP for Saint Maurice, both current architects of Canada's foreign policy, were part of the Special Joint Committee on Canada's International Relations.

Though national unity occupied first place among the new goals, generally speaking it was linked to "the consequences of its vicinity to the United States," a subject ostensibly avoided in the White Paper of 1970. An article by Canada's then Foreign Affairs Minister Mitchel Sharp, entitled "Canada-U.S. Relations: Options for the Future" later corrected this omission (Sharp 1972).

The section more directly related to the objectives of this analysis is undoubtedly the one entitled "Influence Based on the Image and Reputation" in which it is argued that the way Canadians have been viewed abroad often works to their advantage (Canada, Special Joint Committee 1986:27–34).

The Green Paper also offers interesting clues on certain features of Canadian foreign policy, such as "its participation in peacekeeping forces, its advocacy of human rights, its unflagging support of the UN system" and states that "they have favourably influenced how the country is regarded abroad" and have added to its reputation (1986:27).

Lastly, with the 1995 publication of a document entitled *Canada in the World*, Canadian foreign policy clearly assumes the role of promoting the Canadian identity (Canada, DFAIT 1995). In different ways, the three pillars of Canadian foreign policy mentioned in this document support this identity, characterized by a regional identity, but always Canadian. Published under the current Liberal government of Prime Minister Jean Chrétien, this document represents the first time that a new group of Canadian values is openly defined, in addition to the existing ones. Among the economic values of Canada, the promotion of free trade emerges as an integral part of the new strategy of the Liberal government.

Yet economic as well as commercial concerns have occupied a relevant place in the Canadian international strategy since the 1970s when Trudeau introduced them into the institutional structure of the government. However, in the documents issued under his leadership, such as *Foreign Policy for Canadians*, economic values were never offensively defined as central to the axiomatic group that had traditionally promoted Canadian foreign policy. Perhaps the aim was to counterbalance the economic component with the importance and pertinence of such traditional Canadian values as democracy and human rights, not to mention the promotion of culture or Canadian Studies abroad.

Since 1990, promotion of the Canadian identity through its foreign policy has occupied an important place in the financial statements of DFAIT, in the name of Public Diplomacy, described and justified as follows: "The international perception of Canada is often dated and out of step with economic and other realities in Canada. In addressing this issue, the Department is pursuing public diplomacy activities to promote Canada's international academic and cultural relations" (Canada, DFAIT 1999:7).

Until the year 2000, DFAIT published detailed information about contributions to different international institutions and programs in its estimates and reports on plans and priorities. Thus, thanks to a detailed table on transfer payments by business line, we can analyse with certain adequacy the priorities of the federal government concerning foreign policy.

According to the public data published by DFAIT at the beginning of 2000 in *2000–2001 Estimates,* the Department's forecasted expenditure on budgetary policy for the years 1999-2000 was about $1,719.5 million, from which $94.7 million was earmarked for Public Diplomacy. This amount is less than that for "International Security and Cooperation": $479.1 million, "Corporate Services": $308.3 million, "International Business Development": $286.5 million and $215.7 million for "Trade and Economic Policy" (Canada, DFAIT 2000:8).

The Department's *1999-2000 Estimates,* published a year before, contained more detailed and disaggregated information which allows us to compare some important issues. In Forecast Spending 1998-99, grants allocated to "Aid to Academic Relations" amounted to $13,290,000 and those allocated to "Aid and Cultural Relations," $4,997,000, while under the column "Contributions," international institutions such as the Organization of American States (OAS) secured from DFAIT a budget of $12,775,000 in the same period. This is also observed in the case of the UN: $45,359,000 and the Peace Corps: $53,823,000 (Canada, DFAIT 1999:52–54).

These amounts indicate that the financial strategy of DFAIT reflects a prevailing interest in securing a space for negotiations at an international level that naturally allows the projection of a specific image of Canadian values and therefore affirms an identity constructed around the vision of the federal government. This strategy also presumes greater confidence in promoting Canadian identity through multilateral bodies such as the UN, the OAS, or the North Atlantic Treaty Organization than in financing more widely the cultural and academic relations that correspond to the budget line called Public Diplomacy. Clearly, though Canadian identity is promoted through the Public Diplomacy strategy, the definition of Canadian identity and values centres on the business line called "International Security and Cooperation," which considers the following: "Canada is a cosmopolitan country, with economic, security and cultural interests that span the globe. Canada is equally a compassionate country, with a values based foreign policy, backed by diplomatic skills and defense forces, by development assistance and civil society" (Canada, DFAIT 2000:19).

There are six strategic lines associated with Public Diplomacy:

1. Project Canada's image and values abroad.
2. Communicate to Canadians the importance of Canada's role in the world, the international dimensions of the government's priorities as well as the Department's role and the services it provides to Canadians.
3. Promote international, academic, and educational linkages.
4. Promote national unity.
5. Promote identity and attachment to Canada among Canadians through increased awareness of Canada's role abroad.
6. Ensure that foreign governments are aware of the flexibility and evolution of Canadian federalism, as well as the importance of the ongoing international role played by a strong and united Canada (Canada DFAIT 1999:33).

Finally, among the results that DFAIT is expected to accomplish through Public Diplomacy, I quote:

1. Greater public understanding in Canada and abroad of Canadian policies and positions.
2. International public awareness of Canada's characteristics and accomplishments through cultural, scholarly or comparable events.
3. Increased exports of cultural and educational products and services, including choice of Canada as a destination for foreign tourists and students (1999:35).

These strategic lines widely reflect the discourse on otherness that Canadian foreign policy has been developing through Public Diplomacy.

The Public Diplomacy and Human Security strategies are without doubt, the most ambitious and focused projects of Canadian foreign policy at the beginning of the millennium. Its strength lies in the synergy it has been able to establish between its international interests and the new focus of its foreign policy: civil society. Public Diplomacy confers a new status on Canada as a 'facilitator' in the processes of democratic transition and as a mediator in the pacification processes.

As we read through the Public Diplomacy document, one of the most common phrases is: "Canada can make the difference in the region." Contrary to other periods prior to 1990, Public Diplomacy has meant an important investment in the financial and human capital, requiring public officers abroad to change the usual procedures for raising awareness about Canada internationally. The promotion of democracy, defence of human rights, protection of the environment, support of the Canadian culture industry, and strengthening a critical mass of foreigners interested in the study of Canada, support the main objectives of Public Diplomacy.

This sort of diplomacy takes risks because its role as 'facilitator' introduces it to a political field where the national sovereignty of 'the others' is in the way. The political boundary between mediation and intervention is fragile. Such diplomacy fuels a double discourse based on otherness. On one hand, the aim of the above-mentioned objectives is to widen and strengthen the identity of Canada outside the country and in which most of its inhabitants take pride. This is why political mistakes made outside of Canada, such as Canadian intervention in Somalia through the peacekeepers, are more deeply regretted within. At the same time, the presence of Canada through Public Diplomacy is unquestionably useful to explain abroad, through an analysis on Canada, the problems of 'the others.'

This means that analyses of free trade, Aboriginal rights, multiculturalism, or Canadian federalism are often a starting point for explaining other political, economic, and social realities. In this sense, the discourse on otherness fulfills its task.

Notes

1. Bloom analyses the cases of United States foreign policy and the Cold War; the Falklands-Malvinas conflict; unilateral disarmament and American bases in the United Kingdom; the conflict between Greece and Turkey regarding Cyprus, and the Third World foreign policy (Bloom 1990:90–104).

2. According to Miriam Villanueva Ayón, the concept of Human Security was first mentioned in some of the documents published by the General Secretariat of the United Nations Organization as of 1992 and more specifically in the publications of the United Nations Programme for Development in 1993 and 1994 (Villanueva Ayón 2000).
3. Another point of view on the concept of American-ness and North-American-ness may be found in Lachapelle and Balthazar 1999.
4. The name White Paper is usually given to a document officially published by some country that reflects the official position on a certain issue of national concern, in this case, Canadian foreign policy during the 1970s.

References

Badie, B. et M.-C. Smouts. 1999. *Le Retournement du monde. Sociologie de la scène internationale*. Paris: Dalloz.

Bélanger, Louis. 1994. « La Diplomatie culturelle des provinces canadiennes », *Études internationales* 25 (3): 421–52.

_____. 1995. « L'Espace international de l'État québécois dans l'après-guerre froide : vers une compression ? » Dans *L'Espace québécois*, dir. A.-G. Gagnon et A. Noël, 71–103. Montréal: Québec-Amérique.

Bloom, William. 1990. *Personal Identity, National Identity and International Relations*. Cambridge, UK: Cambridge University Press.

Canada. Department of External Affairs. 1970. *Foreign Policy for Canadians*. Ottawa: Queen's Printer.

_____. 1985. *Competitiveness and Security: Directions for Canada's International Relations*. Ottawa: Minister of Supply and Services.

_____. Department of Foreign Affairs and International Trade. 1999. *1999–2000 Estimates. Part III: Report on Plans and Priorities*. Ottawa: Public Works and Government Services Canada.

_____. 2000. *2000–2001 Estimates. Part III: Report on Plans and Priorities*. Ottawa: Public Works and Government Services Canada.

_____. Government. 1995. *Canada in the World*. Ottawa: Minister of Supply and Services.

_____. Special Joint Committee of the Senate and of the House of Commons on Canada's International Relations. 1986. *Independence and Internationalism*. Ottawa: Minister of Supply and Services.

Cooper, Andrew. 1997. *Canadian Foreign Policy: Old Habits and New Directions*. Scarborough ON: Prentice-Hall Canada.

Edelman, M. 1964. *The Symbolic Uses of Politics.* Chicago: University of Illinois Press.

Elder, C. and R. Cobb. 1983. *The Political Uses of Symbols.* London: Longmans.

Fox, W.T.R. 1995. *A Continent Apart. The United States and Canada in World Politics.* Toronto: University of Toronto Press.

Francis, D. 1997. *National Dreams: Myth, Memory and Canadian History.* Vancouver: Arsenal Pulp Press.

Granatstein, J.L. and N. Hillmer. 2000. *Prime Ministers: Ranking Canada's Leaders.* Toronto: Harper Collins Canada.

Hilliker, J. 1990. *Le Ministère des Affaires Extérieures du Canada : les années de formation, 1909–1964.* Québec: Presses de l'Université Laval.

Lachapelle, G. et L. Balthasar. 1999. « L'Américanité du Québec », *Politique et sociétés* 18 (1): 89-165.

Melakopides, C. 1998. *Pragmatic Idealism: Canadian Foreign Policy 1945-1995.* Montréal & Kingston: McGill-Queen's University Press.

Morton, W.L. 1962. *The Canadian Identity.* Toronto: University of Toronto Press.

Nossal, K.R. 1997. *The Politics of Canadian Foreign Policy.* Scarborough: Prentice-Hall Canada.

Pearson, L.B. 1970. *Words and Occasions.* Toronto: University of Toronto Press.

_____. 1975. *Mike: The Memoirs of the Rt. Hon. Lester B. Pearson.* Toronto: University of Toronto Press.

Sharp, M. 1972. "Canada-U.S. Relations: Options for the Future," *International Perspectives*, Special Issue (Fall): 1-27.

_____. 1994. *Which Reminds Me: A Memoir.* Toronto: University of Toronto Press.

Stairs, D. 1994. "Liberalism, Methodism, and Statecraft: The Secular Life of a Canadian Practitioner." *International Journal* 49 (Summer): 673-680.

Story, D.C. ed. 1993. *The Canadian Foreign Service in Transition.* Toronto: Canadian Scholars' Press.

Tully, J. 1999. « Liberté et dévoilement dans les sociétés multinationales », *Globe : revue internationale d'études québécoises* 2 (2): 13–36.

Villanueva Ayón, M. 2000. "Human Security: A Widening of the Concept of Global Security?" *Revista Mexicana de Política Exterior* 59: 106-30.

The Place of Canada in the World of
the Twenty-first Century
Le rôle du Canada sur la scène internationale au vingt et unième siècle

The Canadian Military in the Security Environment of the Twenty-first Century

Donna Winslow*

A T THE TURN OF THE TWENTIETH CENTURY, people predicted an era of peace and prosperity for the coming one hundred years. Nevertheless we found ourselves engaged in vast, blood-letting conflicts that no one could have imagined at that time. It is difficult to guess what the future holds, but we can be certain that the faces of war and peace will change dramatically. New challenges will put greater demands on military personnel than ever before.

Certainly, we will have to place more emphasis on international military cooperation as we did during the Kosovo crisis. We can also anticipate an increase in the number of peace support operations and a broadening of the range of these missions. This carries the risk that the soldier's traditional combat role will change to one of "global street worker."[1] At the same time, military forces are subject to local (i.e. national) pressures. The budget for the military and the number of forces are likely to continue shrinking as the organization becomes more oriented to war deterrence rather than war readiness as in the past. Another local pressure will come from the demand that the military be more accountable to and representative of the Canadian population.

In the following pages, we will examine a variety of issues. We will begin by exploring the changing nature of international conflicts. We will then examine the peace-keeping niche that Canada seems to

* Funding for this research was received from the Defence and Civil Institute of Environmental Medicine [DCIEM], Canadian Department of Defence, and US Army Research Institute Contract No. DASW01–98–M–1868, "Army Culture". I wish to thank my research assistants Jason Dunn and Glenn Gilmour for their good humour and hard work on this project.

have carved out for itself and how that relates to Canada's security interests and its role as a middle power in the international arena, in particular, the interest in "soft power." Throughout this discussion, we will consider the impact of these policies on the Canadian Forces. The final section of the paper deals with national issues such as representativeness and how these impact upon the Canadian Forces.

The Broadening Range of Conflict

The Cold War was a time of relative stability for the armed forces. Today, the rather straightforward, bi-polar conflict has given way to a much messier world. Conflicts are a result of internal state disintegration or civil war rather than the interstate confrontations of the past.

One paradox of future conflict is that it will be simultaneously both extremely high tech and low tech. It will entail the management of highly sophisticated weaponry (such as smart bombs) while fighting is more likely to occur in urban and built-up areas with relatively large numbers of soldiers on foot. This is a particularly messy, dangerous, and time-consuming affair, as the recent fighting in Chechnya has shown.

The battlefield of the future will be bewildering, complex, and fluid. Although some of the technology will be ultra modern; the psychological stresses on soldiers will remain as terrible and lonely as any in the history of warfare.[2] And this will all occur at a time when casualties, both civilian and military, are less politically tolerable. This is a paradox of modern conflicts: asking soldiers to kill without taking any casualties themselves. In terms of civilian casualties, the Kosovo bombing campaign has highlighted the importance of unacceptable civilian casualties. This will continue to be a leadership challenge for the Air Force in the future.

The humanitarian approach to the prevention of harm to noncombatants represents a significant shift in the use of military force in an air campaign. Target selection during the Kosovo campaign was based upon careful consideration of the military importance of the objective, the level of proposed force, the level of anticipated collateral damage and, of course, the anticipated risk to air crews. What would happen if a plane was shot down and aircrew taken prisoner since this was not a mission sanctioned by the United Nations (UN)? In a similar vein, there was the hard choice between using high-level bombing and other risk-avoidance strategies or using lower-level bombing. The first meant greater safety for air crews and higher risk for civilian casualties compared with the second which allowed air crews to abort an attack if the potential for civilian casualties was present.

For the first time in Canadian operations, legal counsel was extensively consulted in target selection during the Kosovo air campaign. Until this point, legalities had little impact on mission planning, but as time went on lawyers had a significant influence on operations. Lawyers often met and briefed pilots prior to missions, and pilots were encouraged to consult with legal counsel on returning from missions. We can see not only that decision-making can be influenced by a larger variety of (non) military actors, but that the influence of these actors, as it relates to ongoing operations, will likely increase.

Another aspect to the high-tech side of war is the threat of cyber attack as economies become increasingly vulnerable to Internet terrorism. The recent spread of the 'love virus' (a computer virus originating in the Philippines which crippled part of the world's electronic mail traffic) illustrates just how fragile the present networked world is. Anyone with a computer and an Internet connection, no matter where, can release an electronic plague with global implications. The Internet has become a powerful tool in the information war. Now, Chechen guerillas have their own websites and are able to communicate in real time.

In the twenty-first century, the face of the enemy is also changing. Some suggest that future militaries will no longer face another soldier but "an unconstrained warrior who has morally run wild."[3] For example, in Sierra Leone, the leader of the Revolutionary United Front, Foday Sankoh, was convicted of war crimes ranging from rape to torture and murder. The events in Sierra Leone have also highlighted the weaknesses of UN peacekeeping that pulls together troops from disparate nations who are ill-equipped and untrained to face a rapid escalation of violence. They also raise the question of whether the Canadian Forces are psychologically prepared to deal with the atrocities found in these forms of violence. Situations like those in Sierra Leone are likely to increase as will asymmetrical warfare such as guerrilla warfare and terrorism.

In the past, Canadians have mostly depended on our southern neighbours to assure our territorial defence. We may continue to support these efforts by becoming partners in a continental missile defence system. Yet the new forms of (cyber) war make us more vulnerable and if terrorists attack the United States, some most certainly will try to come through Canada in order to do so. What role will the military play in combating these threats?

Warriors or Global Street Workers?

As the nature of warfare is changing, Canada seems unclear as to whether it wants its forces to remain interoperable warriors, which implies heavy investments in hardware in order to conduct joint operations with the Americans and its North Atlantic Treaty Organization (NATO) allies, or occupy a niche role as peacekeepers. And while the Canadian military has argued that it is still primarily a combat force, peace operations have become, over the years, its primary business. This ambiguity is reflected in official documents. "Combat capable, multipurpose forces" as described in the 1994 Defence *White Paper* are still being presented as a realistic future. In *A Strategy for 2020*, future forces are described as "high quality, combat-capable, interoperable and rapidly deployable task-tailored."[4] Yet, *Defence Performance and Outlook 2000* tells us that the military is also supposed to advance Canada's human security agenda. This includes, "the ability to fight to protect the fundamental human rights and values that Canadians and the international community espouse ... [and] ... keep the peace once it is achieved."[5] How exactly does an armed force protect values?

Certainly, the peacekeeping image appeals to popular Canadian self-images, to sentiments of altruism and generosity, to helping others who are suffering, and so on. In many ways, peacekeeping contributed to the formation of a Canadian identity in the international arena. Peacekeeping represented Canadian multiculturalism, tolerance, and respect for the rule of law. In the words of Sens, "Peacekeeping had become a mirror, reflecting the finest qualities Canadians ascribed to their own society and national character."[6]

There are, however, other more self-motivated reasons for participating in peace operations. During the Cold War, there were Canadian security matters to consider. As Sens points out, during the Cold War, international security and national security became intertwined:

> Canada's paramount strategic concern during the Cold War was an escalation of superpower hostilities in Europe or elsewhere into a global confrontation which would threaten Canadian territory. As it became evident that the United States and the Soviet Union could

clash in various regional conflicts, Canada acquired an interest in the prevention, control, or containment of hostilities in areas of tension around the world.[7]

This theme appears in Canada's Defence White Papers of that period. Indeed, in 1986, a Special Joint Committee of the Canadian Senate and House of Commons stated that "the threat to Canada is one and the same with the threat to international stability and peace."[8] In the 1990s, then Prime Minister Brian Mulroney talked about the necessity of "rethinking the limits of national sovereignty" in a world of intrastate and transnational problems. This coincided with a surge in peace operations by Canadians.[9]

Peacekeeping also meshes well with Canadian foreign policy conceptions of Canada as a "middle power." Contributions to peace operations are expressions of Canada's commitment to the UN. According to Sens, the desire to be both represented and consulted on international affairs is an important driving force behind Canadian foreign policy, and peacekeeping has helped maintain Canada's profile and influence as an independent sovereign actor in the world.[10] Participation in peace operations also gave Canada some leverage in international forums. According to Wiseman, peacekeeping "enhanced Canada's reputation as a middle power [and contributed] to Canada's stature and influence in the UN."[11] According to Sens: "By contributing contingents to ventures such as peacekeeping Canada hoped to gain a seat at the table, a voice, and therefore some input into decision-making forums."[12] As an example, participation in the operations in the Balkans was an expression of Canada's ongoing commitment to European security and to NATO.

However, as important as participation might be, the question remains as to whether we have the resources and capabilities to honour all our commitments. Canadians have not seen the military as an important national institution and traditionally have not supported defence spending. As Shadwick has stated, "many Canadians seem to aspire to a global security and human security role for their country and their armed forces, but are prone to terminal writer's cramp when it comes to signing the cheques for a credible defence establishment." He indicated that – despite an overwhelming belief that "a strong military is important to Canada's international standing" (88 per cent), "peacekeeping requires combat-ready forces" (94 per cent) and "Canada needs a modern, combat-capable military" (95 per cent –

when it came to a zero-sum choice, defence spending rated last of all choices, with Canadians choosing to allocate an additional tax dollar to propping up the Canadian film industry rather than improving the state of defence.[13]

Dwindling force capacity will affect Canada's ability to sustain prolonged substantial commitments abroad. The ability to work with political objectives in spite of force limitations is not always easy, particularly in a resource-poor environment such as that of the Canadian Forces. In the future, we may have to accept involvement in alliances, not as an ongoing commitment but for specific purposes only. We may still be able to contribute to coalitions but only in a subordinate role with little autonomy of action. This may also have an effect on Canada's standing and ability to exert influence. According to Daryl Copeland, executive director of the Canadian Institute of International Affairs, "Our rhetoric will start to ring hollow unless it is backed up by resources."[14] There was already an indication of this in 1994 when Canada was excluded from the Contact Group, which became the primary mechanism for policy on the Balkans. According to Sens, "Canada's allies were dissatisfied with Canada's contribution to IFOR."[15] In short, we were marginalized for not anteing-up at the international security table.

Soft Power with No Hard Power to Back it Up

Another important trend in Canadian foreign policy has been towards "soft power;"[16] that is, the belief that "knowledge and information confer international influence."[17] The former Canadian Foreign Affairs Minister, Lloyd Axworthy, has described soft power as "punching above your weight. In Canada's case ... ideas, values, persuasion, skill, [and] technique."[18] What this essentially means "is affecting and influencing behaviour by information, by values and by forms of non-intrusive intervention."[19] Besides the fact that 'non-intrusive intervention' may be an oxymoron, we remain somewhat ambiguous about what role hard power plays in support of soft power – if any at all.[20] Yet recent events in the Balkans indicate that peace management is only achievable through military intervention and ongoing military presence. However, in Canada, the emphasis on soft power has coincided with considerable reductions in the defence budget[21] and a resulting loss of hard power capabilities. The new buzzword is "peace building" (efforts to identify and support structures which will tend to strengthen and solidify peace in order to avoid a relapse into conflict[22]). This has led to support for "human security," a concept also championed by Lloyd Axworthy:

> The concept of human security recognizes that human rights and fundamental freedoms, the rule of law, good governance, sustainable development and social equality are as important to global peace as are arms control and disarmament. It follows from this that, to restore and sustain peace in countries affected by conflict, human security must be guaranteed just as military security must. This is where peace building comes in: as a package of measures to strengthen and solidify peace by building a sustainable infrastructure of human security. Peace building aims to put in place the minimal conditions under which a country can take charge of its destiny, and social, political, and economic development become possible.[23]

The concept of human security underlines a fundamental change in the twenty-first century security environment. As the Kosovo bombing campaign shows, territorial integrity and sovereignty can be subordinated to issues of human rights. During the Cold War, territorial integrity superseded human rights. Now the tide seems to have turned in favour of human rights. The Kosovo campaign also shows, however, that human rights have to be robustly defended. What, therefore, is the role for Canada's military in advancing human security interests?

As noted by many, we have a good network of memberships in powerful and comparatively exclusive clubs – G7, the North Atlantic Treaty Organization (NATO), G–20, and the Organization for Economic Co-operation and Development (OECD). These memberships, combined with being in the more universal clubs such as the UN, the Organization for Security and Co-operation in Europe (OSCE), and the Organization of American States (OAS) for example, give us forums for advancing our human security interests. However, we also have to remember that, in contrast to other countries such as the US, the UK, or France, our military instrument is weak, being proportionately smaller, and more poorly funded and equipped. Canada's military continues to innovate in order to use most effectively what little military assets they have. Future governments will have to balance the military's capacity to participate in human security efforts and collective security operations. In order to do so, we will have to tailor our commitments to our resources, instead of always expecting the opposite – i.e. committing the military to an operation and expecting them to come up with the human and material resources to realize it.

If Canada is going to support this package of measures to solidify peace, then interagency co-operation and civil – military co-operation will be an even more important component of peace operations in the future. Non governmental organizations (NGOs) are emerging as important social actors in peace efforts. These actors have become very skillful in adapting to the circumstances and have gained in international influence. The recent NGO protests in Seattle and Washington during the International Monetary Fund and World Bank meetings are an example of this. Non governmental organizations, humanitarian agencies, local representatives, and the military will all have to collaborate closely in future efforts to restore and maintain global peace.[24]

The National Context

The attitudes of society towards its military are subject to various influences depending on the climate within society or the viewpoints of the members of society on questions of war and peace.[25] In Canadian society, social, cultural, and legal changes provide a less robust supporting framework for the core values of military culture. We can say that Canada is not a militaristic society and it is unlikely to become one in the future. Neither can we say that patriotism as it might be expressed in "proud service to one's country" is widespread. Indeed, the new generations of prospective recruits will likely be less accepting of some of the traditional demands of a military way of life.

The military is going to have to adapt to a society that is becoming more individualistic (for example, people wish to be actively involved in how their working lives are structured and expect employers to respect their private and family commitments), egalitarian, and litigious. A higher value is now placed upon social equality and citizens are more disposed to enforce their rights in the courts. Thus, the Canadian Forces have been subject to a number of important legislative acts that have forced change upon the organization. For example, the Canadian Forces were among the first to be fully bilingual and have done away with barriers to homosexual and female participation in all job qualifications, including combat.[26]

Deference to authority figures – especially in institutional organizations – has waned: authority has to be earned and not taken for granted. This trend poses challenges for the armed forces with their highly structured authority relations. Should Service personnel have the right to air and represent their grievances in forums that are outside the formal chain of command? One response has been to set up the Office of the Ombudsman for National Defence and the Canadian Forces that stands outside the military chain of command.

In Canada, the number of people with direct experience of military affairs has dwindled. Along with the long-term decline in the size of the military establishment has come a corresponding diminution in the number of military and ex-military personnel in society. In addition, with base closures and rationalization, the 'footprint' made by the military on society has diminished. The number of people – especially opinion formulaters – who can speak knowledgeably about the Services has declined in recent decades. In Canada, Members of Parliament (MPs) have little direct experience with the military.[27] According to a survey conducted by Dr. Douglas Bland of the Centre for Defence Management Studies at Queen's University, the Canadian MPs responsible for approving $CDN9.5 billion in annual military spending often know little about Canada's defence needs or objectives. Bland commented about the results of his study: "Defence is the only government policy where the government is prepared to deliberately spend the lives of people to accomplish policy ends. You would think if they're going to send people out to get killed, they should think about it." [28]

The families of military members are changing as well. Increasingly, both parents work, placing increased demands on employers for career breaks and more flexible working practices. Demands of the growing number of single parent families must be taken into account. Much work is still to be done in the Canadian Forces to provide more flexible working conditions and to recognize that women are no longer prepared to place their own career second to that of their military partners. Women, of course, are pursuing careers in the military. Career paths will have to take into account the female life cycle, allowing breaks for pregnancy, and ensure career development after women return to work.

While the wider employment of women is still an ongoing process, focus on equal opportunities in the armed services has shifted to address race and ethnicity. Society is also more ethnically heterogeneous than it was twenty years ago, raising issues of equal opportunities for all employing organizations and the need to ensure that the Services are broadly representative of the society they are supposed to defend. A good deal of discussion has centered on the need for the armed services to be broadly 'representative' of Canadian society.

The key question is whether representativeness is achievable. The idea of representativeness can be given at least two rather different interpretations. First, one can refer to a socio-demographic match between the military and society. In this context, representativeness would require the military to match the statistical profile of the wider population – a goal achieved through planned targets if not quotas. As Sir Michael Howard has pointed out, this is very much an American value.[29] Second, one might argue that the armed services should subscribe to core societal values such as equality of opportunity, decency, fairness, careers open to all, and merit-based advancement in the organization. Thus, the Services could feel relatively comfortable about explaining the mismatch between their profile and that of society with but one proviso. The gap would need to be explained, not by the failure to have an effective equality of opportunity programme, but rather by the propensity of particular groups to select certain kinds of occupations, military or civilian.[30] Given this differential propensity rate amongst groups in society, it is most unlikely that the services would be able to achieve the goals of representation in the first sense of that concept. Reaching such a goal would require programmes of affirmative action that are illegal in Canada. One possible result might be that service in the Canadian Forces would become a niche employment for Canadians of British and French ancestry.

Other commentators have identified a number of reasons why meeting equal opportunity objectives is a desirable goal from the point of view of the operational effectiveness of the armed services.[31] First, it provides improved access to a wider recruitment pool as the armed services compete with civilian companies for scarce labour, both in terms of quantity and quality. In Canada, though currently there are twice as many people under fifteen years old as there are over sixty-five, by 2030 the dependent elderly (aged over sixty-five) will outnumber dependants. This trend, combined with declining fertility rates, means that immigration is the only way to maintain or increase the population.[32] Immigrants may come to outnumber those born in Canada and in the future might constitute the major source of recruits

– a very different picture from the predominantly European origin, white force of today. Future forces may become multilingual.

If a force representative of social diversity is achieved, the demands of individual rights, and member-defined fair treatment will become more and more of a challenge. Thus, the supportive links between armed forces and society must be cultivated. Doing so can actually strengthen the Services. In a healthy democracy, it is vital that the armed forces not remain too distant from the society they are charged to defend. After all, society funds them and bestows on them their legitimacy; and it is society from which they recruit and to which their personnel return to continue their lives as civilians.

Conclusions

It is impossible to know for certain what security threats Canada will face in the twenty-first century. We have, however, noted a few significant trends related to international and national developments. In terms of conflict we have noted the increasing importance of technology and the high costs associated with keeping up with high tech weaponry and defence systems. Will Canadians be willing to invest in these costly projects? How can we afford not to? Globalization means not only increased opportunity for investment, but also increased security risks since the stability of Canada's economy can be affected by events in far away places.

What will Canada's defence and security policy be in the twenty-first century? Will we be part of a 'fortress North America' protected by a US defence system? Or will we choose to be an international leader of human rights and security? This entails many elements, from peace operations to the delivery of humanitarian assistance, foreign aid, election monitoring, democracy building, post-conflict reconstruction of infrastructure and social institutions, and preventative diplomacy. It also means a shift from peace operations with a predominantly military focus to a form of new coalitions with NGOs, civilian peacekeepers, human rights monitors, and so on. This makes the task of determining what role the armed forces should play in the future all the more difficult. Not only will decisions have to be made about appropriate equipment, debate is needed on appropriate skill sets and training for future missions. But who can carry out the debate? If Canadian MPs are becoming less familiar with the military, how can they take appropriate decisions? These are some of the challenges facing not only the Canadian military but also the Canadian political leadership.

Notes

1. W. von Bredow, "Global Street Workers? War and the Armed Forces in a Globalizing World," *Defence Analysis* 13 (2) (1997): 169–180.
2. W.L. Hauser, "The Will to Fight," in *Combat Effectiveness: Cohesion, Stress and the Volunteer Military*, ed. S.C. Sarkesian (London: Sage, 1980): 200.
3. US Major R. Peters, cited in *Morale in the Armed Forces*, G. Kummel (Strausberg: German Armed Forces Research Institute, 1999): 11.
4. Canada, Department of National Defence, *A Strategy for 2020* (Ottawa, 1999): 7.
5. Canada, Department of National Defence, *Defence Performance and Outlook 2000: Making a Difference at Home and Abroad* (Ottawa, 2000): 3–5.
6. A.G. Sens, "The Decline of the Committed Peacekeeper." Paper presented at the conference on *Canadian Security and Defence Policy: Strategies and Debates at the Beginning of the 21st Century* (Vancouver, 1999): 7.
7. Sens, "The Decline of the Committed Peacekeeper," 5.
8. Canada, A Special Joint Committee of the Senate and House of Commons on Canada's International Relations, *Independence and Internationalism* Ottawa: Minister of Supply and Services (June 1986): 34.
9. For details, see Sens, "The Decline of the Committed Peacekeeper."
10. Sens, "The Decline of the Committed Peacekeeper," 14.
11. H. Wiseman, "United Nations Peacekeeping and Canadian Policy: A Reassessment," *Canadian Foreign Policy* 1 (3) (Fall 1993): 138.
12. Sens, "The Decline of the Committed Peacekeeper," 6.
13. M. Shadwick, "Canadians and Defence," *Canadian Military Journal* 1 (2) (Summer 2000): 109.
14. D. Copeland, quoted in Marcus Gee, "World's Poor Overlooked as Foreign Aid Stays Low," *The Globe and Mail* (18 February 1999): A20.
15. Sens, "The Decline of the Committed Peacekeeper," 21. IFOR stands for the NATO–Led Peace Implementation Force for Joint Endeavour in Bosnia and Herzegovina.
16. For a review of the debate surrounding soft power in Canada, see D. Oliver, "Soft Power and Canadian Defence," *Strategic Datalinks*, no. 76 (Toronto: Canadian Institute of Strategic Studies, February 1999).

17. Canada, Department of Foreign Affairs and International Trade, "Foreign Policy in the Information Age," *Policy Statement 96/53* (Ottawa: December 1996).

18. Lloyd Axworthy, Minister of Foreign Affairs, quoted in "We're Doing Things Nobody Else Could Do," *Ottawa Citizen* (5 April 1998): A7.

19. Lloyd Axworthy, quoted in M. Trickey, "Canada, Norway Change Their Ways," *Ottawa Citizen* (28 May 1998): A18.

20. For an excellent critique of the soft power see D. Oliver, "Soft Power and Canadian Defence: Square Pegs in Round Holes?" Paper presented to the Centre for International and Security Policy (York University, Toronto, 22 January 1999).

21. The Canadian defence budget fell from $CDN12 billion in 1994 to $CDN 9.25 billion in 1999. This represents a 25 per cent reduction in fiscal outlays, which have resulted in force reduction. Between 1989 and 1999 there was a 30 per cent force reduction. The Canadian Forces have gone from 126,000 in 1962 to 100,000 in 1968 to 80,000 in 1975 and were at 60,600 in 1999. The Land Forces now total 20,900. See Sens, "The Decline of the Committed Peacekeeper," 19.

22. Boutros Boutros-Ghali, *An Agenda for Peace: Preventative Diplomacy, Peacemaking and Peacekeeping* (New York: United Nations, 1992): 32.

23. Lloyd Axworthy, "Building Peace to Last: Establishing A Canadian Peacebuilding Initiative," Notes for an Address by the Honourable Lloyd Axworthy, Minister of Foreign Affairs (York University, 30 October 1996): 2.

24. We have already made some efforts in this, for example, the Canadian Peacebuilding Co-ordinating Committee, the joint working groups of the Canadian International Development Agency, the Department of Foreign Affairs and International Trade, the Department of National Defence, and the Pearson Peacekeeping Centre. In addition, the military is building its civil military co-operation expertise. They now have an exchange with the non governmental organization, CARE, in which an officer is attached to the organization on a six-month basis to learn more about the way NGOs operate.

25. See G. Kummel, *Morale in the Armed Forces* (Strausberg: German Armed Forces Institute for Social Research 1999): 28.

26. Among the important pieces of legislation affecting the Canadian Forces are: *The Canadian Human Rights Act*, 1978; the equality section (Section 15) of the *Canadian Charter of Rights and Freedoms* which came into effect on 17 April 1985; and the *Employment Equity Act*, 1996 which determined that every Canadian citizen has the right to discrimination-free

employment and promotion and that public institutions will strive to be representative of the public they serve.

27. This is not only true for Canada, in the USA the House of Representatives had 320 veterans in 1970, but fewer than 130 in 1994. In 1997, for the first time ever, neither the Secretary of Defence, the National Security Advisor, the Secretary of State, nor any of their deputies had ever been in uniform. J. Hillen, "Must US Military Culture Reform?" *Orbis*, 43 (1) (1999): 54. See also M. Shields, "When Heroes Were Ordinary Men," *Washington Post* (3 August 1998).

28. Quoted in N. Ovenden, "'MPs Know Nothing about Defence': Study," in *The Ottawa Citizen* (5 November 1999): A4.

29. Sir Michael Howard, "Armed Forces and the Community," *RUSI Journal* 141 (4) (August 1996): 10.

30. This point raises difficult and complex issues, especially the extent to which an inclination not to pursue a military career is the result of perceived or real racism in the prospective employing organization.

31. In England, the work of Lt. Col. Stuart Crawford is particularly noteworthy in this connection. The arguments developed here draw on Crawford's work and on a number of conversations with him over the past two years. See Crawford's "Racial Integration in the Army – An Historical Perspective," *British Army Review* 111 (December 1995): 24–8. His Defence Fellowship thesis on this subject is not published to date, therefore not available to the public.

32. J. Verdon, Capt. N.A. Okros and T. Wait, "Some Strategic Human Resource Implications for Canada's Military in 2020." Paper presented to Inter-University Seminar on Armed Forces and Society (Baltimore, MD: October 1999): 11–12.

The Role of Canada in the International Context of the Twenty-first Century

Huguette Labelle

I T IS MOST FITTING THAT THE INTERNATIONAL COUNCIL FOR CANADIAN Studies and the University of Ottawa's Institute of Canadian Studies be the convenors of this conference. They bring strong historical and visionary perspectives to the discussion.

I shall begin by identifying some of the aspects of our international situation that are already setting the scene for the twenty-first century and the role of Canada in our common future.

On the negative side of the ledger, I would give top rating to endemic poverty and to the increasing gap that exists between the rich and the poor of our planet. This gap exists within countries as well as between countries. Expressed in concrete terms, half of the world's population, 3 billion people, live on less than two dollars per day. This figure in itself is startling – yet it masks the fact that, of those, many live on less than two dollars per week. The poorest fifth of the world's population receives 1.4 per cent of the total world income and the richest fifth receives 85 per cent. So if poverty prevails, it is not because of the absence of wealth. Consider how much is spent on arms, recreation, cosmetics, and so on.

In human terms and in terms of social world stability, I would venture to say that ending poverty is the single greatest challenge facing the world as it enters the twenty-first century. It is also the twentieth century's worst legacy.

A close second on the ledger would be the state of the environment. The attention of the world on the state of water, air, and soil degradation has been cyclical, with insufficient sustained attention to the conduct of necessary research and to the application of current knowledge and existing technology. The juxtaposition of the importance of the return on investment for enterprises, of the decline in government budgets, of new industrialization, and of the concentration of people in megacities is leaving an increasing environmental deficit. Each year, for example, human activities, primarily the burning of fossil fuels (80 per cent) and deforestation (20 per cent), release 6 billion tons of carbon dioxide into the atmosphere. Although not the sole factor, environmental degradation has been a contributor to natural disasters. Hurricane Mitch in Central America and the Yangtse floods in China are two significant examples.

To this top group I would also add population growth and its increasing burden on the planet. We need to remind ourselves that 80 per cent of the world's population lives in developing countries and that 95 per cent of the projected growth will take place in these countries. The world population is predicted to increase by about 700 million over the next eight years. The eventual levelling will depend greatly on tackling poverty and illiteracy, especially for women. From a world perspective, this has implications for immigration. It is also interesting to note that Canada and a number of other western countries have ageing populations, whereas in developing countries, anywhere from 48 to 65 per cent of their populations are below the age of twenty-five.

These top three – poverty, environmental degradation, and population growth – have a profound impact on our food and water security. As we meet here today, twenty-six nations are water deficient. By the year 2025, it is estimated that this number will grow to sixty-six countries – home to about two-thirds of the world's population. Similarly, we are losing arable land in a world where we already have more than 800 million who do not have access to enough food.

Of a different order is the increase in civil conflicts. The human costs are high, and the damage to social and physical infrastructures leaves a heavy burden on the world. It also leaves untold and immeasurable human suffering in terms of loss of life, maiming, and loss of property, as well as families torn apart and forced to live in refugee camps for years on end. In 1997, the number of refugees stood at 27.4 million, compared to 2.5 million in 1970. Rwanda, Sudan, Sierra Leone, and Bosnia all serve to remind us of the gruesome reality of these wars. It is not by accident that the majority of these conflicts occur in poorer countries.

Illiteracy and poor health are also contributors to, and the results of, poverty. Pandemics such as AIDS, malaria, and tuberculosis are ravaging parts of the world. In parts of Africa, 40 per cent of the population is afflicted with HIV/AIDS and life expectancy has dropped dramatically to the early thirties. A new generation of children is without parents, with children of seven or eight years of age having to care for their younger siblings.

Local issues are global issues. The people of Sierra Leone are our neighbours. When something goes wrong somewhere in the world, global human security is threatened.

But there is a positive side to the ledger, leaving us room to be hopeful. The world has made tremendous progress in the struggle toward literacy, health status, and life expectancy. A number of countries have emerged from decades of conflict to achieve new accommodations and peace. Central America and Mozambique come to mind. Investments have increased around the world, although they are still minimal in the poorest countries.

Measures are being taken to alleviate the debt of the poorest countries. A number of less endowed countries have seen steady growth in their gross domestic product. Freedom of speech, free and fair elections, and greater gender equity are increasingly apparent. Scientific breakthroughs are announced daily. So there is room to rejoice. And more could be said. Today more than ever before, we have the means to end poverty and to have a more prosperous, equitable, and inclusive world.

At a conference such as this, much will be said about a phenomenon of our time – that is, the impact of the combination of globalization, knowledge build-up, and information technology on societies. This combination has the capacity to contribute further to the increasing gap between the rich and the poor and to marginalize groups of people and countries. Those who hold resources and power have the means to access, to exploit, and to use these to their benefit, thereby expanding their own assets and affording themselves even greater resources and even greater power.

On the other hand, this combination of globalization, knowledge, and information technology has the potential to bridge gaps between the rich and the poor, to connect people to knowledge, and to have the wider world community working together toward common benefits and common goals. Information technology, if placed at the service of communities, can bring them access to educational health services, e-commerce, and knowledge related to many aspects of their daily management.

Keeping this context in mind, I would now like to turn to the role that Canada can play as a helpful member of this world community.

Sharing our experience with multicultural democracy

Our multicultural democracy and our sustained peace is of great interest to many countries as a learning model. One could postulate that this constant accommodation of shared differences has taught Canadians to live with ambiguity, with complexity, and with a certain empathy for differences. Dealing with cultural and linguistic diversity is critical for many countries as we enter this twenty-first century. China, India, Indonesia, and Nigeria, for example, are each comprised of an array of different cultures. In addition, several countries have been affected by population movement for economic or humanitarian reasons, changing the mix of cultures within their borders. Canada can use its multicultural and multilingual capacity to build bridges between nations, to prevent conflicts, to facilitate conflict resolution, and to support countries in the need to become more inclusive societies.

Supporting countries in transition toward new governance models

Currently, many countries are moving from a centralized economy to a market economy. As these governments plan this transition, they must ensure that they have a social system in place to protect their people as they develop new legal, financial, banking, and investment regimes, or as they privatize state-owned enterprises. These countries have outstanding training and retraining requirements and they want to learn from the experiences of others. They recognize that Canada has a reasonable blend of social protection and market approaches and are interested in benefiting from our experience.

Other countries wish to strengthen certain specific aspects of their administration, such as their justice system, their environmental regulatory frameworks and programmes, and their public sector management. Over the past years, there have been many exchanges between Canadians and representatives of these countries. These exchanges should be enhanced to foster mutual benefits.

Finally, our brand of distributive governance is of special interest to a number of countries trying to determine what approach is best suited to their own situation. As South Africa was establishing its new system of governance, it was interested in learning about the federal/provincial balance of responsibilities that has been a key element of Canadian governance for more than a hundred years. And while Ghana was preparing for local elections, it discovered that Canada's municipal governments were elected democratically, without a multi-party approach, an arrangement that seemed more closely suited to its situation.

Pursuing sustainable development through technology transfer and exchange

Because of its size, geography, climate, and population dispersion, Canada has had to invest in advanced technology and in infrastructure building. For example, investment in transportation, energy, water, telecommunications, clean production, agriculture, and waste disposal has been key to Canada's development. The World Bank has estimated that developing countries would require at least $US250 billion per year for the foreseeable future to achieve the infrastructure required to bring equitable prosperity to their people.

Canada can enhance its support to developing countries by sharing its technology in a spirit of mutual learning. Our experience in telehealth and distance education can help other countries provide large segments of their population with access to these essential services. Canada's engineering and telecommunications expertise can be of extra benefit to these countries.

Contributing to the advancement of science and its application

With information technology, it is now easier for universities and research institutions to combine their efforts through virtual alliances in order to deal with the mega-issues of our time. Discovering a vaccine for AIDS or malaria; developing new water-conservation approaches; finding economically viable applications for known sources of alternative energy, including, for example, Canadian fuel cell technology – all these require alliances from a variety of research centres. Canada's universities and research institutions already have a head start in working with scientists from around the world. We need to pursue this partnership approach aggressively in order to influence and contribute to the international research agenda, with its constant evolution, and to ensure that humanity benefits from its results.

Participating in global governance and influencing its adaptation to new imperatives

All countries face an increasing number of situations that cannot be resolved from within their borders. In addition, there are a number of significant global issues that require our attention as we enter this new century. It has been agreed, for example, that we need a global financial architecture better able to deal with the prevention of future financial crises and early management of them when they occur; that we need to have in place a rapid response capacity when conflicts erupt in order to contain them; and that new co-operative mechanisms need to be established in order to correct major environmental problems and conserve our biodiversity.

Canada has been an active participant in all of the global and regional multilateral institutions, from the United Nations (UN) and international financial institutions, to the World Trade Organization (WTO), the North Atlantic Treaty Organization (NATO), the Commonwealth, la Francophonie, the Asia-Pacific Economic Co-operation forum (APEC), the Organization of American States (OAS), and so on. As a mid-power, Canada's effectiveness at the multilateral level will be determined by what it brings to the table. Knowledge, facilitation skills, wisdom, a balanced approach, support for those in need, and financial contributions are all essential. These, however, will be of little impact multilaterally if Canada does not maintain strong bilateral and mutually supportive relations.

As we embrace this twenty-first century, we need to place people and quality of life at the centre of our development. And this quality will be better for all to the extent that we learn to develop new forms of partnerships and concerted alliances between the key players of our societies, nationally and internationally.

A Communications, Technology, and Societal Memory: A Distinct Canadian Archival Voice in the Global Village

Terry Cook*

T O HAVE AN ARCHIVAL TOPIC SOLICITED AS PART OF AN INTERNATIONAL symposium on the nature of Canadian distinctiveness in the twenty-first century is a pleasant surprise. Archives are important to Canadian Studies in two ways: in the familiar sense as the primary source documents that underpin research about Canada in many disciplines and, in a less appreciated sense, as a focus of study themselves that can shed light on the Canadian character and ideal.

This essay analyses the second aspect of the archival voice, and thus will not emphasize archives as essential sources for Canadian Studies. But as this year 2000 is the twenty-fifth anniversary of the release of the two-volume *Report of the Commission on Canadian Studies*, we should at least recall that Tom Symons therein devoted a chapter to archives, where he declared archival records to be the foundation of Canadian Studies.[1] By that report, Symons became the inspirational godfather, if not founder, of Canadian Studies as a recognized university discipline here in Canada. He also served as a kindly uncle to the legitimization of archives as a professional activity for, in the year of his report, the Association of Canadian Archivists was established.[2] For Symons, the underlying purpose of Canadian Studies was

An earlier version of this paper was presented at the Conference of the International Council for Canadian Studies, held 18 to 20 May 2000 at the University of Ottawa. The conference theme of "Canadian Distinctiveness into the twenty-first Century" shaped the following remarks about Canadian archives. The paper intentionally retains the conversational tone of the original presentation, though some limited reference notes have been added to introduce non-archival readers to the discipline of archival studies. I thank Jean-Pierre Wallot and Chad Gaffield for their kindnesses that made this paper possible.

reflected in the title he gave his report: *To Know Ourselves*. It was – and remains – not a bad *raison d'être* for archives as well.

There can be no distinctiveness for Canada and Canadians if we do not know ourselves, if we do not have the capacity to explore our origins, evolution, and characteristics as individuals, groups, communities, and nation. As Symons noted, archives are the underlying bedrock of such self-knowledge, the documentary evidence of past actions and ideas, and the primary sources for research in many disciplines relating to Canada and its peoples.

Without archives, Harold Innis and Donald Creighton could not have written about the Canadian Pacific Railway (CPR) as they did, in ways that fundamentally changed academic perceptions of our past. Without Innis and Creighton, and yet more archives, Pierre Berton could not have written as he did about the CPR that in turn changed popular perceptions of that same past. And without Berton, the various documentaries and docudramas, the high school textbooks and other learning media, the numerous coffee-table books, the novels and stories, the plays and poems, about the great railway itself or reflecting its role as part of other Canadian narratives, simply would not have been the same. Archives are not just the foundation of Canadian Studies and other academic disciplines, they are – by this trickle-down and popularizing process – the roots of our various identities, the fount of our memories, the core reference points by which we come to know ourselves. John Ralston Saul, in his address to the conference, focused on two archival documents fundamental to his analysis of Canada, one of which he says he uses in every speech he gives, to add authority, legitimacy, proof, and evidence for his assertions about Canadianism. Such is the power of archives!

In 1924, National (then Dominion) Archivist Sir Arthur Doughty said, in a phrase that appears on posters and mugs found in many archivists' offices – it is also carved into the base of the only statue ever officially raised in Ottawa to honour a civil servant – that, "of all national assets, archives are the most precious. They are the gift of one generation to another, and the extent of our care of them marks the extent of our civilization."[3] In this essay, I want to focus less on Doughty's archival 'assets' – the actual records that form the foundation of Symons's Canadian Studies or the trickle-down impact on Canadian identity – and more on Doughty's notion of 'care' and his concept of archives as a 'gift.' What is the nature of this 'care' of records by archivists? What do archivists actually do to 'care' for records and, perhaps most importantly, how do they choose the archives in the first place to place under such 'care?' And what is the collective nature of this 'gift' of memory that is communicated across generations with various technologies? How does the present choose the past by which the future will 'know itself?' And in so doing, has Canada developed approaches that are distinctive? And are these, in turn, likely to have an impact internationally in the twenty-first century? Here, then, the issue is not the archives as a warehouse of documents that scholars use to interpret the past, but archives as an active agent in constructing society's memory, deciding who is to be remembered and celebrated and who is to be marginalized and forgotten.

Another National Archivist, and now past president of the International Council of Archives, Jean-Pierre Wallot, has set the inspiring goal for archivists of "building a living memory for the history of our present." In his words, the resulting "houses of memory," will contain "the keys to the collective memory" that the world's citizens can use to open doors to the personal and societal well-being that comes from experiencing continuity with the past, from a sense of roots, of belonging, of forming their various identities.[4] In the rootlessness of the wired global community, where the speed of life makes yesterday recede quickly into the distant past and tomorrow approach with so much uncertainty, French historian Pierre Nora has asserted that "modern memory is, above all, archival. It relies entirely on the materiality of the trace, the immediacy of the recording, the visibility of the image."[5] Here there are resonances to pioneering Canadian work on communications and technology by Marshall McLuhan and especially Harold Innis. Control of recording media and the technologies of communication have formed powerful empires in the past, based on monopolies of knowledge, and the consequent conquest of space or time. All such media have a built-in bias of communication, Innis noted, leading to McLuhan's famous aphorism that the "medium is the message." Archives are the material traces of just such media, the concrete fragments that form our memories, the way we conquer time across generations – as Doughty said, the way our society legitimizes and memorializes itself. What then, in Innis's phrase, are the "biases" of archives as a collective communication medium between the past and the future?[6]

Perhaps readers are now convinced, in theory at least, that archives as institutions and activities should be a subject of Canadian Studies, quite aside from archives as records being the research foundation for Canadian Studies. At this point I want to explore the distinctive Canadian archival voice and its broader ramifications for international affairs, but first I have to set forth, as a background, the traditional thinking about archives, both by archivists and by their traditional major clients, academic historians – and, I dare say, by most other users of archives were they to think consciously about the archival institutions in which they are researching. I then want to look at radically new formulations about archives – what for shorthand might be called "the postmodern archive" – and, with a couple of examples, suggest why Canada has taken the lead in its articulation on a world-wide basis. I will then briefly conclude by suggesting that Canadian distinctiveness in this area has global significance in our new century of networked communications, where the realization of McLuhan's "global village" threatens to homogenize all distinctiveness into a universal blandness.

Archival theory and professional practice was first articulated in nineteenth-century Europe, after centuries of informal development, and then was exported around the world, including to Canada.[7] This development paralleled the emergence of history as a university-based discipline and profession. Most of the early professional archivists were trained as historians at such universities.

Just as much of the early professional history focused on the political, legal, and economic character of the nation state, so too were the first articulations of archival principles strongly biased in favour of the state. Almost all the classic tomes about archival methodology were written by staff members of national archives. Most, not surprisingly, focused on government, public, or state records and their orderly transfer to archival repositories to preserve their original order and classification; and most likewise relegated private and personal archives to the purview of libraries and librarians. Indeed, to this day, archives in Europe, the United States, and Australia generally look after only the official records of their sponsoring governments; national, regional, or university libraries take custody of personal manuscripts. Moreover, these early archival authors lived in an era of document scarcity, where their experience was based on dealing with limited numbers of medieval documents susceptible to careful diplomatic analysis of each page or form, or with records found in well-organized departmental file-registry systems within stable, centralized administrations that exhibited classic Weberian hierarchical structures. Most ignored the appraisal and selection of modern archives as these terms are now understood, where a small percentage alone (typically 5 per cent, and approaching in some jurisdictions, 1 per cent) is preserved as archives from a much larger information universe. Indeed, to the early pioneers of archival thinking, such appraisal and selection activity by archivists was strongly discouraged as nonarchival.

Clearly influenced by Darwinian thinking and metaphors, the pioneers believed that records coming to archives from state departments were simply the natural, organic residue from administrative processes which the archivist then kept in pristine order – archivists in Britain are still called 'keepers' reflecting that earlier mindset. State officials rather than archivists would thus decide which records were to survive. The records themselves were viewed as value-free vessels reflecting the acts and facts that caused them to be created. The archivist kept the records "without prejudice or afterthought," in the words of one influential pioneer writer, and was thus seen (and self-defined) as an impartial, neutral, objective custodian: this same writer asserted that the archivist is "the most selfless devotee of Truth the modern world produces."[8] Such notions of the objective archive were reinforced by historians of the time undertaking what they assumed (in the von Rankean tradition) to be objective, scientific history. On the objectivity question, one archival commentator has suggested that archivists and historians shared "a peculiar form of *disciplinary* repression or blindness," one that was mutually reinforcing.[9]

Traditional approaches to archives, as just outlined, sanction the already strong predilection of archives and archivists to support mainstream culture and powerful records creators. It privileges the official narratives of the state over the documented stories of individuals and groups in society. Its rules for evidence and authenticity favour textual documents from which such rules were derived, at the expense of other media for experiencing the present, and thus of viewing the past. Its positivist and 'scientific' values inhibit archivists from adopting and then documenting multiple ways of seeing and knowing. An original order is sought or re-imposed, rather than allowing for several orders or even disorders to exist among records in archives, and thus in descriptions of them presented to researchers. And so, as a result, researchers see a rationalized, monolithic view of a record collection that may never have existed in reality. And this traditional view seriously hobbles archivists trying to cope with the new technology of electronic records, where active intervention by archivists 'up front' in the creation process of records, rather than passive receipt of records long afterwards, is the only hope that today's computer-based history will be able to be written tomorrow. Moreover, the massive volumes of modern paper records, and the electronic record, require the archivist to appraise records in order to choose the typically 1 to 5 per cent that will be designated as archival; this active construction of the past is of course completely at odds with the notion of a passive (and objective!) keeper of an entire body of records handed over by the records creator. An even greater absence of order or system is present in the record-keeping habits of private individuals and voluntary associations, upon which archivists impose their various orders, rules, and standards.

In addition to these changes in recording technologies, there has been in recent decades a marked change in the very reason why archival institutions exist – or at least in public and publicly funded archives; admittedly, private business archives do not share fully in these changes. There has been a collective shift during the past century from a juridical-administrative justification for archives grounded in concepts of the state, to a socio-cultural justification for archives grounded in wider public policy and public use. Simply stated, it is no longer acceptable to limit the definition of society's memory solely to the documentary residue left over (or chosen) by powerful record creators, whether Richard Nixon or George Bush, state police in South Africa or Olympic Games officials in Tokyo, Canadian military officers posted in Somalia or doctors working with tainted blood products for Health Canada. Public and historical accountability demands more of archives, and of archivists.[10]

As a result, some archivists have begun to think in terms of documenting the process of governance, not just of governments governing.[11] 'Governance' includes cognizance of the dialogue and interaction of citizens and groups with the state, the impact of the state on society, and the functions or activities of society itself, as much as it does the inner workings of government structures. In this newer approach, the archivist, in appraisal and all subsequent actions, should focus on appraising and 'caring' for the records of governance, not just government, when dealing with institutional records. This perspective also better complements the work of archivists dealing with personal papers or private 'manuscript' archives.

All these changes make the archivist an active mediator in shaping the collective memory through archives. Because of the need to research and understand the nature of function, structure, process, and context of institutions and citizen interaction with them, and to interpret the relative importance of these (and other) factors as the basis for modern archival appraisal and description, as well as for making choices for preservation, exhibitions, and website construction, the traditional notion of the impartial archivist is no longer acceptable – if ever it was. Archivists will inevitably inject their own values into all such activities: thus they will need to examine very consciously their choices in the archive-creating and memory-formation process; they will need to leave very clear records explaining their choices to posterity.

In this rethinking of the traditional, state-centred, and positivist framework for archives, and substituting for it, in ways just suggested, a distinctively postmodern alternative, Canadians have led the way internationally. I would estimate that at least 75 per cent of the world's published writing in English, by archivists on the new postmodern archive, has been by Canadians, and much of the remaining 25 per cent has spun off or been inspired by, initially at least, such Canadian writing.[12] These Canadians have repeatedly challenged the five central principles of the archival profession: 1) that archivists are neutral, impartial custodians of 'Truth'; 2) that archives as documents *and* as institutions are disinterested or 'natural' by-products of actions and administrations; 3) that the origin or provenance of records may be found in a single office rather than situated in the complex processes and discourses of creation; 4) that the 'order' and language imposed on records through archival arrangement and description are value-free re-creations of some prior reality; and especially 5) that archives of government are the passively inherited metanarrative of the state.

Some of these generalizations about the postmodern archive are supported by a growing literature on the history of archives, as well as by the wave of multidisciplinary writing that has appeared in academic journals over the past couple of years in the wake of French philosopher Jacques Derrida's recent *Archive Fever*. All show the archive to be extremely problematic as loci for memory.[13] Historian Jacques Le Goff, for example, notes that "the document is not objective, innocent raw material but expresses past society's power over memory and over the future: the document is what remains." What is true of each document is true of archives collectively. By no coincidence, the first archives were the royal ones of Mesopotamia, Egypt, China, and pre-Columbian America. The capital city in these and later civilizations becomes, in Le Goff's words, "the center of a politics of memory" where "the king himself deploys, on the whole terrain over which he holds sway, a program of remembering of which he is the center." First the creation, and then the control of memory, leads to the control of history, thus mythology, and ultimately power.[14] Feminist scholar Gerda Lerner convincingly demonstrates that such power behind the very first documents, archives, and societal memory, was remorselessly and intentionally patriarchal: women were 'de-legitimized' by the archival process in the ancient world, a process that has continued well into this century.[15] Many examples are coming to light of archives collected – and later weeded, reconstructed, even destroyed – not to keep the best juridical evidence of legal and business transactions, as traditionally supposed, but to serve historical and sacral/symbolic purposes, but only for those figures and events judged worthy of celebrating, or memorializing, within the context of their time.[16] But who is worthy? And who determines worthiness? According to what values? Historical examples, in summary, suggest that there is nothing neutral, objective, organic or 'natural' about this process of remembering and forgetting.

Why have Canadian archivists taken this distinctive lead? I think the influence of McLuhan and Innis cannot be discounted: their concern with non-print media, communications technologies, and the bias these carried in shaping past civilizations (and our own) were important insights that were consciously transported to the world of archives and that stimulated thinking by archivists about how records and media shape the past.[17] In their studies of the history of records and the contemporary (and historical) French and English dualism of Canada with its multicultural and First Nations layers, the current generation of senior archivists – trained as historians and who are doing most of this new theoretical writing – perceived the existence of different stories, mixed narratives, and varying interpretations about similar past events, even the same past's texts, that generated doubts about 'Truth' and objectivity in recorded memory.[18] Not just history, but the recording of it, was filled with dissonance and ambiguity, as Jocelyn Létourneau said at this conference. If John Ralston Saul is right, that Canada invented long ago the first postmodern nation, one respecting diversity, complexity, and a culture of minorities rather than insisting on a monolithic national myth, then perhaps it is appropriate that Canada has also invented the postmodern archive.

This Canadian approach to archives has manifestations in working reality; it is not just an academic exercise in definition. Three broad manifestations may be mentioned briefly. The first is appraisal – the most controversial archival activity that determines the tiny trace of all recorded documentation that will survive as society's memory. A decade ago, the National Archives of Canada developed the concept and practice of 'macroappraisal.'[19] Macroappraisal finds sanction for the archival 'value' of determining what to keep and what to destroy – not in the dictates of the state as was traditionally the case, nor in the latest trends of historical research as is more recently so but in the reflection of society's values through a functional analysis of the inter-action of citizen with the state. It focuses on the functions of governance rather than the structures of government; emphasizes the citizen and group as much as the state; encompasses all media rather than privileging text; searches for multiple narratives and hot spots of contested discourse rather than accepting the party line; and deliber-ately seeks to give voice to the marginalized, to the 'other,' to losers as well as winners, through new ways of looking at case files and elec-tronic data. Moreover, macroappraisal is increasingly seen as essential to appraising successfully the electronic record of the automated office. This distinctive Canadian approach to appraisal has caught fire and has already been adopted internationally by several countries and their internal states.

As a second dimension, Canada, alone of first-world nations, for-mally developed the 'total archives' approach, where virtually all public archives in the country – provincial, territorial, city and town, university, and regional – acquire as part of their mandate, within one archival insti-tution, a 'total' archive of a roughly equal proportion of both the public or sponsoring institution's records *and* related private-sector records; and take into their archives the 'total' record in every recording medium (including film, television, paintings, and sound recordings which in many countries are divided among several other repositories).[20] In effect, the separated public archives and historical manuscript maintenance tra-ditions of Europe and the United States are combined in one institution. While there are many reasons why the 'total archives' concept evolved in Canada from the nineteenth century and is now exported to some other countries, and admired in more, this integration of the public and private reflects a wider vision of archives, one sanctioned in and reflective of society at large, of the total historical experience, rather than one limited to being custodians of official state records.

A final example is the Canadian Archival System, a national net-work of archives that is unique, and the envy of every nation that knows about it. First called for by Tom Symons in 1975, and made actual by the leadership of Jean-Pierre Wallot in the mid-1980s, the system is a means of co-ordinating archival activity, standards, and funding by determining local and community archival priorities, and of ensuring that the always too-limited funds go to those projects that reflect a local consensus hammered out in the provincial and territorial councils into a national system. These local perspectives are brought to the national Canadian Council of Archives where such national priorities are then set. Over its first decade, the Council has spearheaded collective lobbying efforts with politicians and the media on behalf of archival issues. More concretely, it has disbursed millions in new-money grant funds to support processing projects of accumulated backlogs in scores of archives across the country, to establish a national conservation initiative, and to develop bilingual, descriptive standards as the backbone of a national, on-line, always-updated inventory of the nation's archives that will allow access to the collective memory of Canada as never before. Creating a national network of archival institutions and soon archival sources adds another dimension to 'total' archives – that of having the total country involved in archives in a co-ordinated, but not monolithic, way. This approach is emphatically not about using standards to impose an Ottawa-based view, but about developing standards to allow our localities and many diversities to be shared more widely. This national system is the archival equivalent of the Canadian tradition of building national canals, railways, airlines, and broadcasting facilities – building, in short, communications technologies and networks for national cohesion across our regions and geography. Perhaps in the archival instance, it is to encourage better communication between our present and future with the past.

Can this Canadian archival distinctiveness contribute internationally in the twenty-first century? I believe the quick answer is yes, and on several levels. A generation ago, Marshall McLuhan wrote optimistically about communication technology creating a global village uniting humanity; at the same time, George Grant lamented the homogenization and eventual destruction of local cultures under the impact of the same technology and its connected American way of life.[21] Those twin attitudes survive as perceptions about the Internet – and the increasingly wired and global village we now inhabit. Some see the Web as a means to think locally and act globally, as a powerful means to rally interests against those very homogenizing forces of global market capitalism, as a flattening of hierarchy and a return to genuine democracy. Others see in the Web the "twilight of sovereignty." Its undermining of the nation state that has protected distinctive cultures and traditions, combined with its Big Brother violations of personal privacy, and, once the global corporations take control of this medium, the emergence of a bland universal commodification and commercialism from its present youthful exuberance – all portend an electronic version of bread and circuses for the masses.[22]

If this conference seems to have developed over these first two days a consensus about the benefits of the Canadian way of diversity, ambiguity, tolerance, and multiple identities as embodied by Saul's postmodern state, then the Canadian parallel way of remembering – of approaching the creation and preservation of memory in archives, will speak strongly to this century's citizens who are concerned about the homogenizing and globalizing 'bias' of the new media and record-creating technologies. Those who desire to construct memory based on celebrating difference rather than monoliths, multiple rather than mainstream narratives, the personal and local as much as the corporate and official, may find in Canada's distinct approach to archives useful tools for their task. William J. Mitchell, media and information technology guru at the Massachusetts Institute of Technology, has observed about photography that "we make our tools and our tools make us: by taking up particular tools we accede to desires and we manifest intentions," an observation that is applicable to all archival media of memory.[23]

But what intentions and desires do we archivists have? What *is* the nature of Doughty's 'gift' to subsequent generations? That question itself is essentially cultural. Steven Lubar, a specialist in the culture of information technology for the Smithsonian National Museum of American History, reminds us, and indeed all heritage professionals, that "we must think of archives as active, not passive, as sites of power, not as recorders of power. Archives don't simply *record* the work of culture; they *do* the work of culture."[24] Archives are not just the foundation of Canadian Studies; they reflect and create, by their very choices and activities, the culture and character of Canada.

Notes

1.   T.H.B. Symons, *To Know Ourselves: The Report of the Commission on Canadian Studies*, 2 vols. (Ottawa, 1975).

2.   The Association of Canadian Archivists (ACA) was created in 1975 in
     Edmonton as the national professional and scholarly body for English-
     speaking archivists in Canada. Before that, archivists had formed a
     special interest group within the Canadian Historical Association. The
     ACA began publishing of *Archivaria* in 1975 as a twice-yearly scholarly
     journal; *Archivaria* has since become the foundation of archival theory,
     strategy and practice in Canada and is recognized world-wide as a
     leader in its field.
3.   A. Doughty, *The Canadian Archives and Its Activities* (Ottawa: F.A.
     Acland, 1924): 5.
4.   J.-P. Wallot, "Building a Living Memory for the History of Our Present:
     Perspectives on Archival Appraisal," *Journal of the Canadian Historical
     Association* 2 (1991): 282.
5.   P. Nora, as cited in the "Introduction,"ed. J.R. Gillis, *Commemorations: The
     Politics of National Identity* (Princeton: Princeton University Press, 1994):
     15.
6.   See H.A. Innis, *The Bias of Communication* (Toronto: University of
     Toronto Press, 1951); and *Empire and Communications* (Oxford: Clarendon
     Press, 1950). For interesting commentaries of McLuhan in terms of mem-
     ory and communications, see P.H. Hutton, *History as an Art of Memory*
     (Hanover VT: University Press of New England, 1993): 13–17; and P.
     Levinson, *Digital McLuhan: A Guide to the Information Millennium*
     (London: Routledge, 1999). For a new assessment of Innis against post-
     modern sensibilities, see C.R. Acland and W.J. Buxton, eds., *Harold Innis
     in the New Century: Reflections and Refractions* (Montréal and Kingston:
     McGill-Queen's University Press, 2000).
7.   See T. Cook, "What is Past is Prologue: A History of Archival Ideas
     Since 1898, and the Future Paradigm Shift," *Archivaria* 43 (Spring 1997):
     17–63. At the risk of charges of self-promotion, this is perhaps the best
     place to start for non-archivists wishing to explore the history and evo-
     lution of archival thinking generally and for Canada.
8.   Sir Hilary Jenkinson of Britain's Public Record Office, who flourished
     there in the first half of the twentieth century and who wrote the first
     major text in the English language of archival theory and practice, *A
     Manual of Archive Administration* (London, 1922, rev. 2d ed. 1937,
     reprinted 1968). For a discussion and citations, see T. Cook, "What is
     Past is Prologue," 23–26.
9.   B. Brothman, "The Limit of Limits: Derridean Deconstruction and the
     Archival Institution," *Archivaria* 36 (Autumn 1993): 205–20, especially
     215.

10. This paragraph reflects my central argument in "What is Past is Prologue." See also E. Ketelaar, "Archives Of the People, By the People, For the People," *South Africa Archives Journal* 34 (1992): 5–16, reprinted in E. Ketelaar, *The Archival Image: Collected Essays* (Hilversum, 1997): 15–26.
11. See I.E. Wilson, "Reflections on *Archival Strategies*," *American Archivist* 58 (Fall 1995): 414–29. For archivists merely (and meekly) to do what they think their government sponsors want regarding their own institutional records, or what archivists think will please these sponsors and thus show that archivists are good corporate 'players' worthy of continued funding, is, as Shirley Spragge says, too easy (and too irresponsible) an abdication of the archivist's cultural mission and societal responsibilities. See her "The Abdication Crisis: Are Archivists Giving Up Their Cultural Responsibility?" *Archivaria* 40 (Fall 1995): 173–81.
12. For a summary, see T. Cook, "Archival Science and Postmodernism: New Formulations for Old Concepts," *Archival Science* 1 (1) (2001): 3–24. The first mention of postmodernism (at least in English) by an archivist in an article title was by T. Cook, in "Electronic Records, Paper Minds: The Revolution in Information Management and Archives in the Post-Custodial and Post-Modernist Era,"in *Archives and Manuscripts* 22 (2) (November 1994): 300–29. The themes were continued in his "What is Past is Prologue," already cited. Two pioneering postmodern archivists before Cook were also Canadian, B. Brothman and R. Brown. Among other works, see B. Brothman, "Orders of Value: Probing the Theoretical Terms of Archival Practice," *Archivaria* 32 (Summer 1991): 78–100; "The Limit of Limits: Derridean Deconstruction and the Archival Institution," *Archivaria* 36 (Autumn 1993): 205–20, and his probing review of Jacques Derrida's *Archive Fever*, in *Archivaria* 43 (Spring 1997): 189–92, which ideas are very much extended in his "Declining Derrida: Integrity, Tensegrity, and the Preservation of Archives from Deconstruction," *Archivaria* 48 (Fall 1999): 64–88; and R. Brown, "The Value of 'Narrativity' in the Appraisal of Historical Documents: Foundation for a Theory of Archival Hermeneutics," *Archivaria* 32 (Summer 1991):151–56; "Records Acquisition Strategy and Its Theoretical Foundation: The Case for a Concept of Archival Hermeneutics," *Archivaria* 33 (Winter 1991–92): 34–56; and "Death of a Renaissance Record-Keeper: The Murder of Tomasso da Tortona in Ferrara, 1385," *Archivaria* 44 (Fall 1997): 1–43. Two recent and incisive analyses are by P. Mortensen, "The Place of Theory in Archival Practice," and T. Nesmith, "Still Fuzzy, But More Accurate: Some Thoughts on the 'Ghosts' of Archival Theory," both from *Archivaria* 47 (Spring 1999): 1–26, 136–50. Some other Canadian

archivists reflecting postmodernist influences, at least in published form in English, include B. Dodge, "Places Apart: Archives in Dissolving Space and Time," *Archivaria* 44 (Fall 1997): 118–31; T. Rowatt, "The Records and the Repository as a Cultural Form of Expression," *Archivaria* 36 (Autumn 1993): 198–204; J. Schwartz, "'We make our tools and our tools make us': Lessons from Photographs for the Practice, Politics, and Poetics of Diplomatics," *Archivaria* 40 (Fall 1995): 40–74; and L. Koltun, "The Promise and Threat of Digital Options in an Archival Age," *Archivaria* 47 (Spring 1999): 114–35. Non-Canadian postmodern archivists include the Netherland's E. Ketelaar, "Archivalization and Archiving," *Archives and Manuscripts* 27 (May 1999): 54–61; and South Africa's V. Harris, "Claiming Less, Delivering More: A Critique of Positivist Formulations on Archives in South Africa," *Archivaria* 44 (Fall 1997): 132–41; as well as his complementary "Redefining Archives in South Africa: Public Archives and Society in Transition, 1990–96," *Archivaria* 42 (Fall 1996): 6–27; and his and S. Hatang's, "Archives, Identity and Place: A Dialogue on what it (Might) Mean(s) to be an African Archivist," *ESARBICA Journal* 19 (2000): 45–58. Planned symposia and publications during the next year to investigate archives and the construction of social memory will do much to expand the numbers and nationalities of archivists involved in considering the implications of postmodernism for their profession.

13. J. Derrida, *Archives Fever: A Freudian Impression* E. Prenowitz, trans., (Chicago and London: University of Chicago Press, 1996, originally in French in 1995, from 1994 lectures). Two issues of the journal, *History of the Human Sciences* 11 (November 1998) and 12 (May 1999), are devoted to essays by almost twenty scholars on "The Archive." For a fine introductory appreciation of the significance of Derrida on archives and archivists, see S. Lubar, "Information Culture and the Archival Record," *American Archivist* 62 (Spring 1999): 10–22.

14. J. Le Goff, *History and Memory*, S. Rendall and E. Claman, trans., (New York: Columbia University Press, 1992): xvi–xvii, 59–60, and passim.

15. Feminist scholars are keenly aware of the ways that systems of language, writing, information recording, and the preserving of such information once recorded, are social- and power-based, not neutral, both now and across past millennia. For example, see G. Lerner, *The Creation of Patriarchy* (New York and Oxford: Oxford University Press, 1986): 6–7, 57, 151, 200, and passim; and R. Eisler, *The Chalice & The Blade* (San Francisco: Harper Collins, 1987): 71–73, 91–93. Lerner's more recent study, *The Creation of Feminist Consciousness: From the Middle Ages to*

Eighteen-seventy (New York and Oxford: Oxford University Press, 1993), details the systemic exclusion of women from history and archives, and the attempts of women, starting from the late nineteenth century, to correct this by creating women's archives. See especially chapter 11, "The Search for Women's History." See also B.G. Smith, *The Gender of History: Men, Women, and Historical Practice* (Cambridge MA and London: Harvard University Press, 1998).

16. As but two stark examples, for mediaeval times, see P.J. Geary, *Phantoms of Remembrance: Memory and Oblivion at the End of the First Millennium* (Princeton: Princeton University Press, 1994): 86–87, 177, especially chapter 3, "Archival Memory and the Destruction of the Past;" and for the First World War, see D. Winter, *Haig's Command: A Reassessment* (Harmondsworth: Penguin, 1991), especially the final section, "Falsifying the Record;" and R. McIntosh, "The Great War, Archives, and Modern Memory," *Archivaria* 46 (Fall 1998): 1–31. For other examples and citations, see Cook, "What is Past is Prologue," 18, 50. We have the sad case in our own time of the deliberate records destruction in Kosovo and Bosnia to efface memory and marginalize peoples.

17. The key thinker here is Hugh A. Taylor, a three-time provincial archivist and influential director (now director general) in the 1970s of the National Archives of Canada. For but five examples of his important articles bringing McLuhan and contemporary social and cultural theory to bear on archival perspectives, see "The Media of the Record: Archives in the Wake of McLuhan," *Georgia Archive* 6 (Spring 1978): 1–10; "Information Ecology and the Archives of the 1980s," *Archivaria* 18 (Summer 1984): 25–37; "Transformation in the Archives: Technological Adjustment or Paradigm Shift?" *Archivaria* 25 (Winter 1987–88): 12–28; "My Very Act and Deed: Some Reflections on the Role of Textual Records in the Conduct of Affairs," *American Archivist* 41 (Fall 1988): 456–69; and "Opening Address," in *Documents That Move and Speak: Audiovisual Archives in the New Information Age. Proceedings of a symposium organized for the International Council of Archives by the National Archives of Canada* (München: K.G. Saur, 1992). For aspects of Taylor's major impact, see T. Nesmith, "Hugh Taylor's Contextual Idea for Archives and the Foundation of Graduate Education in Archival Studies," in B. Craig, ed., *The Archival Imagination: Essays in Honour of Hugh A. Taylor* (Ottawa, 1992), as well as many of the essays by Taylor's disciples and admirers in this festschrift in his honour. The volume also contains a bibliography of his work to that date. An annotated collection of his best archival essays is now being prepared.

18. On the importance of the historical and contextual dimension of archival work, two early advocates were T. Nesmith, "Archives from the Bottom Up: Social History and Archival Scholarship," *Archivaria* 14 (Summer 1982): 5–26; and T. Cook, "From Information to Knowledge: An Intellectual Paradigm for Archives," *Archivaria* 19 (Winter 1984–85): 25–50; both reprinted in T. Nesmith, ed., *Canadian Archival Studies and the Rediscovery of Provenance* (Metuchen, NJ: Scarecrow Press, 1993). Nesmith's introductory essay to this volume, "Archival Studies in English-speaking Canada and the North American Rediscovery of Provenance," is the best description of this fundamental change in archival thinking.

19. For the key conceptual statements, see T. Cook, *The Archival Appraisal of Records Containing Personal Information: A RAMP Study With Guidelines* (Paris: UNESCO, 1991); "Mind Over Matter: Towards a New Theory of Archival Appraisal," in B. Craig, ed., *The Canadian Archival Imagination*; and "'Many are called but few are chosen': Appraisal Guidelines for Sampling and Selecting Case Files," *Archivaria* 32 (Summer 1991): 25–50; and R. Brown, "Records Acquisition Strategy and Its Theoretical Foundation," and his "Macro-Appraisal Theory and the Context of the Public Records Creator," *Archivaria* 40 (Fall 1995): 121–72. See as well Wallot, "Building a Living Memory for the History of Our Present: Perspectives on Archival Appraisal."

20. The classic statement is W.I. Smith, "'Total Archives': The Canadian Experience" (originally 1986), in Nesmith, *Canadian Archival Studies*. For a supportive but critical view, see T. Cook, "The Tyranny of the Medium: A Comment on 'Total Archives'," *Archivaria* 9 (Winter 1979–80): 141–50; and "Media Myopia," *Archivaria* 12 (Summer 1981): 146–57. For a careful analysis of its historical context and more recent developments, see L. Millar, "Discharging Our Debt: The Evolution of the Total Archives Concept in English Canada," *Archivaria* 46 (Fall 1998): 103–46; and "The Spirit of Total Archives: Seeking a Sustainable Archival System," *Archivaria* 47 (Spring 1999): 46–65.

21. Of many possible works, see Marshall McLuhan, *The Gutenberg Galaxy* (1962), and *Understanding Media: The Extensions of Man* (1964); also George Grant, *Lament for a Nation: The Defeat of Canadian Nationalism* (1965), and *Technology and Empire: Perspectives on North America* (1969).

22. As examples, merely, from a wide range of literature, see, for the more pessimistic viewpoint, L.A. Pal, "Wired Governance: The Political Implications of the Information Revolution," in *The Communications Revolution at Work: The Social, Economic and Political Impacts of*

Technological Change, ed. R. Boyce (Montréal and Kingston: McGill-Queen's University Press, 1999): 11–38, especially 18–19; or N. Postman, *Technopoly: The Surrender of Culture to Technology* (New York: Vintage Books, 1993); or more narrowly S. Birketts, *The Gutenberg Elegies: The Fate of Reading in an Electronic Age* (New York: Fawcett Columbine, 1994); and more optimistically, J.D. Peters, *Speaking into the Air: A History of the Idea of Communication* (Chicago and London: University of Chicago Press, 1999): 138, 143, and passim; or P. Levinson, *Digital McLuhan: A Guide to the Information Millennium* (London: Routledge, 1999); or indeed Bill Gates, *The Road Ahead* (New York: Viking, 1995).

23. W.J. Mitchell, *The Reconfigured Eye: Visual Truth in the Post-Photographic Era* (Cambridge, MA: MIT Press, 1992), as cited in Schwartz, "'We make our tools and our tools make us': Lessons from Photographs for the Practice, Politics, and Poetics of Diplomatics," 40.

24. Lubar, "Information Culture and the Archival Record," 15, original emphasis.

Canada One Hundred Years from Now: A Federation of Nations?

Jean Laponce

I N THE FIELD OF HUMAN AFFAIRS, PREDICTING MAY WELL BE THE occupation of fools. Yet, the social sciences are obligated to take that risk, a risk I shall stretch to extremes by addressing my remarks not only to those engaged in the discourse today, but also to those who will be engaged a hundred years from now. Conscious of the danger of appearing foolish in the year 2100, if not before, I am comforted by the thought that a prediction that turns out to be wrong may nevertheless be of help, eventually, in identifying and weighing the role of factors that were either absent, hidden, or simply forgotten when the prediction was made.

If the year 2000 had been the finish line of history, we would have declared the winners to be democracy over authoritarianism, free enterprise over economic statism, the welfare state over l'État gendarme, nationalism over imperialism, and temperate nationalism over its aggressive kin.

In the first three of these competitions, Canada would be counted on the winning side; in the last, on the national question, it is still searching, perhaps with insufficient dispassionate vigor, for solutions to the cohabitation of its national communities. Will Canada of the year 2100 have resolved its national questions, and how?

Let us consider the most likely course of events and, when in doubt, let us point to the future with the help of a double rather than a single pointer. But first, let us take stock of the present.

National vs. Ethnic Cleavages

Canada is variously described as multicultural, multilingual, multiethnic, and multinational. Today, all countries of immigration are bound to be multi-ethnic and multicultural; they are not bound to be multinational. Canada's distinctiveness rests not in its multi-ethnic and multicultural composition but in its enduring national cleavages and confrontations. That distinctiveness is the cause of a problem yet unresolved: how to adjust a federalism of regions to manage a federalism of nations?[1]

Three nations are facing one another (three to simplify the plural into which the First Nations are incarnated): the Canadian, the Québécois and the Aboriginal.[2] Note that for reasons to be spelled out in the next section, I did not say 'English Canadian,' nor 'Anglophone,' but simply 'Canadian.'

What long-term political future awaits these three communities, all engaged in nation building in the same state?

Two Stepping Stones to the Future

At the additional risk of being outrageously economical of the factors involved, I shall set foot on only two stepping stones for a peek at the future: Canadian nation building and demographic evolution.

Nation Building

Considering the obstacles in its way – some inherited from its colonial past (the French fact), others erected by a dysfunctional mix of integration-segregation policies (the Aboriginal fact) – the Canadian nation building enterprise can, at the end of the twentieth century, claim some notable successes. Its major success is in integrating and assimilating its immigrants. To measure this properly, we must set aside the picture of our ancestors given us by a census and turn to the picture of today's collective identities obtained by survey research.

The Canadian Census, like any census, is not simply a statistical tool; it is also a political instrument that may mislead at the same time as it informs. In the case of ethnicity and nationality, its questions – notwithstanding recent improvements (Ornstein 2000) – have become misleading because they have not evolved enough since 1871. The modern census magnifies the multi-ethnic character of the country, while hiding its multinational composition.

The 1871 Census told us that, measured by origin, the population of Canada was roughly 61 per cent British, 31 per cent French, 7 per cent other Europeans, and 1 per cent other non-Europeans. If that same 1871 Census had asked a question about a sense of national belonging, it would very likely have obtained figures similar to those describing the confrontation between the two nations of Lord Durham (1839) and Siegfried (1906): roughly 60 per cent English and 30 per cent French. If we turn to the 1991 Census, we find that the British segment has dropped from 60 per cent to less than 30 per cent, the French from 30 per cent to little more than 20 per cent, while the 'others' have risen to nearly 50 per cent (Tepper 1994). Contemporary censuses show Canada to be a country of 'ethnics.' But what does ethnic origin signify? How often do we think of our origins and in what context? Is the 'ethnic' sense of self embedded within a Canadian identity or is it separate? And, if it is separate, what is its relative importance? To answer these questions we must turn to survey research.

Among surveys treating the subject of group identity, let us consider that of Berry and Kalin, which was conducted the very year of the 1991 Census. One of the questions read (Berry and Kalin 1993):

People may describe themselves in a variety of ways. If you had to make a choice, do you think of yourself as:

a) Canadian,
b) English-Canadian, Scottish-Canadian, etc. summarized by the code British-Canadian,
c) French-Canadian,
d) Other hyphenated-Canadian (the respondent was given examples such as German-Canadian, Jewish-Canadian, but could initiate any term of his or her choice),
e) province (such as Québec, Québécois, British Columbian, Ontario, etc.),
f) any foreign country or nationality, such as German or Germany.

If we ignore the entries scoring less than 5 per cent nationwide, we are left with only three identifications: Canadian which scored 65 per cent, Québec or Québécois which scored 14 per cent, and other-hyphenated (other than French or British) which scored 7 per cent. Note the contrast: the hyphenated-Canadians drop from the nearly 50 per cent recorded by the census to little more than 5 per cent.[3] They appear to be a group on their way to absorption, at least in the public sphere. Like Durham almost two centuries ago and Siegfried almost a century later, we note the juxtaposition of two major communities. But between these two communities, the line of cleavage has changed: no longer is it based on religious differences or the state of origin; it is based on identification with a political institution, state or province – an identification that is typically national in character.

As for Aboriginals who were not represented in sufficient number in the Berry-Kalin survey to warrant a separate analysis, from a survey done by Statistics Canada in 1989 we can infer the transfer of identity to the present status and away from ethnic origins. That survey reported a 3.2 per cent Aboriginal *identification* compared to the 5 per cent Aboriginal *origin* reported by the census.[4]

In the case of Francophones, as for Aboriginals, the majority did not give Canadian as a priority identification, though a significant minority did not identify first with a Québec or French-Canadian nation either. Whereas the 1991 Census recorded 24.3 per cent mother tongue French, the Berry-Kalin survey showed a 14 per cent Québec and a 4 per cent French-Canadian identification. Even if we were to add these last two statistics (that would exaggerate the non-Canadian identification of Francophones) we would still have a significant gap, indicating that, for about 25 per cent of mother tongue French, the dominant identification is neither French-Canadian nor Québécois. In Québec itself, the same statistics indicated that 20 to 25 per cent of mother tongue French did not give their first collective identity as either Québec or French-Canadian.

In short, Canada appears to have been extremely successful in integrating or assimilating its newcomers within the Canadian nation. While less successful with Aboriginals and Francophones, it has drawn a sizeable percentage of each group away from an ethnic or national identity that would have priority over that of Canadian. In terms of 'Canadian content' as defined here by a respondent's dominant collective identity, one cup is nearly full (that of immigrants) and the other two cups (those of Aboriginals and Francophones) are about 30 per cent and 20 per cent full, respectively.

Demography

One hundred years ago, Canada had approximately five million inhabitants. Now, it numbers about six times more. Projecting that trend would give us 180 million inhabitants by the year 2100. If that seems very many, 180 million people would still leave plenty of empty space, even if we do not subscribe to Baade's way of measuring living space (quoted in Neurath 1994). Baade, having noted that the fourteen million people living in the greater New York area spend most of their lives there and seem to like it, took New York's density as his world standard. He then calculated the amount of land needed to feed a world of as many New Yorks as possible and concluded that the earth could accommodate sixty-five billion people. A mere 180 million for Canada would not even come close to satisfying Baade's projections.[5]

But, even as 'low' a figure as 180 million is most unlikely to be reached unless Canada loses relinquishes complete control of its borders. If, over the past hundred years, population grew by an average factor of 1.5 per year, that growth was not due so much to the positive balance of in-migrations over out-migrations as it was to Canada's high birth rate. Now that the birth rate is negative (there are exceptions, notably among Aboriginals) and expected to remain negative (a low birth rate being associated with low infant mortality, high life expectancy, prosperity, education, and urban living), immigration will soon be the sole measure keeping the population stable, let alone growing. It is estimated that by mid-century, barring major changes in life expectancy, retirement age, or productivity, immigration levels of more than 200,000 people per year will be needed to maintain the size of the labour force. When the cradle fails, the immigration officer and the smuggler are bound to take over. A National Health projection done in 1989 estimates that, without immigration, the Canadian population would drop to roughly half its present size in a hundred years; the last Canadian would die in the year 2786 (Canada 1989).

So, unless present trends reverse – barring any major reversal – the future population of Canada, even if not of a size markedly different from that of the present, will be markedly different in its composition. It will reflect, better than now, the changing balance of populations in the world. Canada will have become more globalized, including many more from Asian, Caribbean, Latin-American, and African communities than it does at present. This population renewal will have more profound effects on Québec than on the rest of Canada. Anglophone Canada is already 'mixed wool' – Newfoundland being an exception – while Québec still has, by and large, a *'pure laine'* texture. Québec should continue to approach the Canadian norm of a population increasingly made up of recent immigrants of neither French nor English origin. Furthermore, since the French language has, in North America, a power of attraction much weaker than that of English, the increased proportion of recent immigrants in the population should work to the advantage of Anglophone provinces; they will benefit from the immigrants' willingness, nay eagerness, to learn and to speak English.

Will the changing racial and ethnic composition of the Canadian population be a source of increased social and political tensions? Toronto, Vancouver, and other major cities give us the answer. In 1971, Toronto was about 10 per cent non-white; now the proportion has risen to more than 30 per cent. In 1971, Vancouver was 5 per cent Asian; now it stands at about 30 per cent. These changes occurred remarkably smoothly. The more likely effect of increased racial diversity will be to blur the importance of race, much as national origin has become blurred over the years. While not increasing social and political tensions markedly, however, the new immigration is likely to have a significant effect on the three-nation confrontation, notably on that between Canada and Québec. We shall consider this effect when dealing with the second nation.

The First Nation

The study of First Nations is outside my area of competence. Wisdom would dictate that I refer readers to contributions by my colleagues, notably Alan Cairns (2000).[6] I will proceed, nevertheless, carried by the momentum of my propensity for risk-taking futurology, since there is apparently some virtue to seeing problems from a distance.

Judging by several significant and relatively recent events – the Charlottetown Accords and the types of powers that the federal and provincial governments were prepared to transfer to Aboriginal communities or to Aboriginal representatives in the federal Parliament, the creation of Nunavut, and the outcome of recent negotiations such as those concerning the Nisga'a – one can predict that major land claims will be settled before the end of the century. There will be also likely be wide variety in the forms taken by Aboriginal self-government (depending upon size, location, and resources). The lowest common denominator of local self-government will consist of control over language[7], culture, community membership, some local social services, and property rights associated with the land; the upper limit will likely be the administration of some aspects of criminal justice, though one cannot exclude the possibility that, with the help of a high birth rate, some Native people may obtain territorial and eventually provincial status – in the Northern Cree settlements, for example.

One can thus envisage a future Canada with Aboriginal, self-governing communities, ranging in size from a village to a province and ranging in type from that of a Hutterite settlement turned almost exclusively inward, to a kind of Channel Islands, if not Monaco or San Marino, which look both inward and outward, albeit increasingly outward. Some of those self-governing units will be valued for economic reasons; others, mostly if not solely, for their offering of what Elide calls a "world axis," a "sacred" location which, under community guardianship, links the self to the past and origins, thus providing psychological anchoring and historical comfort.

At the national level, institutions representing the First Nations are likely to be established, though as yet it is too early to tell which form, if any, that representation will take. Will it be along the lines of Courchene's non-territorial Indian province (Courchene 1994), along the lines of the Charlottetown proposal of guaranteed representation in Parliament – a scheme rejected by the Royal Commission on Aboriginal Peoples (Royal Commission 1996) – or along the lines of a separate house of Parliament, as proposed by that same Royal Commission? A Charlottetown-type of representation, embedded in existing structures, seems more likely, but I cannot see a way through that complex problem. It may be too early even to try since it is still unknown how much power the newly-empowered Aboriginal communities will be prepared to delegate and to whom.

The linkage between Aboriginal and Canadian institutions will pose problems outside the areas of Aboriginal self-government, notably in the large urban centers of mixed populations. The obstacles could be overcome by some form of 'personal federalism,' either on the model of the French school boards elected by self-defined populations of interest or on the more formal model of Estonia's minority governments of the 1920s.

Pre-war Estonia had made it possible for its minority groups (Jews, Germans, Russians, and Swedes) to set up non-territorial institutions of self-government with powers limited to language and culture. Jews and Germans took advantage of that possibility and registered on minority rolls (a minimum number of people was required and there was a right to deregister). From registration flowed specific rights and duties: the right to elect a minority government with access to minority schools and the duty to pay the taxes levied by the minority community (Laponce 1960, 1993; Coakley 1994). If such personal federalism appears, it is unlikely to extend beyond cultural and some

social services; it is unlikely to succeed if the number of registrants is
too low to maintain a quality of service comparable to that offered by
the competing institutions of cities and provinces.

Will the multiplication of self-governing Aboriginal communities
fracture Canadian citizenship? In the legal sense of citizenship – no,
but in the sociological sense of citizenship – yes; probably, at least in
the short term. It is normal that building a multination state can lead
to reinforcing attachment to the national segments. It is thus to be
expected that the overarching citizenship will be affectively 'thinner'
than the national solidarities – thinner at least for the minority nations
– since the dominant nation often merges, as it does in Canada, the two
attributes of citizenship, the legal and the sociological and typically
uses only one name for the two. Over time, however, if the national
segments do not feel threatened by one another, one could expect that
the minority segments would add affective and sociological flesh to
their core legal citizenship.

Before the end of the century, the transfer of self-governing power
to Aboriginal communities and institutions should have appeased
resentments and, judging by present trends (high exogamy and migration to cities), may well have facilitated both integration and
assimilation to the Canadian or Québécois nations at the same time as
it secures Aboriginal cultures in their enclave communities. Feeling
secure should facilitate an Aboriginal evolution into whatever modernity means in 2100.

The Second and Third Nations

Will Québec secede? If so, under what conditions? If not, what will be
the alternative? Canadians and Québécois are peaceful and tolerant –
having said that, there is no question in my mind that if enough
Québécois wanted to secede strongly enough they could do so, that
the secession would be of the non-violent, Norwegian type, and that
Québec would be a very good member of the family of democratic
nations. But, the will for independence is not there. The election
returns, the polls, the qualitative evidence gathered from conversations and mood sampling over the years, all of these indicate that the
large majority of Québécois want a restructuring of the Canadian federation, not a separation from it.

Over the years, two processes of nation building have competed
on Québec's territory. Throughout, language flags have been raised.

Other flags, too, appear on the flagpole – the religious in particular – but only the linguistic one has continued to be flown high; it will continue to dominate the confrontation because language cannot, as easily as religion, retreat from the public into the private domain. The denser public communication systems become, the more language will be an issue. We can pray once a day, or go to church once a month, or once a year, or never; we cannot be so economical of our reading, listening, and speaking time.

The sense of nationhood is not, of course, restricted to a single social function. It is not rooted exclusively in culture. It involves a sense of belonging to a global community. It produces an expansion of self in all kinds of directions: cultural, social, economic, and political. It enlarges our sense of achievement in time and space. It takes us on a significant journey from real or imaginary beginnings to a future that we would like to contribute to making secure. Notwithstanding its wholeness, however, there is usually a core, a significant marker, an anchor to the sense of belonging to a nation. It may be a set of shared memories or simply a passport. In the case of Québec, as time passed and as religion and history ceased to be in the daily or even weekly thoughts of its citizens, language gained prominence as 'the' national unifier. It is not frustration with federal economic policies nor is it the memories of the Plains of Abraham that sustain the separatist movement. A random reading of Québec's French newspapers for the past generation will show that rare are the days when concern about language is not in the news or commentaries. The sovereignty movement is sustained by a sense of collective self that vanishes, unlike in Ireland or even in the Basque country, once language is removed as the trigger of identity. Any real or perceived threat to French is perceived by Québécois as a threat to a vital environment. We may thus center our predictions of the future of Québécois-Canadian relations on the language question.

The Canadian Language System

In Canada, two major world languages, by some measures *the* two major world languages, confront each other within the same state.[8] Of the two, English is by far the more powerful. It is the most powerful language the world has ever known, whether we measure power by geographical spread, military capabilities, scientific production, rate of diffusion as a second language, or rate of destruction of other languages (Mackey 1973; Laponce 1987; Van Parijs 2000). The other major language, French, ranks far behind but, having a recent history as *the* world language and having retained very good assets, it does not easily cede that position to English; hence its wanting to have its own playground. French is not prepared to give up and is unlikely to do so within the next hundred years.[9] English can rely on its own power as a language to subdue the other languages in its path. French, by contrast, relies for its protection on territorial concentration and restrictive government legislation. English means English, French means politics.

There are major factors working in favour of French in Québec as well as those working against it. The following lists some:

Factors in Favor:

- Sizable population mass: Québec has more Francophones than either Switzerland or Belgium; French is spoken at home by over 80 per cent of its population.
- Very high level of endogamy (95 per cent of mother tongue French marry mother tongue French).
- All major functions of the polity – cultural, religious, economic, social, and political, can operate in French.
- New migrants must attend French schools with the result that while before 1971 only 27 per cent of Allophones had shifted to French, the post 1971 percentage is 66 per cent (Béland 1999).
- Québec's Anglophones are increasingly bilingual although, in the Montréal metropolitan area, over 60 per cent use English "almost exclusively" in the public domain.

Factors Against:

- Globalization of the economy, popular culture, and science in favour of English.
- Replacement of a significant proportion of the Francophone *de souche* population with one of varied origins, less rooted to the language and the 'old' culture: more geographically and linguistically mobile.
- Advantage of English in attracting new speakers. The index of language maintenance, relating mother tongue to language spoken at home still favours English: 1.24 compared to 1.02 for French (Côté 1999:22).
- Changing ethnic, linguistic, and political composition of the Island of Montréal in favour of Allophones weakens French in a strategic location in economic, cultural, and geopolitical terms. Outside the Montréal region, French is used in public "mostly or nearly exclusively" 96 per cent of the time. On the Island of Montréal, the figure drops to 71 per cent. On the Island, 80 per cent of immigrants with a Latin origin speak predominantly French in public, 78 per cent of immigrants of other origins speak mostly English (Monnier 1993; Béland 1999). Having lost the battle of the cradle, Québécois may well lose the battle of Montréal.
- Decline of Québec's electoral weight within Canada due to the uneven distribution of new migrants continuously more attracted to the West and Ontario. In 2100, Québec should have dropped to less than 20 per cent of the Canadian population compared to 24 per cent now, and 29 per cent in 1960.
- Further decline of Québec's electoral weight even if the electoral system, and the party system, were to be changed by introducing proportional representation. Québec would no longer have the same possibility of affecting the outcome of an election by concentrating its vote on a single party, as it often did in the past.[10]

I am unable to quantify the relative weight of these factors, hence I am unable to summarize them into a positive or negative total score. On balance, I think they work to the advantage of French in the short run but against French in the long run. While the Québécois population is reassured by the remarkable progress French has made in the last generation, its political and intellectual elites are aware of the fragility of these gains. If I am right, then it follows that the Québécois will not achieve independence: too many feel too secure to want it now and they will be too weak to have it – or even want it – later. It also follows that any major revision of the Constitution would have to be obtained in the short term.

At this point, let us consider a few scenarios that involve changing the relations between Québec and Canada so as to lead to some form of federation of nations. We will examine three scenarios, starting with the simplest to implement.

Scenario 1:
From Adversarial to Consensual Government

The Canadian mode of democratic government was inherited from Britain. It is rational in the sense that it satisfies Riker's rule of government by means of minimum winning coalitions (Riker 1962). Since the party winning a Canadian federal election obtains, on average, about 40 per cent of the votes, the minimum size principle is well served. But the system is irrational in that it is not adapted to the governance of a multinational state. If Switzerland had had colonies and if Canada had been one, Canada would have inherited a different mode of government: one based on decision by consensus or at least by very large ruling coalitions. The Swiss government (a coalition of all major parties) does so at a level of about 70 to 80 per cent of the electorate and ensures that its three major national segments – the German, the French, and the Italian – are not subject to a minority position on issues that are essential to any one of them.

Canada has adopted some of the minor features of consensualism (McRae 1997): the federal system puts the French segment in limited control in one province; the Inuit are in control of a territory that could, at some point, become a province; the Supreme Court, the Cabinet, and the chairs of royal commissions have given to Francophones greater weight than that which they could claim on the basis of a strict representation by population. But the dominant mode of decision-making remains majoritarian and the dominant mode of parliamentary government remains adversarial. The constitutional revision of 1982, which was obtained by what looked like a large majority (more than the number of provinces required by the Supreme Court ruling), was in fact the imposition of the will of one national segment (the Canadian) over another (the Québécois). Such a majoritarian and adversarial mode of government is ill-adapted to a multinational polity.

Will the present system evolve into government by co-operation among its national segments? That would be a claim to distinction for a polity that says it does not want to be a melting pot. There has been, in the last decade, a noticeable movement in that direction in the negotiations between First Nations and provincial and federal governments on the the other; but there are no signs of a significant evolution in the relations between the second and the third nations. The result of the Québec referendum of 1995 was viewed, in the words of Prime Minister Chrétien, like that of a hockey game: "Never mind the score, what matters is the win." The appropriate 'consensual' reaction would have been to say: "Never mind the win, let's consider the score. When such a large number of citizens of such an important province – never mind whether it is 50 per cent, 40 per cent, or 30 per cent – is prepared to vote for some form of separation, there must be something fundamentally wrong with the status quo; let's negotiate." I realize the strength of the forces, both federal and provincial, opposing such negotiation, which is why I doubt that the Québécois-Canadian debate will shift from a majoritarian to a consensual mode of operation.

Scenario 2:
Provincial Sovereignty over Language and Culture

A revised Constitution could give Québec (and other provinces wanting them) increased powers[11] and, notably, full sovereign rights in matters of language, education, culture, and related fields. In other words, Québec could be given rights similar to those of a Swiss canton. Unrestricted language sovereignty would enable Québec, at its discretion, to adopt either the unilingualism of Geneva, the bilingualism of Fribourg (which juxtaposes two unilingual areas separated by a language border running through its capital city), or the multilingualism of The Grisons that mixes languages territorially at the level of the municipalities. Under such a constitutional arrangement, the decision either to protect or to assimilate linguistic minorities would be left to the discretion of the provinces. Such a solution might be supported by some Anglophone provinces, provinces where the use of French is so minimal that its privileges offend many electors.

Belgium, which had tried the Canadian policy of protection of language rights on an individual basis, has shifted to the Swiss solution of the juxtaposition of unilingual territories (except in Brussels) in order to moderate its language conflicts (McRae 1986; Laponce 1992, 1997). The likelihood of Canada doing the same is not very high. The Québec Anglophone community is large enough and has enough leverage, outside as well as inside Québec, to block such a change.[12]

Scenario 3:
A Multination Federal Structure

A federal structure joining two or three (or more) nations could be combined with the present federation of regions. A structure of that type had been envisaged some hundred years ago by Bauer (1907, trans. 2000) who proposed reforming Austria by separating economic from national issues. To that effect, he proposed a set of parallel federal structures giving the nationalities their own parliament. His proposal was not implemented but, interestingly, contemporary Belgium adopted a system resembling that proposed by Bauer when it evolved from a unitary into a federal system in the 1990s and created, in addition to the federal parliament, separate parliaments for regions and language communities (Karmis and Gagnon 1996; Delpérée 1996; Laponce 1997).

The questions concerning structure, however, are many. Does Switzerland offer a model that could be adapted to the Canadian scene (Laponce 1984, 1997)? Should the model be Belgium (Karmis and Gagnon 1996; Laponce 1997)? Should it be a federation between a unitary Québec (why not a federal Québec?) and a federal Canada as proposed by Resnick (1991)? Should it be an adaptation of the European Union model as proposed by Québec intellectuals and politicians? Should it be some other scheme to enable the creation of a public space (Taylor 1992) wherein nations could negotiate matters of common interest and regulate separately their own and specific interests? Whatever the structure envisaged, a major political restructuring would be needed. A reformed Constitution that would structure polit-ically a multination federation within the present federal system, by territorializing the three nations as much as feasible – and giving them the powers over language, culture, and citizenship needed to maintain themselves as nations – would give Canada a distinctive model of gov-ernment adapted to a time when nations seek protection from the effects of globalization.[13] Will such a restructuring take place? It is pos-sible but unlikely. In the absence of strong political leadership (such leadership is in the domain of the unpredictable), a major reform of the Constitution would probably require a crisis following a referendum favourable to Québec. A referendum outcome we thought was unlikely.

The Challenge Ahead

I have two conclusions, one drawn on the side of caution, the other on the side of hope.

Conclusion One

If Jesus Christ had been born sixty to seventy years earlier and the mil-lennium and the new century had arrived sooner, would we still be as optimistic about the strength of the democratic system, as optimistic about the economy, and as concerned about the language problem as we are today? Would the First Nations, if not the second nation, not to mention multiculturalism, have been given the same prominence in our futurology? Predicting is, indeed, the occupation of fools. The pre-sent casts auras and large shadows on a future composed wrongly of too much past.[14]

Conclusion Two

Here, however, is a summary of our predictions and hopes given the auras and shadows of the present. We predict that Canada's popula-tion will change fundamentally in looks and origins: it will be much less white, much less French, and much more English-speaking. We think that the structures of integration and assimilation will be strong enough, especially in English Canada, to make Aboriginals – at least a large segment – Asians, Latin Americans, Caribbeans, and Africans become simply Canadians or Québécois, more easily the former than the latter. We predict that the First Nations will settle their land claims and obtain varied forms of territorial self-government; having thus regained their security and dignity, they will more easily converge, economically and socially, with the rest of society. We believe that the French language and Francophones will lose influence but will remain major political actors, thus continuing to pose major problems.

We wish that the governing structures could be changed to make room for a collaboration of nations. We are doubtful that this transformation will occur, thereby redefining the relations between Canada and Québec; our doubts arise from the rigidities of the present structures and modes of government as well as from the very success of the Canadian nation building enterprise. However, I hope that I am wrong in seeing too many obstacles for Canada to resolve its old, two-nations problem with models adapted from Switzerland, Belgium, or the European Union.

The challenge is to bring nations together, as provinces were brought together in the nineteenth century, and avoid this time too symmetrical a federalism. The challenge is to bring harmony out of a great deal of asymmetry.

Notes

1.   For this lack of fit, see among others: Cairns (1993), Resnick (1991), Taylor (1992), Laponce (1997), and Houle (1999).

2.   The term 'ethnic' has become so loaded with myth and politics that it should probably be abandoned. A return to the term 'community' would at least distinguish between a 'system' and that which is merely a 'set.' For the confusion concerning the term ethnic, see Riggs (1985). For a brief history of the use of the term since de la Pouge proposed to distinguish "ethnicity" from "race" in 1896, see Laponce (1992). For a survey of research on ethnicity in Canada see Berry and Laponce (1994). The term 'nation' is also stuck in ideological glue. I use ethnic to mean an historical community perceived as such by its members. The concept would be better rendered by the French *communauté de la longue durée*; I take a nation to be a *communauté de la longue durée* if it governs itself, or wishes to govern itself, politically, at the level of a state, a region, or a locality. Note that the sources I use led me to identify only three nations – Canadians, Québécois, and Aboriginals – where Alan Cairns (1995)

identifies four, by splitting Canadians into "TransCanada Canadians" and "Canadians outside Québec."

3. Note that shifting our attention from census to survey makes the categories of British and French practically disappear. They have been succeeded by Canadians and Québécois. On the one hand we have 65 per cent Canadians, to whom we should add, as related identifiers and political allies, the 3 per cent British-Canadians, many of the 4 per cent French-Canadians, the 7 per cent other hyphenated-Canadians and the 1 per cent identifiers with provinces other than Québec, for a total of roughly 80 per cent. On the other hand we have a Québécois segment of about 15 per cent and an Aboriginal segment of about 3 per cent (see n. 4).

4. The Statistics Canada survey (cat. 89/357) gives the following breakdown: Indians on reserves 1.06 per cent, Indians outside reserves 1.49 per cent, Métis 0.5, and Inuit 0.10 – for a total of 862,485 people or 3.2 per cent of the total population.

5. An immediate reaction to this number of 180 million may well be: where would they fit? They can't be settled in the freezing North. But we should remember the eighteenth century prediction of Buffon, who, having been commissioned to report on prospects for North America, told the king of France: "Sire, in those parts, the climate is so severe that civilization cannot take roots" (author's recollection).

6. Alan Cairns favours giving to Aboriginals special rights in addition to those flowing from their Canadian citizenship but short of the nation-to-nation relationship (Aboriginals vs. non-Aboriginals) advocated by the commissioners in the report of the Royal Commission on Aboriginal Peoples (1996). For an argument against special rights, see Flanagan (2000).

7. Few Aboriginal languages have a chance of survival. The ones that are better placed in the survival competition are those that are isolated and relatively numerous – notably Cree with about 90,000 speakers, Ojibway with about 25,000, and the Inuktitut family of languages with about 30,000. But even those are unlikely to survive unless it be in a diglossic association with English.

8. In only two other states is that the case: Cameroon and Vanuatu.

9. I realize that I reify languages and that I seem to give them a will of their own; I do so for the convenience of shorthand, the kind of shorthand that is used more frequently in describing religions or nations. If languages do not have a government, they have at least a governance.

10. The introduction of proportional representation would satisfy Schattschneider's rule of suffrage expansion (1975) which states that, in

a democratic system, suffrage keeps expanding: first, because it is in the logic of democracy to become more inclusive and second, because it is in the logic of party competition that one of the competing parties will seek to gain new voters by offering the vote to categories of people disfranchised until then. When the age of political maturity cannot be pushed much lower, proportional representation offers an alternative. It would not expand the electorate, but would expand representation in Parliament and, very likely, in the government as well.

11.   For a recent proposal, one among a long series which deal with the transfer of powers to Québec, see Lisée (1999), who suggests a referendum on the transfer of powers over language, culture, communication, immigration, health, social programmes, and research.

12.   Few are the Allophones educated in English who would support a single, universal, French school education. The pro-federalist Greater Québec Movement is an exception (Lachance 1999). Paradoxically, the present *Parti Québécois* government, having set its aims higher than linguistic and cultural sovereignty, quite unreasonably continues to hope to bring to its side the Anglophone and Allophone vote; hence its downplaying of the language issue.

13.   Three or more nations, but at least two; the reason being that the Québécois-Canadian cleavage is the more enduring as it is based on language.

14.   Assuming Canada's national question is solved, what other problem would come to the fore? The logic of a democratic system would favour a problem that raises questions of inequality, but the aura or shadow of the present, as the case may be, prevents us from seeing the problem that will replace the one that remains unsolved.

References

Bauer, O. 1907. *The Question of Nationalities and Social Democracy*. Trans. Joseph O'Donnell. 2000. Minneapolis: University of Minnesota Press.

Beaujot, R. 1991. *Population Change in Canada*. Toronto: McClelland and Stewart.

Béland, Paul. 1999. « Les langues des communications publiques. » *Bulletin du Conseil de la langue française* 15 (4): novembre.

Berry, J. and R. Kalin. 1993. "Multicultural and Ethnic Attitudes in Canada." Paper read at the Fifty-fourth Annual Convention of the Canadian Psychological Association. May 27–29. Montréal.

Berry, J. and J.A. Laponce, eds. 1994. *Ethnicity and Culture in Canada: The Research Landscape.* Toronto: University of Toronto Press.

Breton, R. 1988. "From Ethnic to Civic Nationalism. English Canada and Québec." *Ethnic and Racial Studies* 11 (1): 85–102.

Breton, R. et al. 1990. *Ethnic Identity and Equality* Toronto: University of Toronto Press.

Cairns, A. 1993. "The Fragmenting of Canadian Citizenship." In *Belonging: The Meaning and Future of Canadian Citizenship,* ed. W. Kaplan, 187–220. Montréal and Kingston: McGill-Queen's University Press.

_____. 1995. "Constitutional Government and the Two Faces of Ethnicity: Federalism is not Enough." In *Rethinking Federalism,* ed. K. Knop et al., 15–19. Vancouver: UBC Press.

_____. 2000. *Citizens Plus: Aboriginal Peoples and the Canadian State.* Vancouver: UBC Press.

Canada. Government. 1989. *Charting Canada's Future.* Ottawa: Minister of Supply and Services.

Coakley, J. 1994. "Approaches to the Resolution of Ethnic Conflict: The Strategy of Non-territorial Autonomy." *International Political Science Review* 15 (3): 297–314.

Côté, R., dir. 1998. *Québec 1999.* Montréal: Fides.

Courchene, T.J. and L.M. Powell. 1992. *A First Nation Province.* Kingston: Queen's University, Institute of Intergovernmental Relations.

Delpérée, F. 1996. « Le fédéralisme, forme d'adaptation de l'Etat-nation: le cas de la Belgique. » Dans *Au delà et en deçà de l'Etat-nation,* dir. C. Philip et P. Soldatos, 140–158. Bruxelles: Bruylant.

Durham, J. G. Lambton, Earl of. 1839. *The Report and Dispatches of the Earl of Durham, Her Majesty's High Commissioner and Governor General of British North America.* London: Ridgways.

Flanagan, T. 2000. *First Nations? Second Thoughts.* Montréal and Kingston: McGill-Queen's University Press.

Halli, S., F. Trovato and L. Driedger, eds. 1990. *Ethnic Demography: Canadian Immigrant, Racial and Cultural Variations.* Ottawa: Carleton University Press.

Houle, F. 1999. « Des identités nationales dans le régime fédéral canadien. » Dans *Dislocation et permanence: l'invention du Canada au quotidien,* dir. C. Andrew, 229–81. Ottawa: Presses de l'Université d'Ottawa.

Karmis, D. et A.-G. Gagnon. 1996. « Fédéralisme et identités collectives au Canada et en Belgique: des itinéraires différents, une fragmentation similaire. » *Revue canadienne de science politique* 29 (3): 435–68.

Lachance, A. 1999. « Rififi à l'anglaise. » *L'Actualité.* 18 juin.

Laponce, J.A. 1960. *The Protection of Minorities.* Los Angeles and Berkeley: University of California Press.

_____. 1984. "Tensions between Geography and Politics." *Political Geography Quarterly* 3:91–104.

_____. 1987. *Languages and their Territories.* Toronto: University of Toronto Press.

_____. 1992. "Canada, Switzerland and Talcott Parsons." *Queen's Quarterly* 19 (2): 267–79.

_____. 1993a. « L'heure du fédéralisme personnel est-elle arrivée? » Dans *L'État et les minorités*, dir. Jean Lafontant, 55–65. Saint Boniface: Presses Universitaires de Saint Boniface.

_____. 1993b. "The Case for Ethnic Federalism." *Regional Politics and Policy* 3 (1): 23–43.

_____. 1995. "Ethnicity and Citizenship as Generators of Each Other." In *Ethnicity and Citizenship: The Canadian Case,* ed. J.A. Laponce and W. Safran. London: Frank Cass.

_____. 1997. « *Comment conjuguer le Québec et le Canada,* » Dans *Can Canada Survive?: Under What Terms and Conditions? / Le Canada peut-il encore survivre ? : Comment et dans quelles conditions?* dir. David M. Hayne, 67–90. Toronto: University of Toronto Press.

_____. 1999. "The Québec Sovereignty Referendum of 1995: How Not to Manage a Multinational Polity." *Politikon* 26 (1): 103–19.

Lisée, J.-F. 2000. *Sortie de secours: comment échapper au déclin du Québec.* Montréal: Boréal.

McRae, K.D. 1986. *Conflict and Compromise in Multilingual Societies: Volume 2, Belgium.* Waterloo: Wilfrid Laurier University Press.

_____. 1997. "Contrasting Styles of Democratic Decision-making: Adversary versus Consensual Government." *International Political Science Review* 18 (3): 279–96.

Mackey, W.F. 1973. *Three Concepts in Geolinguistics.* Publication B 42. Québec: Université Laval, Centre international de recherche sur le bilinguisme.

Monnier, D. 1993. *Les choix linguistiques des travailleurs immigrants et allophones.* Québec: Conseil de la langue française.

Neurath, P. 1994. *From Malthus to the Club of Rome and Back.* New York: Sharpe.

Ornstein, Michael. 2000. "The Specificity of Ethnicity." *Newsletter.* York University, Institute for Social Research 15 (1): 1–3.

Resnick,, P. 1991. *Toward a Canada-Québec Union.* Montréal and Kingston: McGill-Queen's University Press.

Riggs, F. 1985. *Ethnicity.* Hawaii: University of Hawaii, Department of Political Science.

Riker, W. 1962. *The Theory of Political Coalitions*. New Haven: Yale University Press.

Royal Commission on Aboriginal Peoples. 1996. *Report*. 5 vols. Ottawa: Minister of Supply and Services.

Schattschneider, E.E. 1960. *The Semisovereign People: A Realist's View of Democracy in America*. Reissued 1975. Hinsdale: Dryden Press.

Siegfried, A. 1906. *Le Canada. Les deux races: problèmes politiques contemporains*. Paris: Colin.

Taylor, C. 1992. « Convergences et divergences à propos des valeurs entre le Québec et le Canada. » Dans *Rapprocher les solitudes*. Québec: Presses de l'Université Laval.

Tepper, E. 1994. "Immigration Policy and Multiculturalism." In *Ethnicity and Culture in Canada: The Research Landscape*, ed. J. Berry and J.A. Laponce. Toronto: University of Toronto Press.

Van Parijs, P. 2000. "The Ground Floor of the World: On the Socio-economic Consequences of Linguistic Globalization." *International Political Science Review* 21 (2): 217–33.

Venne, M., dir. 2000. *Penser la nation Québécoise*. Montréal: Québec-Amérique.

Metaphors and Maps: Imagining Canada into the Twenty-first Century

Lorna Irvine

I N THEIR INTRODUCTION TO *PAINTING THE MAPLE* – A 1998 COLLECTION of essays that, as the metaphor in the title suggests, investigates some of the ways that race and gender influence our perceptions of Canada – Strong-Boag, Grace, Eisenberg, and Anderson (1998), warn that Canada is disintegrating. In illustration, they point to the free trade agreements which, they tell us, facilitate "postmodern corporate capitalism and the related, though less understood, phenomenon of globalization" (1998:3). Such millennial theorizing is not uncommon. For example, in *Millennial Dreams*, the cultural studies theorist, Paul Smith (1997:61), argues that, with the demise of the Soviet Union, capital in the north dominates both time and space, inevitably presenting a "different description of reality." Addressing the cultural, civic, and political life of the United States, he metaphorically personifies the country as "lurching" toward the millennium, "insanely anguished about its future and at the same time wracked by memories of its childhood" (1997:189). While the search for national redefinition goes on, globalization, according to Smith, "has begun to dominate the discursive arena of our time" (1997:262).

Indeed, Smith's insistence that the "millennial dream of capitalism" draws upon "fantasies of domination and exploitation" (1997:262) underlies the conviction of the editors of *Painting the Maple* that globalization is a threat to Canada's distinctiveness because it encourages a uniform, rather than a multivarious, approach to national identity. Deep cultural divisions revolve around issues of diversity, they argue, as the debates about education demonstrate. "The current period, roughly 1980 to the present, has seen a dramatic split in intellectual thought between those who call for a return to the 'core curriculum' and to the questions of universal, national or fundamental importance, and those who argue that the actual problems facing society at the end of the twentieth century cannot be solved by specialized knowledge or homogenous, monological methodologies. For this latter group, interdisciplinarity is a *praxis* that brings together scholars within the university and groups outside the university to work on complex common problems and to produce … transformative knowledge" (Strong-Boag et al. 1998:7). Such knowledge, they go on to argue, recognizes that "the power of words, images, and concepts cannot be underestimated in the construction of Canada. The images of 'Canada First', the 'true North strong and free', and the 'two solitudes', or such terms as 'bilingualism', 'multiculturalism', 'anti-racism', 'First Nations', and 'academic freedom' name realities in order to insert them into the imagining of community. They map the ongoing struggle to construct the nation" (1998:14).

Painting the Maple, indirectly connected to other studies of nation-formation such as Homi Bhabha's (1990) *Nation and Narration*, Benedict Anderson's (1983) *Imagined Communities*, and Néstor Canclini's (1995) *Hybrid Cultures* advocates scrutinizing "the discursive formation of nation to see where, how, and why some discursive practices (stories, texts, voices) install themselves in a narrative of nation and others do not" (Strong-Boag et al. 1998:8). They are just these certain "discursive practices" that William New (1998) questions in his recent *Borderlands*, an essay about how its citizens (mainly its Anglophone citizens) talk about Canada. Because national boundaries, New suggests, are insubstantial and fragile, they allow for numerous metaphoric possibilities, functioning both as "descriptions of concrete agreements *and* as metaphors of relationship and organization" (1998:5). According to New, metaphors conceptualize our world, socially, even ethically compartmentalizing place and space. He points to the familial metaphor of imperialism – mother country, daughter colony – as an illustration of colonial dependency. It is also gendered, reminding us of an earlier conceptualization of Canada by the historian William Kilbourn (1970), who writes that "in a masculine world of the assertive will and the cutting edge of intellect, a certain Canadian tendency to the amorphous permissive feminine principle of openness and toleration and acceptance offers the possibility of healing" (1970:53). Here, Canada is imaged as female, set against a rough assertive male world, and often connected with the United States.

New is interested in more nuanced metaphors; like the editors of *Painting the Maple*, he believes that the borderland works well as an image for contemporary Canada because it implies a "condition of 'interstitiality', *in-between-ness*, an experiential territory of intervention and revision" (1998, 27). A dramatic example of borderland imagery appears in Michael Ondaatje's (1992) *The English Patient*. The Italian villa in which the characters play out the drama is presented as a liminal space, a borderland, which is open to many different kinds of negotiation, all of which oblige readers to question the stability and even the legitimacy of boundaries. At one point, the English patient, speaking of living in the desert, says: "We were German, English, Hungarian, African – all of us insignificant to them [the Bedouin]. Gradually we became nationless. I came to hate nations. We are deformed by nation-states" (1992:138). While not denying the significance of nation, New emphasizes the importance of the uncertainty of in-between-ness: "Inside Canada, a boundary discourse often functions both inclusively and exclusively, as the metaphoric plane on which differing versions of nationhood and nationalism – some with a misconceived faith in the power of definition – declare themselves" (1998:29). Indeed, New thinks of uncertainty as really a "matrix of creation" (1998:30) and quotes the playwright John Gray who, in a sort of excess of metaphors, calls Canada an "internally generated vision, a collective work of art ... an existential fable, a poem packed with personal questions" (1998:68). New quotes Gray, I presume, because he wants all of us to resist certain older nationalist clichés so that we can "imagine our way past the stereotypes of affordability and snowy boredom. And without losing sight of the larger world in which we live ... embrace the local spirit, the creative energy." Canadian Studies will, he hopes, become the "*text* of our lives" (1998:102).

That's probably what Jonathan Kertzer (1998) also hopes in *Worrying the Nation*, his analysis of Anglophone literature. He, too, investigates the tension between politics and culture and argues, as the others have, that without a stable centre, Canada, as a nation, can be imaged only by "permeable" boundaries (1998:136). While he understands that many post-nationalists interpret nations as "tribal remnants" (1998:163), he nonetheless believes that contemporary human beings need, both historically and discursively, the concept of nation, protean as it necessarily is. He writes: "We must continue studying how the nation is imagined: how it defines a body of writing as national; how it informs and validates that literature; how its clashing loyalties impassion citizens for good or ill; how it convokes and disperses communities; how it invokes and subverts the ideal of heroism; how it foresees a fusion of personal and social satisfactions (joy and justice); and how it gives a mission to literary criticism, including the mission to denounce nationalism in its vicious forms" (1998:195). For Kertzer, Canada is a riddle.

Not everyone will agree that Canada should remain a nation in order to give literary critics a mission. Peter Newman (1993), in *The Canadian Revolution: From Deference to Defiance*, might be arguing for Canada's nationhood as a mission for journalists. Situating himself, as he tells his readers in the conclusion, as "the guy in the tunnel. Trying to illuminate the path we've taken and even flash ahead a bit to light our uncertain future" (1993:400), Newman gives us a quantity of numerous potentially guiding metaphors. Former editor-in-chief of *Maclean's* and *The Toronto Star*, he writes with a journalist's panache, a sort of bravura that encourages extravagance. As an analysis of Canadian politics mainly between 1985 and 1995, his book begins with that now clichéd metaphor of Canada as a "Clark Kent" who, Newman argues, may finally be transforming into Superman. While he admits that changes in the political identity of Canada tend to be "glacial" (a not surprising metaphor for such a northern country), he suggests that something happened between 1985 and 1995, when there occurred "a sudden bursting like buds in springtime" (1993:xvi). While this is not an un-Canadian metaphor – buds do, finally, burst even in Canada – the attachment of the metaphor to a renewed connection between thought and emotion is somewhat less Canadian; that is, with the bursting bud metaphor, Newman implies that, at last, Canadians could escape from their lengthy indenture to authority and their northern stoicism, replacing it with individualism and a sort of southern recklessness. In case we miss the point, he underlines it: "the time had come to stop pretending that being Canadian was some kind of inside joke dreamed up by a bored God with a highly-developed sense of the absurd" (1993:xix). Such a God is surely good enough for prime time – a Canadian humorist who might have appeared on *SCTV* or *This Hour Has 22 Minutes*.

Newman's metaphors are certainly rhetorical. They enliven his writing. But they also tell us a good deal about his desires for Canada, most notably that Canada (the peaceable kingdom) is capable of revolution. "Once or twice a century," Newman tells us, "like a hurricane that eludes the meteorologists' charts, the breezes of history unexpectedly accelerate and blow away the touchstones by which people live" (1995:3). While winds are a part of nature, Newman believes that Canadians have always suffered from having an identity so connected with nature; he wants to shift his images in line with the "Darwinian ethic of the 1980s" (1995:65) although surely Darwin has informed Canadian nature imagery all along. For example, Northrop Frye's garrisons image depicts Canada as a series of protective camps surrounded by an often antagonistic nature, a wilderness where, as one of the characters in Margaret Atwood's *Wilderness Tips* imagines: there are trees that are "hardly trees; they are currents of energy, charged with violent colour" (1991:129). Such metaphors describe Canada in terms of a struggle.

Newman's desire to encourage us to see a Canada raw in tooth and claw even affects the now prevalent images of borders that Canadian writers have recently been using. When he tells us that Canada is "delicately poised on the edge of perpetual collapse" (1995:11), unlike the optimistic borders of New's *Borderlands*, this edge is presented as potential disaster. It affects, too, his attention to gender. Newman quotes from his favorite writer, Morley Callaghan: "Canada ... is like a woman waiting in the window of an old house at a crossroads. She is an ageless, wild and hard beauty. Men riding by come to her in the night. They use her but never really possess her. They leave her and ride on, afraid of her fierce domination over them, knowing they can't handle her; she leaves them feeling small." By pointedly setting what he calls Margaret Atwood's "literary ruminations" against, for example, southern Saskatchewan's "folk wisdom born of winters so severe that they couldn't see their own feet in snowstorms and land so tough that it yielded more rock than crop" (1995:35-6), Newman not surprisingly prefers Callaghan's familiar metaphor of male/female struggle in which Canada is perceived as a wild, hard and, of course, used beauty not at all like, for example, the unnamed narrator of Atwood's (1972) *Surfacing*, whose complexity confuses such gendered absolutes.

Newman's particular vision of Canada's future makes it no easier for him to find effective encompassing metaphors than it is for any one else. Earlier, writers such as E.J. Pratt could use the unifying image of a railroad that linked the provinces and emphasized an east-west axis. Now, though, the axes have shifted, more often moving from north to south, or else with further disregard of borders, from North America to Europe and Asia. As Newman notes, "with the demise of nationalism and the CBC that had once been the house organ, Canada would have to find a different set of sustaining mythologies" (1995:103). During a period of economic decline – the decade being discussed in *The Canadian Revolution* – the mythologies are not, on the whole, sustainable. Newman describes a country sharply divided; suffering an identity crisis; overwhelmed by the mass media of the United States; unable to work out its dual cultural, political, and linguistic traditions. He describes Prime Minister Mulroney's policies as calamitous and calls him an "an obsessive beekeeper, walking around the buzzing apiary of Canada punching holes into every hive he could find" (1995:247), succeeding, finally, in dramatically polarizing Canada. In another metaphor (probably owing something to the American poet, Robert Frost), Newman portrays Mulroney as a "lighted match" (1995:261), and the opposition leader, John Turner, as an " iceberg" (1995:265). This fire-and-ice image underlines the bifurcation of Canada that Newman emphasizes.

The images that he repeats from other writers support his vision of a certain Canadian machismo. For example, he quotes the expatriate writer Scott Symons, who, angered by what he believes to be excessive dependence on government money, calls Canada a "crêche, a permanent daycare" (1995:294). Newman objects to the historically dominant metaphor of the Canadian mosaic. Having arrived in Canada in 1940, an "exiled Jew from a Nazi-occupied Czechoslovakia" (1995:329), he recalls feeling very much an outsider, overwhelmed by WASP [White Anglo-Saxon Protestant] ascendancy; he approves of its waning, and supports a revolutionary spirit that might speed its demise. Not surprisingly, then, he interprets the election of 1993 as a revolution during which "Canadians figuratively stormed the walls of Parliament and razed its chambers clean of all but a few traces of the politics they had come to hate" (1995:390). But he is fearful. His conclusion, tellingly entitled "Slouching Toward the Millennium," challenges his country not to abandon the revolutionary spirit as it moves into the twenty-first century. He wants Canadians to jettison the heavy images of the past, as he suggests they did between 1985 and 1995 when "instead of feeling as if they were carrying the Precambrian Shield on their shoulders, Canadians took a break from lugging around the cumbersome baggage of their national virtues and became most untypically Latin" (1995:395). For the "condition" of being a Canadian in the new millennium, he wants Canadians to abandon "deference and blind loyalty" (1995:396) and to begin to look after "their own spirits in the absence of a national soul" (1995:397). The word "soul" introduces, among other things, the jazz metaphors that he loves.

Newman's metaphors are relatively flamboyant. In *Misconceiving Canada* (published two years after Newman's 1995 book), Kenneth

McRoberts (1997) brings us back to a historian's more mundane exposition. Written in a plain style, this book avoids metaphors, except for those overarching images popular with historians that link organicism and nationalism: images of growth, particularly of trees that root, branch, blossom, and so on. Images of war are also used, so naturally that one hardly marks them as metaphors: struggle, mobilization, battle. Occasionally, McRoberts personifies Canada, commenting, for example, on the country's modesty and is inclined to structure space in terms of centres and margins. Arguing against what he calls the "centre-piece" (1997:xv) of Trudeau's policy, that of official bilingualism, with its concomitant rejection of biculturalism in favour of multiculturalism, McRoberts uncharacteristically insists that "cultures may not be water-tight compartments" (1997:118). He also reiterates the metaphor of the struggle for national identity as a "dialogue of the deaf" (1997:188), an image that Atwood (1978) used in *Two-Headed Poems*: "This is not a debate / but a duet / with two deaf singers" (1978:75).

McRoberts' analysis, while quite compelling, is of less help in the pursuit of sustaining metaphors for Canadian nationalism than is Keohane's (1997) *Symptoms of Canada*, an essay on the Canadian identity. Keohane uses metaphors in a whole gamut of ways – to irritate, tease, shock, embolden, and so on. His focus is on language, telling his readers that he is searching for one "that may be employed persuasively in the public sphere" (1997:15). A little like the now notorious David Noble of York University, who has set himself in opposition to the contemporary embrace of technology, Keohane uses the image of the Terminator "a metaphor for a rapacious transnational New World Order" (1997:10), a figure who seeks to end inferior life forms. But Keohane is no Noble. His more positive metaphor of the cyborg, I am sure, would distress the York professor, who particularly opposes the computer's takeover of contemporary life. What is a cyborg? According to Keohane – he picks up the term from cultural theorist Donna Haraway, cyborgs are "fabricated hybrids," who "populate worlds ambiguously natural and crafted,"and a "dialectical antithesis" of the Terminator (1997:11). As "the spectral figure haunting postmodernity", the cyborg's particular metaphoric value as an image for Canada lies, for Keohane, once again in its ability to confuse boundaries (1997:11). Belonging to no particular race, class, or gender, the cyborg, writes Keohane, is committed to "partiality, irony, intimacy, and perversity" (1997:11). This fragmented, hybrid image which occupies "a multiplicity of often contradictory subject positions," offers

Keohane an image not of rebirth, but of regeneration; it allows him to play with the idea of transgressing various boundaries as a positive development in imagining contemporary Canada (1997:11). By using the image, he can create what he calls a "nomadic imaginary" that includes among all Canadians "First Nations, Founding Nations, travelling cultures," and so on (1997:13). Thus equipped, he can do battle with images of the Terminator.

Not everyone will agree with all of Keohane's somewhat outrageous generalizations, but if his work is read as a kind of play, it at least reminds Canadians of the desirability of enjoyment. His metaphors include that of Canada as a house party, with conversation sometimes discordant but always engaged. For Keohane, the Canadian carnival is alive. Witness our comedians, pop singers, mass media, and television (*Kids in the Hall*, for example), moments where the "symbolic order of civilized Canadian society is lifted" (1997:131). Or what about Canada as a restaurant, an image he uses and that can certainly be connected with the sounds that Glenn Gould recorded in his "The Idea of North." Or, Keohane suggests, Canada can be imaged as a Tilley hat, unpretentious and durable. Such playful metaphors remind us of Newman's desire to jettison the Precambrian Shield on our backs.

I conclude with Atwood's *Wilderness Tips*, a collection of stories filled with WASP cages just as restricting as Newman's burden of the Canadian Shield. One of these stories, "The Age of Lead," addresses the decline of the twentieth century (as most of the stories in the collection do). In this story, however, Jane, the ecologically-minded main character, becomes a kind of barometer. She describes her battle against the refuse that nightly collects on the sidewalk outside her house. This is what she says about the objects she finds: "She picks them up, clears them away, but they appear again overnight, like a trail left by an army on the march or by the fleeing residents of a city under bombardment, discarding the objects that were once thought essential but are now too heavy to carry" (1991:175).

Each of the writers I've discussed seems to be trying to discard certain outmoded metaphors that are, as Jane says, "too heavy to carry." Most of them are searching for new metaphors, more appropriate to the global, technologically-connected world in which we now live. Indeed, as Atwood writes in the introduction to *The New Oxford Book of Canadian Short Stories in English*: "we gave up a long time ago trying to isolate the gene for Canadianness" (1995:xiii). Well, yes – but no one seems to have given up the search for encompassing mythologies and the metaphors that populate them. It is this search that can be maintained in a number of ways, through the mapping of the sometimes outrageous and sometimes merely descriptive ideas, images, and symbols that illustrate Canadian hopes and fears as we move into the new century.

References

Anderson, B. 1983. *Imagined Communities: Reflections on the Origin and Spread of Nationalism.* London: Verso.

Atwood, M. 1972. *Surfacing.* Toronto: McClelland & Stewart.

_____. 1978. *Two-Headed Poems.* Toronto: Oxford University Press.

_____. 1991. *Wilderness Tips.* Toronto: McClelland and Stewart.

Atwood, M. and R. Weaver, eds. 1995. *The New Oxford Book of Canadian Short Stories in English.* Toronto: Oxford University Press.

Bhabha, H.K., ed. 1990. *Nation and Narration.* London: Routledge.

Canclini, N.G. 1995. *Hybrid Cultures: Strategies for Entering and Leaving Modernity.* Trans. C. Chiappary and S. López. Minneapolis: University of Minnesota Press.

Haraway, D. 1990. *Simians, Cyborgs, and Women: The Reinvention of Nature.* New York: Routledge.

Keohane, K. 1997. *Symptoms of Canada: An Essay on the Canadian Identity.* Toronto: University of Toronto Press.

Kertzer, J. 1998. *Worrying the Nation: Imagining a National Literature in Canada.* Toronto: University of Toronto Press.

Kilbourn, W. 1970. "The Quest for the Peaceable Kingdom." In *Canadian Writing Today*, ed. M. Richler, 46–53. Middlesex: Penguin.

McRoberts, K. 1997. *Misconceiving Canada: The Struggle for National Unity.* Toronto: Oxford University Press.

New, W.H. 1998. *Borderlands: How We Talk About Canada.* Vancouver: UBC Press.

Newman, P. 1995. *The Canadian Revolution: From Deference to Defiance (1985–1995).* Toronto: Penguin.

Ondaatje, M. 1992. *The English Patient.* Toronto: Vintage.

Smith, P. 1997. *Millennial Dreams: Contemporary Culture and Capital in the North.* London: Verso.

Strong-Boag, V.S. Grace, A. Eisenberg, and J. Anderson, eds. 1998. *Painting the Maple: Essays on Race, Gender, and the Construction of Canada.* Vancouver: UBC Press.

Margaret Atwood, C.C.

Poète, romancière et critique littéraire, Margaret Atwood est l'auteure de plus de vingt-cinq ouvrages dont les plus connus sont sans doute ses divers romans, notamment *La femme comestible*, *La Servante écarlate*, *La Voleuse d'hommes*, *Captive* (prix Giller 1996), *Le Tueur aveugle* (prix Booker 2000) et son tout dernier, *Oryx and Crake* (2003). De nombreux prix et plusieurs grades honorifiques lui ont été décernés, notamment par les universités Queen's et McMaster et par celles de Cambridge, d'Oxford, de Toronto et de Montréal. Membre de la Société royale du Canada depuis 1987, elle a été nommée Compagnon de l'Ordre du Canada en 1981 et Chevalier de l'Ordre des Arts et des Lettres de la France en 1994. En 2001, une étoile a été ajoutée pour Margaret Atwood à l'Allée des célébrités canadiennes.

L'honorable Monique Bégin, O.C.

Monique Bégin est professeure émérite de l'Université d'Ottawa. Secrétaire générale de la Commission royale d'enquête sur la situation de la femme au Canada (1967-1970), elle s'est consacrée pendant deux ans en recherche au CRTC, puis est devenue la première Québécoise élue à la Chambre des communes (Libérale, 1972). Ministre du Revenu national (1976-1977) et Ministre de la Santé nationale et du Bien-être social (1977-1984) dans le gouvernement de Pierre Elliott Trudeau, son nom restera identifié à la *Loi canadienne sur la santé* (1984). Elle est membre de la Société royale du Canada et a été reçue Officier de l'Ordre du Canada en 1998. Doyenne de la Faculté des sciences de la santé à l'Université d'Ottawa de 1990 à 1997, elle enseigne actuellement comme professeure invitée au Programme de maîtrise en administration de la santé.

Alan C. Cairns, O.C.

Alan Cairns est professeur auxiliaire au Département de sciences politiques de la University of Waterloo et professeur émérite de la University of British Columbia, où il a enseigné les sciences politiques de 1960 à 1995. Des grades honorifiques lui ont été décernés par la Carleton University, la University of Toronto et la University of British Columbia. Officier de l'Ordre du Canada et membre de la Société royale du Canada, il est l'auteur et l'éditeur de plusieurs ouvrages et articles portant sur la politique canadienne, l'évolution du fédéralisme au Canada, la Constitution, la *Charte canadienne des droits et libertés* et les relations entre les Autochtones et les non-Autochtones. Sa plus récente publication s'intitule *Citizens Plus: Aboriginal Peoples and the Canadian State* (2000).

Terry Cook

Terry Cook est professeur invité au programme de maîtrise en études archivistiques du département d'histoire de la University of Manitoba, en plus d'être rédacteur indépendant, écrivain et expert-conseil de renommée internationale dans le domaine des archives. Il a travaillé pour les Archives nationales du Canada de 1975 à 1998 et a contribué à élaborer plusieurs politiques et straté-

Margaret Atwood, C.C.
Margaret Atwood is the author of more than twenty-five volumes of poetry, fiction, and nonfiction and is perhaps best known for her novels, which include *The Edible Woman, The Handmaid's Tale, The Robber Bride, Alias Grace* (Giller Prize 1996), *The Blind Assassin* (Booker Prize 2000), and her latest, *Oryx and Crake* (2003). She is the recipient of numerous awards and several honorary degrees, including those conferred by Cambridge, Oxford, Toronto, Queen's, Montréal, and McMaster, and has been a Fellow of the Royal Society of Canada since 1987. She was named Companion of the Order of Canada in 1981 and *Chevalier* of the *Ordre des Arts et des Lettres* of France in 1994. In 2001, Margaret Atwood was inducted into Canada's Walk of Fame.

Hon. Monique Bégin, O.C.
Monique Bégin is Professor Emeritus, University of Ottawa. She served as Executive Secretary of the Royal Commission on the Status of Women in Canada (1967-1970), followed by two years in research at the Canadian Radio-Television and Telecommunications Commission (CRTC), before becoming the first woman from Québec elected to the House of Commons (Liberal, 1972). She held the office of Minister of National Revenue from 1976 to 1977 and Minister of National Health and Welfare from 1977 to 1984 in the Trudeau Government. *The Canada Health Act*, 1984, is her political legacy. She is a Fellow of the Royal Society of Canada and was invested as Officer of the Order of Canada in 1998. She served as Dean of the Faculty of Health Sciences, University of Ottawa from 1990-1997, and currently teaches in the Master's Health Administration Programme.

Alan C. Cairns, O.C.
Alan Cairns is Adjunct Professor of Political Science at the University of Waterloo and Professor Emeritus, University of British Columbia where he taught Political Science from 1960 to 1995. He has received honorary degrees from Carleton University, University of Toronto, and the University of British Columbia. Officer of the Order of Canada and Fellow of the Royal Society of Canada, he is the author and editor of books and articles on Canadian politics, historical development of Canadian federalism, the Constitution, the Canadian Charter of Rights and Freedoms, and Aboriginal/non Aboriginal relations. His most recent publication is *Citizens Plus: Aboriginal Peoples and the Canadian State* (2000).

Terry Cook
Terry Cook is Visiting Professor in the Master's Programme in Archival Studies, Department of History, University of Manitoba, as well as an international archival consultant, freelance editor, and writer. He worked at the National Archives of Canada from 1975 to 1998 and was involved in initiating several influential national archives policies and strategies on regional

gies nationales importantes sur les dossiers régionaux, l'évaluation, l'échantillonnage et les documents informatiques. Au moment de son départ, il était directeur de l'évaluation et de l'élimination des documents gouvernementaux (tous supports). Ancien rédacteur en chef d'*Archivaria* (1982-1984), ses écrits portent sur la théorie archivistique en général, l'évolution historique des documents sur l'Ouest et le Nord canadiens, l'histoire des concepts archivistiques et les documents informatiques.

Maya Dutt

Maya Dutt est professeure d'anglais à l'Université de Kerala à Thiruvananthapuram, en Inde, et codirectrice du centre d'études canadiennes de la même université depuis 1991. Elle est associée aux études canadiennes de plusieurs façons : en présentant des exposés à des conférences, en publiant des articles dans des revues de recherche et en dirigeant des dissertations de maîtrise ou de doctorat en études canadiennes.

Chad Gaffield

Chad Gaffield est directeur de l'Institut d'études canadiennes de l'Université d'Ottawa. Il a étudié à l'Université McGill, où il a obtenu un baccalauréat ès arts en 1973 et une maîtrise ès arts en 1974 et à la University of Toronto, où il a fait son doctorat (1978). Il a enseigné à la University of Victoria de 1979 à 1985 avant d'entrer à l'Université d'Ottawa où il est titulaire d'une chaire de recherche en histoire canadienne. Son enseignement et ses activités de recherche sont centrés sur l'histoire sociale du Canada aux dix-neuvième et vingtième siècles. Parmi les distinctions qui lui ont été décernées figurent le Prix d'excellence en recherche de l'Université d'Ottawa pour l'année 1995 et celui du Professeur de l'année en 2002. Président de la Société historique du Canada en 2000-2001, il est actuellement chef d'équipe pour le projet de l'Infrastructure de recherche sur le Canada au XXe siècle.

Karen L. Gould

Karen L. Gould est doyenne du McMicken College of Arts and Sciences de la University of Cincinnati. Elle est l'auteure et la coéditrice de cinq ouvrages, dont *Writing in the Feminine: Feminism and Experimental Writing in Quebec* (1990) et de plus de 40 articles et essais sur l'écriture et la culture des femmes au Québec et sur le nouveau roman français. Elle est présidente sortante du Conseil international des études canadiennes, ancienne présidente de l'Association des études canadiennes aux États-Unis et ancienne rédactrice en chef du journal interdisciplinaire *Québec Studies*.

Maria Teresa Gutiérrez-Haces

Maria Teresa Gutiérrez-Haces est professeure chargée de recherche à l'Instituto de Investigaciones Económicas de l'Universidad Nacional Autónoma de México (UNAM) et professeure au Département de sciences

records, appraisal, sampling, and electronic records. At the time of his departure, he was director responsible for the appraisal and disposal of government records in all media formats. A former general editor of *Archivaria* (1982-84), his writings have focused on archival theory in general, the historical evolution of records relating to the Canadian West and North, the history of archival ideas, and electronic records.

Maya Dutt

Maya Dutt is Professor of English at the Institute of English, University of Kerala, Thiruvananthapuram, India and co-director of the Centre for Canadian Studies at the University of Kerala since 1991. She has been associated with Canadian Studies in manifold ways, presenting papers at conferences, publishing articles in research journals, and guiding MPhil and PhD theses in Canadian Studies.

Chad Gaffield

Chad Gaffield is Director of the Institute of Canadian Studies at the University of Ottawa. He was educated at McGill University (BA 1973; MA 1974) and at the University of Toronto (PhD 1978). He taught at the University of Victoria (1979-1985) before coming to the University of Ottawa where he holds a University Research Chair in Canadian History. His teaching and research activities focus on Canadian social history during the nineteenth and twentieth centuries. He was selected the University's Researcher of the Year for 1995 and Professor of the Year in 2002. In 2000-2001, he was President of the Canadian Historical Association. He is currently team leader of the Canadian Century Research Infrastructure Project.

Karen L. Gould

Karen L. Gould is Dean of the McMicken College of Arts and Sciences at the University of Cincinnati. She is the author or co-editor of five books, including *Writing in the Feminine: Feminism and Experimental Writing in Quebec* (1990), and over 40 articles and essays dealing with women's writing and culture in Québec and the French *nouveau roman*. She is Past President of the International Council for Canadian Studies, former President of the Association for Canadian Studies in the United States, and former editor of the interdisciplinary journal *Québec Studies*.

Maria Teresa Gutiérrez-Haces

As Research Professor at the *Instituto de Investigaciones Económicas* of the National Autonomous University of Mexico (UNAM), and Professor in the Faculty of Political Sciences, she is a member of the National Research System

politiques. Elle est également membre du Système national de recherche du Conseil national des sciences et de la technologie (CONACYT). En 1992, elle a contribué à fonder l'Association mexicaine d'études canadiennes (AMEC), dont elle a assuré la présidence de 1993 à 1996. Elle a également siégé au Comité exécutif du Conseil international d'études canadiennes. Depuis 1986, elle participe activement au débat entourant le libre-échange et en 1990, elle a été invitée à témoigner devant un comité de la Chambre des communes. Sa plus récente publication s'intitule : *Canada: A Postmodern State* (2000).

C. Michael Hall
C. Michael Hall est professeur au Centre for Tourism de la University of Otago en Nouvelle-Zélande. Il détient des grades de la University of Western Australia et de la University of Waterloo au Canada. Il est membre de l'Association d'études canadiennes de l'Australie et de la Nouvelle-Zélande (AECAN-Z) depuis 1988 et président sortant de cette même association. Son enseignement et ses travaux de recherche portent sur des sujets variés comme le tourisme, le patrimoine, le développement régional et l'histoire de l'environnement. Il a également écrit ou édité de nombreux ouvrages, articles et chapitres de livres. Ses intérêts en études canadiennes se concentrent surtout sur les questions de développement régional urbain et rural lié au tourisme, à la promotion des lieux et aux études comparatives du développement des parcs nationaux.

Lorna Irvine
Lorna Irvine est professeure d'anglais, d'études culturelles et d'études des femmes à la George Mason University de Fairfax en Virginie. Ses publications comprennent *Sub/Version: Canadian Fictions By Women Collecting Clues: Margaret Atwood's « Bodily Harm »*, *Critical Spaces: Margaret Laurence and Janet Frame*, ainsi que de nombreux articles et chapitres de livres consacrés aux oeuvres d'écrivains canadiens. Elle a siégé au comité de direction de l'Association d'études canadiennes aux États-Unis (ACSUS), aux comités de rédaction des revues *Québec Studies* et *American Review of Canadian Studies*. À l'heure actuelle, elle étudie les écrits de l'auteure canadienne Carol Shields.

Hugette Labelle, C.C.
Huguette Labelle est chancelière de l'Université d'Ottawa. Titulaire d'un doctorat en éducation de l'Université d'Ottawa, Huguette Labelle s'est vu décerner des doctorats honorifiques par dix universités canadiennes. Elle a été présidente de l'Agence canadienne de développement international de 1993 à 1999, administratrice générale du Bureau du Canada pour le millénaire en 1998, sous-ministre des Transports de 1990 à 1993, présidente de la Commission de la fonction publique de 1985 à 1990 et sous-secrétaire d'État de 1980 à 1985. Elle a également été secrétaire associée du Cabinet et sous-greffier du Conseil privé. Compagnon de l'Ordre du Canada, elle a reçu la Médaille Vanier de l'Institut d'administration publique du Canada, le Prix pour ser-

of the National Council of Sciences and Technology (CONACYT). In 1992, she was the founder of the Mexican Association for Canadian Studies (AMEC) and served as its president from 1993 until 1996. She served as a member of the executive committee of the International Council for Canadian Studies. Since 1986 she has been very active in the debate about Free Trade and in 1990 was invited to testify at a House of Commons committee. Her most recent publication is *Canada:A Postmodern State* (2000).

C. Michael Hall
C. Michael Hall is a Professor at the Centre for Tourism at the University of Otago, New Zealand. He holds degrees from the University of Western Australia and the University of Waterloo in Canada. He has been a member of the Association for Canadian Studies in Australia and New Zealand since 1988 and is a Past President of the Association. He has wide-ranging teaching and research interests in tourism, heritage, regional development, and environmental history and has authored or edited numerous books, articles, and book chapters. His Canadian interests have primarily focused on issues of urban and rural regional development associated with tourism, place promotion, and comparative studies of national park development.

Lorna Irvine
Lorna Irvine is Professor of English, Cultural Studies, and Women's Studies at George Mason University in Fairfax, Virginia. Her publications include *Sub/Version: Canadian Fictions By Women; Collecting Clues: Margaret Atwood's Bodily Harm; Critical Spaces: Margaret Laurence and Janet Frame*, as well as many articles and book chapters devoted to the work of Canadian writers. She has been a member of the executive committee of ACSUS, the editorial boards of *Québec Studies* and the *American Review of Canadian Studies*. Her current research investigates the writing of Canadian author Carol Shields.

Hugette Labelle, C.C.
Huguette Labelle is Chancellor of the University of Ottawa. She holds a PhD (Education) from the University of Ottawa and has received honorary doctorates from ten Canadian universities. She was President of the Canadian International Development Agency from 1993 to 1999, Deputy Head of the Millennium Bureau of Canada in 1998, Deputy Minister of Transport Canada from 1990 to 1993, Chair of the Public Service Commission from 1985 to 1990, and Under Secretary of State from 1980 to 1985. She was also Associate Secretary to the Cabinet and Deputy Clerk of the Privy Council. She is a Companion of the Order of Canada and has been awarded the Vanier Medal of the Institute of Public Administration of Canada, the Outstanding

vices insignes de la Fonction publique du Canada et l'Ordre de la Pléiade de l'Assemblée parlementaire de la Francophonie.

Denis Lacorne

Denis Lacorne est agrégé supérieur de recherche au Centre d'études et de recherches internationales (CERI) de la Fondation nationale des sciences politiques. Il est diplômé de l'Institut d'Études Politiques de Paris et détient un doctorat en sciences politiques de la Yale University. Il a enseigné les sciences politiques aux États-Unis, en Suisse, au Mexique et à l'Université du Québec à Montréal. À Paris, il donne des cours à l'Institut d'Études Politiques, à l'Université Paris 1 Panthéon-Sorbonne et au campus parisien de la Stanford University. Ses plus récents livres sont *La politique de Babel. Du monologuisme d'État au pluralisme des peuples*, avec Toni Judt (2002) et *La Crise de l'identité américaine. Du melting-pot au multiculturalisme* (1997).

Jean Laponce

Jean Laponce est professeur émérite à la University of British Columbia où il a enseigné les sciences politiques. Il est diplômé de l'Institut de Sciences Politiques de Paris et a obtenu son doctorat à la University of California, à Los Angeles. Il a été directeur de l'Institut des relations interethniques de l'Université d'Ottawa de 1992 à 2001 et professeur invité au Département de sciences politiques durant cette même période. Ancien président des associations canadiennes et internationales de sciences politiques ; il est depuis 1974 membre de la Société royale du Canada. Il est l'auteur de nombreux articles et ouvrages, notamment *The Protection of Minorities* (1961) et *Langues et territoires* (1984). Ses recherches portent présentement sur l'étude comparée des états multiethniques et multinationaux.

Jocelyn Létourneau

Jocelyn Létourneau est professeur titulaire au Département d'histoire de l'Université Laval et chercheur au Centre interuniversitaire d'études sur les lettres, les arts et les traditions (CÉLAT). Au cours des dernières années, il a publié un grand nombre d'articles savants dans des revues scientifiques internationales et canadiennes, ainsi que plusieurs livres, dont *Les années sans guide. Le Canada à l'ère de l'économie migrante* (1996) et *Passer à l'avenir : Histoire, mémoire, identité dans le Québec d'aujourd'hui* (2000). Il est maintenant titulaire de la chaire de recherche du Canada en histoire et en économie politique du Québec contemporain, à l'Université Laval.

Gilles Paquet, C.M.

Gilles Paquet est directeur fondateur du Centre d'études en gouvernance de l'Université d'Ottawa. Il est présentement chercheur supérieur du Programme de recherche sur la gouvernance et l'intendance et professeur émérite à l'École de gestion de l'Université d'Ottawa. Il a étudié la philosophie, les sciences

Achievement Award of the Public Service of Canada, and the *Ordre de la Pléiade* of the *Assemblée Parlementaire de la Francophonie.*

Denis Lacorne
Denis Lacorne is Senior Research Fellow at the Centre d'études et de recherches internationales (CERI) of the Fondation nationale des sciences politiques. He studied at the Institut d'Études Politiques, Paris and received his PhD in political science from Yale University. He has taught political science in the United States, Switzerland, Mexico, and Canada at l'Université du Québec à Montréal. In Paris, he teaches at the Institut d'Études Politiques, at the Université Paris 1 Panthéon-Sorbonne and at the Paris campus of Stanford University. His most recent books are *La Politique de Babel. Du monologuisime d'État au pluralisme des peuples* with Toni Judt (2002) and *La Crise de l'identité américaine. Du melting-pot au multiculturalisme* (1997).

Jean Laponce
Jean Laponce is Professor Emeritus, University of British Columbia, where he taught political science. He graduated from the Paris Institute of Political Science and obtained his PhD at the University of California, Los Angeles. He was Director of the Institute of Interethnic Relations of the University of Ottawa from 1992 to 2001 and Visiting Professor at the University's Department of Political Science during that period. He is a former president of the Canadian and International Political Science Associations and has been a Fellow of The Royal Society of Canada since 1974. He has published numerous articles and books, among them *The Protection of Minorities* (1961) and *Languages and their Territories* (1987). His present research interest is in the comparative study of multi-ethnic and multinational states.

Jocelyn Létourneau
Jocelyn Létourneau is Professor of History in the History Department at Université Laval and a researcher at the Centre interuniversitaire d'études sur les lettres, les arts et les traditions (CELAT). He has published scholarly articles in Canadian and foreign journals and books such as *Les Années sans guide. Le Canada à l'ère de l'économie migrante* (1996), and *Passer à l'avenir: Histoire, mémoire, identité dans le Québec d'aujourdhui* (2000). He now holds the Canada Research Chair in Contemporary Political History and Economy in Québec, at l'Université Laval.

Gilles Paquet, C.M.
Gilles Paquet was the founding Director of the Centre on Governance, University of Ottawa and is presently Senior Research Fellow with the Program of Research on Governance and Stewardship, and Professor Emeritus of the School of Management at the University of Ottawa. He stud-

sociales et l'économie à l'Université Laval, à la Queen's University et à la University of California, où il a reçu une bourse de perfectionnement post-doctoral en économie. Il a été doyen de la faculté des études supérieures et de la recherche à la Carleton University au cours des années 1970 et de la faculté d'administration de l'Université d'Ottawa durant les années 1980. Il est président élu de la Société royale du Canada pour la période de 2003 à 2005 et Membre de la Royal Society of Arts of London. Il a été nommé Membre de l'Ordre du Canada en 1992. Actif en radiodiffusion, il a écrit un grand nombre d'articles et des livres traitant de l'histoire de l'économie canadienne, des politiques publiques et des questions de gouvernance.

Susan D. Phillips
Susan D. Phillips est professeure agrégée d'administration publique à la Carleton University, où elle donne des cours sur le gouvernement urbain, la recherche stratégique et le secteur bénévole. Elle a été rédactrice en chef du rapport d'examen annuel *How Ottawa Spends* et rédactrice associée de la revue *Canadian Public Policy / Analyse de politiques*. De 1997 à 1999, elle a été directrice de recherche du Groupe d'experts sur la saine gestion et la transparence dans le secteur bénévole. Elle est Fellow au Centre canadien de gestion et conseillère en politique auprès de l'Initiative sur le secteur bénévole et communautaire, un regroupement des organisations nationales bénévoles et de plusieurs ministères. Parmi ses nombreuses autres fonctions, mentionnons celle de directrice du Centre for Voluntary Sector Research and Development à la Carleton University.

Jean-Louis Roy
Jean-Louis Roy est Chancelier de l'Université Sainte-Anne en Nouvelle-Écosse. Il a été secrétaire général (1990-1998) de l'Agence de la Francophonie, Paris, délégué général du Québec à Paris (1986-1990) et directeur du quotidien montréalais *Le Devoir* (1981-1986). En août 2002, il a été nommé président du Droits et Démocratie/Centre international des droits de la personne et du développement démocratique (Montréal). Il est présentement chercheur invité à l'Université de Moncton, professeur invité à la University of Toronto et à l'École polytechnique de Montréal. Il a publié de nombreux ouvrages consacrés à la politique internationale et à l'histoire ainsi que des essais et des oeuvres littéraires.

John Ralston Saul, C.C.
Romancier et essayiste, John Ralston Saul est reconnu pour ses études et ses romans contemporains aux multiples intrigues politiques et morales. Sa trilogie philosophique *Les Bâtards de Voltaire: la dictature de la raison en Occident*, *Le compagnon du doute* et *La Civilisation inconsciente* a inspiré de nombreux débats, tout comme son ouvrage sur le Canada au vingtième siècle, *Réflexions d'un frère siamois: le Canada à la fin du XXᵉ siècle* (1997) et son livre le plus récent

ied philosophy, social sciences, and economics at Laval, Queen's, and at the University of California where he was a Postdoctoral Fellow in Economics. He was Dean of the Faculty of Graduate Studies and Research at Carleton University in the 1970s and of the Faculty of Administration at the University of Ottawa in the 1980s. He is a President-elect of the Royal Society of Canada (2003-2005), a Fellow of the Royal Society of Arts of London, and was named Member of the Order of Canada in 1992. He has been active in broadcasting and has written numerous books and articles on Canadian economic history, public policy, and governance issues.

Susan D. Phillips
Susan D. Phillips is Associate Professor of Public Administration, Carleton University, where she teaches courses in urban government, policy research, and the voluntary sector. She is past editor of both the annual review, *How Ottawa Spends* and of the journal *Canadian Public Policy / Analyse de politiques*. From 1997-99, she was the Research Director of the Broadbent Panel on Accountability and Governance in the Voluntary Sector. She is a Fellow with the Canadian Centre for Management Development and acts as Policy Advisor to the Voluntary Sector Initiative, a coalition of national voluntary organizations and several government departments. Among her many other functions, she is also the current Director of the Centre for Voluntary Sector Research and Development at Carleton University.

Jean-Louis Roy
Jean-Louis Roy is Chancellor of l'Université Sainte-Anne in Nova Scotia. He served as Secretary General of the international Agence de la Francophonie (1990-1998), Paris. He was Québec's Delegate General to Paris (1986-1990) and editor of the Montréal newspaper, *Le Devoir* (1981-1986). In August 2002 he was appointed President of Rights & Democracy/International Centre for Human Rights and Democratic Development, (Montréal). He is currently a visiting researcher at the Université de Moncton, visiting professor at the University of Toronto, and visiting professor at the École polytechnique de Montréal. He has published many books on international politics and history, along with essays and literary works.

John Ralston Saul, C.C.
Novelist and essayist, John Ralston Saul has earned recognition as the author of studies and densely plotted novels on contemporary political issues and moral intrigue. His philosophical trilogy – *Voltaire's Bastards: The Dictatorship of Reason in the West, The Doubter's Companion: A Dictionary of Aggressive Common Sense*, and *The Unconscious Civilization* – has generated much debate in Canada and abroad, as has its sequel, *On Equilibrium*, published in 2001 and

On Equilibrium (2001). Il a été nommé Chevalier de l'Ordre des Arts et des Lettres de la France en 1996 et Compagnon de l'Ordre du Canada en 1999. Il a obtenu son doctorat du King's College de la University of London (Angleterre), détient aussi des doctorats honorifiques des universités McGill, Victoria, Simon Fraser, McMaster, Québec à Montréal, Manitoba et Western Ontario et a été nommé Senior Fellow du Massey College de la University of Toronto.

Shirley Thomson, C.C.
Shirley L. Thomson a été directrice du Conseil des Arts du Canada (1998-2002). Auparavant, elle a été directrice du Musée des beaux-arts du Canada (1987-1997), secrétaire générale de la Commission canadienne pour l'UNESCO (1985-1987) et directrice du Musée McCord, à Montréal (1982 à 1985). Elle détient un doctorat en histoire de l'art de l'Université McGill, une maîtrise ès arts de la University of Maryland et un baccalauréat ès arts de la University of Western Ontario. Elle a reçu en outre plusieurs doctorats honorifiques et a été nommée Chevalier de l'Ordre des Arts et des Lettres par la France et Officier de l'Ordre du Canada en 1994, puis Compagnon en 2001.

W. Michael Wilson
W. Michael Wilson est détenteur du poste de vice-président principal des initiatives stratégiques de RBC Groupe financier. Récemment, en tant que vice-président principal de la réassurance, il a été chargé de la gestion et de l'expansion des activités de réassurance de Groupe financier de la Banque Royale du Canada. Il est membre du Comité de direction de RBC Assurances et siège au conseil d'administration de plusieurs filiales de cette dernière. Il a fréquenté la Queen's University, où il a obtenu un baccalauréat en droit et une maîtrise en histoire. Reçu au Barreau de la province de l'Ontario en 1986, il est actuellement membre du Barreau du Haut-Canada.

Donna Winslow
Donna Winslow a remporté plusieurs prix à titre d'anthropologue. Elle est actuellement présidente du département d'anthropologie culturelle et de sociologie du développement de la Faculté des sciences socio-culturelles de la Vrije Universiteit à Amsterdam (Pays-Bas). Avant cette nomination, elle a été professeure agrégée à l'Université d'Ottawa, où elle a dirigé le Programme de recherche sur la paix, la sécurité et la société du Centre d'études en gouvernance, et a coordonné le programme de Military Officer Degree. Elle détient un doctorat de l'Université de Montréal. De 1995 à 1997, elle a été conseillère technique auprès de la Commission d'enquête sur le déploiement des Forces canadiennes en Somalie. Elle a également publié *Le Régiment aéroporté du Canada en Somalie, une enquête socio-culturelle* (1997). Ses recherches actuelles portent sur les problèmes de mondialisation et de localisation et de développement, de paix et de sécurité.

his 1997 study of Canada in twentieth century, *Reflections of A Siamese Twin*. He was named *Chevalier* of the *Ordre des Arts et des Lettres* of France in 1996 and Companion of the Order of Canada in 1999. He earned his PhD at King's College, University of London (UK), holds honorary doctorates from the universities of McGill, Victoria, Simon Fraser, McMaster, UQAM, Manitoba, and Western Ontario, and is a Senior Fellow of Massey College, University of Toronto.

Shirley L. Thomson, C.C.
Shirley L. Thomson was Director of the Canada Council for the Arts from January 1998 to December 2002. She was Director of the National Gallery of Canada from 1987 to 1997, Secretary General of the Canadian Commission for UNESCO from 1985 to 1987, and Director of the McCord Museum in Montréal from 1982 to 1985. She received her PhD in art history from McGill University, her MA from the University of Maryland, and her BA from the University of Western Ontario. She has received a number of honorary doctorates and is a *Chevalier* of the French *Ordre des Arts et des Lettres*. In 1994, she was made an Officer and, in 2001, a Companion of the Order of Canada.

W. Michael Wilson
W. Michael Wilson holds the position of Senior Vice-President, Strategic Initiatives, RBC Financial Group. Most recently he was Senior Vice-President, Reinsurance, where he was responsible for managing and expanding the reinsurance business for Royal Bank Financial Group. He is a member of the senior executive committee for RBC Insurance and serves as a director of various RBC Insurance companies. He attended Queen's University where he obtained a Bachelor of Laws degree and an MA degree in history. He was called to the Bar of the Province of Ontario in 1986. He is a member of the Law Society of Upper Canada.

Donna Winslow
Donna Winslow is an award-winning anthropologist and currently Chair of the Department of Cultural Anthropology/Sociology of Development, at the Faculty of Social-Cultural Sciences, Vrije Universiteit in Amsterdam (The Netherlands). Prior to this appointment she was Associate Professor at the University of Ottawa where she directed the Program for Research on Peace, Security, and Society at the Centre on Governance, in addition to co-ordinating the Military Officer Degree Program. She received her PhD from l'Université de Montréal. From 1995 to 1997 she served as a technical advisor to the Commission of Inquiry into the Deployment of Canadian Forces to Somalia and published the book *The Canadian Airborne Regiment in Somalia: A Socio-cultural Inquiry* (1997). Her current research involves issues of globalization and localization, development, peace, and security.